VOYAGES
IN ENGLISH
Writing and Grammar

Elaine de Chantal Brookes

Patricia Healey

Irene Kervick

Catherine Irene Masino

Anne B. McGuire

Adrienne Saybolt

LOYOLAPRESS.

Grateful acknowledgment is given to authors, publishers, photographers, museums, and agents for permission to reprint the following copyrighted material. Every effort has been made to determine copyright owners. In the case of any omissions, the publisher will be pleased to make suitable acknowledgments in future editions. Continued on page 543.

Cover Design/Production: Loyola Press, Steve Curtis Design, Inc.
Cover Illustration: Jeff Parks
Interior Design/Production: Think Design Group, Loyola Press

ISBN: 0-8294-2089-4

Manufactured in the United States of America.

LOYOLAPRESS.
3441 N. ASHLAND AVENUE
CHICAGO, ILLINOIS 60657
(800) 621-1008
www.LoyolaPress.org

CONTENTS

PART 2

Grammar

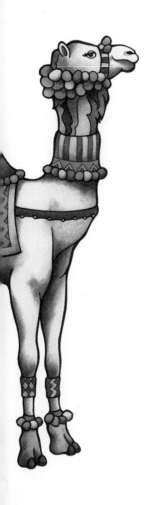

What do all of these

people have in common?

They all use writing in their jobs.

How do you think that writing helps them in their everyday lives?

PART

1

Written and Oral Communication

Our Wide Wide World

In ancient Egypt only about 1 out of 100 people were literate, so scribes, who were trained to read and write, were very important members of society. Scribes performed clerical tasks, drew up marriage and property contracts, or took high-level positions as tax collectors, treasurers, or architects. Even though few people could read, scribes wrote down everything from lists of food to stories about the Egyptian people, which is why we know so much about this ancient society today.

Personal Narratives

Hi Mom,

I just had one of those days when I wish I had just stayed in bed.

   I got up early yesterday in order to get to my new job down at the docks on time. My dock crew's task for the day was to remove large boxes of granite from shipping containers and put them on the waiting trucks. At about 11:20 A.M. it started to drizzle, just as I was in the process of moving a large box up the ramp onto the truck bed. The ramp was slippery from the rain, and in spite of my heavy, rubber-soled shoes, my foot went out from under me. In an effort to keep the granite from sliding all the way down, I fell off the ramp. I landed on my side and heard a loud CRACK! A few of my coworkers quickly ran over. When they saw how badly my leg was twisted, they called an ambulance to take me to San Francisco Memorial Hospital.

   I got to the hospital about 20 minutes later, where x-rays revealed a broken leg, a fractured elbow, and the news that my cast-induced, mummified appearance would make me a dock sitter rather than a dockworker for about eight weeks.

   Now, Mom, I know you're worried, but don't be. I've had lots of visitors, and several people from work have brought magazines and snacks to keep me busy until the hospital sends me home. I'm thankful to those who came to my assistance and for the foreman saying that my job will be waiting when I'm well. Things could have been worse, but that doesn't stop me from wishing I had overslept yesterday!

Your clumsy son,

Ernie

What Makes a Good Personal Narrative?

Most of the short stories and novels that you read are narratives. A narrative is a story in which events are usually told in order. A personal narrative is the account of a true incident that the writer experienced. Here are some things to remember when you write a personal narrative.

Audience

Before you begin to write, consider your audience, the people who will be reading your narrative. What are their ages? What do they know about your topic? How interested are they in it? What are you trying to express to them? The tone of your narrative depends on your audience.

Introduction

In the introduction to your narrative, it is important to catch your audience's attention. Say something that will make them want to continue reading. Set the stage for the body of your story.

Body

The body of your writing contains all the relevant facts or details. It might be one paragraph, or it might be many. Make notes before you write and review them step by step to be sure you haven't omitted anything. Be sure you don't include events that are not important to your story. Put the events in the order they actually occurred.

Conclusion

End your narrative in a way that makes your audience know it is complete. Don't introduce new information in the conclusion.

You might want to briefly summarize your main points or relate a lesson that you learned from your experience. Reread your introduction and tie in your ending with what you stated at the beginning. Share your thoughts and personal feelings about the outcome.

Point of View

The point of view in a personal narrative is yours. You are relating your own experience. This point of view is called the first-person point of view, so you will use words like *I* and *me*.

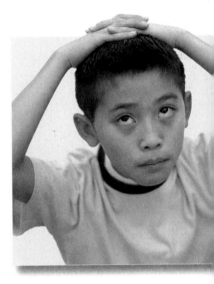

• Activity A •

The following sentences are from the body of a personal narrative about a day that the writer had been dreading. Their order has been scrambled. Look for words that will give you clues about the order in which events actually occurred. Write the sentences in logical order.

To my surprise, I felt relaxed as I faced the class and began to speak. I barely had time for breakfast before I had to run for the bus. Everyone congratulated me and took time to look at the pictures and diagrams that I made of the pyramids. I awoke at the sound of the alarm with a feeling of dread at what the day would bring. All my practicing paid off as I gave a nearly flawless presentation. Morning classes passed uneventfully, but I had difficulty concentrating and participating in discussions. Before I knew it, the time for my presentation had arrived.

Writer's Corner

Think about events in your own life that might make good personal narratives. Did something strange or funny happen to you? Did you receive good news or praise for something that you did? Did you experience something sad or serious? Do some brainstorming to help you think of things to write about. Make a list of the topics that you think would make good personal narratives. Save your notes to use later.

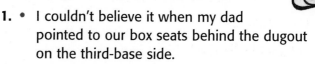

Activity B

Each group of sentences comes from a different personal narrative. Decide which sentence would be part of the introduction, which would be part of the body, and which would be the concluding statement of the narrative.

1. • I couldn't believe it when my dad pointed to our box seats behind the dugout on the third-base side.

   • A stop at our favorite pizza restaurant on the way home was the perfect ending to my perfect day.

   • It had started out being an ordinary Saturday, when all I wanted to do was sleep in.

2. • The butterflies are quiet, I've already made some new friends, and I know this will be the best school year ever.

   • It was the night before my first day at middle school, and the butterflies in my stomach were in a flutter.

   • I smiled as a friend from my last school sat down next to me.

3. • After three stories and two glasses of water, she finally gave in and took a nap.

   • With a crying toddler, milk spilled on the floor, and the doorbell ringing I wondered if I would make it as a babysitter.

   • An exhausted but proud first-time babysitter, I beamed and said, "Everything's fine!" when the parents returned.

Activity C

Think about an interesting event from your own life. Write a sentence that could be part of the introduction about that event, a sentence that could in the body, and a sentence that could be part of the conclusion. Keep in mind the things you read about personal narratives on pages 8 and 9.

• Activity D •

Whenever you do any type of writing, it is important to keep to the topic. The following are notes that an Egyptian scribe took to prepare for writing a report to the pharaoh. Select two items in each set that probably don't relate to the topic of that particular report.

1. Request for Supplies to Build Tomb of Pharaoh
   - stone from local quarries
   - pictures to hang on walls
   - stone to be transported from other locations
   - worker's tools: mallets, chisels, drills
   - gifts and offerings for inside the tomb
   - scaffolding to support teams of workers

2. Government Report on Job Opportunities for Scribes
   - farm the fertile Nile River Valley
   - prepare annual citizen tax records
   - draw up contracts for rental of land
   - sail the boat to Aswan for granite
   - write official letters from the pharaoh
   - compose and write tomb inscriptions

Writer's Corner

Take a look at the topics you listed for the Writer's Corner on page 9. Choose two topics and list details you would include in narratives about those topics. Include details such as who was involved, where the event took place, what the end result was, and so on. Try to remember as much as possible. Save your notes for future use.

Introductions and Conclusions

The introduction is your first chance to entice people to read your personal narrative. Interesting sentence structure and sensory images can catch the reader's attention. Use your opening sentences to preview what you will discuss in the body of your personal narrative.

Your narrative's conclusion should help the reader remember what is most important. You can summarize what you have said, share your final feelings, or tie everything together. The conclusion is your last chance to leave your reader satisfied.

Activity A

Read each pair of sentences. Which sentence would grab the reader's attention and be a better introduction to a personal narrative?

1. **a.** My mouth watered in anticipation of the sundae that awaited me after our family bike ride.

   b. Our family always goes for a bike ride after dinner, and then we stop for ice cream.

2. **a.** I found out this morning that my dog, Ginger, had puppies last night.

   b. Mom woke me up early to see the tiny bundles of fur huddled close to my dog, Ginger.

3. **a.** A crash of thunder, a bolt of lightning, and then suddenly total blackness—I was scared!

   b. There was a storm last night that caused our electricity to go out.

Activity B

For each topic below, write an opening sentence that will convince people to continue reading. You might use colorful descriptions, unusual sentence structures, elements of surprise, or opening questions.

1. your first experience at any sport
2. a party you attended
3. buying something at the store
4. riding with your family on a long car trip
5. a funny story about you and a friend

Activity C

Read the example of an effective introductory paragraph and think about what makes the paragraph work. Then write an introductory paragraph about each of the topics that follow.

I heard the noise just after I pulled up the covers and opened my book. What could it be? The noise sounded like it was coming from my closet. Did something fall? Did I dare look?

1. a time you were frightened
2. a time you did something kind for someone
3. an event you dreaded, but that turned out to be fun
4. an outdoor activity ruined by bad weather
5. a time you were late for something

Writer's Corner

Take a look at the notes you saved from Lesson 1. Write introductions for the two topics that you think would make interesting personal narratives. Keep these introductions to use again later.

• Activity D •

A report can be a type of personal narrative. Choose the sentence in each pair that would best conclude a report by an ancient Egyptian scribe. Remember an effective conclusion will summarize what has been said previously, tell how the experience affected the writer, or tie everything together.

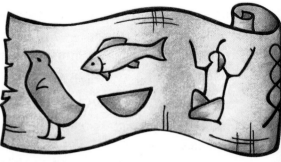

1. for a report on the status of tax bills

    a. The final household taxes for Imahoket, the stone mason, were nearly double those of last year.

    b. After the taxes were calculated, I returned to each household and personally delivered a final itemized accounting.

2. for a report on food needed for tomb builders

    a. As explained above, I considered the numbers of workers, approximate hours of labor required, and average amount of food per person in preparing this food request.

    b. I suggest that we feed the workers in three shifts.

3. for a report on stone required for building a pyramid

    a. Finally, I think we will need to use a finer limestone to cover the outer casing.

    b. I have personally visited the quarries from which these stones will come and have carefully calculated quantities as well as boats and workers required for transport.

4. for a report on the mummification of Pharaoh's cat

    a. The divine feline now rests in a funerary urn waiting to join Pharaoh when he begins his journey to the glorious afterlife.

    b. All members of Pharaoh's household have shaved their eyebrows, mourning the passing of the beloved cat, Bastet.

Activity E

Write a good concluding paragraph for each of these personal narratives. Pay attention to details in the introduction and body so that you tie everything together.

1. Harder Than It Looks!

I awoke before my alarm clock, anticipating my first swing dance class. Would I be able to keep up with the music and with my friends? I wasn't a beginning dancer, but I wanted to try something different.

We lined up for class, and I took my place in the back row, where I thought I'd be more comfortable. Ms. Joanne, the teacher, welcomed me warmly. She assured me that while I might feel lost at first, the dances would eventually become second nature. We followed warm-up exercises with swinging music and lively dance routines.

2. The Good-Bad Day

I dreaded getting out of bed last Friday. I had argued with Keilani, my best friend, the day before. I didn't feel prepared for a huge math test. And to top it all off, my parents said if my room wasn't cleaned by the end of the day, there would be no TV for two weeks. I forced myself to get up a little earlier than usual, determined to make the best of a bad situation.

I had a quick breakfast while doing a final math review, and then I was off to school. As soon as I got there, I found Keilani and apologized. He felt bad too, and we settled our disagreement with a handshake. Math class followed and my early morning review paid off because I got a very good grade.

Writer's Corner

Look at the introductions that you wrote for the previous Writer's Corner. Write a conclusion that ties in to each introduction.

Dictionary

The dictionary is a tool that writers use frequently. A dictionary lists words in alphabetical order. It gives the correct definitions of the thousands of words it contains. It also shows how to pronounce the words and what part of speech each one is. If you can't remember exactly how a word is spelled, you can use the dictionary to find the correct spelling.

Entry Words

When you open a dictionary, you usually see two columns printed on each page. Listed along the left side of the columns are words in dark type. These are the entry words, the words that you want to find definitions for.

Guide Words

The two words printed at the top of every dictionary page are called guide words. They help you locate words quickly. The first guide word is the first entry word on that page, and the second guide word is the last entry word on the page. If a word comes between the two guide words alphabetically, it should be on that page.

• Activity A •

Alphabetize the words in each set.

by first letter	by second letter	by third letter
honorable	persevere	devotion
suite	profile	decline
windmill	pagoda	determine
criticism	piccolo	defraud
venture	pyramid	deposit

Activity B •

Here is a sample dictionary page with its guide words.

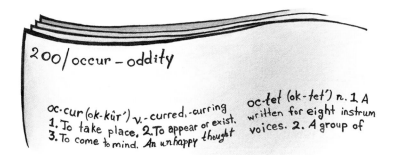

200/occur – oddity

oc·cur (ok-kûr´) v. -curred, -curring
1. To take place. 2. To appear or exist.
3. To come to mind. An unhappy thought

oc·tet (ok-tet´) n. 1. A
written for eight instrum
voices. 2. A group of

Use the guide words shown on the dictionary page above to indicate whether each of the following words would be located before page 200, on page 200, or after page 200.

occupy   oddball   ocean

Oklahoma   obtain   occasion

onion   octopus   ocelot

Activity C •

Use *opossum* and *orchestra* as guide words. Write two words that would appear in your dictionary right before this page, four words that would appear on this page, and two words that would appear after this page. Do the activity again with *genealogy* and *gerbil* as guide words.

Writer's Corner

Open your dictionary to any page and look at the guide words at the top of the two pages. Look at the entries for these guide words. Browse through the other entries on the pages. Find a few particularly interesting words or words you've never seen before. Write a short paragraph about one of the entry words. Define the word. Tell why it appealed to you. Tell how and when you might use it now that you're familiar with it.

A Dictionary Entry

Knowing all the parts of a dictionary entry can help you discover important information about a word. The following sample shows what is included in most dictionary entries.

A   **B**   **C**   **D**

hug·ger-mug·ger (hug′er-mug′er) *n.* **1.** Confusion.

E

The spy escaped in the hugger-mugger of the air raid.

2. Secrecy. *adj.* **1.** Disorderly. **2.** Secretive. *There was a*

hugger-mugger mood in the locker room before the game.

    F

v. **-ered, -ger·ing, -gers** To act in a secretive manner.

A strange man hugger-muggered around the back door.

A. division into syllables

B. dictionary respelling for pronunciation

C. part of speech

D. definition

E. sample phrase or sentence

F. spelling of last syllable with endings added

Activity D

Refer to the sample dictionary entry above to respond to the following.

1. What parts of speech are listed for *hugger-mugger* in the entry?

2. How many pronunciations are listed for *hugger-mugger*?

3. How many meanings does *hugger-mugger* have as an adjective?

4. Write three sentences using *hugger-mugger*. Each sentence should demonstrate *hugger-mugger* as a different part of speech.

Activity E

Look up each of these words in your dictionary. Write two different meanings for each word.

fast	rest	run	concrete	utter	grant
safe	point	strike	lame	ram	heel

Activity F

Look in your dictionary for five other words that have multiple meanings. Write down the words and their meanings. Trade your word list with a classmate. Have a race to see which of you is first to finish writing sentences for two different meanings of each word.

Activity G

Your dictionary can help you find the correct spelling for words when you aren't sure of the exact spelling. Find the correct spelling for the following misspelled words in dark type.

malases	sweet brown syrup made from sugar cane
furlow	time off from official duties
markey	movie theater sign
personell	people employed in a business
vaccum	a space that contains no solid, liquid, or gas
restaraunt	a business that prepares meals
refridgerator	an appliance that keeps food cold
jewlery	rings, necklaces, bracelets

Our Wide Wide World

The discovery of the Rosetta Stone in 1799 led to the translation of hieroglyphics. The stone showed the same message in three types of writing: hieroglyphic, demotic writing, and Greek. By matching the hieroglyphics, which were unknown, to the Greek, which is a known language, scholars were finally able to decipher hieroglyphic signs. You might say that the Rosetta Stone was a type of dictionary.

Writer's Corner

Look at the introductory and concluding sentences that you wrote on page 15. Choose at least three words and look them up in a dictionary. For each word, find and write out its definition, dictionary respelling, and part of speech. Then use the word in a new sentence.

Revising Sentences

Rambling Sentences

Good writers use sentences of different lengths to make their writing more interesting. They know that using too many short sentences sounds choppy. If a writer tries to cram too many ideas into one sentence, however, readers can become confused even if the sentence has proper grammar and punctuation.

Read these two examples. Notice how they are alike and how they are different. Which one makes more sense to you?

A. This was my best summer ever because my family spent the entire month of August in Wisconsin, where we rented a cabin on a lake and we could swim, row our boat, dive off a raft, windsurf, or just lie in the sun on the sandy shore.

B. This was my best summer ever! My family spent the entire month of August in Wisconsin, where we rented a cabin. We were on a lake where we could enjoy all kinds of water activities. We went swimming and dove off the raft. We rowed our boat and even tried windsurfing. When we wanted to rest, we just lay in the sun on the sandy shore.

Both examples include the same fun summer activities. In example A, one very long sentence contains too many ideas. In example B, that same sentence was divided into several shorter sentences. The shorter sentences are clearer, and the variety of sentence length makes the narrative more interesting.

Activity A

Improve these rambling sentences. You may add or change words to make your improved sentences read smoothly.

1. The forests of the world are one of our most valuable resources, but they are disappearing so we should do what we can to protect them because it would take many years to replace trees when they are all cut down.

2. The nib, or point, on a quill pen got flat quickly and had to be sharpened over and over, which meant quill pens didn't last long, but it wasn't until 1884 that a man named Lewis Waterman invented a fountain pen with a steel nib that could be used a long time.

3. Copper is a strong, tough metal that carries heat and electricity well and has many important uses including the manufacture of wires of all kinds, such as telephone wires, television cable, and power lines.

4. We live near the airport, and when planes fly directly overhead the noise is so loud that we can hardly hear each other speak, and so we asked the mayor to help us get the flight patterns changed.

5. Books are better than movies for many reasons like the fact that you get to imagine what the characters and setting look like in a book and because movies are over much more quickly than books which you can enjoy for a long time.

Writer's Corner

Think of all the things that you did yesterday from the time you got home from school until you went to bed. Using complete sentences, write down everything you can remember as quickly as you can. Afterward, exchange lists with a partner. Look for rambling sentences in each other's paper. If you find any, rewrite them into shorter, more understandable sentences. Discuss any changes.

Run-on Sentences

Run-on sentences can be just as confusing as rambling sentences. A run-on sentence is actually two or more sentences that have been put together without the proper punctuation to show where one sentence ends and the next one begins. There are several ways to correct run-on sentences. Look carefully at the following examples.

A. Underground, some people in the Sahara find water and shelter from storms it is also cool there on hot days.

B. These people build their homes below the ground, they dig 25 feet deep.

Each of the above sentences is a run-on sentence because each one contains two separate ideas written as one sentence. Sentence A has no punctuation between the ideas, and sentence B has the wrong punctuation mark—a comma.

The ideas in sentence A are very closely related. They both tell what the people find underground. This sentence could be fixed by adding a comma and a conjunction.

> Underground, some people in the Sahara find water and shelter from storms, and it is also cool there on hot days.

The ideas in sentence B are related but not as closely as those in sentence A. Sentence B could be fixed in one of two ways, with a period and a capital letter or with a semicolon.

> These people build their homes below the ground. They dig 25 feet deep.

> These people build their homes below the ground; they dig 25 feet deep.

If you use a conjunction to fix a run-on sentence, be sure you don't create a rambling sentence. If the ideas are not closely related, it's better to make two separate sentences.

Activity B

Correct each of the following run-on sentences. Use a period and a capital letter; a semicolon; or a comma and a conjunction.

1. A camel is a large desert animal it can travel long distances.

2. The camel's hump is like a storage tank it stores fat.

3. Camels can survive with little food or water, they draw on their reserve in their storage tanks for energy.

4. Some camels have one hump and some have two it depends on what type of camel they are.

5. Some Middle Eastern camels called dromedaries are used for riding and racing, they can travel about 10 miles an hour and about 100 miles a day.

6. The dromedary has one hump the Bactrian camel has two humps.

7. Camels are well adapted for desert life, their feet are padded for walking on hot sand.

8. A camel's milk is used for drinking and for making cheese it is so thick that it forms lumps in liquids.

9. The hair of the Bactrian camel can be woven, blankets, tents, and clothing are made from this hair.

10. Camels are useful animals they are a source of milk, meat, wool, and hides.

Writer's Corner

Trade the paper that you wrote for the Writer's Corner on page 21 with that of a different partner. This time look for run-on sentences. If you find any, rewrite them into separate, complete sentences. Discuss each other's changes.

Exact Words

In a personal narrative, you want your audience to picture the incident that you are retelling. Using exact words can help your readers visualize the events as they happened. Using fresh language will hold your readers' interest and make them want to continue reading.

When you revise your writing, look for words that are dull and overused. Try to think of words that will create vivid pictures in your readers' minds. Think about how you felt during the experience. When you were *angry*, were you *upset, irritated, enraged,* or *incensed*? When you *placed* the book on the table, did you *lay it, toss it, throw it,* or *slam it* down? If you were *irritated*, you probably *tossed it* down; if you were *enraged*, you probably *slammed it* down.

Picture each of these sentences in your mind. Which one paints a more vivid picture for a reader?

- I was awakened by a loud noise.
- I was startled from my sleep by a shrill scream.

Activity A

For each italicized word below, think of two other words that are more exact or that express the idea more precisely. Use a thesaurus for help.

1. a *bad* storm
2. a *pretty* painting
3. my *aim* in life
4. a *brave* knight
5. to *hold* a life preserver
6. a *big* glacier
7. a *fast* antelope
8. a *trip* down the Mississippi
9. an *interesting* dream
10. the *increasing* popularity of soccer

Activity B

Write a sentence for each of the following images. Replace the italicized word with one that is more descriptive.

1. a *crying* baby
2. a snake *moving*
3. two cats *fighting*
4. the *splash* of a waterfall
5. an angry *crowd* in the street

Activity C

Look at the word in dark type in each row. Arrange the other words in the row according to how exactly they describe the word in dark type. The first one is in the correct order. Pants are a type of clothes, shorts are a type of pants, and bermudas are a type of shorts.

1. **clothes**	pants	shorts	bermudas
2. **move**	sprint	hurry	run
3. **color**	crimson	hue	red
4. **utensil**	pan	cookware	skillet
5. **male**	son	youth	boy
6 **food**	hamburger	beef	meat
7. **sport**	race	hurdles	track
8. **meal**	eggs	omelet	breakfast
9. **creature**	fish	shark	hammerhead
10. **music**	popular	punk	rock

Writer's Corner

Word webs can be used to help you choose exact words. Take a look at a recent piece of writing and choose an overused word. Create a synonym word web with the overused word in the center and synonyms branching out. If you find that you often overuse a particular word in different pieces of writing, you might consider making a synonym word web to save for future use.

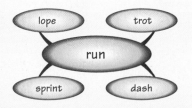

Activity D

Write one or two adjectives you could use in place of *old* if you were writing about each of these things.

1. a grandfather clock
2. a style of clothing
3. a book
4. a friend
5. an Egyptian pyramid
6. a tree
7. a bike
8. a house
9. shoes
10. a myth

Activity E

Replace each italicized adjective with a more precise descriptive word or group of words. You may use a thesaurus.

1. We had a *nice* time at the surprise party.
2. Trying to appear very *brave*, he entered the deserted house.
3. The apple in my lunch tasted *good*.
4. When we finished working on the car, we were *dirty*.
5. The principal thought our class play was *great*.
6. With the *loud* noise outside, it was hard to concentrate.

Activity F

The following are overused verbs. They express action, but there are more vivid or precise words that can give a reader a clearer picture of what is happening. How many colorful words can you list for each verb below?

say	walk	laugh
look	eat	do
carry	throw	hold

Activity G

Think of a more exact word to replace the verb *moved* in each of the items below. Then add an ending to complete each sentence.

1. The space shuttle moved . . .
2. An old car moved . . .
3. The supersonic jet moved . . .
4. The lame dog moved . . .
5. The lion moved . . .
6. The marathon runner moved . . .

Activity H

Rewrite each of these sentences. Change at least two words in each sentence to make it a more vivid picture.

1. The small dog ran into the field, chasing the squirrel.
2. Red leaves fell from the tall trees.
3. When I saw the funny picture, I laughed.
4. The mean stepmother made Cinderella work hard.
5. The fire burned in the empty barn.
6. As the storm came closer, dark clouds appeared.
7. The coach yelled at the boys for being too loud.
8. My old bike can go really fast.
9. The smell in the alley was very unpleasant.
10. The little girl was bothering all the guests.

Writer's Corner

Reread the sentences that you have written for earlier Writer's Corner activities. Look for overused or inexact words that wouldn't help your reader visualize your ideas. Replace the words with vivid, precise words that will engage your reader.

Speaking and Listening Skills

Oral Personal Narratives

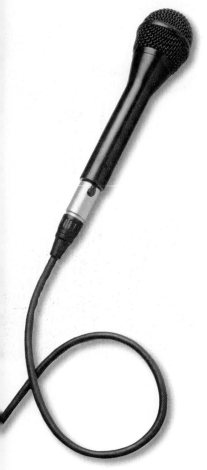

Every day you probably tell your friends or family about a personal experience. You know that they will be interested in what you have to say because they like you. There will be times when you have to speak to audiences in less familiar situations. When you do, you must keep in mind the same things that you do when you are writing a personal narrative.

Audience

Think about the ages and experiences of the people you are talking to. You speak differently to friends than you do to strangers. You speak differently to small children than you do to your parents. Match your language to your audience.

Introduction

You want your opening to grab your audience's attention just as you do in your writing. Body language, tone of voice, and facial expressions can help spark your listeners' interest.

Body

Relate all the parts of your experience in time order. When you put events out of order in an oral presentation, listeners are more likely to become confused because they can't go back to reread as they could in a written narrative. If a listener has to interrupt you for an explanation, you lose momentum. Finally, just as you do with a written narrative, leave out unnecessary details.

Conclusion

Conclude your story so that your audience knows that you have finished. If it's a funny experience, end on an amusing note. If you want your audience to share your feelings, tell how the experience affected you.

Voice

Let your personality show as you speak. Be yourself and try to relax. If you are stiff and nervous, your audience will recognize it. Often they will respond by losing interest in your presentation. Vary your pitch to show emotion and meaning. Use stress and tone for emphasis.

• Activity A •

Think of a day that you recently enjoyed at school. Maybe it was Career Day, or a book fair, or a special assembly. Jot down some notes about a good opener to get people interested in hearing about the day. Make notes for how you would describe your good feeling at the end of the day in a closing remark.

• Activity B •

Review the personal narrative at the the beginning of this chapter with your partner. Retell the dockworker's story to each other in two different ways. First tell the story in a humorous way. Then tell it in a dramatic way. Discuss the differences with each other and suggest ways that each of you could improve your delivery.

Speaker's Corner

Often it's easier to speak in a small group than in front of a large audience. Work in pairs or groups of three and use the notes you made for Activity A to tell your classmates about your special day. Take turns listening to one another's narratives. After each person speaks, give feedback about what you liked and what you would like to hear more about, and ask any questions you have. Use the suggestions to prepare a speech that you can present to the class.

Practice

Many people don't like to give speeches. They get nervous and forget what they want to say. The best way to overcome this nervousness is to practice. The better you know your material, the less nervous you will be. This is true if you are telling a one-minute joke or an eight-minute book report.

First, practice aloud by yourself. Make note cards with key words. Practice glancing at your notes to jog your memory, but don't come to rely on them so much that you forget to look at your audience. Imagine that you have an audience when you practice. Move your eyes around the room as though you are talking to people in the back row as well as in the front seats.

When you feel confident that you can present your narrative, ask a family member or friend to be a practice audience. Ask for suggestions on how you can improve your presentation.

- Did my introduction grab your attention?
- Did I tell my experiences in a way that you could follow my story?
- Were my voice and body language effective?
- Did I finish my speech in a way that you knew it was over?

Listening Tips

Think about how you listened when you took turns practicing with your partner. Did you listen to your partner the way you wanted your partner to listen to you? Here are some suggestions for good listening.

- Look at the speaker so that he or she will know you are paying attention.
- Picture in your mind the experiences being described.
- Watch the speaker's facial expressions and body language.
- Listen carefully to the speaker's tone of voice, stress, and volume for hints about meanings and emotions.
- When the speaker has finished, ask questions politely and give the speaker some positive feedback about the presentation.

An audience of good listeners can actually improve the speaker's delivery by helping him or her relax. The result is a speech that is clearer and more enjoyable for everyone.

• Activity C •

Choose one of the topics below or think of one of your own and plan to share it with the class. As you prepare, reread the suggestions on pages 28 and 29. Your audience will be your classmates, so plan to talk the way you would with your friends. Think of a clever way to get their attention and jot it down. List the details of the experience in time order. Remember the highlight of this experience—the reason you chose the topic. Be sure this is part of your conclusion.

* my stroke of good luck
* a special holiday tradition in my family
* starting a band with my friends
* putting on a play
* a funny time with my pet

Our Wide Wide World

The pyramid shape is special all over the world. The Transamerica Building in San Francisco and the entrance hall to the Louvre Museum in Paris are pyramids. Do you know what denomination of U.S. paper money has a pyramid on the back?

• Activity D •

Work with a partner. Take time to read over your notes from Activity C and think about how your voice and body language can help you tell your story. What will you stress with your voice and gestures? What will be your mood? Take turns sharing your personal experiences with each other. When it's your turn to be the listener, pay close attention so you can give your partner positive feedback after he or she finishes.

Speaker's Corner

Share your narrative from the previous Speaker's Corner with the class. Consider using the suggestions and questions from your partners to give the best presentation that you can. Remember to actively listen as classmates tell their stories. Note what speakers do to draw you into their narratives.

Prewriting and Drafting

It's time to use the skills that you developed in this chapter as you go through the writing process to produce a personal narrative about one of your life experiences. Today you will begin to write a personal narrative. Your classmates will be your audience.

Prewriting

Prewriting is a time to choose a writing topic and free write to explore ideas. It is also a time to develop a plan for how you will organize and structure your writing. In a personal narrative you should think about time order while prewriting.

Choosing a Topic

Before writing a personal narrative, writers give a lot of thought to what they're going to write about. A personal narrative should be about an event that was significant in the writer's own life. One way you can think of an event to write about is to brainstorm. In other words, quickly list all the ideas that come to mind. When you have finished, choose a topic that you believe you will be able to write an interesting narrative about.

Your Turn

Brainstorm events in your life that stand out in your memory and had some effect on your feelings. They could be things that made you feel pleased or angry, happy or sad. Jot down all your ideas.

Then choose the one idea that most appeals to you. Think for a few minutes about the experience. How did it affect you? Did you learn anything from it?

Free Writing

After choosing a topic, many writers use free writing to explore and expand their ideas about the subject or event. When free writing, they record whatever comes to mind about the topic. The more ideas they have, the more there will be to choose from when they write their narrative.

Last year, Matt was chosen to be the piano accompanist for the fifth-grade Spring Sing. Now, as a sixth-grader, he considers this one of his proudest achievements. He wants to use his experience as the subject of a personal narrative. Here are his free writing notes about attaining his goal.

- knew piano lessons paid off when I got to play at Spring Sing last year
- aunts and uncles, grandparents, mom and dad came
- everybody clapped and I did an encore
- wanted to learn to play when I saw the music program in second grade
- moved here in first grade
- glad I never gave up my lessons
- almost did in second grade, but mom made me go one more year
- By third grade I knew some good songs
- grandparents like me to play at holidays
- Mrs. Egan let me play for my class sometimes
- I'm going to keep taking piano lessons

Your Turn

Think about your experience. What would you call the beginning? How did events progress from there? Write down everything that you can remember about it. Let your ideas flow. If you add details that aren't important, you can take them out later. If you forget important details, you can add them later.

Organizing Ideas

In a personal narrative, ideas usually are put in time order. That is how Matt organized his ideas. He used each school year as his guide.

- I came to Lincoln School when I was in first grade.
- saw Spring Sing in second grade & wanted to learn the piano
- started piano lessons
- Sometimes I didn't like to practice but Mom always made me
- wanted to quit the first year, mom said I had to try for a year
- By third grade I knew six songs
- played for grandparents at holidays
- teacher sometimes let me play for the whole class
- in fifth grade, Mrs. Egan asked me to play for the Spring Sing.
- grandparents, aunts and uncles came as well as my parents and friends
- did well, played an encore
- I was proud to reach my goal
- I'll keep taking lessons.

Your Turn

Look at your free-writing notes and put them in time order. If you see details that aren't important to your narrative, cross them out. If you remember details that you should include, add them.

Drafting

A draft is your first chance to develop and organize your prewriting notes into a coherent narrative, including an introduction and conclusion. Matt got rid of a few of his notes that didn't relate to the main idea. As he began his

Achieving My Personal Goal

This is the story of how I achieved my personal goal of playing the piano for the Spring Sing program. Accompanying my class chorus was the most exiting thing in my life. We moved here when I was in the first grade. At first I didn't like Lincoln, but then I made friends. I started piano lessons in the second grade. I wasn't always a good learner. I didn't like to practice. My mother told me that if I still hated the lessons after a year, I could quit but before a year was up, I was hooked because I went to my first Spring Sing and I was so impressed with the piano player that I decided that by fifth grade, I would be the one playing the piano.

So I kept taking lessons and by third grade I could play some good songs. I played at holidays and my grandparents liked it. Mrs. Egan let me play for her music class. She encouraged me even when I goofed up.

Now we're at forth grade. One time I didn't want to go to my lesson so I hid behind the drapes. My Mom found me though and after a lecture, I decided not to try that again.

Now we're at fifth grade. Mrs. Egan asked me in February to be the fifth-grade accompanyist for Spring Sing. I couldn't believe it I said "Me?" She said that I was good enough and I said I would try. It was my goal and I had reached it.

My whole family came to the Spring Sing. I played a short solo at the end. Some people shouted. "Encore!" I knew they wanted me to play some more. Mrs. Egan gave me a nod, so I did. And I'm going to keep playing the piano.

first draft, he realized that mentioning every family member who came to the recital was unnecessary, so he didn't list them separately. Be aware that, like Matt, you can adjust your plan when writing. On page 34 is the draft that Matt wrote.

Your Turn

Review your notes and write your first draft. Double-space so you will have room to edit and make changes. Keep in mind that you will probably rewrite your narrative more than once.

Keep your audience—your classmates—in mind as you write. Continue to eliminate information that isn't necessary. Include new details that you think will add interest.

Remember how you practiced writing introductions and conclusions. Be sure these parts to your narrative are strong. Let your audience know how you feel at the end.

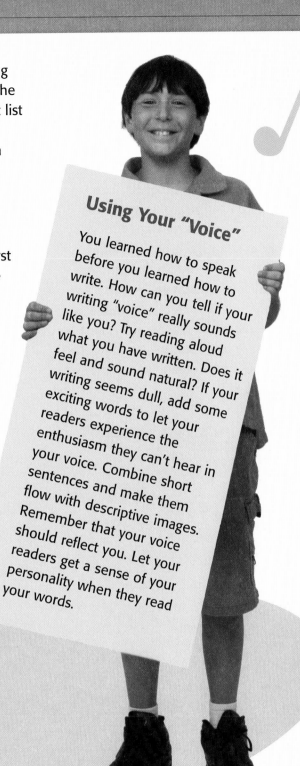

Using Your "Voice"

You learned how to speak before you learned how to write. How can you tell if your writing "voice" really sounds like you? Try reading aloud what you have written. Does it feel and sound natural? If your writing seems dull, add some exciting words to let your readers experience the enthusiasm they can't hear in your voice. Combine short sentences and make them flow with descriptive images. Remember that your voice should reflect you. Let your readers get a sense of your personality when they read your words.

Content Editing

A draft is a work in progress. Good writers edit and revise, sometimes many times, when they are writing a personal narrative. A content editor checks to make certain that all the necessary information is included and that the writing is clear, ordered, and logical. Many editors use a checklist to make sure they review everything. This is a checklist for editing your narrative.

Good writers read their own work many times before they're finished. In many cases writers read their own writing so often that they don't always see what might be confusing to others. That's why writers often want to have new eyes read their work to see what might have been missed.

Matt knew that a classmate could be a big help editing his narrative. His friend Andre was always a careful worker, and Matt knew that Andre would suggest good changes. The two teamed up to edit each other's narratives.

Andre read Matt's narrative all the way through once. Then he read it two more times, looking carefully at the Content Editor's Checklist. He made notes for himself so he would remember his ideas. When Andre finished, the boys had a conference.

Content Editor's Checklist

✔ Does the introduction make the reader want to continue reading?

✔ Are the details told clearly and in time order?

✔ Does the body tell only the relevant details?

✔ Does the body tell all of the relevant details?

✔ Does the writer use exact words to help the reader more clearly share the experience?

✔ Is there a good conclusion that ties everything together?

First, Andre told Matt how cool it must have been to be the pianist for Spring Sing. Then Andre told Matt what he liked about his narrative. He liked how Matt organized the narrative by school year. He also liked the way Matt shared his feelings of not always wanting to practice. Then Andre made his suggestions.

- The introduction states your goal, but it doesn't really make me want to keep reading.

- It isn't important that people know when you moved here and how you felt about Lincoln at first.

- Details of what happens at the Spring Sing might be helpful to people who are unfamiliar with it.

- Maybe you could tell what you learned from this experience. Just saying that you're going to continue playing doesn't seem like enough.

Matt respected Andre's opinions. Although Matt didn't agree with all of Andre's suggestions, he liked most of them, and he knew that his narrative would be better because of Andre's help.

Your Turn

Reread your first draft, looking at the Content Editor's Checklist as you do so. When you use a checklist, don't try to check all the items at once. Read through your writing several times looking for only one or two types of problems each time. Is your introduction engaging? Are your details in order? Did you include all the important details? Does your conclusion satisfy you and the reader?

Work with a partner and read each other's narratives. Take notes as Andre did and confer with each other, making positive suggestions for improvement. Be sure you both use the Content Editor's Checklist. When it is your turn to share your comments about your partner's work, remember to start with the things you liked. You've both worked hard, and there are many good things about your writing.

After hearing your partner's suggestions, consider all of them, but remember that the final product is yours. You don't have to make all the suggested changes. You may find other things on your own that you can improve in your final revision.

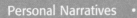

Personal Narratives

Revising

This is how Matt revised his narrative based on his own and his partner's suggestions.

need new title

Achieving My Personal Goal

It was the night of the Spring Sing and all eyes were on the piano player—me! ~~This is the story of how I achieved my personal goal of playing the piano for the Spring Sing program.~~ Accompanying my class chorus was the most exiting thing in my life. It was a goal I set for myself in second grade. ~~We moved here when I was in the first grade. At first I didn't like Lincoln, but then I made friends.~~ I started piano lessons in the second grade. I wasn't always a good learner. I didn't like to practice, especially when I heard other kids playing ball. My mother told me that if I still hated the lessons after a year, I could quit but before a year was up, I was hooked because I went to my first Spring Sing and I was so impressed with the piano player that I decided that by fifth grade, I would be the one playing the piano.

So I kept taking lessons and by third grade I could play some familiar ~~good~~ songs. I played at holidays and my grandparents were delighted ~~liked it~~. Mrs. Egan let me play for her music class. She encouraged me even when I goofed up. ~~One day when I was in the forth grade.~~ Now we're at forth grade. One time I didn't want to go to my lesson so I hid behind the drapes. My Mom found me though and after a lecture, I decided not to try that again.

Mrs. Egan surprised me last February and asked if I would be ~~Now we're at fifth grade. Mrs. Egan asked me in February to be the fifth-~~ grade accompanyist for Spring Sing. I couldn't believe it I said "Me?" She said that I was good enough and I said I would try. It was my goal and I had reached it. Boy, am I glad I did!

My whole family came to the Spring Sing. I played a short solo at the end. Some people shouted. "Encore!" I knew they wanted me to play some more. Mrs. Egan gave me a nod, so I did. And I'm going to keep playing the piano. That experience taught me what hard work can accomplish. Here I come Carnegie Hall!

Look at some of the things that Matt did to improve his personal narrative.

- He took Andre's suggestion and changed the introduction to make the reader want to know what's coming next. He realized he wasn't happy with the title and decided to try and come up with a better one.

- He agreed with Andre to leave out the part about how he felt about his new school when his family moved to town.

- He decided not to include an explanation about the Spring Sing. Most of his audience would know what it was, and Matt wanted to focus his narrative on his accomplishment.

- Matt concluded by saying that he's glad he played in the Spring Sing and that he learned the value of hard work from this experience. However, Matt still wasn't happy with his conclusion, and he kept thinking of ways to improve it.

As Matt looked at his paper again, he saw something else that he wanted to change. He knew he had been much more excited than the paper made him sound. He tried to add some exact words that better expressed his emotions about the experience such as *Mrs. Egan surprised me* instead of *Mrs. Egan asked me,* and *my grandparents were delighted* instead of *my grandparents liked it.* To show more of his own emotion, he also added the exclamatory sentence *Boy, am I glad I did it!*

Your Turn

Use any new ideas you have and the ideas you got from your partner conference to revise your narrative. When you have finished, go over the Content Editor's Checklist again. See if you can answer yes to each question.

Copyediting and Proofreading

Copyediting

When you copyedit, you should look for accurate word meaning, word choice, and sentence structure. Matt realized that his narrative was greatly improved after making his own changes and following Andre's suggestions. But since he had made extensive changes to his draft, Matt wanted to make certain that his sentences flowed well. He decided that one of his sentences rambled. Can you find it?

Matt also noticed a run-on sentence. See if you can spot it. Matt then used the rest of the Copyeditor's Checklist to finish editing his personal narrative.

Copyeditor's Checklist

✔ Are there rambling sentences?

✔ Are there run-on sentences?

✔ Is there variety in sentence length?

✔ Are exact words used that help the reader visualize the events?

✔ Is there variety in word choice?

✔ Is the structure of sentences logical and grammatically correct?

Your Turn

Look over your revised draft. Use the Copyeditor's Checklist to edit your narrative. Vary your sentences. Too many short, choppy sentences are boring to read. Make sure you don't have any run-on or rambling sentences. Read your story aloud or ask someone else to read it while you listen.

Proofreading

Before writing the final copy of a narrative, a good writer proofreads to check for spelling, punctuation, capitalization, and grammar. A checklist can help.

Proofreader's Checklist

✔ Are the paragraphs indented?

✔ Have any words been misspelled?

✔ Is the grammar accurate?

✔ Are capitalization and punctuation correct?

✔ Were new errors introduced during the editing process?

Good writers ask others to proofread their work because a proofreader can give a fresh look at the piece. He or she will probably spot errors that the writer missed. It is also important to check that no new errors were introduced during the editing process. A writer may add or delete a sentence or a word by accident while correcting other errors.

Charlotte was happy to proofread Matt's narrative. She found just three spelling errors and one capitalization error. Can you find them? Use a dictionary if you aren't sure of a spelling.

Your Turn

Read your paper carefully, using the Proofreader's Checklist. Look only for one kind of error at a time. It's easy to miss errors if you're looking for too many things at once. You will have to read your story several times, and errors that you missed on previous readings will jump out at you. Use the proofreading marks in the box below to mark changes on your paper.

When you have finished the Proofreader's Checklist, trade papers with a partner. Go over each other's papers in the same way. Be sure to have a dictionary handy.

Common Proofreading Marks

Symbol	Meaning	Example
¶	begin new paragraph	over. ¶Begin a new
◯	close up space	close u p space
∧	insert	students ^should think
℘	delete, omit	that the the book
/	lowercase letter	Mathematics
∩	letters are reversed	letters are reversed
≡	capitalize	washington
ᵛᵛ	quotation	ᵛI am,ᵛ I said.

Chapter 1 Writer's Workshop

Personal Narratives

Publishing

Publishing is the moment when you decide to share your finished work. You know it is your best work and you are ready to show it to your audience. After several editing sessions, Matt felt he had done his best. It was now time for

Continue On!

The lights dimmed. The audience was hushed. Their eyes all focused on the piano player–me! Accompanying my fifth-grade class for our part of the Spring Sing was the most exciting thing that has happened to me in my life. It was a goal that I set for myself in second grade.

I began taking piano lessons in the second grade, and I admit that I wasn't always enthusiastic. I didn't always want to practice, especially when I heard other kids playing ball. My mother told me that if I still hated my lessons after a year, I could quit. But I was hooked on piano before a year was up. I had gone to my first Spring Sing, and I was so impressed by the piano player that I decided that by fifth grade, I would be the one playing the piano. It was a pretty ambitious goal for a second grader.

By the time I was in third grade, I could already play some familiar songs. I played at holidays and my grandparents were delighted. Mrs. Egan let me play for her music class. She encouraged me even when I goofed up.

One day when I was in the fourth grade, I hid behind the drapes. I was hoping Mom wouldn't find me to take me to my piano lesson because I hadn't practiced. She found me though and after a lecture, I decided not to try that again.

Mrs. Egan surprised me last February when she asked if I would be the fifth-grade accompanist for the Spring Sing. It made me so nervous to think of performing in front of my schoolmates and all the parents that I just gulped and said, "Me?" When she assured me that I could do it, I said that I would try. Boy, am I ever glad I did! It was the greatest.

My whole family came to listen to me play. As the program ended with my short piano solo, I heard some people call out, "Encore! Continue on." Mrs. Egan gave me a nod, so I did. Not only did I continue on to play an encore, but I also plan to continue with my piano lessons. This experience taught me what hard work can accomplish. Here I come, Carnegie Hall.

the finished version. He printed out his narrative onto a clean sheet of paper. After all his work, Matt was actually pleased that he would have a chance to share it with his classmates.

Your Turn

Eventually, a professional writer submits his or her personal narrative to a magazine or book publisher. This is an exciting moment for the writer because he or she is making the work available to an audience for the first time.

Although the writing that you do in school may not be printed in a book or magazine, the moment you share your work with your class or teacher should also be an exciting moment. Make certain that your work is in its best form before you present it.

To publish your work, follow these steps:

- Use your neatest handwriting or a computer to make a final copy of your revised draft.

- Proofread your copy one more time for correct spelling, capitalization, and punctuation. If you can, use your computer's spell checker.

There are many ways you can publish your narrative. One way is to put together a book of all the personal narratives from your class. Some students may have photographs, illustrations, or other souvenirs of their experience. These would be interesting items to attach to the narratives.

If your school has a library, ask the librarian if your class's book of personal narratives could be a checkout book for a limited time. Advertise in the school newsletter or on the activities bulletin board that your book is available for other students to read.

You might also have your class book on hand for Parents' Night. That way you will have an even larger audience. Whenever you publish any of your work, your goal is to share your thoughts and experiences with other people.

CHAPTER

2

Our Wide Wide World

A simple click on *Print* sets the computer and printer in motion. They work together to send us our final product—the fruits of our written labor on a sheet of paper. Can you imagine your life without writing? How does the printed word influence your life every day?

How-to Articles

Replacing an Ink Cartridge

Your Franklin XL-805 printer uses a XLP-800 series black ink cartridge and a XLP-800c color ink cartridge. Check the expiration date on the carton before installing the replacement cartridge.

CAUTION: Ink may be harmful if swallowed. Avoid contact with the eyes.

Carefully open the outer and inner boxes and remove the replacement cartridge. Lift the printer cover. The print cartridges will automatically move to the center of the printer. The black ink cartridge is on the left, and the color ink cartridge is on the right. With your thumb and index finger, lift the plastic latch holding the empty cartridge in place and remove the cartridge from its slot.

Holding the new cartridge upright, remove the protective tape from the bottom of the cartridge. DO NOT TOUCH THE INK NOZZLE. Place the cartridge firmly in position and push it down until it clicks. Close the latch. Finally, close the printer cover. The cartridges will return to the proper place for printing, and the ready light should appear.

Before starting to print, align the print cartridges. To do this, click on the printer icon on your desktop or use the Start menu to locate the printer. Go to Printer Services and choose the alignment service. Follow the directions to align the cartridge and get test printouts. This will take several minutes, but it is an important step.

Use the box that contained the replacement cartridge to mail the used cartridge to Franklin Printers for recycling. Franklin will send you a $5-off coupon for each empty cartridge you return.

What Makes a Good How-to Article?

Written directions are a large part of our modern world. There are directions for programming cell phones, televisions, DVD players, and even coffee makers. Directions tell us how to play games and how to bake cookies. These are all examples of how-to writing. Here are some things to remember when you write a how-to article.

Audience

Think about the people who will be reading your directions. Don't assume that your audience knows what you know. On the other hand, don't make your directions too easy. Instructions for installing a car engine shouldn't tell mechanics how to use a wrench.

Introduction

People who read a how-to piece are looking for information, so starting with an attention-grabbing sentence isn't important. Instead, start out by telling readers what your directions teach—what they will be able to do when they finish reading.

Correct Order of Steps

Writing your directions as you perform the task yourself will help you make sure that you put each step in the proper sequence and that you list all the necessary materials and tools. If you can't perform the task as you write, very carefully review in your mind each step and what is needed to perform it. Use imperative sentences to tell your readers how to do the steps.

Conclusion

The conclusion of a how-to article should explain what the end result of the process should be or what should have been learned. The reader ought to feel assured that by following the directions, he or she will be able to complete the task as it was described in the introduction. This is also the place to include suggestions or tips for the reader to use when performing the steps in the future.

• Activity A •

Read the following explanation of how to get your school day off to a good start. You may notice that if you were to follow the suggestions exactly, you might not have a good day at all! Rewrite the sentences in a logical sequence so they could be followed with successful results.

Have your clothes laid out before you go to bed.

Get up when your alarm rings.

Catch the bus to school.

Get dressed.

Eat a healthful breakfast.

Shower and brush your teeth.

Make your lunch.

Make sure you have all your homework and supplies.

Go to your first class with a positive attitude.

Meet your friends and compare notes to make sure you are ready for all your classes.

Writer's Corner

Sometimes the simplest actions can be the hardest to explain. Pretend you are instructing a creature from another planet to do something you do every day such as buttoning or zipping a jacket, tying shoes, or brushing your teeth. Write four or five step-by-step directions. Then work with a partner taking turns being the creature to see if your how-to piece is accurate and complete.

Activity B

Select one of these sentence starters as an introduction to a short how-to article that you would like to write. Try to include at least three or four steps in your explanation. Then write a concluding sentence.

A. Have you ever wondered how to _____?

B. _____ is not as difficult as it looks.

C. If you're tired of the card games you know, try _____ for a change.

D. You may be surprised at how _____.

E. Before you can drive the boat, you need to know _____.

F. Just imagine the fun you could have if _____.

Activity C

Many how-to pieces are written as numbered steps. Others are written in paragraph form just as the directions for replacing an ink cartridge were.

The following steps are used to prepare paper for recycling. Change the directions from numbered steps into paragraph form. Add a suitable introduction and conclusion.

1. When recycling paper, be sure to take out staples and remove all traces of glue.

2. Tear the paper into small squares, about one inch on a side.

3. Put the torn paper in a bucket of water and let it soak for at least two hours.

4. Put batches of the paper into a blender, making sure there is plenty of water (about one-third paper with two-thirds water). The blender will break up the wet paper into a pulp.

5. Fill a rectangular plastic tray with about two inches of water and pour in a blender full of pulp.

6. Now you are ready to form pages, using a screen and frame.

Activity D

Look at the following titles for how-to articles. For each one write who the intended audience probably is—adults, teens, or children. Some how-to articles may have more than one audience.

1. Makeup Tips for School Days and Saturday Nights

2. How to Soup Up Your Bicycle

3. Improve Your Swing and Lower Your Golf Score!

4. Games for Babysitters and Young Children

5. Growing Vegetables All Year Long

6. How to Be a Deejay at Parties

7. Cleaning Your Doll's Clothes

Activity E

For each set of directions, match the how-to language with its intended audience.

1. Blanch four tomatoes.

   Dip four tomatoes in boiling water to loosen the skin.

   a. professional chef

   b. amateur cook

2. Tighten the bolt firmly.

   Tighten the bolt to 20 foot-pounds.

   a. mechanic

   b. teenager

3. Reboot the computer.

   Turn the computer off and on again.

   a. beginning computer user

   b. computer technician

Writer's Corner

Have you ever made a paper-bag puppet? Look at the illustration on the right. Then write a how-to article for second graders explaining how to make a paper-bag puppet. Remember to use imperative sentences.

How-to Articles

Order, Accuracy, and Completeness

The purpose of a how-to article is to teach readers to do something that they couldn't do before. Just as a builder does not begin with the roof of a house, the how-to writer does not begin with the last step of the process. The careful writer makes sure that each step connects to and builds on the one before it to produce the final product or outcome.

• Activity A •

A how-to article with missing steps can result in frustration when readers don't get the results they expected. Read the following how-to article and the missing steps that follow. What will happen if the instructions are followed as presented? Rewrite the paragraph to include the missing steps. Remember that each step should build on the one before it.

Cheesy Eggs for Breakfast

Here is how you can make cheesy eggs, a great breakfast dish that is particularly good when served with toast and juice.

First, shred enough cheddar cheese to make one-half cup. Next, break eight eggs into a bowl. Add about four tablespoons of water or milk to the eggs and mix well with a fork or whisk. After that, heat a medium skillet on low. Then pour the egg mixture into the skillet and heat until it begins to thicken, stirring often. Mix until the cheese is melted and eggs are firm. Salt and pepper to taste.

Missing Steps: **1.** Melt two tablespoons of butter in the skillet to prevent the eggs from sticking. **2.** When the eggs are almost firm, sprinkle the grated cheese into the mixture.

• Activity B •

Imagine that you are going to meet friends at a new ice-cream parlor in your neighborhood. If you give your friends the following directions, they might get lost. What information is missing? Rewrite the directions to make sure your friends won't get lost.

Get off the westbound Maple Avenue bus at the Dover Street terminal. Walk north on Dover two blocks to Front Street. Turn on Front Street and walk past the post office to the second street on your left, West Avenue. Turn left, and continue down West Avenue to 112. It will be on the left side of the street, across from the pet shop.

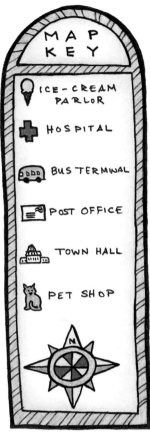

• Activity C •

Suppose that your friends are ready to go home. However, for variety they want to take a different route back to the bus terminal. Write directions to the terminal that will take your friends on different streets than they used to get to the ice-cream parlor. They won't mind a longer route.

Writer's Corner

Write a paragraph that gives directions to get from school to someplace that your classmates will recognize. Don't tell what the place is. When you have finished, exchange papers with a partner to see if you can determine each other's destinations.

• Activity D •

Read through the following recipe and imagine that you are making the cupcakes. Three important pieces of information are missing. What missing information do you need to make your cupcakes?

Cranberry Cupcakes

1/2 cup shortening	1 cup light brown sugar
eggs	1/2 cup sour cream
1 1/2 cups flour	1/2 cup cranberries
1 tbs. cinnamon	1/2 cup nuts
salt	1/2 tsp. baking soda

Cream shortening and sugar. Add eggs, one at a time and beat until light and fluffy. Stir in sour cream and cranberries. Add dry ingredients and blend well. Mix in nuts. Fill paper-lined (or well greased) muffin tins two-thirds full. Bake for 20–25 minutes.

• Activity E •

Read the following directions for how to paint a room. Some of the steps are out of place. Determine the correct order of the steps and rewrite the directions in paragraph form.

1. Lay out your drop cloths.
2. Move furniture away from the walls.
3. Paint the ceiling first.
4. Repair cracks and holes with spackling paste.
5. Use a brush to paint close to windows, doors, and fixtures.
6. Use a roller and pole to paint the walls.
7. Remove pictures, wall plates, and outlet covers.
8. Clear cobwebs out of corners with a dust mop.
9. Put masking tape around fixtures.
10. Return furniture to original positions.
11. Pick up drop cloths and remove masking tape.
12. Replace pictures, wall plates, and outlet covers.
13. Wait for paint to dry.

Activity F

Suppose that you are writing how-to pieces on three activities from the following list. Go through the steps for each activity in your head and think of all the items that it requires. Write down the items. Then compare your lists with your classmates' lists. For each activity the person with the longest list of necessary items wins.

1. Playing baseball
2. Cooking a hot breakfast
3. Tending a garden
4. Fixing a flat bicycle tire
5. Washing a car
6. Painting a room
7. Fishing

Activity G

The following directions explain how to play a game called Odd Man Out. Some important information is missing. Write the information you need to know to play the game.

1. Remove one king from a deck of playing cards.
2. Deal out cards to each player.
3. Players look at their hands and lay down any pairs of cards.
4. The dealer takes one card from the player to the left.
5. The player to the left takes one card from the next player.
6. Play continues until all pairs are on the table.
7. The player holding the extra king is the "Odd Man Out."

Writer's Corner

Think of something that you like to make such as something good to eat or something to wear. Make a list, in proper sequence, of the steps involved in making this item. Be sure to include everything and to eliminate unnecessary steps. Keep your list to use again.

Transition Words

Our Wide Wide World

Quill pens were used for about 1,200 years—from roughly AD 600 to 1800. These pens were made from bird feathers. After the feathers were plucked, the nibs were heated by fire to harden them. They were then shaped and sharpened by a special tool called a penknife. Each pen lasted about a week.

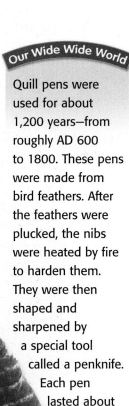

When directions are written in paragraph form, writers use transition words to help their readers follow along. Words such as *first*, *second*, *then*, *next*, and *finally* are some transition words that help readers keep track of the order of steps needed to perform a task. They signal to the reader that it is time to do the next thing. Here is a list of common transition words and phrases.

first	third	then
begin by	after that	soon
second	next	finally
the second step	while	to finish

Keep track of the transition words that you use when you write. If you use only number transition words such as first, second, third, and so on, your directions will be easy to follow, but they won't be very interesting. Read the following paragraph:

> First, fill the pot about half full with potting soil. Second, place the plant cuttings in the center. Third, hold them while you loosely pack more dirt around them. Fourth, water the cuttings thoroughly. Fifth, place them near a window where they will get lots of sun.

Read the same directions with other transitions words.

> The first step in planting cuttings is to fill the pot about half full with potting soil. Next place the plant cuttings in the center and hold them while you loosely pack more dirt around them. Then water the cuttings thoroughly. Finally, place them near a window where they will get lots of sun.

Write transition words that will complete these how-to paragraphs. You may choose to omit a transition word in a sentence, or you may use a different word or phrase of your own. Change and add words as necessary.

1. Your assignment is to set the table. _____ place a dinner plate on each placemat. _____ put the silverware beside the plate, with the forks on the left and the knife and spoon on the right. _____ fold the napkins. Be creative! _____ put a napkin at each place. _____ add a glass above and slightly to the right of the plate. _____ the addition of flowers on the table would be an elegant touch.

2. Let's get started on our class project to send greeting cards to senior citizens. _____ look at the list on the board to obtain the name and address of a person who would like to receive a card. _____ locate the card-making program on the computer. _____ choose one of the sample cards on display or create a card of your own design. _____ write a short, cheery note to the person. _____ put the card into an envelope and address it. Remember to put a stamp on the envelope. _____ drop it in the mailbox and feel happy that your effort will make someone else happy too!

Writer's Corner

Look at the list of steps you wrote for making something in the previous Writer's Corner. Write the steps in paragraph form, making sure you keep them in the correct order. Use appropriate transition words. Remember to vary your sentences to make your directions interesting.

Activity B

Read the two sets of directions below. Rewrite the steps in each set into paragraph form. Use the transition words and phrases on page 54 to help readers keep track of the order of the steps.

1. **a.** Using a computer mouse is not difficult.

   b. Grasp the mouse in your hand.

   c. Place one finger on the left button and one finger on the right button.

   d. Slide the mouse around your desktop and observe how it affects the arrow on your computer screen.

   e. Move the mouse so that the arrow is directly on top of an icon on your computer screen.

   f. Click the left button on the mouse two times quickly.

   g. The application that your arrow was on will open.

2. **a.** Front stoop baseball can be played by 2 to 6 players.

   b. You'll need a front stoop with three to five steps, chalk, and a tennis ball or a rubber ball.

   c. Mark out zones away from the stoop: 10 feet = out; 15 feet = a single; 20 feet = a double; 25 feet = a triple; 30 feet = a home run.

   d. The team that is up bounces the ball against any step. Players take turns "batting."

   e. If the fielding team stops the ball in the "out" zone, the batter is out.

   f. If the fielding team catches the ball on a fly, the batter is out.

   g. If the fielding team catches the ball after it bounces, the batter is "on base" according to the zone where the ball is caught.

   h. After three outs, teams switch positions. Play as many innings as you can before your mom calls you for dinner.

Activity C •

Where could you put transition words to make this paragraph flow more smoothly? Rewrite the paragraph.

Try my dad's system for washing a car. He does the roof. He soaps it down. He rinses it off. He soaps and rinses the hood. He repeats the process for the trunk. He does the car's sides. He does the grillwork. He uses a chamois cloth to soak up the water droplets on the car. He scrubs the wheels and tires with a stiff brush. He applies chrome polish. He buffs the chrome until it shines. He uses window cleaner and newspapers to make the windshields and side windows sparkle. Your vehicle will look like new.

Activity D •

Healthful snacks are a smart way to keep us going between meals. Snacks can be delicious to eat, easy to prepare, nutritious, and just plain fun! Read about the colorful and yummy Snack on a Stick. Then rewrite the paragraph with transition words to make it read more smoothly.

Create healthy snack sticks by using wooden skewers. Cut Swiss cheese and cheddar cheese into chunks. Cut green and red peppers into cubes. Slice and roll thin slices of ham. Drain stuffed green olives. Thread ingredients onto a skewer, alternating colors, until it is almost full. Make a lot and enjoy them with friends.

Writer's Corner

Write your own healthy Snack on a Stick recipe, using your favorite nibble foods. You might use fruits, vegetables, meat, or any combination of these. Be sure to make your recipe read smoothly with transition words. Write your recipe in paragraph form with an appealing introductory sentence and a mouthwatering conclusion to make people want to try it.

Writing Skills

Sentence Types

Varying the types of sentences in your writing will make it more interesting. There are different types of sentences you can use.

Simple and Compound Sentences

A simple sentence is one independent clause (group of words) with a subject and a predicate. It expresses a complete thought.

> Max wanted to start a rock group.

A compound sentence is made up of two or more independent clauses joined by coordinating conjunctions such as *and, but,* or *or.* Long independent clauses need a comma between them. If the clauses are short, they usually don't need a comma.

> Ed may go, *but* he must take his sister Dina with him.
> They might go to the movies, *or* they might play softball.
> Dina will pitch *and* Ed will catch.

Coordinating Conjunctions	
and	The conjunction *and* connects two independent clauses that are similar or that happen at the same time. **Judy will wash and I will dry.**
or	The conjunction *or* connects two independent clauses that indicate a choice is possible. **You can paint the bench or you can stain it.**
but, yet	The conjunctions *but* and *yet* connect two independent clauses that are opposite or that contrast each other. **I would like to play, but I don't know how.** **Mehmud speaks little English, yet he reads it very well.**

Activity A

Choose the best coordinating conjunction to combine the following pairs of simple sentences into compound sentences. Use each conjunction one time.

or   **and**   **but**   **yet**

1. Proper tools are important. Know-how is more important.
2. You can pop corn on a stove. You can pop it in a microwave.
3. We were late when we left. We were held up in traffic.
4. I saw the crash about to happen. I couldn't prevent it.

Activity B

Add an independent clause to each of these simple sentences to make a compound sentence. Join the clauses with a coordinating conjunction.

1. I took my dog for a walk.
2. Jessica did not get the best score.
3. The whistle blew to start the game.
4. I want a new guitar.
5. Chris can stay here with me.

Activity C

Write two sentences for each coordinating conjunction: *and*, *but*, and *or*. Then show that you have connected independent clauses by taking the coordinating conjunction out of each sentence and writing the two simple sentences that made up the compound sentence.

Writer's Corner

Look at the recipe that you wrote for the previous Writer's Corner. Rewrite the paragraph so that it contains simple sentences and compound sentences.

Complex Sentences

Using some complex sentences is another way to make your writing clearer and more interesting. The following conjunctions are called subordinate conjunctions. They show a time relationship within a sentence. They help your readers understand the order of events in your writing. When you use these conjunctions, you write complex sentences.

after	before	when
as	once	whenever
as soon as	since	while

Read these examples of complex sentences showing time relationships. Tell what the conjunction is.

A. Once the leaves are dead, remove the bulbs from the soil and store in a cool spot.

B. While the potatoes are boiling, prepare the other vegetables to be added later.

C. Remove the doughnuts from the oil as soon as they float to the top.

In sentences A and B, the subordinate conjunction is in the first clause. When the conjunction is in the first clause, use a comma to separate the two clauses. If the subordinate conjunction is in the second clause, as in sentence C, no comma is needed.

• Activity D •

Rewrite these pairs of simple sentences to make them complex sentences. Use a conjunction from the list above. Draw a line below the clause that contains the conjunction. If the clause with the conjunction comes first, put a comma between the two clauses. If it comes second, you don't need a comma.

1. Maria and I heard the call for volunteers. We went to help.

2. I hurried to catch the school bus. I ate a quick breakfast.

3. Tamika worked on the ladder. Jorge held it steady.

4. The fire was under control. Firefighters arrived on the scene.

Activity E

Make each of these simple sentences into a complex sentence by adding a clause and a conjunction that shows time relationship. Add the clause to the beginning or end of the sentence.

1. I opened my last birthday gift.
2. It was time for the fireworks to start.
3. Beginning skiers should take classes.
4. Remove the bread from the oven.

Activity F

Rewrite these short paragraphs. Make them more interesting by changing the simple sentences to compound or complex sentences. You may add words or change word order.

Shoes that are well polished can make you feel good about yourself. They also give others a good impression of you. Choose the proper polish. Wax gives a better shine. Cream preserves leather better. Remove the laces from the shoes. Use an old T-shirt or sock to remove dirt from the shoes.

For very grimy shoes, use saddle soap to soften the dirt. Wipe off the saddle soap and dirt. Let the shoes dry for about five minutes. Apply the polish. Use a clean cotton cloth to rub the polish into the leather. Do one shoe at a time. Start at the front of the shoe. Work your way back. Don't forget the tongue. Let the polish sit on the leather for about 10 minutes. Do the other shoe.

Put your hand into the first shoe to hold it. Use a soft-bristle brush to quickly buff back and forth until you have a lustrous shine. Repeat for the other shoe.

Writer's Corner

Choose any how-to piece or other article you have written. Rewrite as many sentences as you can into complex sentences. Compare the two versions of the paragraph. Which is more interesting to read?

Instructional Graphics

Our Wide Wide World

In the fifteenth
century, Johann
Gutenberg
revolutionized
the way books
were produced. He
had the idea to cast
individual letters
out of cheap but
durable metal. The
letters could be
rearranged in any
order. Using his
press, Gutenberg
published 180
copies of the
two-volume
Gutenberg Bible.

Flowcharts

Writers have different ways to show information to their readers. Sometimes tables can be useful. Sometimes charts work best. How-to writers often present their instructions with flowcharts. A flowchart gives step-by-step directions. The following figures are common flowchart symbols.

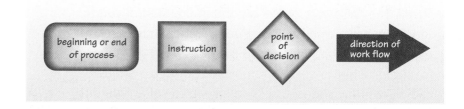

Try to follow this troubleshooting flowchart for determining why a car does not start.

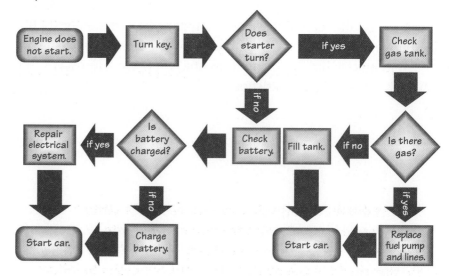

Activity A

Read through the troubleshooting flowchart for a car engine that does not start. Convert the flowchart into directions written in paragraph form.

Activity B

Read the following directions for starting a lawn mower. Then copy the flowchart below and fill it in, using the steps in the directions.

1. Turn the ignition switch to "On."
2. Adjust the choke to "Full."
3. Push the primer bulb 3 times.
4. Pull the starter rope 1 time.
5. Move the choke to "Half."
6. Pull the starter rope until the engine starts.
7. If the engine does not start after 5 pulls, repeat from Step 2.
8. When the engine starts, move the choke to "Off."

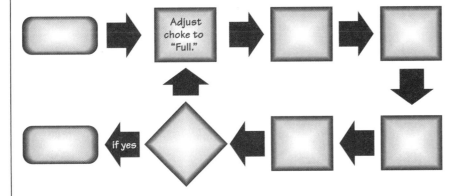

Writer's Corner

Look at the list of steps that you wrote for the Writer's Corner on page 53. Convert the written steps into a flowchart. Trade papers with a classmate and decide whether the flowcharts or the written directions are easier to follow.

Diagrams

Another helpful tool to use when explaining how to do something is a diagram. If you can give your readers a picture to refer to as they read the directions, they can often understand better what they should do to complete the task.

The following directions explain the rules for barrel racing, an event in rodeos and horse shows. Cover the diagram and read the directions. Then read the directions again, this time referring to the diagram. Does the diagram help you to understand how barrel racing is done?

Barrel Racing

1. Set up three barrels at the corners of a triangle.
2. The barrels at the base of the triangle should be 90 feet apart.
3. The barrels that make up the sides of the triangle should be 105 feet apart.
4. The starting line should be 30 feet from the base of the triangle.
5. The time starts as soon as the horse crosses the starting line.
6. The rider can circle either base barrel first.
7. When circling each barrel, the horse must cross over its own path.
8. The rider proceeds to the second base barrel.
9. The rider circles the top barrel last.
10. The time stops when the horse crosses the starting line.
11. A penalty of five seconds is added for each barrel knocked over.

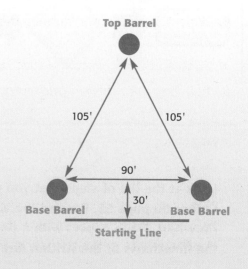

Activity C

In addition to the layout of the barrel-racing course, the National Barrel Horse Association has safety rules about how close the corral fences can be to the barrels. The distances are (1) a minimum of 15 feet between each of the first two barrels and the side fences, (2) a minimum of 30 feet between the third barrel and the back fence, and (3) a minimum of 30 feet between the start/finish line and the front fence. Copy the diagram from page 64. Add lines and measurements to show the minimum distances between the barrels and the fences.

Activity D

Just as written directions must be accurate for people to follow them properly, diagrams must be accurate or they will confuse people who try to follow them. The diagrams to the right don't match the order of the steps as they are written. Determine which diagrams are out of place and tell which steps they belong with.

1. Slide the tie around the collar so that the wider end *A* is longer than the thinner end *B*. Cross *A* over *B*.

2. Wrap *A* behind *B*.

3. Bring *A* up.

4. Thread *A* between the collar and the tie.

5. Wrap *A* over *B*, from left to right.

6. Wrap *A* behind *B* and through the loop between the collar and the tie.

7. Push *A* down through the knot in front.

8. Pull the knot tight and draw it up to the collar.

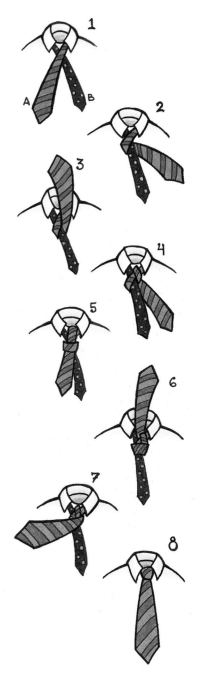

Writer's Corner

Choose any set of directions that you wrote for a Writer's Corner in this chapter. Draw a diagram to accompany the directions that will make them easier to understand.

Speaking and Listening Skills

How-to Talks

Our Wide Wide World

Early typewriters of the 19th century seem like strange machines today. They typed only in capitals and the typist couldn't see the letters being typed. Not surprisingly, many writers at the time found them difficult to use.

When you write a how-to piece, you want readers to be able to follow your directions. You keep your audience in mind, you write your directions in a step-by-step sequence, and you explain things as clearly as possible. When giving an oral how-to presentation, you must follow similar rules. Keep your audience in mind, list your steps, and be clear.

Audience

Speak loudly and clearly enough to be heard in the back of the room. Use language your listeners will understand. If there are many things that are important to remember, you might provide a handout with those details to your audience.

Visual Aids

Use visual aids when you can. Find out what equipment and materials are available to you and plan to use them in your presentation. Make your own displays to aid your presentation. Flowcharts can be useful when giving how-to talks. If you are explaining how to make something, display examples of the product at different stages of completion. Demonstrate each step as you discuss it.

Organization

In the opening of your presentation, explain what you will teach your audience to do. Tell them what materials they will need to accomplish the task. If there are many items, hand out a list so that they won't miss anything important while trying to write.

Just as you would for a written how-to piece, explain the steps in the proper sequence. Encourage your listeners to ask questions about anything they don't understand.

Practice

Talking in front of an audience makes most people nervous. The best way to overcome nervousness is to practice. Practice on your own until you feel confident. Then if you can, recruit family members or friends who don't know how to do the task that you are explaining. Ask them to follow along with your presentation and see if they understand your directions. This will help you make sure that your directions are accurate and complete.

• Activity A •

Make a list of the steps you would use to teach someone how to do these simple everyday activities.

1. Brushing your teeth
2. Sharpening a pencil
3. Doing a physical exercise
4. Folding a paper airplane

• Activity B •

Choose one of the lists of steps that you made for Activity A. Work with a classmate to give each other directions. When you are giving the directions, speak slowly and clearly. Wait for your partner to complete each step before moving on to the next one. Afterward, discuss the completeness of each other's directions and how they could be improved.

Speaker's Corner

Work in small groups to do this activity. Choose one person to give detailed directions for drawing something while the others draw what is being described. The speaker cannot look at the drawings-in-progress or tell the group what they are drawing. Compare the completed pictures. Are you surprised at how differently directions can be interpreted? Take turns being the person giving the directions.

Listening to How-to Presentations

Listening to how-to presentations is different from listening to other oral presentations. You want to learn how to do something, so you have more reason to listen closely. Other members in the audience also want to learn how to do something. Each audience member owes it to the others not to cause any distractions. That means that there should be no unnecessary talking, paper shuffling, or fidgeting. Turn off any electrical devices such as cell phones before the speaker begins.

When you were the listener in the previous activities of this lesson, were you able to follow the instructions? Keep these things in mind when you are listening to instructions and explanations.

- Focus on the speaker. If you begin to glance around the room, you're more likely to be distracted from what the speaker is saying. You might miss something important.

- If you don't understand a step, politely raise your hand. A good speaker will stop to let you ask your question. If you don't understand a step, other listeners might not understand either.

- Watch carefully if the speaker demonstrates how to do any of the steps.

- Take notes, but don't try to write down everything. Write down key words and important numbers.

- After the presentation is over, go over your notes as soon as possible. Compare your notes with those of another audience member. You can fill each other in on any details that were missed.

Activity C

Select any activity that you enjoy, such as baseball, fishing, dancing, or cooking. Then think of an action that is performed in the activity. For example, for baseball it might be batting or throwing a curve ball. For fishing it might be cleaning a fish or casting. For cooking it might be the proper way to knead dough. Write down the steps needed to perform that action. Explain things like how to stand, position of fingers, motions, and so on. List any equipment or materials needed to perform the action.

• Activity D •

Find a partner who wrote directions for a process other than the one that you chose in Activity C. Take turns explaining to each other how to perform the actions that you chose. As you listen to your partner's directions, practice the movements and try to think of any steps that seem incomplete or out of sequence. Give your partner positive feedback and help him or her to create the best instructions possible.

• Activity E •

After you and your partner feel that your directions are accurate and complete, practice delivering your instructions to each other. You know that the steps are accurate. Now make sure that your delivery is solid. Practice using visual aids. Practice adjusting your tone of voice and using gestures to make your presentation more interesting for your audience. When you have practiced enough to feel confident, find other classmates to listen to your how-to presentation.

Speaker's Corner

During this chapter you have written several how-to pieces that you might present orally. Choose one to practice and present to your class. Keep in mind the speaking tips covered in this lesson as you prepare your presentation. Remember to give your audience a chance to ask questions before you return to your seat.

How-to Articles

Prewriting and Drafting

In this chapter you had a chance to think about many things that you know how to make and do. Now it's time to combine your writing skills with your knowledge to create and publish your own how-to article.

Prewriting

Prewriting is a time to choose your topic, to decide what you want to say about it, and to organize the way that you will present your ideas. For how-to articles, you brainstorm to determine what topic you know enough about to teach to someone else. Then you review the steps in the process, making certain that nothing is left out. Finally, you organize your notes to make sure that the steps are in the proper sequence.

Before starting to write about a how-to project, writers list the steps they follow from beginning to end. After all of the steps have been listed, the writers review them to determine what materials and tools are needed.

Your Turn

Today you will begin to write your own how-to piece. Your classmates will be your audience. First, you must choose a good topic. It should be an activity that you are good at and enjoy doing.

Think of things that you do well. What interests you the most? What are you enthusiastic about sharing? Ask yourself these questions:

- What do I really enjoy doing?

- Would others be interested in this activity or project?

- Is it something that I am confident enough about to share my knowledge?

- Is it something that my audience— my classmates—can learn to do?

- Will the required materials be easily available to my audience?

Listing Steps

Alexandra loves scrapbooking. Her first experience was helping her mother make a family scrapbook for her grandparents. Scrapbooking is now Alexandra's favorite hobby. When her class was given an assignment to write a how-to article, she decided to write about scrapbooking. Here are the notes she made for writing about her hobby.

1. Gather souvenirs to be displayed: photos, postcards, ticket stubs, and so on. Spread them on table.

2. Decide how to organize the items.

3. Position but don't glue items on sheets of paper. Craft paper works best.

4. Arrange pages with room for writing and gluing words and notes. Crop and mat pictures.

5. Glue items in place and add writing and lettering.

6. Write captions or short descriptions for each item.

7. Punch holes and put pages in binder.

Basic materials include pens, markers, glue, scissors, construction paper, craft paper, three-hole punch, binder, magazines or newspapers, various other decorative items.

Alexandra numbered each step to make sure she didn't forget anything. At the end she listed the necessary tools and materials.

Your Turn

Think about the activity that you chose for your how-to topic. Think about all of the things you do when you participate in the activity. Start at the beginning and picture every step or every action in your mind. Write them down in the exact order that you do them. Leave room to add any details that you may think of later or notes that you think are important for your readers. Keep track of all the materials and tools that are needed to perform the activity.

Organizing Ideas

Alexandra decided to write her how-to piece in paragraph form. This is how she organized her notes.

1. Scrapbooking is a lot of fun.

2. Basic materials for making a scrapbook include pens, markers, glue, scissors, 3-hole punch, 3-ring binder, and craft paper.

3. Spread souvenirs out on the table. Plan how to group items.

4. Place items on as many pages as you need. Vary the layout to be artistic.

5. Glue items in place. Write captions to identify and explain each item.

6. Glue down lined "boxes" for journal entries.

7. Write journal entries.

8. Punch holes in pages and put everything in your binder or folder.

Your Turn

Look at your steps and your notes. Write them in the order that the reader will use the information.

Drafting

A how-to writer's draft is your first attempt to organize your prewriting notes into an understandable explanation of a process. The goal is to enable readers to successfully perform the task being described.

Alexandra read through her notes several times. She added some items and removed some others. She changed the order of some steps. When she felt that her notes were complete and accurate, she wrote her first draft, double-spacing it to have room for editing changes that she knew she would eventually make.

Learning How to Scrapbook

Scrapbooking is great fun. You'll really enjoy it if you try it. I put together my first scrapbook with my mother two years ago. We made a scrapbook of our family to give to my grandparents for Christmas.

Here's how to get started. The basic supplys you will need are inexpensive and readily available. You need heavy paper, pens and markers, a ruler, scissors, glue or glue stick, and the binder to display your pages.

Asemble the items you want to display. Spread them on the table so you can plan where to put them on each page. Vary the arrangements to be artistic, mix the types of items that you put on dfferent pages. You may want to use things like photos, postcards, ticket stubs, newspaper articles, and anything else you have saved.

Crop the pictures. Position the pictures and other items on the page. Save room to write captions for each item. Cut out squares of notebook paper to write longer notes. When you are pleased with your arrangement, glue everything down.

Then have fun adding page and section titles with stenciled letters, or with words or phrases cut out of magazines and newspapers. Use colored markers or pencils to write captions directly onto the pages. Write your journal entries on the notebook paper.

Punch holes in the pages. Put them in your binder. Decorate your cover. Add finishing touches to personalize your scrapbook Use stickers, rubber stamps, and stencils. You can use a stamp pad and press thumbprints on the pages. Make your book reflect you. Have fun sharing it!

Your Turn

Reread your notes and write your first draft. Double-space your work so you will be able to make changes easily. Remember that you will probably rewrite your piece more than once.

Keep in mind your audience—your classmates—as you write. Don't expect them to be experts the first time they read your directions. Always give the easiest way to do a step. Your goal is to have your audience complete the project successfully. If they do, and they like the result, they can learn to do the expert stuff later.

Content Editing

Good writers know that most writing needs to be edited and revised several times before it is completely clear and accurate. A content editor notices how well the ideas of a piece are expressed and checks to make sure that all of the necessary information is included.

Writers edit their work themselves to make it as good as they can. But sometimes they read it so often that they don't notice if something is out of place or missing. That's why it's a good idea to have someone else check the writing before it is published.

Alexandra asked Steve to be her editing partner. She knew that Steve was in the advanced art class and would have good ideas for her craft project. She would read his how-to article in return and give him feedback on ways that he could improve it.

Alexandra and Steve both used the Content Editor's Checklist to help them look for common mistakes. They read each other's work and wrote notes about ways to improve it.

Content Editor's Checklist

✔ Does the introduction tell the reader what he or she will learn to do and why it is fun to do it?

✔ Are the steps presented in order?

✔ Are all the details complete and accurate?

✔ Are transition words used effectively to help the reader follow the sequence?

✔ Is the writing clear so that the reader knows exactly what to do after reading each step?

✔ Does the conclusion tell the reader how to use or enjoy the end product?

Steve read Alexandra's instructions for scrapbooking several times, picturing himself doing each of the steps. There were a couple of spots that puzzled him. He read it again, using the Content Editor's Checklist. Steve had many helpful comments when Alexandra and he met to discuss each other's work.

First, Steve told Alexandra that she must have done a good job because he thought he'd like to try scrapbooking now. He told her he thought she had included a lot of ideas and possibilities that a beginner might try. These are some of Steve's specific suggestions.

- The introduction might be more appealing if you mentioned books you've made and that kids could make, instead of one book you made with your mother.

- You talk about supplies and hint that you can use different kinds of things. Maybe it would be good to mention using your imagination and creativity.

- Definitely add words to help with the sequence of steps. Words like *first*, *next*, and *finally* will help the reader to follow your steps more easily.

- The order is good except for one place. In the third paragraph, make the last sentence the second sentence so that the list of materials to mount follows the sentence about assembling the materials.

- Many people don't know what *crop* means. You should explain this word for those who might not know it.

Alexandra thought Steve had given her some good ideas. She agreed that she should define the word *crop*. She especially liked the introduction idea because she could share the kinds of scrapbooks she had made.

No one is perfect. Steve missed one detail that Alexandra forgot to include. Check the list of materials against the directions and see if you can spot what Steve missed.

Your Turn

Reread your first draft and check it against the Content Editor's Checklist. Can you answer "yes" to each of the questions?

Trade your how-to article with a partner. Read each other's work and make suggestions for improvement. Imagine that you are following the steps. Take notes on any changes you want to suggest. Confer with each other when you have both finished. Be positive and point out the good features of the writing first. Be sure you both use the Content Editor's Checklist.

Take your partner's suggestions into consideration. Remember that the final product is yours. You don't have to make changes that you determine would not improve your piece. Read your own work carefully. You may find more changes you want to make.

Revising

This is Alexandra's revision of her scrapbooking piece.

Learning How to Scrapbook (need catchier title)

a great way to keep memories alive. scrapbooking too,
Scrapbooking is ~~great fun.~~ You'll ~~really~~ enjoy it if you try it. ~~I put~~
I made
~~together~~ my first scrapbook with my mother two years ago. We

made a scrapbook of our family to give to my grandparents for

Christmas. Now I have six scrapbooks of my own, covering
everything from vacations to gymnastics meets.
Here's how to get started. The basic supplys you will need are
lined notebook paper,
inexpensive and readily available. You need heavy paper, pens and

markers, a ruler, scissors, glue or glue stick, and the binder to

display your pages. Your imagination and creativity are also
important tools.
First, ^semble the items you want to display. Spread them on the table

so you can plan where to put them on each page. Vary the

arrangements to be artistic, mix the types of items that you put on

dfferent pages. You may want to use things like photos, postcards,
or any other souvenirs
ticket stubs, newspaper articles, ~~and anything else~~ you have saved.
by cutting out unnecessary trees, people, and so on.
Crop the pictures. Position the pictures and other items on the

page. Save room to write captions for each item. Cut out squares

of notebook paper to write longer notes. When you are pleased

with your arrangement, glue everything down.

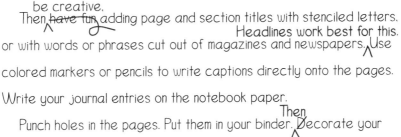

be creative.
Then ~~have fun~~ adding page and section titles with stenciled letters,
Headlines work best for this.
or with words or phrases cut out of magazines and newspapers. Use

colored markers or pencils to write captions directly onto the pages.

Write your journal entries on the notebook paper.

Punch holes in the pages. Put them in your binder. Then Decorate your

cover. Add finishing touches to personalize your scrapbook Use

stickers, rubber stamps, and stencils. You can use a stamp pad and

press thumbprints on the pages. Make your book reflect you. Have

fun sharing it!

Look at the editing changes that Alexandra made to improve her piece.

- She changed the introduction to tell about her books. She's working on the title because she recognized that she needed something catchier.

- Suggesting that the reader use his or her imagination and creativity was a good idea, she thought, so she added that to the supplies she listed. She also noticed that she had forgotten an item from her list of supplies. Did you see what she needed to add?

- She agreed that it would be best to add some transition words to make the sequence easier to follow.

- She agreed with Steve's change of order in the third paragraph to get the materials closer to the beginning of the paragraph.

- She added a short explanation about cropping photographs.

Your Turn

Revise your how-to article. Use any new ideas you have and make changes your partner suggested if you agree with them. When you have finished, go over the Content Editor's Checklist to see if you can answer yes to each question.

Chapter 2 Editor's Workshop

How-to Articles

Copyediting and Proofreading

Copyediting

When copyediting, look for accuracy in word meaning, word choice, sentence structure, and the overall logic of the writing.

Alexandra looked at the changes she had marked. She felt that her how-to piece was getting better with every revision, but she knew that more improvements could be made.

She saw that the sentences in her final paragraph lacked variety. They were short and choppy and didn't flow well. She decided to combine some of them to make compound and complex sentences. She was pleased with the improvements.

Alexandra used a checklist to help her copyedit her work. The following checklist can help you make your how-to article clear and coherent.

Copyeditor's Checklist

✔ Are the direction steps in the correct order?

✔ Are the steps accurate and complete?

✔ Are transition words used to help readers follow the steps easily and in order?

✔ Is there a variety of sentence types and lengths?

✔ Did you include any instructional graphics to make your directions clearer?

Alexandra also decided on a title she thought had a little more life: *Memories in the Making*.

Your Turn

Look over your revised draft using the Copyeditor's Checklist. Look for ways to vary your writing with simple, compound, and complex sentences. Picture yourself following your directions step by step. If possible, read your article aloud while someone else acts out making or doing what you are explaining.

Proofreading

Before making the final copy of any written piece, good writers proofread to check for spelling, punctuation, capitalization, and grammar. They also check to make certain that no new errors have been introduced during the revising process.

A checklist like this one can help.

Proofreader's Checklist

✔ Are the paragraphs indented?

✔ Are all words spelled correctly?

✔ Is the grammar accurate?

✔ Are capitalization and punctuation correct?

✔ Was the revision checked to make certain that no new errors were introduced?

Writers find it helpful to have others proofread their work because fresh eyes can often spot errors that writers miss.

Alexandra asked Catori, a classmate, to proofread her writing. Catori followed the Proofreader's Checklist and found two misspelled words and a run-on sentence. Can you find these three errors on pages 76–77?

Your Turn

Read and review your paper carefully, using the Proofreader's Checklist. Look for only one kind of error during your first reading. Then do a second reading and look for another kind of error. Additional readings will help you spot errors you may have missed.

When you have finished the Checklist, trade papers with a partner. Go through each other's how-to articles in the same way. Check a dictionary if you think words are misspelled.

Publishing

Publishing is the moment when writers share their finished work. Alexandra felt that she had done her best. She had read and revised her article several times.

After all that work, she was glad she would have a chance to share her paper with interested classmates.

Memories in the Making

Scrapbooking is a great way to keep your memories alive. I made my first scrapbook two years ago as a Christmas gift for my grandparents. Now I have six scrapbooks of my own, covering everything from vacations to gymnastics meets. You'll enjoy scrapbooking, too, if you try it.

Here's how to get started. The basic supplies needed for scrapbooking are inexpensive and readily available. You need heavy paper; lined notebook paper; colored pens, pencils, and markers; a ruler; scissors; a hole punch; glue or glue stick; and the binder to display your pages. Your imagination is your most important tool because your creativity is what personalizes your scrapbook.

First, assemble the materials that you want to display. Items such as photos, postcards, ticket stubs, newspaper articles, or any other souvenirs are good scrapbook materials. Spread the items on the table so you can plan where to put them on the pages. Vary the page layouts to be artistic. Mix the types of items that you put on each page.

Crop the pictures by cutting out unnecessary people or things. Then position the pictures and other items on the page. Make sure you leave room to write captions for the items. Cut out squares of notebook paper to write longer journal notes. When you are pleased with your arrangement, glue down everything.

Then be creative, adding page and section titles with stenciled letters or with words or phrases cut out of magazines and newspapers. Headlines work best for this. You can write shorter captions directly onto the page with colored markers. Write your longer journal notes on the notebook paper squares.

After you punch holes in the pages, put them in your binder. Then decorate your cover with some finishing touches. Personalize your scrapbook with stickers, rubber stamps, and stencils. You can use a stamp pad and press ink thumbprints onto the pages. Make your scrapbook reflect you and then have fun sharing it!

Your Turn

By now you have spent a good deal of time crafting your how-to article. You have brainstormed a topic and organized your information. You have written a draft and discussed it with at least one classmate. You've revised your work, perhaps several times. You have copyedited and proofread it. Your article is as good as you can make it and you have a right to be pleased with your achievement.

It is time to publish, to share your work with your audience. Prepare your article for publishing by following these steps:

- Use your best handwriting or a computer to make your finished work.

- Proofread your copy one last time for spelling, grammar, capitalization, and punctuation. If you can, use your computer's spell checker.

- If possible, add a photo or other visual that illustrates your how-to piece. Bring in a sample if it is about something to make.

How will your class publish your how-to articles? Discuss with your teacher and classmates different ways to publish your how-to articles.

CHAPTER 3

One of the most common places to find descriptive writing is in advertisements. The earliest ads were colorful signs painted on buildings. Archaeologists working in Rome and Pompeii have found many examples of these. One sign in ancient Rome advertised property for rent. A sign painted on a wall in Pompeii invited travelers to visit a restaurant located in another part of town. What is today's equivalent of this kind of advertising?

Descriptions

Boa Roller Coaster:
A Snake You're Going to Love!

by Alexis Major
Coaster Island Marketing Group

IN APRIL, COASTER ISLAND released an enormous, fearsome snake onto its main avenue. The beast is 60 feet long, and it ferociously twists and turns as it carries terrified human victims in its belly. Of course, this snake is the roller coaster *Boa,* the newest and most exciting coaster designed by King Koaster Unlimited.

Made especially for Coaster Island, *Boa* is one of the fastest, longest, and tallest roller coasters in the world. At 250 feet high and boasting a top speed of 78 miles per hour, this coaster will squeeze shrieks from even the most experienced riders.

Each of the three 36-passenger trains rounds the track in just under three minutes. The ride begins with a slow, clanking climb up the initial hill. The tension explodes into screams at the 250-foot drop, followed by a thrashing stretch of snakebite twists that leads riders to another plunge called the "Sting." *Boa* bites again with a drop of 150 feet before riders squeal their way through twists and turns that squash them first left, then right, then left again.

The final thrill comes as riders hop along six camel bumps and make a lightning-quick stop at the loading station. Survivors stagger down the exit ramp and back into the popcorn and cotton candy aromas of the midway. ●

If you want to know how it feels to have a Boa take your breath away, visit Coaster Island!

What Makes a Good Description?

Our Wide Wide World

During the Middle Ages, merchants hired "criers" to advertise their wares. The criers would walk around town shouting their praises for their employer's goods.

A description can be part of a longer composition, such as a biography or a personal narrative, or it can be a complete composition by itself, such as a character sketch or a travel article. A good description takes readers into a scene as the writer pictures it. A good description helps readers to feel involved in a story's action rather than just being told about it.

Here are some things to remember when you write a description.

Visualizing

When you describe any subject in your writing, first picture it in your mind. Don't think only about how your subject looks. Think about everything that you see, hear, smell, taste, and feel as you visualize. Then describe the subject in as much detail as you can.

Organization

Good description is organized to make it easy for the reader to picture what the writer is saying. You can organize spatially: left to right, up to down, near to far. You can organize by sense: sight first, then sound, then smell, and so on. You can organize by importance: the aroma of a baking apple pie masking the smell of fresh paint.

It is usually best to lead your reader along a straight path. If you describe a meal, don't talk about the salad and then go to the dessert and then describe the meat and vegetables. Finish describing one area before moving to a new one.

Audience

Who will be reading your description? Adults or children? People who are familiar with the subject or people who know nothing about it? Keep your audience in mind as you choose words and phrases. If you are describing a country scene to a city audience, don't use language that city dwellers won't recognize. If you are describing a building for a group of architects, don't use oversimplified terms that will bore them.

Activity A

Copy and complete the following chart. Use sensory words to describe the persons, places, and things in the first column.

Subject	Sight	Sound	Smell	Taste	Touch
pudding					creamy, hot
lawn mower				none	
playground		laughing, shouting			
short-order cook	white-aproned				
autumn leaves					feathery, light
shoe store			new leather		
bridegroom	nervous				
pizza				tangy sauce	

Writer's Corner

Choose one person, one place, and one thing that you see every day. Write two sentences describing each, using two different senses.

Activity B

Picture your last holiday or birthday meal with your family. Use the following questions to help you visualize. Answer each question as completely as you can. If you can't remember things exactly, make up something.

1. What is the occasion?
2. Who is seated around the table? Is it crowded?
3. How are people dressed? Is anyone dressed strangely?
4. What are people talking about? How do their voices sound?
5. What does your place setting look like? Are the dishes paper, plastic, or china? Are the utensils plastic or silver?
6. Who is bringing the food out to the table?
7. What are the main dishes? What are the side dishes?
8. What is the strongest scent that you can smell?
9. What are some other scents that you notice?
10. What foods are on your plate? How does each one taste?
11. What are you drinking?
12. What sounds do you hear while everyone is eating?
13. What desserts are served? How do they taste?
14. When you have finished eating, how do you feel?

Activity C

Look over your answers to the questions in Activity B. Choose one sense and write two or three sentences describing one part of the meal.

Activity D

Look over your sentences from Activity C. Write two or three new sentences about the same thing but use a different sense to describe it.

Activity E

Create a fictional character. Answer the following questions to visualize a man or woman named Pat.

1. How old is Pat?
2. Is Pat a man or a woman?
3. What color is Pat's hair?
4. What else can you see about Pat's hair?
5. What color are Pat's eyes?
6. Is there anything unusual about Pat's eyes? What?
7. What does Pat's nose look like?
8. What does Pat's mouth look like?
9. What else do you notice about Pat's face?
10. What is unusual about Pat's build?
11. Is there anything unusual about the way Pat walks? What?
12. What are Pat's hands like?
13. What are Pat's clothes like?
14. What does Pat's voice sound like? Is there an accent?
15. Does Pat have a distinctive smell? Is it pleasant or unpleasant?

Activity F

Use the same questions you answered in Activity E to visualize someone you know really well. After you answer the questions, write a description of the person.

Writer's Corner

Write two paragraphs to describe Pat, using your answers to the questions in Activity E. If you think of anything else about Pat that you want to include, write as many paragraphs as you wish.

Writing a Description

A good description will lead the reader along a straight path that gives a structured picture of the subject being described. A clearly organized structure will help your reader follow your description without getting lost.

Spatial Order

There are many ways that you can organize a description. One way is by spatial order, arranging the paragraphs so that a subject is described from top to bottom, from front to back, from side to side, or from inside to outside. Spatial order is the most common form of organization in descriptions.

Read the following excerpt about a character from *The Red Pony* by John Steinbeck. Picture the man as you read.

. . . In a few moments he had trudged close enough so that his face could be seen. And his face was dark as dried beef. A mustache, blue-white against the dark skin, hovered over his mouth, and his hair was white, too, where it showed at his neck. The skin of his face had shrunk back against the skull until it defined bone, not flesh, and made the nose and chin seem sharp and fragile. The eyes were large and deep and dark, with eyelids stretched tightly over them. Irises and pupils were one, and very black, but the eyeballs were brown. There were no wrinkles in the face at all. This old man wore a blue denim coat buttoned to the throat with brass buttons, as all men do who wear no shirts. Out of the sleeves came strong bony wrists and hands gnarled and knotted as hard as peach branches. The nails were flat and blunt and shiny.

The description starts at the top and moves down, expanding upon significant details along the way. Can you follow the path of Steinbeck's organization?

Activity A

Read the following description from *My Side of the Mountain* by Jean Craighead George. Picture the images as the author describes them. Then answer the questions that follow.

I am on my mountain in a tree home that people have passed without ever knowing that I am here. The house is a hemlock tree six feet in diameter, and must be as old as the mountain itself. I came upon it last summer, and dug and burned it out until I made a snug cave in the tree that I now call home.

My bed is on the right as you enter, and is made of ash slats and covered with deerskin. On the left is a small fireplace about knee-high. It is of clay and stones. It has a chimney that leads the smoke out through a knothole. I chipped out three other knotholes to let fresh air in. The air coming in is bitter cold. It must be below zero outside, and yet I can sit here inside my tree and write with bare hands.

1. What senses does the author appeal to in her description?

2. Where does the author's description begin? Where does it end?

3. What words does the author use to organize her description spatially?

4. Do the descriptive words make the "home" seem pleasant or unpleasant? Point to examples in the excerpt that support your opinion.

5. Can you picture the "home" that the narrator created or do you have questions about it? Explain.

Writer's Corner

Reread one of your descriptive pieces from Lesson 1. Are the sentences in a logical order? Should you rearrange them in any way? Revise your writing so that the sentences are ordered logically.

Chronological Order

Another way to organize a description is chronological order, which is usually used when describing a process. Paragraphs that are arranged chronologically are arranged in the order in which things occurred. Imagine that you are describing yourself building a campfire. You might start with the search for firewood. Then you describe laying out the wood and lighting the kindling. You might finish with a description of the burning fire. At each step, you describe things you see, hear, smell, or touch.

• Activity B •

Imagine that you are walking to a favorite place, such as a park or a friend's house. Describe what you see, hear, smell, touch, and taste as you walk along. Use chronological order to organize your description.

• Activity C •

Choose a topic from the list. Write a short description using sensory words and phrases to describe the topic. Use chronological order to organize your description.

babysitting job	baseball game	birthday party
day at school	summer vacation	dance class
school field trip	family celebration	music recital

• Activity D •

The following descriptive passage is poorly organized. Rewrite it, putting the sentences into a logical order. (Hint: It will be easier if you divide the passage into two paragraphs.)

Coach used to be a Big Ten athlete. His hair, once coal-black, now is steely gray. Coach's face still reflects the determination of a competitor. The legs that propelled him through opponents' lines are still rock-hard from exercise. His nose is slightly off-center from a head-on collision with a linebacker. His shoulders look almost as though he is still wearing pads. His eyes dart back and forth, seemingly looking for an opening to run through. Although he is nearly 60 now, Coach still has a powerful build.

Activity E

Study the picture below. Then choose one of the following options:

1. Write a short description about the picture using spatial organization.

2. Imagine that the girl in the picture is a character in a story. Describe what she might be doing using chronological order.

Writer's Corner

Think of someone close to you, and write a paragraph describing that person. Before you begin writing, think about the best way to organize the piece. Are you describing the way the person looks? Are you describing the person's actions? When you have finished writing, save your description to use again later.

Sensory Language

To create images in the minds of your readers, it helps to "show" them what you mean, not just tell them. One way to do this is to use sensory language. Just as you use your senses to visualize the subject you wish to describe, you can appeal to your readers' senses by using language that helps them picture the image.

Read these two sentences and notice the difference between them. Both sentences tell what happened. Which sentence makes you feel more like you are in the scene?

A. The campfire blazed brightly.

B. The crackling campfire cast an orange glow on our hot faces and left a smoky smell on our skin.

In sentence A, the writer wrote only about what she saw. In sentence B, the writer used more of her senses to visualize the scene. Then she used sensory language to help her readers see what she visualized.

• Activity A •

Read the following sentences. Tell which sense each sentence appeals to.

1. Mandy was surprised that the snake's skin was dry and pleasantly cool.

2. Six snow-white horses were hitched with shining silver harnesses to the brightly painted circus carriage.

3. The foghorn's deep, muffled groan rolled across the harbor.

4. A mixture of aromas flooded the outdoor market as vendors sold fresh fish, strong cheeses, and exotic spices.

5. Mrs. Kessel makes her mouth-watering apple pies with tart Granny Smith apples.

Activity B

Write a one-sentence description of each item below. Include as many sensory details as you can.

1. a flag flying in the wind
2. a pet
3. the coldest or warmest day of the year
4. a snowstorm
5. an athlete finishing a 100-meter sprint
6. a peach tree full of fruit
7. a running lawn mower

Activity C

Choose one of the topics below and write a descriptive paragraph about it. Use as many sensory details as you can. Try to create a clear picture in the reader's mind.

A. shopping at the local supermarket
B. sitting in church before the service begins
C. racing with your friends on bicycles
D. buying food at the school cafeteria
E. watching a building under construction
F. attending a baseball game at the ballpark
G. riding a Ferris wheel at the carnival

Writer's Corner

Choose any description that you wrote in Lesson 1. Reread it and try to visualize the subject. Then think of stronger sensory language to make the image clearer. Rewrite the description with the new language. Read both versions to a classmate and ask which one projects the better image.

Using Similes and Metaphors

A *simile* describes one thing by comparing it to another thing. Similes always use the words *like, than,* or *as.*

> The insult hurt *like* a slap to the face.
> Ernest is as happy *as* a pig in slop.
> My first loaf of bread was harder *than* a rock.

A *metaphor* also describes one thing by comparing it to another thing. Metaphors do not use the words *like, than,* or *as.*

> Willy is the *big frog* in the pond at band practice.
> My father's writing is *chicken scratches* to most people.

When using similes or metaphors, writers need strong images that are generally recognized by most people. Anything that projects a special quality can be a simile or a metaphor.

People can be used as metaphors or similes.

> My brother is an Einstein when it comes to fixing motors.
> Pablo came to our rescue like Spiderman.

Animals can be used as metaphors or similes.

> I'm going to get you, you dirty rat!
> The baby has been as quiet as a mouse all morning.

Things can be used as metaphors or similes.

> You are the light of my life.
> The movie's heroine was as cool as a cucumber.

Places can be used as metaphors or similes.

> It would be heaven to have a good air conditioner.
> It's like a desert outside.

Metaphors and similes can add interest and depth to a description. But if a metaphor or a simile has been used so often that it becomes commonplace, it becomes a cliché. Rather than adding interest, a cliché can make writing seem dull and flat.

Activity D

Copy the following sentences. Circle the two things in each that are being compared. Tell whether the comparison is a simile or a metaphor. Then tell which sentences you think are clichés.

1. Giant redwoods are the skyscrapers of the forest.
2. The other team's fullback was as wide as a garage door.
3. From the space station, Earth is a huge, blue-green ball.
4. The sun was like a child playing hide-and-seek in the clouds.
5. The halls of the new school were like a maze to me.
6. Dina brightened up the room like a flash of lightning.
7. On Fridays the last half-hour of school is an eternity.
8. The skunk raised its tail and Bob took off like a shot.
9. Mr. Maples was as mad as a wet hen when Mary Jane got home.
10. "Don't be a chicken," I taunted my brother.

Activity E

Match the simile parts in the first column to the ones in the second column to create complete similes.

1. as gentle as
2. as bossy as
3. shaking like
4. running like
5. scolding like

a. a scared puppy
b. a summer breeze
c. a mother blue jay
d. an Olympic star
e. an older sister

Writer's Corner

Look at the description you revised in the previous Writer's Corner. Add at least one simile or metaphor to make your description more interesting to a reader.

Misused and Confusing Words

The English language includes some confusing words that are often misused in writing. Writers often misuse these words because they are misused in casual speech, because the words sound alike, or because the words are quite close in spelling.

Read this chart to help you understand how to use some of these commonly misused words correctly.

Word	Correct Usage
can	*Can* means "to have the ability to do something." **Sam can ride a skateboard.**
may	*May* gives or asks permission. **You may go to the store. May I buy candy?**
lay	*Lay* means "to put something down." **Lay the books on the table.**
lie	*Lie* means "to recline or rest." **Lie down and take a nap.**
set	*Set* means "to put something down in a certain place." **He set the tools on the bench.**
sit	*Sit* means "to be seated." **You may sit in the front row.**
good	*Good* is an adjective that describes something positive. **I read a good book last night.**
well	*Well* is usually an adverb that gives more information about a verb by telling *how*. **Pablo sings well.**

Activity A

Use each example word in the chart in a sentence. Trade your paper with a partner, and make changes if necessary.

Activity B

Following are some other words that are often misused. Write sentences for the words in each pair. Use a dictionary if you need help.

1. its it's
2. loose lose
3. passed past
4. accept except
5. than then
6. right write
7. their they're
8. to too
9. whose who's
10. your you're
11. desert dessert
12. stationary stationery
13. principle principal
14. threw through
15. breath breathe

Writer's Corner

Reread your descriptive pieces to find any of the commonly misused words in the chart or in Activity B. Look up the words in a dictionary to be sure you used them correctly. Make changes as necessary.

By the beginning
of the 20th century,
railroads crisscrossed
the United States.
Items with brand
names such as Ivory
soap, Wrigley gum,
and Coca Cola could
now be advertised in
magazines and
newspapers and
sold throughout
the country.

Activity C

Complete each sentence with the correct word in parentheses.
Use a dictionary to check your answers.

1. The baseball team could not _____ defeat.
   (accept except)

2. Where is the best place to _____ the basket? (sit set)

3. My mom said that I _____ go with you. (can may)

4. _____ book is this? (Whose Who's)

5. I like to _____ under a tree and write in my journal.
   (lay lie)

6. Did you _____ your hat? (loose lose)

7. He doesn't feel very _____ today. (good well)

8. Claudia chose all of the _____ answers. (right write)

9. _____ grandfather is very kind. (They're Their)

10. The teacher wants to talk with _____ parents.
    (your you're)

11. Kyle _____ the test with flying colors. (passed past)

12. Megan runs faster _____ Jake. (then than)

13. The golf ball crashed _____ the window.
    (threw through)

14. My favorite part of eating out is the _____.
    (dessert desert)

15. _____ a great day for a trip to the beach. (Its It's)

Activity D

Complete each sentence with the correct word from the list of often misused words in Activity B.

1. The light switch is to the _____ of the window.

2. _____ time to write descriptions of our field trip.

3. The blue whale is larger _____ the elephant.

4. The dog is wearing _____ collar.

5. Did anyone here _____ a black and white ski glove?

6. May I go _____?

7. The _____ doorknob came off in my hand.

8. Go _____ the shoe store, and it's the first door on the left.

9. Jules Verne began to _____ his stories in 1863.

10. Is that _____ new jacket?

11. Larry knows _____ lunch that is.

12. They ate _____ sandwiches.

13. Just _____, a firecracker popped!

14. _____ going to the movies tonight?

15. Throw the ball _____ the first baseman.

Writer's Corner

Write a description of a room in your home, using at least two pairs of words that are often misused.

Thesaurus

When you write, the more precisely you choose your words, the better you are able to communicate your ideas. The dictionary is a wonderful tool for finding information about a single word, but if you want to find words to fit an idea, you need a thesaurus.

A thesaurus is a book of synonyms. If you can't think of the exact word to use in a sentence, you can look up a word with a similar meaning in a thesaurus. Listed along with the word you looked up, you will find many other words that mean the same thing or nearly the same thing. Look through that list and you will often find a synonym that has the exact shade of meaning that you are looking for. A thesaurus is also helpful if you are using a word too often and want to use synonyms for variety.

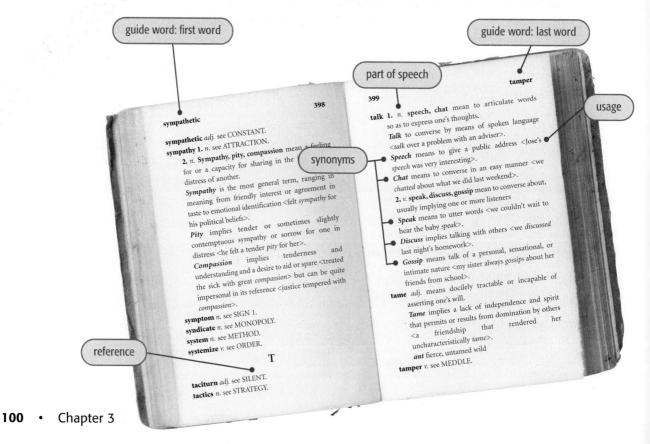

guide word: first word

guide word: last word

part of speech

usage

synonyms

reference

Dictionary Thesaurus

A dictionary thesaurus lists entry words in alphabetical order just as a dictionary does. There are also guide words at the top of the pages to help you find entry words quickly. You use the guide words just as you would in a dictionary. Some thesauruses also provide antonyms because writers sometimes need to know the opposite of a word.

If a word can be more than one part of speech, such as a noun and a verb, the thesaurus will give synonyms for each part of speech.

talk *noun* speech, lesson, chat; *verb* speak, discuss, gossip

The synonyms given for a word may have several shades of meaning. If you aren't sure what a synonym's exact meaning is, you can look it up in a dictionary.

Activity A

The italicized words are not as precise as they could be. Use a thesaurus to find a more precise synonym. Rewrite the sentence with the synonym in place of the italicized word.

1. The airplane flew at a *height* of 35,000 feet.
2. We want to start a bird *retreat* in the woods behind the school.
3. You must go to the children's library for *immature* books.
4. I wanted to sit next to you, but the seat was *inhabited*.
5. There is a beach at the northern *border* of the lake.

Writer's Corner

Choose three words from any of the descriptions that you wrote earlier in this chapter. In a thesaurus, find a synonym for each word. Rewrite the sentences, replacing the original words with their synonyms. Which word works better—the original or the synonym? Explain.

Indexed Thesaurus

Another type of thesaurus is the indexed thesaurus. An indexed thesaurus is divided into two sections, and you must go through two steps to find synonyms. First, you look up the word that you want a synonym for in the back section of the book, the index. The index lists words alphabetically. It gives a number for each word that tells where in the front section you can find that word and all its synonyms. The indexed thesaurus is more complicated than the dictionary thesaurus, but it is also much more thorough.

talk

nouns
speech 722
lesson 731.8
report 742.43
conversation 777.2
chat 779.4

verbs
betray 555.11
speak 724
gossip 760.13
discuss 774.9
chat 779.8

> **779.4**
> **visit, chat,** *tête-à-tête*, little talk, heart-to-heart

• Activity B •

Use the index segment above to determine what section numbers you would look under to locate a synonym for *talk* in each of the following sentences.

1. The doctors had a long talk about the operation.

2. Dad gave a talk to his bosses about the new project.

3. People will talk!

4. Aunt Phoebe can talk on the phone for hours.

5. Professor Weber gave a talk about the Dark Ages.

Activity C

Use a thesaurus to find synonyms for *little* that would complete the following sentences. Do not use a synonym more than one time.

1. We have only a _(adjective)_ time to get ready.

2. I was _(adverb)_ bothered by the change.

3. Gina ate a _(noun)_ of the soup to keep up her strength.

4. The dollhouse contained _(adjective)_ furniture.

5. I _(adverb)_ knew my cousin.

Activity D

For each of the following words, find in a thesaurus three synonyms that have different meanings. The first one has been done for you.

run: sprint, operate, campaign

scale

match

party

fall

plot

Writer's Corner

Use a thesaurus to find one word that has at least three synonyms. Write a sentence for each different meaning of the word. For example, for *run* in Activity D:

1. I *sprint* every day for exercise.

2. Can you *operate* this copier?

3. George will *campaign* for class president.

Speaking and Listening Skills

Oral Descriptions

You often describe things to your friends and family. You might tell your parents about a poster you want to hang in your bedroom or you might tell your friends about a pizza you had last night. You might describe the newest song by your favorite group. Describing things is a part of our everyday life. Sometimes we must describe things in a more formal setting. Here are some things to keep in mind when giving an oral description.

- Consider your audience. Choose language that will be understood by your listeners.

- Your introduction should tell what you are describing and grab your listeners' attention.

- The body of your oral description should be organized just as a written description should be. You may want to organize your description spatially, by sense, or by chronological order. Make sure that whatever method you choose, the organization is logical. Use vivid and precise words in your description.

- The conclusion of your presentation should give your listeners a feeling of closure. You might end by explaining why your topic interested you enough to have given an oral presentation about it. You might suggest that your audience do further research about the topic if it interests them.

Using Visual and Audio Aids

Oral description comes alive when you use different media to help your audience picture what you are describing. Some useful visual and audio aids include:

- posters
- diagrams or maps
- photographs
- objects or props
- projected or computer-generated images
- videotapes or DVDs
- audio tapes or CDs

Practice

The more you practice, the more comfortable you will feel standing in front of an audience. Make note cards to guide you and audio or visual aids to help your audience understand what you are describing. When everything is ready, practice in front of a mirror or with a friend or a family member.

Voice

Be enthusiastic about your subject. Vary the volume and speed of your delivery. Speak in varied tones and use movement and body language to emphasize important parts of your description.

● Activity A ●

Choose any object in the classroom, such as a desk, bulletin board, flag, poster, or map. Prepare a short oral description using the object as a visual aid. Take turns with other students delivering and listening to each other's speeches.

● Activity B ●

For each of the topics listed below, suggest one or two audio or visual aids that would be useful in an oral description.

1. the Grand Canyon
2. a vacation by car
3. a country music festival

4. a Thanksgiving Day parade
5. a family reunion
6. a tour of a cookie factory

Speaker's Corner

Choose an idea that you could describe in detail. List some sensory words that you could use in your description. Try to think of ways that visual or audio aids could help the description.

Listening Tips

Show the speaker the same courtesy that you expect when you are in front of the class.

- Look at the speaker so he or she will know you are paying attention.
- Picture the description in your mind.
- Look carefully at the materials the speaker displays. The visual aids might contain information that the speaker does not directly state.
- Do not interrupt the speaker.
- When the speaker has finished, give him or her some feedback. Ask questions or say things like "In my mind, I could see the frog coming out of the mud," or "I could almost smell the warm spring air."

Activity C

Take turns with a partner being speaker and listener. The speaker chooses an object in the room and describes it to his or her partner without saying what the object is. The listener draws the object as it is being described. The listener should draw only what the speaker describes, even if the listener can guess what the object is.

Afterwards, both partners should discuss the drawing, identifying what the speaker forgot to include in the description or what the listener forgot to include in the picture. Then switch roles as speaker and listener.

Activity D

Work in small groups. Think of a movie that you have seen recently either on television or in a theater. Picture the most memorable character in the movie and form a strong picture of that character in your mind. Then take turns with the rest of your group in describing your characters without naming the movies in which they appear. Describe their physical appearance, their personalities, the way they speak, and any other characteristics that made them stand out. After each description the audience should try to guess who the character is and in what movie he or she appears.

Activity E

Read the following description from *The Trumpet of the Swan* by E. B. White. Use any of the visual aids suggested on page 104 to create a multimedia presentation of the paragraph. Be prepared to deliver it to the class.

But one day a change came over the woods and the pond. Warm air, soft and kind, blew through the trees. The ice, which had softened during the night, began to melt. Patches of open water appeared. All the creatures that lived in the pond and in the woods were glad to feel the warmth. They heard and felt the breath of spring, and they stirred with new life and hope. There was a good, new smell in the air, the smell of earth waking after its long sleep. The frog, buried in the mud at the bottom of the pond, knew that spring was here. The chickadee knew and was delighted (almost everything delights a chickadee). The vixen, dozing in her den, knew she would soon have kits. Every creature knew that a better, easier time was at hand—warmer days, pleasanter nights. Trees were putting out green buds; the buds were swelling. Birds began arriving from the south. A pair of ducks flew in. The Red-winged Blackbird arrived and scouted the pond for nesting sites. A small sparrow with a white throat arrived and sang, "Oh, sweet Canada, Canada, Canada!"

Speaker's Corner

Find or create a couple of audio or visual aids that would work with an oral presentation of the description you chose in the previous Speaker's Corner. Practice your presentation, and then deliver it to the class.

Chapter 3 Writer's Workshop

Descriptions

Prewriting and Drafting

All the people you know, all the places you go, and all the things you experience can become topics for written descriptions. Use the skills you learned in this chapter as you follow the writing process to produce a written description.

Prewriting

Prewriting helps a writer choose a subject, capture mental images and vivid details, and make a plan for how a description will unfold. Alan, a sixth-grader, wanted to be a writer. He knew that professional writers get assignments to write descriptions for travel brochures, restaurant or movie reviews, or radical race cars. He thought that kind of work would suit him perfectly.

Choosing a Subject

When he got the assignment to write a description, Alan wanted to write about something his classmates already know and enjoy. His plan was to write about an everyday thing in an unusual way. No subject caught his attention. So he used these questions to help choose a subject.

- Who are your role models?
- Whom do you want to help your friends get to know better?
- What is your favorite possession?
- What makes you really annoyed?
- What places have you been that you really liked or really disliked?
- What are some things that people see every day, but rarely notice?
- What is your favorite, or least favorite, food?

Your Turn

Choose a topic that interests you. Perhaps you already have a subject that you are interested in and that you would like to share with your classmates.

If there is no subject that has grabbed your attention recently, use Alan's list of questions to get ideas.

When you have chosen a subject, think about it. Picture it in your mind. What is the quality that stands out most, the thing that you notice first? Is it something that you see, hear, feel, smell, or taste?

Using a Graphic Organizer

Once Alan had a subject to describe, he used a graphic organizer to keep track of his ideas. A sensory chart is a useful tool when writing descriptions. Here is part of a sensory chart that Alan created for a description of his favorite food, popcorn.

Sight	small, fluffy, yellow, clouds
Sound	snap against bag, muffled pop
Touch	hot steam, feathery greasy fingers
Smell	heavy, buttery
Taste	delicious, filling

Notice that Alan used vivid words, even at this stage. He used phrases instead of complete sentences because he wanted to get his ideas down on paper quickly.

Your Turn

Make a sensory chart for the subject that you chose to describe. Remember, you don't need to have a quality for each sense.

Organizing a Writing Plan

After a writer has a strong image of the subject, he or she can begin to organize the description. It's important to open with a strong lead paragraph that tempts the readers to keep reading.

The body of the description should take the reader on a straight, logical path, finishing each element before moving on to the next.

The conclusion should give a feeling of closure. Think of any questions that the reader might ask and make sure you answer them.

Alan decided to organize his description based on chronological order. He would write about the process of making and eating the popcorn. He could add the sensory details as they occurred in the process.

Your Turn

Decide how you want to organize your description. Would it be most clear if you did it spatially? Would it be better to organize it by sensory details?

Drafting

Alan was writing his description as part of a class guessing game. He would read aloud his final draft without naming his topic and then have the class guess what he wrote about.

He knew that he needed to use vivid verbs and adjectives to help his classmates. Alan wrote his first draft. He double-spaced the lines because he knew that he would be making changes and corrections later.

Good Eating

This is a description of my favorite snack.

I place the folded bag into the microwave and enter the time. Then I hit the start button and wait for the fun to begin. Soon muffled popping sounds echo in the oven as if tiny drummers were beating out uneven rhythms.

Its not long before a heavy, buttery aroma fills the room. I almost drool as I carefully remove the bag from the microwave. as I tear it open, the steam nearly burns my fingers. The smell becomes overpowering and I can't wait to dig in!

I pour the small, fluffy, yellow clowds into a big bowl and watch them.

My hand reaches in for the hot, feathery kernels. I pick up a handful as a few extras escape back into the bowl. I open my mouth as wide as I can and try to cram the whole fistful past my lips. After the last delicious handful, I lick the salty grease from my fingertips.

The next time your hungry, make yourself a bag of popcorn. Nothing is better then this delicious snack!

Your Turn

Write your first draft. You will probably rewrite your description several times. Double-space your lines so that you have room to make changes later. Refer to your sensory chart often to make sure you don't leave out any details. If you think of any new details, add them.

As you write, keep your audience—your classmates—in mind. Remember that your writing is meant to paint a picture for them. Use words and phrases that help them feel as if they are there with you.

Remember, you want a good lead to catch your readers' attention, a body with sensory details, and an ending that gives your audience a feeling of completeness.

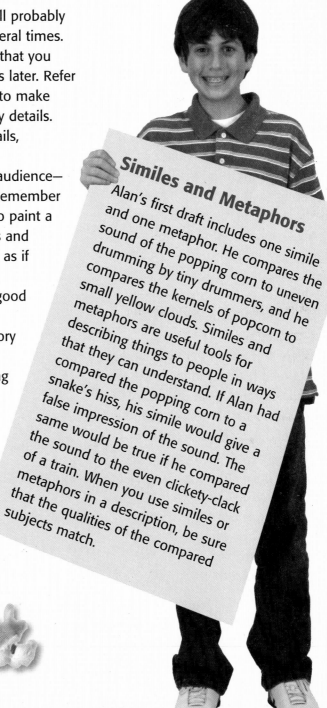

Similes and Metaphors

Alan's first draft includes one simile and one metaphor. He compares the sound of the popping corn to uneven drumming by tiny drummers, and he compares the kernels of popcorn to small yellow clouds. Similes and metaphors are useful tools for describing things to people in ways that they can understand. If Alan had compared the popping corn to a snake's hiss, his simile would give a false impression of the sound. The same would be true if he compared the sound to the even clickety-clack of a train. When you use similes or metaphors in a description, be sure that the qualities of the compared subjects match.

Content Editing

Writers usually write several drafts, constantly revising to make their work better and better. After a while, however, they have read their own writing so often that they don't see problems that fresh eyes would notice. That's when writers ask a friend or colleague to edit their work.

Alan edited the first draft of his description. He liked it, but he wanted to make it even more interesting and correct.

He knew that he needed to have a classmate read his description. After all, his classmates were his audience. Alan chose Lauren to be his content editor.

Lauren and Alan were in the same study group. They often read each other's writing. Alan felt comfortable with Lauren because she would make sure that his writing was clear, ordered, and logical. They agreed to use this checklist.

Content Editor's Checklist

✔ Does the introduction grab the reader's attention?

✔ Is there a good use of sensory language?

✔ Does the description use spatial order or chronological order?

✔ Are there any misused or confusing words?

✔ Can any of the descriptive words be improved by using a thesaurus?

✔ Is there a satisfying conclusion?

Lauren read Alan's description several times. She went through the Content Editor's Checklist carefully. Then she and Alan met to talk.

First, Lauren told Alan how impressed she was by the clear and logical way the description was organized. She also told Alan that the conclusion was very effective. Then Lauren and Alan went over her comments for improving the piece.

- Your introduction could be more effective. I know we can't name our topics until the end, but can you think of a better introduction?

- Does popcorn echo? Tiny drummers sounds like you are trying too hard to be poetic.

- You say that you pour the clouds into the bowl and watch them. What are you watching them do?

- You say that the smell becomes *overpowering.* That doesn't sound very good to me. Can you think of a better word? I also think that *feathery* is a funny word to describe popcorn. Who wants a mouthful of feathers? Try using a thesaurus.

Alan listened closely to Lauren's comments. Then he gave her suggestions for ways to improve her description.

Your Turn

Read your first draft and think about how to improve it. Does your lead-in grab your readers and make them want to read more? Do you include well-organized sensory details? Does your conclusion give a sense of closure? Is there any confusing information?

Trade descriptions with a classmate. Read your classmate's description several times, using the Content Editor's Checklist.

When you finish reading your partner's first draft, talk with him or her about ways to improve it. Make sure you begin with positive comments. Your partner should do the same for you.

Alan made changes for most of Lauren's suggestions, but not for all of them. You are the writer, and you get to decide which changes you want to make and which ones you will not make.

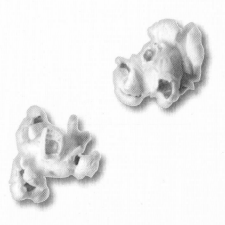

Revising

What makes my mouth water, just to hear its name? What tastes
Good Eating
so incredible that I want to eat more even when I'm stuffed? It's my
favorite snack, and I make it myself.

~~This is a description of my favorite snack.~~

I place the folded bag into the microwave and enter
the time. Then I hit the start button and wait for the fun to
begin. Soon muffled popping sounds echo in the oven as if
tiny drummers were beating out uneven rhythms.

Its not long before a heavy, buttery aroma fills the room.
I almost drool as I carefully remove the bag from the
microwave. as I tear it open, the steam nearly burns my
fingers. The smell becomes ~~overpowering~~ *irresistible* and I can't wait
to dig in!

I pour the small, fluffy, yellow clowds into a big bowl
and watch them. *gently fall like snowflakes*

My hand reaches in for the hot, *puffy* ~~feathery~~ kernels. I pick
up a handful as a few extras escape back into the bowl. I
open my mouth as wide as I can and try to cram the whole
fistful past my lips. After the last delicious handful, I lick
the salty grease from my fingertips.

The next time ~~your~~ *you're* hungry, make yourself a bag of
popcorn. Nothing is better ~~then~~ *than* this delicious snack!

Look at some of the things that Alan did to improve his description.

- He agreed that his introduction needed improvement. He changed it to really grab his reader's attention.

- He decided that he would leave in the part about the popcorn echoing in the microwave. Alan also liked the image of the tiny drummers even if Lauren didn't.

- He agreed that he should add an explanation of what he watches the popcorn do. He added the simile *gently fall like snowflakes* to describe what the popcorn looks like as he pours it in to the bowl. He was glad Lauren had made that suggestion.

- He thought Lauren had a point about the overpowering smell of the popcorn. He looked in his thesaurus and decided that *irresistible* was a much better word. He also agreed that the word *feathery* wasn't very precise. He decided that the word *puffy* was less confusing and more accurate.

As he revised his draft, Alan noticed that Lauren had missed one of the points on the checklist. He noticed that in the last paragraph he misused the words *your* and *then.* He checked his dictionary and changed the words to *you're* and *than.*

Your Turn

Use your ideas and the ideas you got from your partner to revise your description. When you have finished, go over the Content Editor's Checklist again. Make any additional changes to your draft.

Copyediting and Proofreading

Copyediting

Alan had made revisions based both on Lauren's comments and on some things that he had noticed. Now he was ready for the next step—copyediting. He used the following checklist to look for accuracy in word meaning, word choice, sentence structure, and the overall logic of the description.

Copyeditor's Checklist

✔ Are there overused words that could be replaced with synonyms?

✔ Are vivid adjectives and verbs used?

✔ Are a variety of sentences used?

✔ Are transition words used to show logical order?

✔ Are sentences structurally logical and grammatically correct?

Your Turn

Look over your revised draft using the Copyeditor's Checklist. Use a thesaurus to find synonyms for any overused words you might find. When you have gone through the checklist, read the description aloud and listen for words that don't mean exactly what you want to say. Use a dictionary and your textbook to check that words are spelled correctly and that sentences are grammatically correct.

These Tools Can Help You Edit

Use these tools to help you edit your descriptions:

Dictionary: to check for usage and spelling

Thesaurus: to vary your language and use interesting, descriptive words

Teacher: to answer questions when you're not sure if your change is necessary or correct

Proofreading

Before writing a final copy of a description, a good writer proofreads to check for spelling, punctuation, capitalization, and grammar.

A checklist like this one can help.

Proofreader's Checklist

✔ Are the paragraphs indented?

✔ Have any words been misspelled?

✔ Is the grammar accurate?

✔ Are capitalization and punctuation correct?

✔ Were any new errors introduced during the editing process?

Alan asked Jomei to proofread his description. She used the Proofreader's Checklist and found one missing apostrophe, one capitalization error, and one spelling error. See if you can find these errors on page 114.

Your Turn

Read your description carefully, using the Proofreader's Checklist. Look for only one kind of error at a time. First, check each paragraph to see that you indented correctly, then check to make sure each sentence begins with a capital letter, and so on. You will read your writing several times. When you finish, trade papers with a partner. Go through your partner's paper in the same way.

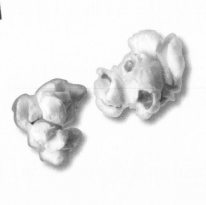

Descriptions

Publishing

After several editing sessions, Alan felt that his description was as good as he could make it, so he copied it carefully onto a sheet of paper. Then he read it aloud to his class, omitting the word *popcorn* until the very end. All of his classmates knew what he was describing. Alan had done a great job!

Good Eating

What makes my mouth water, just to hear its name? What tastes so incredible that I want to eat more even when I'm stuffed? It's my favorite snack, and I make it myself.

I place the folded bag into the microwave and enter the time. Then I hit the start button and wait for the fun to begin. Soon muffled popping sounds echo in the oven as if tiny drummers were beating out uneven rhythms.

It's not long before a rich, buttery aroma fills the room. My mouth begins to water as I remove the bag from the microwave. As I tear it open, the steam nearly burns my fingers. The smell becomes irresistible and I can't wait to dig in!

I pour the small, fluffy, yellow clouds into a big bowl and watch them gently fall like snowflakes.

My hand reaches in for the hot, puffy kernels. I pick up a handful as a few extras escape back into the bowl. I open my mouth as wide as it will go. The popcorn is delicious and filling.

The next time you're hungry, make yourself a bag of popcorn. Nothing is better than this delicious snack!

Your Turn

Publishing is the moment that you turn your work in to your teacher, read it aloud to your classmates, or post it on the bulletin board for others to read. Be sure that you like your description before you publish it.

To publish, follow these steps:

1. Make sure you have not left out anything important or left in anything unnecessary.

2. Use your neatest handwriting or a computer to make a final copy of your description.

3. Proofread your final copy one more time for correct spelling, grammar, capitalization, and punctuation. If you can, use your computer's spell-checker.

As a class, decide how you will publish your descriptions. You might even choose different publishing methods, depending on your topic. Perhaps give these ideas a try.

For Descriptions of Places: Make dioramas that show the place you described. Attach your written descriptions to these models.

For Descriptions of People: Paint portraits. Hang your paintings and written descriptions in a classroom gallery.

For Descriptions of Things: Play a guessing game. Read aloud your descriptions, omitting the name of the topic. Have your classmates guess what you are describing.

Invite your classmates to help you improve your description, but remember that this is your work. You have the final say and can choose whether or not to make changes.

Pay attention when your classmates read aloud their descriptions. Offer helpful suggestions and listen for ways to improve your own writing.

CHAPTER
4

A study of ancient civilizations sheds light on the origins of many aspects of modern life. Democracy had its roots in Athens, where citizens for the first time were able to speak up and take part directly in governmental decision making. In our democratic system, we can make our wishes known to the representatives we elect, and they speak for us. Another legacy of the Greeks was their concern for the whole person and their emphasis on physical fitness for all citizens. This resulted in gymnasiums, gymnastics, and the Olympian Games—the forerunner of the modern Olympics.

120

Persuasive Writing

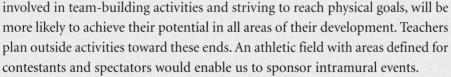

A proposal to the Lakeside Park Board:

On behalf of the Oak Middle School PTA, I am writing to urge members of the Park Board to consider our proposal for the new park adjacent to our school. We feel that the addition of an athletic field, a running track, and playground equipment to the plans for a new park would greatly benefit the community.

State standards for physical educational programs recognize the many benefits of proper physical exercise. We know that children who are active at least one hour a day, involved in team-building activities and striving to reach physical goals, will be more likely to achieve their potential in all areas of their development. Teachers plan outside activities toward these ends. An athletic field with areas defined for contestants and spectators would enable us to sponsor intramural events.

Our school is enrolled in the Presidential Champions program. Through this program children earn recognition for their achievements in various categories of activity and sports. The program also encourages families to work together toward these goals. Therefore, families could also make use of these facilities during nonschool hours.

We were thrilled to hear that this land had been allocated by the Lakeside Park District to be a community park. We are confident that you will agree with us that the nearness of the park to our school provides a great opportunity for us to work with you in a way that will benefit the health and physical development of our students as well as the community in general. We look forward to hearing from you and working with you.

Sincerely,

Linda Navarro

Linda Navarro
President, Oak Middle School PTA

Persuasive Writing

What Makes Good Persuasive Writing?

Persuasive writing tries to make readers agree with the writer's position on an issue. It is easy to state an opinion, but to persuade others to agree with it, the position must be supported with solid reasoning and relevant facts. These are some of the things you should keep in mind when you write to persuade others.

Audience

Consider who your readers will be and how they may feel about your topic. If they are already likely to agree with your position, appeal to their emotions to further convince them. If they have no set opinion yet or if they are likely to disagree with your position, use hard facts and logic to sway them to your way of thinking.

Introduction

State your position in the introduction. Let your readers know what side of an issue you are taking. Briefly state your main reasons, which you will explain more fully in the body of your writing.

Body

In the body, state arguments supporting your position. Provide logical reasons, examples, or facts to convince your readers that your position is the correct one. Be sure your supporting details are relevant to your position. The body of your persuasive writing can also be used to rebut arguments against your position. State the opposing arguments, then show why they are weak or unimportant.

Conclusion

Briefly summarize your strongest evidence. Don't add any new reasons in the conclusion, but restate your position in a positive, convincing manner. Call on your audience to take action based on your arguments.

• Activity A •

Look at the model on page 121. Answer these questions.

1. Who is the target audience of the proposal? Write one reason they might be in favor of the proposal and one reason they might be against it.

2. What position does the writer take in her introduction? What reason does she give for that position?

3. What are two reasons she offers in the body of her proposal that support her position?

4. What action does the writer want her audience to take?

• Activity B •

Brainstorm in small groups about an issue in your school that you think the teachers and students should consider. Be sure there are two sides to the issue. Choose two students to list the group's suggestions for two opposing position statements and three or four main reasons to support each statement. Share issues, positions, and reasons with your class.

Writer's Corner

Consider the topic "Our school should arrange more field trips." Decide what your position is. List as many reasons as you can for your position. Choose the reason that you think is strongest and write a persuasive piece using that reason to support your position.

Pierre de Coubertin, the founder of the modern Olympic Games, believed that physical education and sports should play a large role in young people's lives. To see his ideas come to life, he persuaded a number of countries to hold the first modern Olympic Games in Athens in 1896.

• Activity C •

You make your reader interested in reading your opinion when you state it clearly and immediately. Choose two of the following topics and write an effective introduction for each, expressing your opinion and suggesting that you have convincing evidence to present to the reader.

1. Students should be allowed to use calculators for math tests.

2. Schools should/should not sell junk food to students.

3. Homework should be eliminated.

4. Schools should teach only language arts, mathematics, and science.

5. Computers should be distributed to all students.

• Activity D •

Read the following paragraphs. Decide what position each writer has about his or her topic. Write introductions and conclusions for both persuasive paragraphs.

A. The musical chime of a cell phone is a major distraction in a classroom. All ears tune in, trying to determine who is getting the call. Attention to the teacher or any student making a point in the class discussion is lost. I know this because after one ill-timed chime, I stopped my lecture immediately and asked who could name the melody. All hands went up. When I asked for a brief summary of what we had been discussing, only two hands went up. Enough said?

B. You are sitting in your car, listening to your radio and waiting for the light to change. Then you hear the steady BOOM, BOOM, BOOM, BOOM grow louder as some apparently deaf music fan pulls up next to you. He has probably spent more money on his sound system than he has on his car. Not only can't you hear your own radio, you can't even hear yourself think. Don't these noise addicts understand the damage they are doing to their ears? Studies show that listening to over-amplified music for 30 minutes a day eventually causes hearing loss. That's why so many rock musicians wear earplugs when they play. They want to be able to listen to their music in their twilight years. I guess their fans will have other ways to fill their time.

• Activity E •

Look at the following arguments for and against Lakeside Village hosting the next Summer Olympic Games. Write whether each argument is based on facts or on an appeal to emotions.

Lakeside should enter a bid for hosting the next Summer Olympic Games

1. because it would generate much-needed tourist dollars for the local economy.

2. because Lakeside would be in the same league as Los Angeles, Tokyo, London, and Paris.

3. because we already have the park space developed for many of the events.

4. because we could rub elbows with the greatest athletes in the world.

Lakeside should not enter a bid for hosting the next Summer Olympic Games

1. because the cost of building athletes' housing and support facilities would bankrupt our village.

2. because cities that host Olympic Games often lose money.

3. because we would have a lot of foreigners walking our streets.

4. because we don't have enough hotel rooms for so many tourists.

Writer's Corner

Choose one of the issues discussed in Activity B. It can be the issue that your group brainstormed or one brainstormed by another group. Decide on the position that you agree with and then write an introduction and a conclusion for a persuasive article supporting that position.

Fact and Opinion

Facts Support Opinions

A fact is a statement that can be proved. An opinion is a person's view about something. It cannot be proven either true or false. An opinion supported by facts is more persuasive than an opinion that stands alone.

Read the following statements about a political candidate:

A. Yolanda Jones is the best candidate for mayor.

B. Yolanda Jones is a lifelong resident of the city who has served three terms on the city council.

Statement A is an opinion. Other people may have a different opinion about who the best candidate for mayor would be. Statement B expresses facts. It can be proved how long Yolanda Jones has lived in the city, and her political background can be checked.

Statement A, the opinion, is supported by statement B. Statement B states a fact explaining why Yolanda Jones is the best candidate. One good way of supporting opinions is by using facts.

Use Relevant Facts

When you are trying to persuade someone to think as you do, it is important that the statements supporting your opinions be convincing and relevant.

> This is an excellent novel.
> *It cost $14.95.*
> *It won the Newbery Medal.*

The book's price is a fact, but the price does not prove the book is excellent. The supporting statement about the Newbery Medal is also a fact. Winning a major book award gives convincing evidence that the novel is excellent.

• Activity A •

The first sentence in each pair is a statement of opinion. Tell whether the second sentence supports the opinion and is convincing and relevant. If it is not convincing, provide a sentence that is.

1. Speedy Airlines is the best airline. Its on-time departures and safety record are unmatched in the industry.

2. For a class party, it is better to serve cupcakes than a sheet cake. Cupcakes bake faster than a sheet cake.

3. Our class is the best in the school. We have the most popular students, and we drive the hottest cars.

4. Religion played a large part in the lives of ancient Greeks. The Olympian Games were played to honor the gods and goddesses.

• Activity B •

Most persuasive pieces use both fact and opinion. Choose one of the following topics and decide on a favorable or an unfavorable position to argue. Then write one sentence using fact and one sentence using opinion to support your position.

1. Your city wants to tear down a historic mansion and replace it with a recreation center.

2. A larger city wants to pay your town to use its garbage dump.

3. The town council wants to pass a law making all businesses close on Sundays.

Writer's Corner

Look back at the issue for which you wrote an introduction and conclusion in the Writer's Corner on page 125. Write a short body for a persuasive article supporting your position. Include opinions with supporting facts or examples.

Propaganda Techniques in Persuasive Writing

Propaganda is often used in persuasive writing. Propaganda techniques appeal to people's emotions rather than to common sense. Writers who use propaganda are trying to persuade people with ideas or opinions that are biased or irrelevant. Advertising and political commentary often use propaganda. These are a few of the common techniques:

- Bandwagon—tells you to do something or buy something because everybody else is doing it
- Testimonial—tells you to use something because a famous person uses it
- Loaded words—uses words that appeal to your emotions, either positively or negatively
- Vague generality—uses broad statements that can't be proved one way or the other

• Activity C •

Identify the propaganda technique used in each of these examples.

1. Roasty Toasty cereal is really better! You'll agree after the first bite!
2. If you want to be like Spike, you've got to wear Mercury basketball shoes.
3. Yolanda Jones is a careless conservative.
4. Join the crowd breaking down the doors to see Tim Holt's latest movie.
5. Mayor Baker is a lazy liberal.
6. Drink Sports-Ade, the thirst-quencher of champion athletes.
7. Everybody's raving about Choco-Gum. Try it and you'll see why!
8. Are you man enough to drive the AlphaAmigo SUV?

• Activity D •

Write four more statements like the ones in Activity C, one for each type of propaganda technique. Then switch papers with a classmate and try to match statements to techniques.

• Activity E •

Here are two students' views on whether to open the school gym during the summer vacation. Which statements are facts and which are opinions? Which of the four supporting statements is most convincing? Explain why you think so.

1. Pablo feels that the gym should be open during the summer.

   a. Keeping the gym open will provide a safe place for children of working mothers while their mothers are away from home.

   b. An open gym will help children keep physically fit.

   c. The gym is more fun than the playground.

   d. It's a waste of money to let the gym go unused for so long.

2. Jill feels that the gym shouldn't be open during the summer.

   a. Children should be outside when the weather is nice.

   b. We would have to pay adults to supervise activities.

   c. The older children won't play with the younger ones.

   d. The school's insurance rates would skyrocket.

• Activity F •

Write two news items about a mayoral candidate. In one, provide facts about the mayor's achievements. In the other, make an emotional appeal.

Writer's Corner

Look at the issues that that you listed for the Writer's Corner on page 123. Choose one issue on which you could use a propaganda technique to support your point of view. Write several sentences, including at least one fact and one propaganda technique.

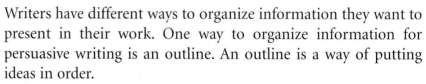

Outline

Writers have different ways to organize information they want to present in their work. One way to organize information for persuasive writing is an outline. An outline is a way of putting ideas in order.

The first step in making an outline is to write the title. For persuasive writing, the title might be your position statement. Then you can begin to organize your ideas.

Divisions of an Outline

An outline shows ideas in their level of importance. Main ideas are labeled with Roman numerals (**I, II, III, IV**, and so on). Each main idea could become the topic sentence of a paragraph.

Subtopics that are related to a main idea are labeled with capital letters (**A, B, C, D**, and so on). There should be two or more subtopics under each main idea. Subtopics are supporting details in a paragraph.

Details connected to the subtopics are labeled with Arabic numerals (**1, 2, 3, 4**, and so on). It is not necessary to have details under each subtopic. Details add more information related to the main idea of the paragraph.

No level of an outline may have only one entry. If you have Roman numeral I, you must have a II. If you have an A, you must have a B. If you have a 1, you must have a 2, and so on.

Outline Structure

Outlines are easy to follow if they are properly laid out. The periods for each type of number or letter must line up. If the periods line up properly, the numbers and letters will also line up.

Outlines list all ideas in complete sentences, in phrases, or in words. Sentences, phrases, and words should not be mixed in an outline.

Why Mass Transit Must Be Funded

I. Trains most efficient way to move people (main idea)
  A. Popular everywhere (subtopic)
    1. European railway systems (detail)
    2. Japanese railway system (detail)
    3. Indian railway system (detail)
  B. Railroads unaffected by road congestion (subtopic)
    1. Surface trains (detail)
    2. Elevated trains (detail)
    3. Subways (detail)
II. Buses good option within cities (main idea)
  A. Can reach all districts (subtopic)
    1. Most shops and businesses close to bus stops (detail)
    2. Bus/train terminals convenient for commuters going from home to office (detail)
  B. No need to find parking (subtopic)
III. Private cars wasteful and inefficient (main idea)
  A. Usually only one passenger per car (subtopic)
  B. Not enough parking for all (subtopic)

 **Activity A**

Read the following paragraph. Then create an outline section with Roman numerals, letters, and Arabic numerals, using the information from the paragraph.

Subways are an efficient form of travel for cities. Because they run below ground, they can avoid traffic jams and stoplights. They also can travel on direct routes between stops because they don't have to follow street layouts. When used in combination with buses, they provide all the transportation a city-dweller needs.

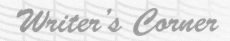

Writer's Corner

Write a paragraph based on main idea II, subtopic A of the model outline. Incorporate all of the details from the outline. If you can think of other details that support the main idea, add them to your paragraph. Compare your paragraph with the paragraphs of several classmates.

• Activity B •

Below are parts of two different outlines. Identify the subtopic in each example that doesn't support the main idea. Replace the item with a subtopic that does support the main idea.

Example 1

I. Global warming is a threat that we should address before it is too late.

   A. The ice sheet covering much of Greenland is melting, and in 1,000 years it will raise the sea level by seven meters.

   B. The Arctic Ocean ice pack has melted by 30 percent over the past three decades.

   C. The melting ice will be fresh water, centuries old.

   D. Coastal areas will be submerged, and island nations will disappear.

Example 2

I. Limited homework benefits student growth

   A. Sports activities necessary for physical fitness

   B. Cheap Saturday movie matinees at the Twin Cinema

   C. Outside reading habits strengthened

   D. Families interact, build strong bonds

• Activity C •

Identify which of the following items is the title, which are main ideas, and which are subtopics. Then sort the ideas and subtopics into an outline. Use the outline on page 131 as a model.

- Global warming shown to cause global climate changes
- Why we should recycle
- Immediate effects in our society
- Fewer landfills save money and resources
- Deforestation will cause animal and plant species extinction
- Cleaner water leads to fewer health hazards
- Preserving the earth for the future

Activity D

Following is an outline for a persuasive article by a physical education teacher supporting her school's participation in the Presidential Champions program. Some items have been left out. Find the items in the box and tell where they belong.

Presidential Champions Program Participation

I. Promotes physical fitness
    A. 30 minutes exercise per day
        1. Lowers blood pressure
        2. _____
        3. Builds strong bodies
    B. _____

II. Encourages parental involvement
    A. Can be done at home
        1. _____
        2. Isometric exercises
    B. Presidential recognition for parents when commitment fulfilled
        1. Certificate for each child
        2. Trophy for three or more children
    C. _____

III. Minimal cost to school and parents
    A. _____
        1. Can use existing facilities
        2. Pays for participation awards only
    B. Parental costs
        1. No financial costs
        2. _____

> School costs
>
> Controls weight
>
> Parents exercise with children
>
> Calisthenics
>
> Time and commitment
>
> Helps cut down TV viewing

Writer's Corner

Choose a persuasive article topic. Develop an outline for the topic, including at least two main ideas and two subtopics for each main idea.

Prefixes

A prefix is one or more syllables added to the beginning of a word that changes the meaning of the word.

A trick to remembering that the prefix *pre-* means "before" is to think about going to the movies. Before the feature you see *previews* of other movies. Previews are the views of movies that are shown before the entire movie comes to the theater.

If you know the meanings of some words that share the same prefix, you can usually figure out the meaning of the prefix. See if you can think of other words with these prefixes.

Common Prefixes		
Prefix	**Meaning**	**Example**
dis-	not, opposite of	disapprove
im-	not	impatient
under-	below, less than	undersea, undercooked
mis-	badly, wrongly	misspell
non-	not	nonfiction
pre-	earlier, before	prepay
re-	again, back	reunite
un-	not, opposite of	unusual
in-	not	inappropriate

Activity A

Choose one of the prefixes above to make each of these words opposite in meaning. You may need to check a dictionary to make sure you have used the correct prefix.

agree	active	violent	possible
sense	secure	honest	certain
fire	behave	fair	perfect

Activity B

Copy the chart below and fill in the missing parts.

Prefix	Root	New Word	Meaning
1. re-	_____	restart	_____
2. under-	_____	_____	draw a line below
3. _____	_____	unlucky	not lucky
4. non-	returnable	_____	_____
5. _____	satisfied	dissatisfied	_____
6. _____	arrange	_____	arrange earlier
7. un-	_____	_____	not forgiving

Activity C

Complete each sentence with the correct word by adding a prefix from the list on page 134 to the word at the left.

set

1. Because of the electrical failure, we had to _____ the clocks.

sense

2. Humorous poems are often called _____ poems.

agreed

3. "Strike three!" yelled the umpire, but the batter _____.

information

4. She got lost because she was given _____ about the party's location.

proper

5. He was penalized for an _____ play.

launch

6. Astronauts must undergo an extensive _____ examination before they can take off.

touched

7. Fortunately, our home was _____ by the tornado.

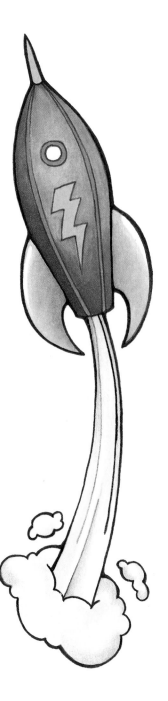

Writer's Corner

For three minutes, list as many words as you can that begin with the same prefix. Refer to the list of common prefixes on page 134. Then use as many of your words as you can in a paragraph. Choose some words that could be related to a topic you would like to write about.

Number Prefixes

There are many prefixes that have a number-related meaning. You probably know many of them. Knowing their meanings can help you figure out the meanings of new words you read. Here is a list of common number prefixes.

Prefix	Meaning	Example
uni-	one	unicycle
bi-	two	bicycle
tri-	three	triangle
quadr-	four	quadrangle
pent-	five	pentathlete
dec-	ten	decigram
centi-	one hundred	centiliter
milli-	one thousandth	millimeter
mega-	one million	megaton
giga-	one billion	gigabyte

• Activity D •

Even though you may not have seen some of these italicized words before, you can probably answer the questions about them if you think about the meanings of the number prefixes.

1. How many horns did the dinosaur *triceratops* have?

2. How many years are there in a *decade*?

3. If I buy the entire *trilogy*, how many books will I purchase?

4. If an animal is a *quadruped*, how many feet does it have?

5. If my computer disk has one *megabyte* of free space, how many bytes of free space does it have?

6. A *millisecond* is what fraction of a second?

7. How long must you live to be a *centenarian*?

8. Which polygon has more sides, a *decagon* or a *pentagon*?

9. If Genghis Kahn *unified* the Mongol tribes, what did he do?

10. In how many Olympic events does a *biathlete* complete?

11. Two *gigawatts* is how many watts?

Activity E

Answer these questions by thinking about what the italicized words in each sentence have in common.

1. If a *bibliography* is a list of books and a *bibliophile* is a lover of books, what do you think *biblio-* means?

2. If something *automatic* works by itself and an *autograph* is a person's name written by himself or herself, what does *auto-* mean?

3. If *biology* is the study of living things and a *biography* is an account of a person's life, what does *bio-* mean?

4. If *antifreeze* keeps a car from freezing and *antiwar* protestors work for peace, what does *anti-* mean?

5. If a *beneficial* act helps people and a *benefactor* is someone who does good things, what does *bene-* mean?

6. If a *hyperactive* child cannot sit still and *hyperbole* is great exaggeration, what does *hyper-* mean?

Activity F

Use the prefix meanings in Activity E to answer the following questions.

1. How does an *antisocial* person behave toward others?

2. Is there life in the *biosphere*?

3. If *bibliotherapy* is used to help a person with a problem, what does that therapy include?

4. What is the subject of an *autobiography*?

5. If a malediction is a curse, what would a *benediction* be?

6. If people ventilate their blood by breathing, what do they do when they *hyperventilate*?

Writer's Corner

Prefixes can be fun! Use some of the number prefixes to write a humorous paragraph. You may use other prefixes besides those listed.

Writing Skills

Expanded Sentences

Some people make their cars more interesting by adding chrome wheels, fancy windshield wipers, or colorful running lights. Writers want their work to be more interesting too, so they expand their sentences with modifiers such as adjectives, adverbs, and prepositional phrases.

Adding Adjectives and Adverbs

Occasionally you may decide that a sentence you have written is dull. Even though it tells the facts, it doesn't give readers a good picture of what you want them to see. Such sentences can come to life in the reader's mind if you add colorful and expressive adjectives and adverbs.

Look at the following example:

The lanterns swayed.

The colorful Chinese lanterns swayed rhythmically.

The first sentence is a complete sentence, but it is not very interesting. Adding the adjectives *colorful* and *Chinese* and the adverb *rhythmically* gives the reader a more appealing image.

Now study this example. Note the words that are added to the second sentence.

The tightrope walker balanced herself.

The daring tightrope walker balanced herself effortlessly.

The writer has added the adjective *daring* to modify the noun *tightrope walker* and the adverb *effortlessly* to modify the verb *balanced*. Expanding the sentence with only two words makes it much more descriptive and interesting to read.

• Activity A •

Write two vivid adjectives to describe each noun below.
Then work with a partner and read each other's descriptions.
Compare the mental pictures you created.

swamp	cloud	parrot
shack	baboon	bramble
meadow	barber	kite

• Activity B •

Make these sentences more colorful by adding one or more adjectives or adverbs.

1. The rain fell.

2. The hikers walked through the forest.

3. Bees swarmed over the rose garden.

4. The puck flew past the goalie.

5. The campfire blazed.

6. The artist made paintings.

7. Two shadows emerged from the spaceship.

8. The frog leaped from the log.

Writer's Corner

Work with a partner to write a description. Brainstorm and agree on a topic. One of you write the first sentence without using any modifying words. Then have the partner expand the sentence by adding an adjective and an adverb. Then have the partner write a second sentence to be expanded. Continue this way until the paragraph is finished.

Adding Prepositional Phrases

Adjectives and adverbs can make your sentences come to life. Prepositional phrases are another helpful tool that you can use to add life to your writing.

Look at this sentence.

> The colorful Chinese lanterns swayed rhythmically.

By adding a prepositional phrase the writer made the image even more vivid for readers.

> The colorful Chinese lanterns swayed rhythmically in the light breeze.

Study the example below. Note the prepositional phrase that was added to the second sentence.

> The daring tightrope walker balanced herself effortlessly.

> The daring tightrope walker balanced herself effortlessly above the crowd.

The writer has added the prepositional phrase *above the crowd.* It modifies the verb *balanced* and does the work of an adverb by telling where she balanced herself. Prepositional phrases can also modify nouns. Look at the following example.

> A clown made balloon animals for the children.

> A clown in a hobo costume made balloon animals for the children.

The prepositional phrase *in a hobo costume* modifies the noun *clown.* It does the work of an adjective.

• Activity C •

Add a prepositional phrase or phrases to each of these sentences to make them more specific.

1. The Mars Explorer landed.

2. Doug dribbled the ball.

3. The river overflowed.

4. Forty drums boomed.

5. Wind-swept snow drifted.

6. Weeds grew.

Activity D

Expand the following sentences. Add colorful adjectives, adverbs, or prepositional phrases. Do this activity in two steps. First, add adjectives or adverbs. Then go back and add prepositional phrases.

1. David enjoys riding his bike.
2. He wants to start a bicycle club.
3. His friend, Miguel, competes at BMX rallies.
4. Miguel thinks that starting a bicycle club would be a great idea.
5. Debra rides in bicycle rallies that cover long distances.
6. She has several friends who would join the club.
7. Coach Fiyuja believes that bicycling is good exercise.
8. He agreed to sponsor the club.

Activity E

Copy the following sentences. Circle the descriptive adjectives and the prepositional phrases that modify nouns. Underline the adverbs and the prepositional phrases that modify verbs.

1. The multicolored hot-air balloon drifted lazily into the clouds.
2. My gray-haired grandmother loves to watch brawny professional wrestlers roughly throw each other around the ring.
3. A scruffy mongrel with matted hair pitifully followed my little sister from the playground.
4. The uneven sidewalk in front of my house has caused many unwary pedestrians to stumble to the ground.
5. The thunderous roar of the powerful nitromethane engines drowned out the enthusiastic cheers of the drag-racing fans.

Writer's Corner

Write five sentences that could be made more interesting by adding prepositional phrases, adverbs, and adjectives. Below each of the original sentences, write an expanded sentence with interesting modifiers added.

Our Wide Wide World

Artistic gymnastics includes events such as the horizontal bar, uneven bars, parallel bars, pommel horse, rings, and vault. This competition has been part of the modern Olympics since they began in 1896.

Television coverage of Olympic gymnastics has played a part in the increasing interest of children in these events. Gymnastics requires much discipline of mind and body. It helps develop muscles, flexibility, and balance.

Persuasive Speech

Have you ever tried talking your parents into letting you stay overnight at a friend's home? Have you ever tried to talk your friends into seeing a movie that you wanted to see? If you have, you've done persuasive speaking. Persuading people face-to-face is very much like persuading them in writing. To convince others to share your point of view, you must give reasons and facts to support your viewpoint.

Audience

Know the people in your audience before you prepare your speech. Try to anticipate how they feel about your position and how difficult they will be to convince. If they are likely to agree with your viewpoint, you may use more emotional arguments. If they are more apt to disagree, you should stick to facts and logic. Use language that your audience will understand.

Introduction

Grab your audience's attention with an interesting insight connected to your topic. State your position on the topic and the main reasons for your point of view.

Body

In the body of your speech, list the arguments for your position along with facts, statistics, reasoning, personal experiences, and expert opinion that support your arguments. You can also use the body of your speech to point out weaknesses in any opposing points of view.

Conclusion

End your speech with a brief restatement of your position and your strongest arguments in support of that position. If you asked your audience to take some action in the introduction, repeat your request in the conclusion.

Voice and Body Language

Speak with confidence when you are trying to persuade people. Avoid using verbal fillers such as *um* and *uh*, leaving long pauses, and shuffling through your notes. An audience is more likely to believe a speaker who is forceful than a speaker who is timid. The way that you stand and move also can affect your audience's opinion of what you say. Stand facing forward and use hand gestures to emphasize important points.

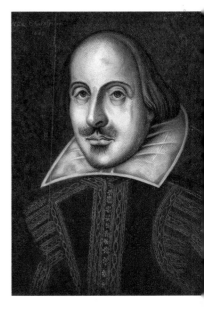

• Activity A •

Work with a partner. Take turns reading each of these quotations in two different ways. Vary the volume, speed, and pitch each time to show different levels of emotion. Practice using gestures and body language to emphasize your voice.

1. Ask not what your country can do for you, ask what you can do for your country. *(John F. Kennedy)*

2. Some are born great, some achieve greatness, and some have greatness thrust upon them. *(William Shakespeare)*

3. Tart words make no friends: a spoonful of honey will catch more flies than a gallon of vinegar. *(Benjamin Franklin)*

4. I know not what course others may take; but as for me, give me liberty or give me death! *(Patrick Henry)*

Speaker's Corner

Prepare a speech to convince your friends to see your favorite movie. Include a catchy introduction, a body that supports your choice, and a conclusion that restates your reasons. Practice presenting your speech.

Propaganda in Persuasive Speaking

The propaganda techniques that were discussed in Lesson 2 are often used in persuasive speaking. You can hear them in commercials. When you hear commercials on television or radio, pay attention to the various techniques and decide whether they are convincing or whether they make you doubt their claims.

Writers of political speeches use propaganda techniques to make their candidate look better than the opposing candidate. For example, the slogan "Ed Jones, the people's choice for honest government" uses the bandwagon technique to suggest that all the people support Ed Jones. It also uses the adjective *honest* to describe government, implying that Ed Jones's opponent is not honest. During election campaigns, listen for techniques designed to sway voters to vote for specific candidates.

Being an Alert Listener

When you were a listener for Activity A on page 143, did you listen actively? Keep these things in mind for active listening when the speaker's goal is to persuade:

- Be open-minded, but evaluate the reliability of the speaker's facts, reasoning, examples, and evidence.
- Politely question the speaker when appropriate.
- Be alert for the speaker's use of propaganda techniques.

Activity B

Write an advertising slogan, using one of the following techniques: bandwagon, testimonial, loaded words, or vague generality. You may review the definitions on page 128. Then read your slogan for your classmates and have them tell which propaganda technique you used. As you read your slogan, remember to follow the voice and body language suggestions on page 143.

Activity C

Pretend that you are running for president. Write a 30-second campaign speech that tells why you are the best person for the office. Use propaganda techniques and adjectives to make yourself look better than your opponent.

Activity D

Work in small groups to discuss various commercials or advertisements that you see every day. Think of the audience at which each commercial is aimed. How does advertising aimed at adults differ from advertising aimed at your age group? Are any propaganda techniques used? What are the techniques? List four commercials, their target audiences, and the propaganda techniques, if any, that are used. Be prepared to discuss your choices with the rest of the class.

Activity E

Many of the following ideas could actually be put into action. Choose one position and think of arguments that support it. Then improvise a speech in favor of the position. As you deliver your speech, include an introduction, a body, and a conclusion as described on pages 142–143. Listen to your classmates as they present their speeches. Then discuss the presentations and decide who made the strongest arguments.

A. We should change the way our desks are arranged.
B. We should leave the desk arrangement as it is.

C. We should make one day a week a "dress-up" day.
D. We shouldn't be forced to dress up if we don't want to.

E. School vending machines should carry snack foods and soft drinks.
F. School vending machines should carry only healthful foods.

G. Our class should have a picnic during summer vacation.
H. Our class should not have a picnic during summer vacation.

Speaker's Corner

Practice the speech that you wrote for Activity C. Take turns with your classmates delivering your speeches. After each speech offer suggestions for improvement. Then decide which of your classmates you would vote for.

Prewriting and Drafting

Have you ever tried to make someone agree with your point of view? For example, you may have tried to talk your parents into letting you have a puppy. Today you will begin the process of writing a persuasive article. Your challenge will be to convince a particular audience—your classmates—to agree with you.

Prewriting

Persuading other people to agree with you is not always easy. However, if you choose a topic you care about, do your research, and plan your writing, you have a better chance to persuade others.

Choosing a Topic

Ms. De Note, the Harris School principal, presented a challenge to the Student Council. Some funds were available for a new club and she wanted input from the students about the kind of after-school club they would like. The teachers would be the judges to choose the most convincing proposal.

Tatiana, a sixth grader, was thrilled to find that the majority of her classmates wanted a gymnastics club. Tatiana had been in gymnastics since she was seven. She volunteered to write the sixth-grade proposal because she felt strongly that a gymnastics club would be fun for all Harris School students.

Your Turn

Choose a topic that you feel strongly about. Think of an issue that has opposing viewpoints. Then consider your audience. Will your classmates be interested in the topic? Will many of them have a different point of view? Use the following questions to help you think of a topic:

- Are you involved in any clubs, organizations, or athletic teams? If so, is there something about the activity that you feel needs to be changed?

- Is there an issue at school that your classmates are always talking about?

- Is there something that you'd like to see changed to improve your community?

Researching a Topic

As Tatiana spoke with her classmates, she recorded their reasons for wanting a gymnastics club. She also had her own ideas, but she knew that in order to persuade the judges, she needed to include facts that back up the opinions. Tatiana did some research on the Internet.

Here are Tatiana's notes:

- Most sixth graders like our idea.
- Lots of kids already take gymnastics.
- I've been taking classes since second grade.
- Arguments to use: 1) health and fitness, 2) helps build friendships and school spirit, 3) wouldn't cost school much
- President's Council says that physical activity indicates how healthy you are (from Internet)
- Team activities help kids to work well together and to make new friends.
- Helps flexibility in the body, balance, and muscle development
- Mental discipline and concentration are important in gymnastics
- Can use school's gym equipment
- Can also get free materials from USAmerica Gymnastics (online)

Your Turn

Write down your opinions. They are what your persuasive piece is about. However, opinions without facts to back them up are not likely to persuade an audience. Use the library or the Internet to find supporting facts for your opinions.

Making an Outline

Tatiana decided that an outline would help her present her ideas logically.

In Favor of Gymnastics

I. Hope to convince judges
   A. Many students already involved
   B. Reasons
      1. Health and fitness
      2. Improved student attitude
      3. Low cost to school
   C. Most sixth graders in favor
II. Health and physical fitness
   A. President's Council urges exercise
   B. Aids balance, flexibility, muscles
   C. Good for concentration and mental discipline
III. Student attitudes improve
   A. Teaming makes friends
   B. School spirit built by competing with other schools
IV. Low cost of club
   A. Uses school gym equipment
   B. Research USAmerica Gymnastics and other organizations for funding
V. Thanks for the opportunity
   A. Glad our opinion was asked
   B. Sure our reasons will convince teachers and administrators

Your Turn

Use your notes to make an outline similar to Tatiana's. Glance back at the example outline on page 131 if you need help.

Drafting

Tatiana knew that her draft was her first chance to form her opinions into a convincing argument. So, she used her outline to guide her. Each Roman numeral entry in the outline became the main topic in a paragraph. The entries for the capital letters and numerals became supporting ideas and details.

In Favor of Gymnastics

I couldn't believe I was chosen to present the sixth-grade opinion! I love gymnastics so much I take classes outside of school, so I'm delighted to explain why we should have a gymnastics club. I know I like the idea of a gymnastics club the best and so do most of my friends. I hope to convince you, the judges, to agree. The reasons are better health, improved student attitudes, and low cost.

First, there's health. The President's Council says that physical activity is a requirement for good health. Gymnastics is terrific exercise. It helps develop flexability and coordination. Muscle development and better balance are made apparent in improved strength and physical appearance. Mental concentration sharpens as gymnasts work to develop their routines.

Second, student attitudes will improve. Gymnasts develop their skills while working with partners and on teams. Lasting friendships develop as teammates help each other build confidence and self-esteem. Competing in turnaments will develop school spirit.

Finally, a gymnastics club would would be unexpensive. The physical education department already has a lot of the equipment. Outside gymnastics organizations provide free instructional videos and pamphlets.

We are grateful that we were asked for our opinion. I hope my arguments convince you that this would be a worthwhile and popular club.

Your Turn

Use your notes and outline to write your first draft. Double-space your lines so you will have room to make changes later. Keep in mind that you will probably rewrite your article more than once.

Use the introduction to briefly tell your audience about the issue, your position, and your main arguments. Explain the details about the arguments in the body of your persuasive piece. Express a tone of confidence in your conclusion.

Content Editing

In persuasive writing, the content editor checks to make sure that the arguments are logical and well supported. Tatiana worked to make sure that her proposal was as strong as it could be. Still she knew it's always a good idea to have someone else take a look.

Tatiana's classmate Kyle had developed an interest in gymnastics when his PE teacher taught tumbling

last winter. He also was very enthusiastic about a gymnastics club when Tatiana surveyed the sixth-grade students. Kyle agreed to content edit her proposal before she gave it to the judges.

Kyle read Tatiana's proposal through one time. His first comment was "Gee, I hope the gymnastic club wins!" Then he read her paper again several times, looking for ways to make it even more convincing.

Kyle used the Content Editor's Checklist to guide him, checking only two or three things each time he read it. He made notes on the suggestions he would make. After Kyle finished, the two met for a conference.

Kyle told Tatiana that she supported her arguments well, and the arguments sounded convincing to him. He could see that she was enthusiastic about starting a gymnastics club. He also mentioned ways she might improve her paper.

Here are Kyle's comments.

Content Editor's Checklist

✔ Does the introduction state your position clearly and briefly state the reasons for the position? Does it catch the reader's attention?

✔ Does the body explain the reasons and support them with facts?

✔ Have you included all important details?

✔ Have you taken out details that are not important?

✔ Does your conclusion summarize your arguments and express confidence that they are convincing?

- The beginning needs work. You don't say that most sixth graders voted for a gymnastics club. The judges don't care how happy you are to explain what we chose. They want to know what the choice is.

- Try not to use the pronoun *I* so much. That could make it seem like the club is all about you.

- Don't gush about how much you and your friends like gymnastics. It looks like a clique thing, instead of something the class wants.

- I think they're going to want to know about a club sponsor. Have you talked to any PE teachers about becoming involved?

- I'm not sure exactly what to suggest, but you need a stronger ending.

Tatiana respected Kyle's opinion and knew his ideas were on target. She hadn't realized that she didn't mention the sixth graders' votes. She knew it was important to mention their support in the introduction. She agreed that she had to share her enthusiasm without making it sound like "me, me, me!"

Tatiana also saw that she made a claim that wasn't supported. Kyle missed it, but Tatiana knew she needed to name at least one organization that supplied free training materials. Naming a group would make her persuasive essay stronger.

Tatiana also eyed several words that did not look right. Using her dictionary, she found that she had misspelled two words and had used an incorrect prefix on a third. Can you find the words that needed fixing?

Tatiana also saw that she had used the word *develop* five times. She took out her thesaurus and looked up some synonyms.

Kyle's suggestion to find a faculty sponsor for the club was an excellent one, Tatiana thought. She decided to ask Mr. Karpov, a boys' PE instructor, if he would be interested.

Your Turn

Reread your first draft carefully and check it against the Content Editor's Checklist. Does the introduction grab your audience's attention and state your position? Do you provide support for each argument? Are you sure you're stating evidence and not an unsupported opinion? Is your conclusion positive?

Work with a partner and read each other's persuasive articles. Make notes as Kyle did, using the Content Editor's Checklist. See if you are convinced by your partner's arguments. Confer with each other when you have both finished. Point out writing that is strong, but be honest if you think parts are weak. Make suggestions for improvement. Use your partner's suggestions as you revise your article, and keep looking for things you both may have missed.

Revising

This is Tatiana's revision of her persuasive article.

~~In Favor of Gymnastics~~ *Need better title*

~~I couldn't believe I was chosen to present the sixth-grade~~
The sixth-grade votes are in, and we have flipped over a club that would
~~opinion! I love gymnastics so much I take classes outside of school.~~
serve all students at Harris: a gymnastics club. We have three strong reasons
~~so I'm delighted to explain why we should have a gymnastics club.~~
that we hope will convince you that our school needs a gymnastics club.
~~I know I like the idea of a gymnastics club the best and so do most~~
~~of my friends. I hope to convince you, the judges, to agree.~~ The
When you examine these reasons, we know that you will agree with us.
reasons are better health, improved student attitudes, and low cost.

on Fitness and Sports
First, there's health. The President's Council says that physical

activity is a requirement for good health. Gymnastics is terrific

flexibility
exercise. It helps develop ~~flexability~~ and coordination. Muscle

enhance
development and better balance ~~are made apparent in improved~~

strength and physical appearance. Mental concentration

perfect
sharpens as gymnasts work to ~~develop~~ their routines.

hone
greatly
Second, student attitudes will improve. Gymnasts ~~develop~~ their

emerge
skills while working with partners and on teams. Lasting friendships

~~develop~~ as teammates help each other build confidence and self-

tournaments   increase
esteem. Competing in ~~turnaments~~ will ~~develop~~ school spirit.

Finally, a gymnastics club would would be ~~unexpensive~~ **inexpensive**. The physical education department already has a lot of the equipment. **Mr. Karpov has volunteered to be the club's sponsor.**

Outside gymnastics organizations **such as Gymnastics USAmerica** provide free instructional videos and pamphlets.

We are grateful that we were asked for our opinion. ~~I hope~~ **We're sure that the** exercise and health benefits. the improved student attitudes. and the low cost will ~~my arguments~~ convince you that this would be a worthwhile and popular club.   And who knows? Maybe our school has a future olympic star waiting to be discovered!

Take a look at the changes Tatiana made to improve her persuasive article.

- She wrote a livelier beginning and put the voting results first. While this definitely helped, Tatiana still thought her title needed more work.

- She changed the first-person singular pronoun *I* to the first-person plural *we* to avoid sounding as though the club was for her.

- She dropped the part about how her friends want a gymnastics club so that the judges wouldn't think that it was for just a few students.

- She persuaded the boys' PE teacher to sponsor the club. Adding this fact made her arguments stronger.

- Tatiana used the synonyms for *develop* she had found.

- She wrote a stronger ending.

As Tatiana revised, she realized that she had left out an important detail. The judges might not know what the President's Council was, so she inserted the whole name—the President's Council on Fitness and Sports—so that the judges would know what she was quoting.

Tatiana liked the changes she had made. Still, she wanted her paper to be the winning proposal, so she went over her work again.

Your Turn

Revise your persuasive article. Use your partner's suggestions and any new ideas you want to incorporate. When you have finished, use the Content Editor's Checklist once more to be sure you can answer yes to each question.

Chapter 4 Editor's Workshop

Persuasive Writing

Copyediting and Proofreading

Copyediting

Tatiana felt that she was really getting there. She had followed many of Kyle's suggestions and incorporated changes of her own. Her article was sounding better to her, but now she needed to polish it. She started looking more closely at word meaning, word choice, and sentence structure. She used this Copyeditor's Checklist to help her.

Copyeditor's Checklist

✔ Are there rambling sentences?

✔ Are there run-on sentences?

✔ Is there variety in sentence length?

✔ Are exact words used to help the reader visualize and understand the issue?

✔ Is there variety in word choice?

✔ Is the structure of the sentences logical and grammatically correct?

Tatiana wanted her first sentence to capture the judges' attention. She thought she could use the multiple-meaning word *flip* to make a strong image. *The sixth graders at Harris School flip over gymnastics!*

She knew she needed a better title. *Get Moving for a Healthy Life* was the one she chose.

She added some "healthy" adjectives.

Tatiana checked her conclusion to be certain it was clear how much kids would benefit from gymnastics.

Your Turn

Look for ways to make your sentences more persuasive. Try using adjectives, adverbs, and prepositional phrases to coax your audience to see your point of view. Make a last check to make certain you have evidence to support your opinion. Be sure that your feelings are clearly conveyed in your writing. If your readers don't think you're passionate, they won't be persuaded. Finally, make sure that your title and first and last sentences are just right!

Support your opinion with **F-E-E-L**ing:

Facts
Evidence
Examples
Logic

Proofreading

Any persuasive article is stronger when it has been proofread for spelling, punctuation, capitalization, and grammar. Using a checklist can help writers and editors search out errors that might distract the reader.

Proofreader's Checklist

✔ Is the first line of each paragraph indented?

✔ Does each sentence and proper noun begin with a capital letter?

✔ Are punctuation marks used correctly?

✔ Are all words spelled correctly?

✔ Are all run-on sentences corrected?

Most writers find it helpful to have another person act as a proofreader. Lea offered to proofread for Tatiana because she wanted this club to succeed. She went through the Proofreader's Checklist one item at a time to look for errors. She could find only one error in capitalization. When Lea reminded Tatiana that organization names are proper nouns, Tatiana saw the capitalization error right away. Can you find it?

Also, Lea wondered if *Gymnastics USAmerica* was spelled correctly. Tatiana researched the spelling of the organization online and found that they spelled their name without periods or a space.

Your Turn

Read your paper carefully, using the Proofreader's Checklist. Read it once through for each question on the checklist. This is an efficient way to spot errors and make last-minute changes to improve your piece. When you have finished making your last revisions, ask your partner to use the checklist to proofread your writing.

Chapter 4 Writer's Workshop

Persuasive Writing

Publishing

Tatiana was confident that she had written a very persuasive article. She was ready to write her final copy. For Tatiana, publishing would be when she delivered her proposal to the judges. She carefully typed her persuasive article and printed it for the next Student Council meeting.

Getting Moving for a Healthy Life

The sixth-grade votes are in, and we have flipped over a club that would serve all students at Harris. We have three strong reasons that we hope will convince you that our school needs a gymnastics club. The reasons are better health, improved student attitudes, and low cost. When you examine these reasons, we know that you will agree.

First, there's health. According to the President's Council on Fitness and Sports, physical activity is a requirement for good health. Gymnastics is terrific exercise. It improves flexibility and coordination. Muscle development and better balance enhance strength and physical appearance. Mental concentration sharpens as gymnasts work to perfect their routines.

Students' attitudes will also improve. Gymnasts hone their skills while working with partners and on teams. Lasting friendships develop as teammates help each other build confidence and self-esteem. Competing in tournaments with other schools will increase school spirit.

Finally, a gymnastics club would be inexpensive. Our school already has most of the necessary equipment. Our PE teacher, Mr. Karpov, has volunteered to be our club sponsor and coach. Also, there are gymnastics organizations like Gymnastics USAmerica that provide free instructional videos and pamphlets.

We are grateful that we were asked for our opinion. We are sure the exercise and health benefits, the improved student attitudes, and the very low cost will convince you that this would be a worthwhile and popular club. And who knows? Maybe our school has some Olympic stars waiting to be discovered!

Your Turn

Although you probably aren't planning to formally publish your persuasive article, your writing will still be finalized the moment you share it with your teacher and classmates.

Follow these steps to be sure you share your most persuasive words:

- Make sure you have not left out any convincing facts or evidence.

- Use your neatest handwriting or a computer to make the final copy of your revised draft.

- Take a last look for spelling, grammar, capitalization, and punctuation. If you can, use your computer's spell checker.

Decide with your classmates and teacher how you will share your persuasive articles with one another. Think about posting the articles on a class bulletin board or in your class or school newspaper. If possible, you and your classmates might want to share your articles on your school's Web site.

If your persuasive article discusses an issue or a change in your school or community, talk with your teacher and parents about how you might share your view with a wider audience.

Our Wide Wide World

In the Middle Ages, people relied on word of mouth and posted notices for information. News traveled with people on ships, on horseback, and on foot, and it took a long time for news to spread. Books were copied by hand, one at a time, often by monks. These books were rare and valuable objects.

Today, if something happens on the other side of the world, we find out almost immediately. We can find information on just about anything quickly and easily. How do you get news of the world around you?

Expository Writing

Hats Off to These Caring Students

FROST MIDDLE SCHOOL — Don't just take off that hat! Donate it to the Warm Fuzzies clothing drive. After reading last month's article about this winter's severe cold in the *Village Crier,* three very special sixth graders at Frost Middle School sprang into action. They organized a drive to collect warm hats, gloves, and coats and to distribute them to people in need. With support from family and friends, the students planned their drive, carried it out, and last Saturday brought it to a successful conclusion.

Sonia Valesky, Juan Edelman, and Melissa O'Meara read the article and were moved by the number of children and adults in the community who do not have adequate winter clothing. The three students were discussing the report as they bundled up for lunch recess. Melissa explained, "We realized how lucky we were and just kind of all decided that we could do something to help." The three met after school to plan the details of advertising and collecting. The Frost School principal agreed to let the school be a collection place. The local fire station also joined in the effort.

"Because my dad's a firefighter," Juan explained, "I asked him if his crew would agree to use their station as a drop-off point. They were more than happy to help."

Upon hearing of the compassionate venture, other classmates eagerly volunteered to help. Students made hundreds of colorful signs promoting the campaign and even spent their recess time contacting business sponsors. Local merchants were cooperative, opening their businesses to posters and donation boxes. Large drop boxes were placed in the school office, the fire station, and several other locations throughout the town. The Warm Fuzzies clothing drive was on its way.

The response of the community was immediate. In just two weeks they had collected 112 pairs of gloves and mittens, 89 hats, and 46 coats and jackets. The proud parents of the trio volunteered to help sort, pack, and deliver the Warm Fuzzies to the two agencies they chose.

"We're proud of our children," Melissa's mother, Kathleen, boasted. "We never had any idea how this project would blossom from a lunch-table conversation to such a successful community outreach. I guess they showed us all how to make a difference!"

Expository Writing

What Makes a Good Expository Article?

Expository writing gives information about a specific topic—an actual person, place, thing, or event. Everything in an expository article should be factual, not made up. Expository articles are usually written in the third-person point of view. Newspaper articles, such as "Hats Off to These Caring Students," are examples of expository writing that people see every day.

Introduction

Introductions in expository writing tell what the topic is. Because writers like to have many people read their work, however, good writers use a catchy beginning to entice readers to keep on reading. In newspaper articles a catchy beginning is called a "lead."

Body

The body of an expository article presents the most important information. It answers the questions *who, what, why, when,* and *where,* and often *how.* The information can be presented in different ways, depending on the topic. A writer may explain a relationship between two different things, using comparison and contrast or cause and effect. A writer may give information about a topic, using expert or eyewitness quotations, facts and statistics, explanations, and/or examples.

Conclusion

Conclusions to expository articles should sum up the main ideas and tie them together. An interesting conclusion might include a profound insight, a summarizing quotation, or a thought-provoking statement. In newspaper articles the conclusion is called a "wrap-up."

Activity A

Read the following book titles. Which ones would be appropriate for an expository article? Explain why you think so.

1. *No Unicorns Allowed on the Bus*
2. *Mark Twain's Years as a Steamboat Pilot*
3. *Rock and Roll: The Golden Years*
4. *Invaders from Venus*
5. *The Pigeon That Wanted to Play the Tuba*
6. *London Sightseeing Tours for Under Twenty Dollars*
7. *Pyramids of Egypt and the Americas*
8. *No Way to Tickle a Troll*

Activity B

Each sentence below uses one of the following methods to present information: cause and effect, comparison and contrast, expert or eyewitness quotation, facts and statistics, example, or explanation. Tell which method is used for each sentence.

1. Some Aztec technology, especially technology concerning agriculture, was superior to technology used in Europe.
2. The ash from Vesuvius quickly buried Pompeii, preserving a snapshot of Roman life at the end of the first century.
3. The Pony Express ran some 1,800 miles between St. Joseph, Missouri, and Sacramento, California.
4. Before railroads set standardized time zones, towns across America set their clocks in whatever way was most convenient for their citizens.
5. Although television presents news more quickly, newspapers present news in much greater detail.
6. "The driver was out of control," Sheriff Garcia commented.

Writer's Corner

Use one method of presenting information from Activity B to write a description of the last meal that you ate.

Newspaper Writing

Because many people read only the first few paragraphs of a news article, news reporters often address *who, what, where, when, why,* and *how* early in their writing. Then the article continues with supporting facts, examples, and quotations.

Reporters interview people who were involved in an event or who witnessed it. Often reporters are eyewitnesses themselves, gathering information at political rallies, sporting events, natural disasters, and other newsworthy occasions.

• Activity C •

Look back at the model "Hats Off to These Caring Students." Then copy and complete the following chart.

What	donated winter clothes for people in need
	Frost Middle School and throughout the town
Who	
When	
	They were affected by a news article.
How	

• Activity D •

Select the best lead for this paragraph about bleachers being installed at a high school football field. Then write a wrap-up to end the paragraph.

1. Frost High School will be losing a piece of its history Saturday.

2. The Frost Fliers better have a winning season this year.

3. Students no longer need to bring lawn chairs to Fliers games.

New bleachers are being installed for the Frost High School football field. They will seat approximately 200 spectators along each side of the field. The old bleachers, which were installed shortly after World War II, were becoming dangerous, and most students avoided sitting on the shaky structures. Returning veterans constructed the old bleachers, which were only half the size of their replacements. Student enrollment after the war was much lower than today.

Activity E

The following newspaper article has important information that is not presented until near the end. Write four new sentences to begin the article. Make sure they answer *who*, *what*, *where*, *when*, *why*, and *how*. Then add an interesting lead to the beginning of the article.

City crews were kept busy cleaning up the storm damage in the Frostville downtown area. Broken tree limbs and flooded streets made Main Street impassable throughout much of the day. The weather bureau reported that just under three inches of rain fell in less than an hour, a record for the town. Power lines were down, cutting electricity to homes and businesses south of Sandberg Avenue. The Fliers game with the Park Ridge Hornets was cancelled because the diamond was under four inches of water. The storm, which happened early Tuesday morning, was a total surprise because the forecast was for a cool day with clear skies. The rain stopped as suddenly as it began. City crews used chain saws and pumps to clear the streets of debris and water.

Activity F

Use the information from Activity E that you did not include in your opening sentences. Rewrite the rest of the article. Close with an interesting wrap-up.

Writer's Corner

Work with a partner. Choose a topic you are both familiar with. Each of you create a list of answers to *who*, *what*, *where*, *when*, *why*, and *how* about that topic. Then trade lists with your partner. See who can use the answers to write the best opening paragraph to a newspaper article.

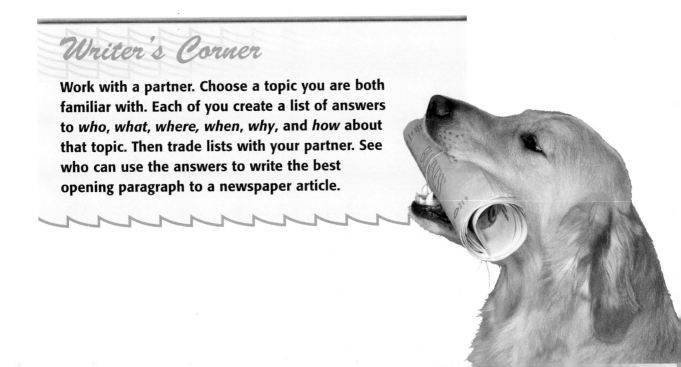

Interviewing

When writing expository articles, you will occasionally need to talk to people to gather information. For example, you might want to write about an upcoming charity dinner or about a political candidate. An interview will help you gather the most current information and a personal view of the event or person.

Setting Up the Interview

Call the person you wish to interview. Explain who you are and why you would like an interview. If the person is agreeable, make an appointment for a time and place that is convenient for both of you. Remember to exchange phone numbers in case either of you has a change in plans.

Preparing for the Interview

Write out your questions in advance, leaving spaces for the responses. The five *w*'s—*who, what, where, when,* and *why*—provide a good guideline for questions to ask. Avoid questions that require a simple yes or no answer. Save time by finding the answers to easy questions through research. If any questions will require complex answers, alert the subject in advance so that he or she can be prepared. Don't ask questions that will embarrass the subject.

Conducting the Interview

Come to the interview on time, neatly dressed, and prepared. Bring your questions, a notebook, pens or pencils, and a tape recorder if your subject agreed to let you tape the interview. (Never record people without asking them first.) Ask permission if you want to quote the subject's exact words. Also ask if you may contact him or her with follow-up questions later.

After the Interview

Immediately after the interview, review your notes and fill in any missing details. If you recorded the interview, check your notes against the tape recording. If something is confusing, contact the subject to be sure you don't make a mistake in your article.

No later than one day after the interview, send the subject a thank-you letter. Also send a copy of your article after it's finished.

Guidelines for Interviewing

- Be prepared.

- Be courteous before, during, and after the interview.

- Ask your questions clearly. Then allow the subject to respond fully.

- Listen carefully; take notes even if you are recording answers.

- Ask the subject to clarify responses that you don't understand and to spell names of people and places you don't know.

- If the subject strays from the topic, listen politely and then bring the interview back on track.

• Activity A •

A famous author is coming to visit your school. You have been chosen to interview the author for the school paper. Write a question to ask about each of these topics. Add three questions of your own.

Source of ideas
Workday of a writer
Person who most influenced
   the author

Rewards of writing
The author's background
Favorite books and authors

Writer's Corner

Brainstorm with a partner about a topic for an interview. Write your questions individually. Then take turns being the interviewer and the subject. Keep your notes to develop into an expository article later.

Interviewing Eyewitnesses

A news reporter often must travel to the scene of a newsworthy event to gather information. The reporter interviews people who witnessed the incident. This is much different from formally interviewing people by appointment. Different eyewitnesses often give different accounts of what happened. The reporter must decide how reliable each eyewitness is.

The five *w*'s are useful when questioning eyewitnesses. They help make sure that the same questions are asked of all the witnesses. In that way the reporter can compare answers and get a good idea of what actually happened.

Activity B

Read the following descriptions from three eyewitnesses to a single incident. Try to decide which parts are accurate and which are not. Then write a short description of the incident as you think it happened.

From Adele H., a 32-year-old bank teller:

A man in his thirties entered the bank. He had blond hair and blue eyes and was over six feet tall. He wore jeans, a blue sweatshirt, and red basketball shoes. He stepped up to my window and handed me a note saying that he had a gun and telling me to hand over all my cash. Before I could react, he noticed Ralph, the guard, at the other end of the lobby. He became nervous and rushed out of the bank without waiting for the money.

From Tyrone D., a 19-year-old bank customer:

I was depositing my paycheck when this old guy, about 40, went to the window next to me. I'm six foot, two, and he was a good six inches shorter than me. He had blond hair. I didn't see his eyes. He wore jeans, a gray sweater, and red high-tops. He said something to the teller, and I could see that she was nervous. I was going to do something, but he suddenly got scared and ran out.

From Ralph M., a 53-year-old bank guard:

I first noticed the suspect when he was nervously standing at Adele's cage. He looked to be in his late 20s or early 30s. He had sandy brown hair and was about five foot, ten. He wore blue jeans, a blue sweater, and orange running shoes. I didn't know anything was going on until he suddenly wheeled around and dashed through the lobby door.

Our Wide Wide World

Magazines and periodicals appeared soon after the first newspapers. Early English magazines had titles like the *Tattler, Spectator,* and *Rambler.* The English periodical *Gentleman's Magazine* was the first to use the word *magazine* to mean a periodical meant for entertainment.

• Activity C •

Work with two classmates. Brainstorm an important occasion that all three of you experienced and remember, such as a school or community event. Write down your own memories about it. Then compare your description with your partners' descriptions. Discuss how your three reflections are alike and how they are different.

• Activity D •

Read the following questions and decide who would be the best person to interview to learn the answer to each one. Explain why you think so.

1. What streets will be closed for the Independence Day parade?

2. Which sixth-graders are taking advanced placement classes?

3. How many high school seniors will graduate in June?

4. Who will be the starting quarterback for next week's game?

5. When is the new east side fire station due to open?

6. Where will the new downtown parking lot be located?

7. When will the library's computer room be available to patrons?

Writer's Corner

Work with a partner. First each should write a list of interview questions about a recent event at school. The five *w*'s would be a good starting point.

After writing your questions, use them to interview your partner. Record his or her responses. Then answer your partner's questions. Compare your responses. Determine which questions worked best to bring out an accurate account of the occasion.

Using Quotations

Direct quotations are another person's exact words—either spoken or in print—that are incorporated into your own writing. They can be used in expository writing to make it come alive and add interest. Direct quotations can also provide evidence to help support an opinion. They can be used to explain or express something in a special way, to clarify something with a good example, or to summarize your point.

The use of direct quotations in an expository piece can make a strong impact on the reader when they are relevant to the topic and carefully placed. If you are writing about people and something that they know about or have done, using their own words can reveal an important fact or a thought-provoking insight. When quoting people in your writing, always indicate that you are using their words and not your own.

When including direct quotations in your writing, be sure to use quotation marks before and after every quotation. The first word of a quotation, no matter where it is located in a sentence, should be capitalized, and punctuation marks should come before the closing quotation marks.

Activity A

Look back at the chapter opener article "Hats Off to These Caring Students." Reread the paragraphs that include quotations. Then answer the questions.

1. How many direct quotations did the writer use?

2. Whom did the writer quote?

3. What did each quotation tell you about the person speaking?

4. Which quotations seem most relevant to the topic? Why do you think so?

5. Which quotations make the most impact? Why do you think so?

6. Can you think of quotes from other people that might have improved the article? Explain.

Activity B

Identify the quotations that would be most relevant in an expository piece titled "The Truth about King Arthur." Explain your reasoning for each choice.

1. "Charlemagne was a medieval king who has many legends told about him," said Mrs. Nagra, the librarian.

2. "Arthur really was a war hero," Professor Carter explained, "whose exploits were recorded in the *Historia Brittonum* by a monk named Nennius."

3. "Alexander the Great was also a noted military leader," Mrs. Nagra continued.

4. "Although the location of Arthur's battles are recorded, most of the place names are no longer used, which has made pinning down Arthur's origins quite difficult," stated Professor Carter.

5. "It is likely that Arthur was not a king as we understand kings today," continued Professor Carter, "but a tribal leader who controlled an undefined region."

Writer's Corner

Imagine that you are a newspaper reporter writing an article about a classmate. Conduct a short interview with a partner, asking questions such as "Where were you born?" and "What do you like about your community?" Record the answers as quotations, referring to the speaker in each sentence. Save your work to use again later.

Did you ever wonder how small newspapers all over the country with few reporters can still carry stories from places as far off as Africa and Asia? Most likely, they get their stories from a news agency, like the Associated Press (AP) or Reuters. Today's news agencies share resources to provide content for newspapers, magazines, radio, television, and the Internet.

Kinds of Quotations

There are different ways to present quotations. One way is as a complete quotation. The speaker reference comes either at the beginning or at the end of what was said.

A. "Why don't we meet at the theater box office?" Jose suggested.

You might also have a divided quotation, in which the speaker reference comes in the middle of what was said. Divided quotations can add variety to sentences in your writing.

B. "I'm just tired," said Sarah, "because I got up early this morning."

Be careful not to overuse the word *said*. For expository articles, you might use words such as *explained, reported,* or *stated.*

• Activity C •

Change each undivided quotation into a divided quotation. Remember to use correct capitalization and punctuation.

1. "The Eiffel Tower was built between 1887 and 1889," explained Madame Durand.

2. "There are nine joined square structures that make up the Sears Tower, which are actually individual skyscrapers of varied height," revealed Mrs. Lang.

3. "For 41 years the Empire State Building was the tallest building in the world," stated Mr. Ross.

4. "The top of the Leaning Tower of Pisa is about 17 feet off-center," Professor DeMateo began.

• Activity D •

Rewrite the following sentences, adding and correcting the punctuation and capitalization as necessary. Change each *said* to a more precise word to fit the context.

1. Roberto said the teacher please locate Japan on the map for us.

2. Where is the lettuce for the salad said Mother looking puzzled.

3. Enjoy yourselves at the dance said Dad but be sure to come home on time.

Stephanie interviewed her Aunt Gerry and recorded quotations using her aunt's exact words. She recorded as many as she could, knowing that she could choose the most relevant quotations later. Read the notes and imagine that you are writing an expository article about Aunt Gerry's life. Discuss with a partner which quotations you would include and where they would make the most impact—the introduction, the body, or the conclusion.

Stephanie's notes:

"I was born in Indiana in 1946. I have three brothers and one sister."

"I'm a baby boomer!"

"Television had been invented shortly before I was born. My family didn't have TV till I was seven. My favorite show was *Howdy Doody*."

"I liked to play outdoors with my friends. We loved Red Rover and Freeze Tag. We played outside till it got dark."

"I went to two different schools because my family moved."

"I was around for several historic events. The Sputnik satellites were a huge advance in technology. And I remember the assassinations of President Kennedy and Martin Luther King Jr."

"I love teaching. That's what I went to college to study for."

"I still get letters from many of my ex-students. That is the greatest reward of all."

"I think my life was and is interesting. Experiencing happy events and sad events has made me who I am."

"I wouldn't change a thing."

"I know the best is yet to come."

Writer's Corner

Take a look at the quotations that you wrote for the Writer's Corner on page 169. Did you use both undivided and divided quotations? If not, revise some of the quotations so that you have a mixture. Check to make certain that you have not overused the word *said*. If you did, change *said* to another word that also fits the context.

Taking Notes

There are two situations in which you need to take notes. One is when you write as you listen, such as when you take notes as your teacher presents a lesson, when you interview someone, or when you write down the words of a song as you listen to it. The second note-taking situation is when you record information from books, magazines, or the Internet.

Taking Notes as You Listen

Taking notes while someone is speaking can be harder than taking notes from printed materials because you can't write as fast as people can talk. Since you are writing for yourself, however, you can use shortcuts to make sure you get the most important information down. Here are some shortcuts.

Omit the articles *the*, *a*, and *an*; other small connecting words; and pronouns:

pledge   allegiance   flag

Use abbreviations and symbols:

w/ = *with*   e.g. = *for example*   etc. = *and so on*

& = *and*   x or X = *don't*   @ = *at*

Use numerals for number words:

1st base   42nd state   5-piece band   3 stooges

Drop vowels from words or leave off endings:

(Ftbll stad. 2 gt new blchrs.)

Use anything that will help you to remember what was said. Try to spell out proper names as well as you can. You may have to look them up later for accuracy.

● Activity A ●

Mr. Jamison, a sixth-grade teacher, was listening to the radio. He heard a host interviewing a teacher about "Make A Difference Day." He thought it sounded like a worthwhile project for his class, so he grabbed his pencil and took notes of the interview. Read his notes and answer the questions.

Make A Difference Day—4th Sat. in Oct. every yr.
    volunteer program—biggest commun. serv. event in US.
    makes people aware—help others
    3+ million vols in 2003—millions more benefit
Sponsors
    Started by USA WEEKEND magazine (mag. section in
        500+ nwspaprs) 1991/92
    Points of Light Foundation, Wash, DC helps people volunt.
        in commun. serv.—helps w/many volunt. progs.
    Paul Newman gives $ to 10 best projects
Who & what
    groups/individuals—all help others. commun. projects—decide
        on own or get suggests.
    register to get ideas & help—big/small projects companies.
        schools, indivs., movie stars
    all diff. projects e.g., visit elderly, grant wishes of sick children.
        collect & make baby things
How to get involved
    register online diffday@usaweekend.com
    call 1-800-416-3824

1. Is Make a Difference Day held on a specific date?

2. How is Paul Newman connected to Make a Difference Day?

3. Are projects assigned to participants?

4. What are four types of projects that participants have worked on?

5. What is the minimum number of people required?

Writer's Corner

Listen to a song you don't know. Write the lyrics to the song, using as many note-taking shortcuts as you can. When you have finished, compare your notes with the written lyrics. Were you able to get down most of the lyrics?

Taking Notes as You Read

One way to take notes from written sources is to make a KWL chart. This kind of chart is especially helpful when you are taking notes to use in an expository piece. First, record in the Know column what you already know about a topic. Then record in the Want to Know column what you want to find out about this topic. These questions will guide your research. As you do research about the topic, record notes in the Learned column.

Below is a KWL chart that a sixth-grade student made when she did research for an expository article about Make a Difference Day. The student included additional notes at the bottom of the chart because she wanted to include the information in her article.

What I Know	What I Want to Know	What I Learned
1) 1-day community service event (biggest in U.S.)	1) What if people can't help on that day?	1) leeway for religious and other reasons
2) Occurs every year on 4th Saturday of Oct.	2) What is the deadline for signing up?	2) no deadline, but to be eligible for award, must sign up by mid-November
3) Sponsors: 1000 Points of Light, Paul Newman, USA WEEKEND	3) Who else is connected to the event?	3) Boy Scouts; Girl Scouts; Farm Aid; Kiwanis; U.S. Air Force; U.S. Army; U.S. Navy; Boys & Girls Clubs; Catholic, Protestant, Jewish organizations; many others
4) volunteers include groups and individuals	4) Can 6th-grade students join in the activities?	4) no age limit; any type of group can join
5) Call 1-800-416-3824 or register online at diffday@usaweekend.com	5) What kind of projects can 6th graders do?	5) clean up parks; collect food, toys, clothes for the needy; babysit for working mothers; visit kids in hospitals

Additional Notes:

all information on Internet

benefits elderly people, sick children, the poor

Activity B

Work with a small group. Think of a topic you all know something about, are interested in, and about which you can easily find additional information in your classroom or library. Then do the following:

1. Choose a person to act as recorder for your group.

2. Draw a blank KWL chart.

3. As a group, brainstorm what you already know about the topic. Record your ideas in the Know column.

4. Fill in the Want to Know column by recording what your group members want to know about the topic.

5. Locate and read additional information about the topic. Take notes from the written information and record them in the Learned column.

Activity C

Make an outline from the KWL chart that your group wrote for Activity B. Compare your outline with those of your other group members. How are they similar? How are they different?

Writer's Corner

Listening for information while taking a telephone message is a common experience. Work with a partner. Make up a realistic phone message for someone in your partner's family. Make certain that the necessary information includes names, dates, activities, and times. Take turns being the caller and the message-taker. The message-taker should listen carefully and take notes. After both partners have listened to the other's messages, each one should rewrite his or her notes into a short memo to give to the family member. Exchange memos and have the message-giver check for accuracy.

Word Study

Homophones

Homophones are words that sound alike but have different spellings and meanings. Some of the most common words in English are homophones. Because many homophones are used so frequently, writers often confuse them. Find the homophone pairs in each of the following examples.

A. Into the pitch-black night, the knight rode on his white charger.

B. Where are the pants that I want to wear to the dance?

C. I heard the toy boat creak as it sank into the creek.

Did you find the homophones? What does each word mean? When you write, be careful to use the correct spelling of words that are homophones. Always check the dictionary if you are unsure of a word's spelling or usage.

• Activity A •

Give definitions for each pair of homophones below. Use a dictionary if necessary. Brainstorm three new homophone pairs.

1. bough, bow

2. patience, patients

3. peace, piece

4. root, route

5. stationary, stationery

6. some, sum

7. threw, through

8. weather, whether

9. road, rode

10. tide, tied

Activity B

Complete each sentence with the correct homophone from Activity A. Use each word only once.

1. Vegetables, such as turnips, that grow underground are called _____ vegetables.

2. The tree lost a _____ in the storm.

3. Radar is an instrument used in _____ forecasting.

4. Sam _____ a horse last week.

5. _____ seabirds travel thousands of miles in their migrations.

6. Tricia fielded the ground ball and _____ it to first base.

7. Brett could not decide _____ to study math or play volleyball.

8. After one week working on the exhausting paper _____, Juan added up the _____ of his earnings.

9. Making a tiny model plane requires much _____.

10. I made a deep _____ as the audience clapped for my performance.

11. We drove _____ the long tunnel on our way into Manhattan.

12. I _____ a big white ribbon on the gift.

13. Afraid his arm was broken, Alex sat in the emergency room among the other _____.

Writer's Corner

Write a narrative that uses the following homophones: *bored, board, wade,* and *weighed.* Use a dictionary if you need help. Compare your work with a partner's. Did you both use the words in the correct context?

Eight Troublesome Homophones

Writers often misuse the following homophones. The best way to remember how to use these homophones is to associate the spelling with their common uses. Study the chart. Do you use these homophones correctly when you write?

Homophone	Common Use	Example
you're	contraction for *you are*	He thinks you're kind.
your	possessive adjective	Grace likes your sweater.
they're	contraction for *they are*	Jamal will go when they're done.
their	possessive adjective	Jane went to their house.
there	adverb that tells where	I'll go there tomorrow.
two	adjective meaning "one more than one"	Emma has two clock radios.
to	preposition meaning "toward"	Let's go to the movies.
too	adverb meaning "also" or "overly"	May I see too? This soup is too hot.

• Activity C •

Use homophones from the chart to complete the paragraph. Check the context of each sentence before placing a word. Use each homophone only once.

Mario's family is going ——————— the beach this Saturday.

They will stay for _____ days. Mr. Sanchez will go ahead

of time and set up _____ tent. _____ going to

have a great time, and Mario can't wait to get _____.

Mario asked Luke to go _____. I heard Mario ask Luke.

He told Luke, "_____ going to love camping at the beach

with us. This will be _____ best vacation yet!"

• Activity D •

Write a homophone pair for each set of definitions. The first one is done for you.

Definition	Definition	Homophone Pair
1. pipe in a chimney	past tense of fly	flue, flew
2. want, require	mix and squeeze	_____
3. masculine gender	something sent by post	_____
4. glue, adhesive	walked back and forth	_____
5. a step	look fixedly at	_____
6. pulled, dragged	small, frog-like amphibian	_____
7. fly aloft, glide	painful, sensitive	_____
8. school leader	basic truth or law	_____
9. agreement, treaty	filled completely	_____
10. breakfast food from grain	story published in parts	_____

• Activity E •

Use each pair of homophones in one sentence. Use a dictionary if you need help.

1. cells, sells
2. week, weak
3. plain, plane
4. break, brake
5. deer, dear
6. ring, wring
7. beet, beat
8. brows, browse
9. days, daze
10. horse, hoarse
11. kernels, colonels
12. sow, sew

Writer's Corner

Content edit a piece of writing that you have been working on. Find at least three words that have homophones. Check a dictionary to make sure that you used each word correctly. Revise any mistakes.

Speaking and Listening Skills

Current-Event Reports

Have you ever watched a report on the news about local or national events, or seen a special-interest program about the parents of quintuplets? These are expository presentations—they inform an audience. One common form of expository presentation is a current-event report. Besides describing the event itself, a current-event report might include the history or meaning behind the event, as well as related anecdotes or interesting tidbits. Keep the following things in mind when reporting current events.

Choosing a Topic

The topic of your report is determined by the event that you choose. With current-events reporting, the topic usually finds the reporter. It is usually something of importance to the audience that has happened recently or will happen in the near future.

Audience and Angle

Think about who your audience is going to be and consider what you want them to know about your topic. This consideration is called an "angle." If your topic is a new fountain in the park, decide what you want to tell your audience about the fountain. Choose an aspect of the event that your audience might find intriguing.

Five *W*s

Always keep the five *w*'s in mind. Who is the subject or who is the report going to effect? What happened or what will happen? When did, or will, the event happen? Where did the event take place? Why is the event important? Keeping the five *w*'s in mind will keep your report relevant and engaging.

Activity A

Choose one of the following story ideas. Describe who your intended audience will be. Jot down two ideas for angles and include three questions you might research for each angle. Write down one person whom you would interview for information. Save your notes to use later.

- Retirement party for the local librarian
- 6th-grade class field trip to an ostrich farm
- Town centennial festivities
- Interview with a local musician

Activity B

Choose one of the story ideas from Activity A and answer the following questions.

1. Who is the subject?
2. What is important about the event?
3. When did, or will, the event take place?
4. Where did, or will, the event take place?
5. Why will people be interested in the event?
6. What special angles will you discuss?

Speaker's Corner

Prepare to deliver a current-event report. Choose a topic and jot down ideas about your angle, audience, and supporting facts. Name any people you might interview to gather information. Share your ideas with a group. Offer other group members feedback about their ideas, such as another angle that they might take for their story, or facts that they might include to make their story stronger.

Visual Aids and Props

Using visual aids and props when reporting current events can help you focus what you are saying. You already know about using props and visual aids such as objects, charts, and maps. In a current-event report you might even include video clips, such as an interview with an expert or an eyewitness, or shots of the location where your event occurs.

Anticipate difficulties that you might have by practicing your report using the visual aids or props. If you use a video clip, make sure that you know how to operate the video player. Check the volume and make sure that the television is on the right channel. Play the tape section and rewind it to the proper spot so that you know it is properly set up. Practice in front of someone to get feedback about whether the visual aids or props enhance the report or if they are distracting.

Being an Active Listener

Make sure that you are an active listener. The following questions can help you listen to a current-event report.

- Why is the reported event newsworthy?
- How is the report relevant to you?
- Does the speaker have a bias for or against the event?
- When does the reported event take place? Is it ongoing news or old news?
- What is the reporter's desired effect on the audience?
- Does the reporter use an interesting angle to present the report?

• Activity D •

Make an outline for a presentation about a current-event topic that interests you. Include facts you would plan to research and people you might interview. Picture the presentation in your mind and write down a list of visual aids or props that you plan to use.

Activity E

Imagine that you are a student news anchor for an after-school news and information television show. You are responsible for selecting, writing, and presenting a three-minute informative segment for middle-school students. Choose a topic and write what you already know about it. Do research to gather more information, taking notes. Write questions that you would ask an expert. Then write an outline, including just the information that you would include in your segment.

- vacation spots with special facilities for children
- how an older person in a family can influence a younger person's life
- a look at a popular sport—reason for its popularity, ways to participate on a team, community support, and so on
- pets in the community—local rules, guidelines for care, how the community feels about pets
- bicycle safety
- video games and their effect on children's health and study habits
- disadvantages of some students not having computers at home when they do homework

Speaker's Corner

Work with a partner and choose a topic from Activity E. Take turns interviewing one another as though you are conducting an actual TV news report. Create note cards to use when you are the interviewer. For your presentation, the interviewer should sit at a news-anchor desk. Trade places when you switch interviewers. If possible, have someone tape your presentations for the class to watch. If this is not possible, take turns presenting your reports to your classmates.

Expository Article

Prewriting and Drafting

Now it's time to apply the writing process to produce an expository article.

Prewriting

Andrew has two great interests. He is an avid writer, and he is passionate about the environment.

Aaron Lyons, the faculty sponsor of the school newspaper, asked Andrew if he would write an article about Earth Day. Frost Middle School had observed Earth Day since 1972, almost from the beginning. The time was rapidly approaching for this year's celebration. Mr. Lyons wanted Andrew to write an article that would make students aware of the event. Andrew eagerly agreed.

Your Turn

When writing an expository article, choose a subject that matters to you. Think about your interests. They may be related to things that you are learning in school, or to family activities, sports, hobbies, music, pets, or places you've visited with family or friends.

Plan to interview someone for some of your information. Choose a topic that requires you interview classmates, teachers, family members, or friends to get information.

Gathering Information

Andrew knew how Frost Middle School was planning to observe Earth Day. He had already made plans to join other students to clean up Dobb's Creek.

For more facts about Earth Day, he knew that he would have to research on the Internet. He also decided to interview this year's sponsor, Principal Marsha Nichols, to see how she felt about Earth Day. He wanted to talk with Ms. Eleanor Arrado as well. As a science teacher, she had sponsored the event more than 20 times.

In order to decide what questions he would ask in his interviews, he made a KWL chart. In the first column, he wrote the things that he knew.

What I Know

Earth Day = April 22, every year

Frost Middle has been participating since before today's students were born

E.D. started in 1970s (1960s?) by Gaylord Nelson.

Frost school project this year: clean up Dobb's Creak

This years sponsor is Ms. Nichols

Mrs. Arrado usually sponsors; has been since beginning

When Andrew had filled in the first column with things that he knew, he thought about things that he wanted to know. He put these questions in the middle column.

What I Want to Know

When was Earth Day first observed?
Who is Gaylord Nelson?
How was Dobb's Creak chosen?
Why is Ms. Nichols (school principle) sponsor this year?
How did Mrs. Arrado become so active in environmental issues?

Your Turn

Write your topic at the top of a sheet of paper. Spend some time writing notes detailing what you already know about the topic. Try using a KWL chart to organize your ideas for your article.

Taking Notes

Andrew did his Internet research first. He found information about Gaylord Nelson and the beginnings of Earth Day. The more he learned, the more questions he had. He knew that he wouldn't use all of the information, but he was glad there was a lot to choose from.

Then Andrew contacted Mrs. Arrado and Principal Nichols. They both said that they would be happy to speak with him. He could even bring a tape recorder if he wanted to use some direct quotes in his article. He met with Principal Nichols first. Here are his notes of her interview:

always wantd to wrk 4 envrnmt
bn a spnsr of E.D. 4X. Eleanor Arrado 20+X.
Choz Dobb's Creak cause trsh is bcoming isore & ndangring ecosystm.
13 volnteers now, need mor
just sho up—lots of work

The next day, Andrew met with Mrs. Arrado. Here are his notes from that meeting:

becam spnsr 1st year teaching.
wantd 2 do smthng to make stdnts no me.
red about polution, nvirnmnt, ecolgy—got hookd.
bin spnsr 22 X

Andrew combined the information that he gathered from the interviews with the facts that he found on the Internet. He completed his KWL chart. Then he created an outline using the information. The outline would help him organize his article.

Your Turn

Ask the people you need to speak with if you may interview them. Use the notes to fill in your KWL chart or whatever graphic organizer you chose to use. Then decide how you will present the information in your article. You may want to use an outline as Andrew did.

Drafting

Andrew used his outline to write his draft. He double-spaced the lines on his computer because he knew he would be editing and making changes.

Dobb's Creek Will Sparkle Again

This year in honor of Earth Day, Frost Middle School is sending student volunteers to clean out Dobb's Creak. Years of people illegally dumping trash have placed the local ecosystem in danger. There is room for more volunteers. Last year there were 20 of us. Just come at nine-thirty on Sunday morning. You will be put to work.

Earth Day has been around for more than 30 years, and it is still going strong. The first Earth Day was on April 22, 1970. Since then it has been celebrated every year on April 22.

Frost became involved in 1972. Mrs. Arrado, who will retire at the end of this school year, was just a first-year science teacher back then. She volunteered to sponsor Frost's initial participation in Earth Day events. "At first, I just wanted to do something that would help students get to know me," she confessed, but as I read more and more about the subject, I became a convert to the cause."

Since then, Mrs. Arrado has been an Earth Day sponsor more than twenty times. She has hauled newspapers and aluminum cans in her car, planted trees along Devon parkway, cleaned up vacant lots, and contributed to improving the environment in numerous other ways. Principle Nichols is this year's Earth Day sponsor. However this is only her fifth turn.

Earth Day was instituted by former Wisconsin Senator Gaylord

Nelson. In the 1960s he became concerned about the degradation of the environment. He realized that the best approach to addressing the problem was to involve America's youth. He takes little credit for his part however, he makes the following statement on the Earth Day Web site, "Earth Day worked because of the spontaneous response at the grassroots level. We had neither the time nor resources to organize 20 million demonstrators and the thousands of schools and local communities that participated. That was the remarkable thing about Earth Day. It organized itself."

Since that first Earth Day celebration, the movement has spread worldwide. Many groups even make it Earth Week and Earth Month.

Your Turn

Reread your notes and your graphic organizer. Then write your first draft. Double-space your lines so you have room to make changes. Remember that you will make revisions as part of the writing process.

Keep your audience in mind as you write. Leave out unimportant information. Keep in mind that expository writing is informational. Don't make it too personal, but do include material from your own experiences.

Chapter 5 Editor's Workshop

Expository Article

Content Editing

After completing a first draft, a writer edits it for content. In this step the writer makes sure that all of the necessary information is included and that the ideas are presented in a clear, ordered, and logical manner. Andrew used a checklist for expository articles to make sure he didn't overlook any important information.

Content Editor's Checklist

✔ Does the introduction tell what the article is about?

✔ Does the article answer the questions *who, what, why, where, when,* and *how?*

✔ Are the paragraphs well-developed with main ideas and supporting details?

✔ Is information presented by using examples, cause and effect, statistics, and explanations?

✔ Are there eyewitness or expert quotations to support ideas?

✔ Are the quotations meaningful to the story?

✔ Does the conclusion tie things together?

Andrew knew he had a ready-made content editor to read his work. A classmate, Hailey DiGanis, had been the student editor for the school newspaper for two years. She checked every article before it went into print. She was thorough and always had constructive suggestions for writers' submissions.

Hailey read Andrew's expository article through one time to get the general tone. Then she read it twice more, using the Content Editor's Checklist to make certain that she wouldn't miss anything. She took notes so she would remember what she wanted to ask or to tell Andrew. She had many useful comments when the two had a conference.

First Hailey told Andrew that his article made her decide that she wanted to join the Dobb's Creek cleanup. She complimented him on all the interesting information he had included. She said she hadn't realized that Earth Day was such an important event. Then she pointed out ways in which Andrew could improve his article. These are some of her specific suggestions.

- You say that a lot of trash has been dumped into Dobb's Creek over the years. It would give readers a clearer picture if you named the types of trash that have been dumped.

- I don't think you need to mention how many volunteers there were last year.

- The quote from Mrs. Arrado is interesting, but it makes her look as though she started sponsoring Earth Day activities for a selfish reason. Is there another quote you can use?

- When you say that this is only the fifth time Principal Nichols is the Earth Day sponsor, it seems as though you are belittling her efforts. Can you rephrase the statement so it doesn't sound critical?

- Your article really got me interested in Earth Day. I think you should add some information about how your readers can learn more about it.

Andrew liked Hailey's ideas. It helped to have someone else's opinion. He could see that describing the kinds of trash that had been dumped in Dobb's Creek would help readers visualize the problem. Also, he hadn't meant to make Principal Nichols's Earth Day contributions look small. He saw a few other changes that he wanted to make in his revision.

Your Turn

Reread your first draft, using the checklist as you do so. After you have gone over your work, trade articles with a classmate. Take the role of content editor reading each other's article several times. Use the Content Editor's Checklist as you read and take notes so that you can make good suggestions.

When you have your conference, remember to start with some positive comments. Remember, your partner worked hard on this paper, just as you did on yours.

When you do your revision, take your partner's suggestions into consideration but remember that the final product is yours, so you must make the final decisions. Always be looking for new ways to improve your article during the revisions.

Expository Article

Revising

This is how Andrew revised his expository article.

Dobb's Creek Will Sparkle Again (Terrible Title!)

This year in honor of Earth Day, Frost Middle School is sending student volunteers to clean out Dobb's Creak. Years of people illegally dumping trash have placed the local ecosystem in danger. There is room for more volunteers. ~~Last year there were 20 of us.~~ Just come at nine-thirty on Sunday morning. You will be put to work.

Earth Day has been around for more than 30 years, and it is still going strong. The first Earth Day was on April 22, 1970. Since then it has been celebrated every year on April 22. Frost became involved in 1972. Mrs. Arrado, who will retire at the end of this school year, was just a first-year science teacher back then. She volunteered to sponsor Frost's initial participation in Earth Day events. "At first, I just wanted to do something that would help students get to know me," she confessed, but as I read more and more about the subject, I became a convert to the cause."

Since then, Mrs. Arrado has been an Earth Day sponsor more than twenty times. She has hauled newspapers and aluminum cans in her car, planted trees along Devon parkway, cleaned up vacant lots, and contributed to improving the environment in numerous other ways.

Principal
~~Principle~~ Nichols is this year's Earth Day sponsor. ~~However~~ this is only her fifth turn. "I'll never match Mrs. Arrado's record," she admits. "I'm just happy to do what I can to improve the quality of our air and water." Earth Day was instituted by former Wisconsin Senator Gaylord

Nelson. In the 1960s he became concerned about the degradation of the environment. He realized that the best approach to addressing the problem was to involve America's youth. He takes little credit for his part however, he makes the following statement on the Earth Day Web site, "Earth Day worked because of the spontaneous response at the grassroots level. We had neither the time nor resources to organize 20 million demonstrators and the thousands of schools and local communities that participated. That was the remarkable thing about Earth Day. It organized itself."

Since that first Earth Day celebration, the movement has spread worldwide. Many groups even make it Earth Week and Earth Month.

If you are interested in learning more about this vital movement, visit the Web site at http://earthday.envirolink.org.

These are the revisions Andrew made in his article.

- He visited Dobb's Creek to see the trash dumped there and added that information.

- He agreed that the number of volunteers last year didn't add to his story so he deleted the sentence.

- The quote from Mrs. Arrado was natural. He left it in.

- He added a quote from Principal Nichols that showed her feelings about ecology and Mrs. Arrado.

- He added the URL where he found information about Earth Day.

- He saw that he had used *Principle* instead of *Principal.*

Your Turn
Use your own ideas and the ideas you got from your partner to revise your article. Use the checklist. Can you answer yes to each question?

Copyediting and Proofreading

Copyediting

When you copyedit your work, you should look for mistakes in sentence structure and word choice. You should also pay attention to how well your sentences flow together.

Andrew saw he could improve the flow of ideas in his first paragraph, by combining two sentences. He did the same in the paragraph about Senator Nelson. Can you see how he might have combined sentences in the two paragraphs?

Finally, Andrew read his article using the Copyeditor's Checklist to finish editing his expository article.

Copyeditor's Checklist

✔ Are there rambling sentences?

✔ Are there run-on sentences?

✔ Is there variety in sentence length?

✔ Is there variety in word choice?

✔ Have all commonly misused words been checked for accuracy?

✔ Are all quotations correctly punctuated?

✔ Do sentences flow together smoothly and logically?

By using the checklist, Andrew found a run-on sentence that he previously missed. Can you spot it?

Your Turn

Look over your revised draft. Use the Copyeditor's Checklist to edit your article. Are your sentences varied? Have you checked for run-on and rambling sentences? Have you punctuated quotations correctly?

Proofreading

Before writing the final copy of an expository article, a good writer proofreads to check for spelling, punctuation, capitalization, and grammar. It is also a good idea to make sure that no new errors have been introduced during the revising process. It is helpful to to refer to a Proofreader's Checklist.

Proofreader's Checklist

✔ Are paragraphs indented?

✔ Are capitalization and punctuation correct?

✔ Is the grammar correct?

✔ Are all words spelled correctly?

✔ Has the text been checked for any new mistakes that may have been introduced?

Writers often find it helpful to have others proofread their work. A proofreader, like a content editor, will often find mistakes that the writer has overlooked. It's best to have someone who hasn't seen the writing before do the proofreading. Hailey had read Andrew's article when she content edited it. He wanted another pair of eyes to proofread. Mr. Lyons, the school newspaper's faculty sponsor, agreed to look over Andrew's article.

In the first paragraph, Mr. Lyons found a spelling mistake. In the third paragraph there was an error in punctuation, and in the fourth paragraph there was a capitalization mistake.

Your Turn

Read your paper carefully using the Proofreader's Checklist. Look for only one kind of error at a time. It will be easier to spot errors that way. It also makes you read your story several times. With each reading you will probably find something you missed previously.

When you have finished checking your own paper, trade papers with a partner. Go through each other's papers in the same way. Check the dictionary for spelling errors. Use proofreader's marks to indicate any changes that you think should be made.

Expository Article

Publishing

After several revisions, Andrew felt he had done his best. It was now time for the final copy. He typed in all of his hand-written revisions and ran a spell check to make sure he hadn't misspelled any words. He double-checked all homophones because he knew the spell checker would not catch them.

Then he printed out his article. He felt confident as he handed the writing in to Hailey. After all that work, Andrew was glad he would have a chance to share it with his classmates. He hoped that some of them would join in cleaning up Dobb's Creek.

A Touch of Frost at Dobb's Creek

This year in honor of Earth Day, Frost Middle School is sending student volunteers to clean out Dobb's Creek. Years of people illegally dumping shopping carts, appliances, tires, and assorted other pieces of trash have placed our local ecosystem in danger. There is room for more volunteers. Just show up at nine-thirty on Sunday morning, and you will be put to work.

Earth Day has been around for more than thirty years, and it is still going strong. The first Earth Day was held on April 22, 1970. Since then it has been celebrated every year on April 22.

Frost became involved in 1972. Mrs. Arrado, who will retire at the end of this school year, was just a first-year science teacher back then. She volunteered to sponsor Frost's initial participation in Earth Day events. "At first, I just wanted to do something that would help students get to know me," she confessed, "but as I read more and more about the subject, I became a convert to the cause."

Since then, Mrs. Arrado has been an Earth Day sponsor more than twenty times. She has hauled newspapers and aluminum cans in her car, planted trees along Devon Parkway, cleaned up vacant lots, and contributed to improving our environment in numerous other ways.

Principal Nichols is this year's Earth Day sponsor. This is her fifth turn. "I'll never match Mrs. Arrado's record," she admits. "I'm just happy to do what I can to improve the quality of our air and water."

Earth Day was instituted by former Wisconsin Senator Gaylord Nelson. In the 1960s he became concerned about the degradation of the environment and realized that the best approach to addressing the problem was to involve America's youth. He takes little credit for his part, however. He makes the following statement on the Earth Day Web site, "Earth Day worked because of the spontaneous response at the grassroots level. We had neither the time nor resources to organize 20 million demonstrators and the thousands of schools and local communities that participated. That was the remarkable thing about Earth Day. It organized itself."

Since that first Earth Day celebration, the event has spread worldwide. Many groups even make it Earth Week and Earth Month. If you are interested in learning more about this vital crusade, visit the Web site at http://earthday.envirolink.org.

Your Turn

When a writer's final copy is ready, he or she submits it to a publisher for printing and distribution. Although the articles you write in school are not formally printed, you turn in your work or share it with the class.

To publish, follow these steps:

- Make sure you have not left out any main or supporting details.

- Use your best handwriting or a computer to make a final copy.

- Proofread your copy one more time for correct spelling, grammar, capitalization, and punctuation.

Decide as a class how you will publish or share your expository articles. If you have a class newspaper, you might include a few of the articles in each issue.

Some people might videotape their expository pieces in a TV news setting as if they were special feature segments on a daily news show.

Others may prefer to have theirs in a class book of expository writings. Everyone has done a lot of work to share a lot of interesting information. Learn from each other by sharing these expository writings.

CHAPTER 6

In 1803 Thomas Jefferson asked Congress for money to send Meriwether Lewis and William Clark on a journey to the uncharted French and British lands west of the Mississippi. On the journey Lewis and Clark discovered people, landscapes, and wildlife that Americans back home had never seen. The trip took two and a half years, so long that many people thought the entire expedition had perished.

Why do you think people are so eager to explore the unknown?

Business Letters

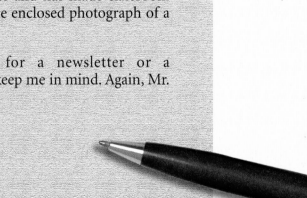

Jasper Middle School
110 George St.
Lynn, MA 01901

March 16, 20—

James Duffy
Exhibit Coordinator
Lynn Museum of Visual Arts
25316 Oakdale Ave.
Lynn, MA 01901

Dear Mr. Duffy:

I am writing on behalf of the sixth-grade students at Jasper Middle School. As the students' fine arts teacher, I would like to thank you for the excellent presentation on the artists of the Impressionist period, which we experienced on March 5.

Your docents were obviously well trained and did a wonderful job of providing interesting, vital information. The students especially liked the slide show that highlighted artworks by Monet and Manet. The presentation has enriched my students' lives and has made classroom learning more relevant. I hope you enjoy the enclosed photograph of a student's interpretation of Monet.

If you ever need a positive quote for a newsletter or a recommendation from an educator, please keep me in mind. Again, Mr. Duffy, thank you for a terrific presentation.

Sincerely,

Kathleen Schmidt

Kathleen Schmidt

Enc: photograph

Business Letters

What Makes a Good Business Letter?

1 Heading
The writer's return address is typed in the top left-hand corner of the paper. The date should be placed below the return address.

2 Inside Address
The inside address includes the receiver's name and job title, as well as the company's name and address.

3 Salutation
The salutation is a greeting. It should read "Dear" (followed by the name of the receiver) or "To whom it may concern" and a colon.

4 Body
The body is the main part of a letter, where the message is conveyed. The body is single-spaced, with a line between paragraphs and a line after the last paragraph. The paragraphs are not indented.

5 Closing
The closing of a business letter is brief and complimentary, such as "Sincerely" or "Respectfully." A comma follows the closing.

6 Signature
The sender's name is typed four lines below the closing. The sender's handwritten signature is written directly above his or her name. *Enc* after the signature means *enclosure*.

Kathleen Schmidt's letter on page 197 is a business letter. A business letter is a formal letter with a specific business-related purpose. In the case of Kathleen's letter, the purpose is to thank someone for exceptional service. Look at Kathleen's letter, shown below, to see where the parts of a business letter are placed.

Jasper Middle School **1**
110 George St.
Lynn, MA 01901

March 16, 20—

James Duffy
Exhibit Coordinator
Lynn Museum of Visual Arts **2**
25316 Oakdale Ave.
Lynn, MA 01901

Dear Mr. Duffy: **3**

I am writing on behalf of the sixth-grade students at Jasper Middle School. As the students' fine arts teacher, I would like to thank you for the excellent presentation on the artists of the Impressionist period, which we experienced on March 5. **4**

Your docents were obviously well trained and did a wonderful job of providing interesting, vital information. The students especially liked the slide show that highlighted artworks by Monet and Manet. The presentation has enriched my students' lives and has made classroom learning more relevant. I hope you enjoy the enclosed photograph of a student's interpretation of Monet.

If you ever need a positive quote for a newsletter or a recommendation from an educator, please keep me in mind. Again, Mr. Duffy, thank you for a terrific presentation.

Sincerely, **5**

Kathleen Schmidt **6**
Kathleen Schmidt

Enc: photograph

Crafting the Body

Good business letters are always written with a specific purpose in mind. The best business letters are also confident, polite, and concise. Here are some guidelines for crafting effective bodies of business letters.

- Begin the first paragraph with a professional and polite opening that states the purpose of the letter. In some cases you might want to identify yourself right away so that the recipient better understands why you are writing. Leave out any unnecessary details as you state your purpose.
- In the next paragraph or paragraphs, offer information, examples, explanations, or persuasive reasoning to support your main point.
- In the last paragraph, restate the purpose of the letter and ask for action if appropriate. If you are making a request, thank the recipient in advance for his or her help.

Activity A

Study the body of the letter on page 197. Answer these questions.

1. What is the purpose of the letter?

2. How does the sender identify herself?

3. What is one example that the sender gives to support her main point?

4. What invitation to action does the sender give in the last paragraph?

5. How does the sender restate the purpose of her letter in the last paragraph?

Writer's Corner

Think of a person or company to which you could write a complimentary business letter. Write a sentence that describes why you would write the letter.

Letters of Thanks or Congratulations

Some business letters are written to apply for a job, to request information, or to order a product. Often business letters are written to thank people for extraordinary service or for an outstanding product. The following are some reasons you might write this kind of positive business letter.

- It lets recipients know to continue providing the service or to continue carrying the product.
- It provides recipients with documentation that could be used to commend or promote an individual.
- It lets recipients know that their hard work is appreciated.

Some business letters are also written to congratulate a person or a company on a specific accomplishment. This kind of business letter is often written by someone who has worked with the recipient in the past and who would like to continue working with that person. Therefore, this kind of business letter is useful because it nurtures business relationships.

• Activity B •

Read the following opening paragraphs from two different business letters. Identify each paragraph as being from a business letter of thanks or one of congratulations.

> I received an e-mail from Kendra Martin yesterday notifying me that your company has just received the prestigious Best Family Commercial Award. I hope that I am among the first to applaud your efforts. What a wonderful accomplishment!

> I am writing to let you know how much I appreciate the fine efforts of Annie Howe, one of the night managers at your motel. When the fire alarm sounded last Thursday at 3 a.m., she went from room to room notifying sleeping guests. I was one of them. I am eternally grateful for her selfless act of courage.

• Activity C •

Imagine that you will write a business letter for each of the following purposes. For each purpose, write a sentence for the opening of a business letter that tells why you are writing. You can add creative details as necessary.

1. to apply for a job as a lifeguard at Water World, a local water park

2. to thank a store manager for taking back a leaky inflatable pool toy

3. to ask for pamphlets or brochures about vacations to Silver Spur Dude Ranch

4. to order a music CD titled *Today's Top Hits*

5. to complain about a defective video game

6. to ask a local store to carry your favorite brand of shoes

7. to complain that a product doesn't really perform the way that its commercials show it performing

• Activity D •

Choose one of the sentences from Activity C. Write a closing paragraph for the body of that letter. Use your imagination as you restate your purpose for writing and perhaps invite some sort of action from the sender.

Writer's Corner

Brainstorm a list of business-related purposes for which you could write a business letter. Then choose one and develop an opening paragraph for the body of a business letter. Be sure to leave out any unnecessary details and use confident, polite, and concise language.

Audience, Tone, and Formal Language

When writing a business letter, determining the correct audience, using the proper tone, and using formal language can clearly bring across a message as well as get results for a writer.

Audience

When writing a business letter, it is important to get the message into the hands of the right person. Letters that use the greetings *To whom it may concern* or *Dear Sir or Madam* can be set aside as belonging to no one. Use these greetings only as a last resort.

Do research before writing your letter. Make phone calls if necessary. If you are writing to thank or congratulate someone, be sure to find out the first and last name and the title of the person you want to compliment. For this kind of letter, you might write to a worker's manager so that good work gets rewarded. If you are writing to complain about a product or service, be sure to find the name and title of a person who can quickly get results for you. When writing, keep in mind that your audience is probably busy. Get to the point early.

Tone

The tone of a business letter should be polite and professional. If the purpose of the letter is to thank or congratulate, don't exaggerate your enthusiasm with exclamations or over-the-top compliments. Be honest, but choose your words carefully. If you write a business letter to make a complaint, be respectful, not insulting or threatening. If the purpose of your letter is to apply for a job, be direct and confident as you explain why you are the right person for the position.

Formal Language

Good writers know how to use formal language when crafting a business letter that is polite and professional. Because a business letter should use formal language, avoid contractions such as *you've*, *they've*, *I'll*, and *I'm*. Spell out the words that make up the contractions. Also avoid clipped words, such as *photo* for *photograph* and slang such as *cool* to mean "good."

• Activity A •

Under each company or organization is a purpose for writing a business letter. Name the job title of a person you think would best be able to respond to each letter. Explain how you might do research to find the person who has that title.

1. Scarsdale Public Library
   to apply for a job as a library assistant during the summer

2. Krispy Krunchies Cereal Company
   to complain about stale cereal inside a closed box and request a refund

3. Barry's Burgers
   to thank a waiter for calling about a wallet that you left in his restaurant

Writer's Corner

Read a piece of direct mail advertising that has been delivered to your home and see how well it matches the guidelines in this lesson. Make lists of ways that it matches the guidelines and ways it misses them. Bring your letter and lists to class and compare them with those of your classmates.

Checking for Audience and Tone

Once you have written a business letter, it is a good idea to reread it with audience, tone, and formal language in mind. For a letter of thanks or congratulations, ask yourself questions such as these:

- Am I writing to the correct person, or is there someone else who should be reading this letter?
- What might the recipient think or feel about my letter?
- Will the reader think that any words are inappropriate or too informal?
- Am I stating my gratitude or congratulations in an honest, respectful way, or am I exaggerating?
- Is my tone professional and polite?

Activity B

Rewrite the contraction in each sentence to give the sentence a more professional tone.

I can't thank you enough for your help.

They're my favorite kind of running shoes.

I'm writing to apply for the position of camp counselor.

I am so glad that you've won the prize.

I know they'll work if you replace the charger.

I'd love to have the job if there is an opening.

It doesn't turn on when I push the power button.

I am delighted that he's going to continue working at your store.

Activity C

Revise each group of sentences so they have a polite, professional tone that uses formal language.

1. I totally want to thank you for helping me fix my bike. You are so cool for taking the time!

2. If you don't give me a refund, I'm going to come down to the store and make a fuss. Then you'll have to help me.

3. I'm writing to say congrats on your award for the Best Recreational Vehicle of the Year. That Roadracer ATV is awesome!

Activity D

For each audience and purpose, write two polite, professional sentences for the body of a business letter. You can use your imagination to fill in details.

Audience: Miss Lynch, choir director of Hydesburg Middle School
Purpose: to thank her for a wonderful week at Choral Camp

Audience: Omar Hernandez, Public Relations Director for WRET radio
Purpose: to ask for a T-shirt from the last WRET Battle of the Bands Contest

Audience: Nikita Lewis, owner of Beads and Baubles
Purpose: to thank her for restringing your favorite necklace free of charge

Audience: Soonhee Pak, Customer Service Manager
Purpose: to ask for a replacement for a defective cell phone battery

Audience: Jesse Willow, Shipping Manager
Purpose: to congratulate her on her promotion to manager from assistant manager

Audience: Lyndon McFinch, owner of Lincoln Records
Purpose: to ask for a replacement for a scratched CD

Audience: Mr. Pickle, professional clown
Purpose: to ask for a chance to train with him to become a professional clown

Audience: Cecil Lubinski, manager of the Danish Cheese Factory
Purpose: to thank him for taking your class on a tour of the factory

Writer's Corner

Read the revision you wrote for number 2 in Activity C. Use the questions on the top of page 204 to check for audience, tone, and formal language. Revise your sentences as necessary.

Suffixes

A suffix is a syllable or syllables that can be added to the end of a word to change its meaning or to make it a different part of speech. Knowing the meanings of suffixes can help you increase your vocabulary.

Adverb and Adjective Suffixes

The suffix *-ly* changes adjectives to adverbs. Adding *-ly* to the adjective *happy* makes the adverb *happily*. Often the spelling of a base word changes when you add a suffix. In the word *happy*, the *y* becomes an *i* before the suffix is added.

Some suffixes change nouns into adjectives. The suffix *-ful*, meaning "full of," can be added to the noun *beauty* to form *beautiful*. *Beautiful* is an adjective that means "full of beauty."

The suffix *-ish*, meaning "relating to" or "like," can be added to the noun *child* to form *childish*. *Childish* is an adjective that means "like a child."

Adjective Suffixes		
Suffix	**Meaning**	**Example**
-able, -ible	capable of being	manageable, credible
-al	relating to	natural
-ful	full of	skillful
-ic	relating to, like	athletic
-ish	resembling, like a	childish
-like	resembling, like a	catlike
-y	full of	cloudy

Activity A

Copy the chart below and fill in the missing parts.

Base Word	Suffix	New Word	Meaning
1. sorrow	-ful	_____	_____
2. _____	-ish	_____	like a fool
3. mud	-y	_____	_____
4. child	_____	childlike	_____
5. _____	_____	bendable	able to be bent
6. critic	-al	_____	_____

Activity B

Add an adjective suffix from the chart on page 206 to the base word at the left so the new word correctly completes the sentence. Use a dictionary to check spelling.

tickle   **1.** I never knew Ewen was so _____.

wind   **2.** It was a cold, _____ day with the snow a foot deep.

grace   **3.** The _____ ballerina seemed to float on the stage.

comfort   **4.** My new shoes are very _____.

life   **5.** The figures in the wax museum were very _____.

music   **6.** Playing piano is one of her _____ talents.

Writer's Corner

Brainstorm a list of 10 words with suffixes. Trade lists with a partner. Find the suffix in each word on each other's list. Then work together to use each word in a sentence.

Noun and Verb Suffixes

There are many suffixes that change base words to nouns or verbs. Here are some common noun and verb suffixes.

Noun Suffixes		
Suffix	**Meaning**	**Example**
-ant, -ent	person who	assistant, resident
-ion	act of, state of	celebration
-ist	person who	pianist
-ment	act or process	placement

Verb Suffixes		
Suffix	**Meaning**	**Example**
-ate	make	activate
-en	cause to	awaken
-ize	cause to be	realize
-fy	make	falsify

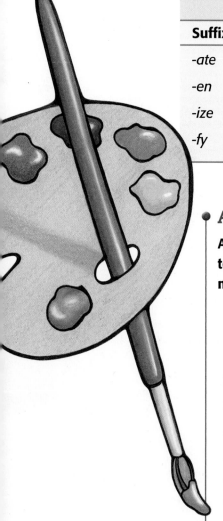

• Activity C •

Add a noun or verb suffix from the charts to each base word to make a new word that fits each definition. Identify the new word's part of speech.

simple	wide	familiar	serve
collide	art	move	active

1. to acquaint someone with something
2. to make bigger in width
3. person who takes care of the needs of another
4. the act of going from one place to another
5. to make something easier
6. the act of coming together, as in a crash
7. person who creates original artworks
8. to make something become active

• Activity D •

Complete each sentence with the correct word from each pair.

1. lengthen, lengthy

He made a _____ campaign speech.

I will _____ the coat that is too short.

2. agreement, agreeable

Our teacher was _____ to our recess plan.

The boys made an _____ not to fight.

3. solidify, solidly

When it is chilled, the gelatin will _____.

We stood _____ behind our candidate.

4. cheerful, cheerfully

She is always such a _____ person.

I _____ accepted the second-place prize.

• Activity E •

Complete the chart by writing the new word, its meaning, and another word that ends with the same suffix. Use a dictionary to check each spelling.

Suffix	Base Word	New Word	Meaning	Another Word
1. -*ment*	merry	_____	_____	_____
2. -*ize*	fertile	_____	_____	_____
3. -*ist*	column	_____	_____	_____
4. -*en*	strength	_____	_____	_____

Writer's Corner

Reread a piece of writing you have been working on. Find at least five words with suffixes. Look up each word in a dictionary to be sure you used each word correctly in context and that each word is spelled correctly.

Writing Skills

Expanding Sentences

When writers vary sentences, their writing is often clearer and more interesting. Using compound parts can be a useful way to vary sentences.

Compound Subjects and Predicates

A sentence can have a compound subject, a compound predicate, or both. The subject of a sentence names the person, place, or thing that the sentence is about. Two or more subjects and their modifiers form a compound subject in a sentence. Compound subjects are often connected by the word *and* and usually require a plural verb. What is the compound subject in this sentence?

Monet, Renoir, and Pissarro are famous French artists.

The predicate of a sentence tells what the subject is or does. Two or more simple predicates and their modifiers form a compound predicate. Compound predicates are often joined by the word *and*. What is the compound predicate in this sentence?

Camille Pissarro arrived and settled in France in 1855.

• Activity A •

Identify the compound subjects and compound predicates in the sentences. Some sentences may have both.

1. Many people admire and collect Impressionist paintings.

2. Rajan saw and purchased a modern-art poster at the museum.

3. Apples and bananas are my favorite fruits to bring for lunch.

4. Rick and Jorge painted and framed pictures for the art exhibit.

5. Taidje read and reread all of the Harry Potter books.

6. Brittany and I are going to the Fun Fair tonight.

7. Weeds and dandelions grew and overran our flower garden.

Activity B

Complete each sentence with a compound subject.

1. _____ are pleased to be on the same soccer team.
2. The _____ are frozen, so we can't eat them.
3. _____ need plenty of water to grow.
4. _____ are my favorite team sports.
5. _____ make the most delicious sandwiches.
6. _____ send e-mails to Jane every day.
7. _____ are good books.
8. _____ work with my father.
9. _____ are reptiles.
10. The _____ are in the garage.

Activity C

Complete each sentence with a compound predicate. Be sure the verbs agree with the subjects.

1. At the water park, Mai and Erin _____.
2. My cousin and her friend _____.
3. The monster movie _____.
4. Top athletes Jake and Bijan _____.
5. Her pet rabbit _____.
6. The skilled acrobat _____.
7. Cars and trucks _____.
8. Whales and dolphins _____.
9. That video game _____.
10. Guitar players _____.

Our Wide Wide World

In the early 1840s, California was a sparsely populated territory. That changed in 1848 when John Sutter began construction of a sawmill on his property. Pea-sized nuggets of gold were discovered throughout the building site. Sutter tried to keep the discovery a secret so that he could continue building an agricultural empire, but news leaked out. By 1849, about 80,000 gold prospectors had flooded the California territory.

Writer's Corner

Write a journal entry about your day. Use at least three compound subjects and three compound predicates as you write.

Compound Direct Objects

A direct object is a noun or pronoun that receives the action expressed by a verb. Two or more direct objects and their modifiers form a compound direct object in a sentence. What is the compound direct object in this sentence?

Before the guests arrived, Dad moved the truck and the car from the driveway.

Compound Objects of a Preposition

The noun or pronoun following a preposition is the object of the preposition. Two or more objects of a preposition and their modifiers form a compound object of a preposition. What is the compound object of a preposition in this sentence?

The artist created a dramatic effect with light and shadows.

• Activity D •

Find a compound object in each sentence. Tell whether it is a direct object or an object of a preposition.

1. We have our warmest weather in July and August.
2. Jason went to the movie with Nick and me yesterday.
3. My aunt planted parsley and chives in her herb garden.
4. Maria studies ballet and tap.
5. In astronomy we studied the planets and stars.
6. She will weave the strips into baskets and purses.
7. Louisa was surprised at the many cards and gifts.
8. The mechanic carefully replaced the oil and filter.
9. My grandmother loves to eat olive oil and bread.
10. After a rainstorm, our sidewalk is always covered with slugs and snails.
11. Her dress was covered in rhinestones and sequins.
12. We met both the artist and the writer at the comic book store to sign autographs.

Activity E •

Rewrite the sentences below, using compound subjects, predicates, direct objects, or objects of prepositions.

1. I am writing to request information on family resorts in northern Michigan. I would like information on bike trails in the area too.

2. I admire your writing very much. I loved reading *The Giver*. I enjoyed *The Silent Boy*.

3. I would like to order a one-year subscription to the magazine *Muse*. I would like a one-year subscription to *Dog Fancy*.

4. Your loan representative, Mr. Chambers, handled my loan quickly and courteously. Mr. Chambers handled my request for a new account in the same way.

5. The sunglasses are defective. The jacket zipper is defective as well.

Activity F •

Use each compound phrase in an original sentence as indicated.

1. celery and carrots (subject)

2. dove and swam (predicate)

3. pen and pencil (direct object)

4. chair and couch (object of a preposition)

5. babies and young children (subject)

6. song and dance (direct object)

7. flowers and shrubs (object of a preposition)

8. crouched and hid (predicate)

Writer's Corner

Reread a piece of writing that you have been working on. Find at least two sentences that you can expand or combine by using compound parts. Revise your writing.

State Abbreviations	
Alabama	AL
Alaska	AK
Arizona	AZ
Arkansas	AR
California	CA
Colorado	CO
Connecticut	CT
Delaware	DE
District of Columbia	DC
Florida	FL
Georgia	GA
Hawaii	HI
Idaho	ID
Illinois	IL
Indiana	IN
Iowa	IA
Kansas	KS
Kentucky	KY
Louisiana	LA
Maine	ME
Maryland	MD
Massachusetts	MA
Michigan	MI
Minnesota	MN
Mississippi	MS
Missouri	MO
Montana	MT
Nebraska	NE
Nevada	NV
New Hampshire	NH
New Jersey	NJ
New Mexico	NM
New York	NY
North Carolina	NC
North Dakota	ND
Ohio	OH
Oklahoma	OK
Oregon	OR
Pennsylvania	PA
Rhode Island	RI
South Carolina	SC
South Dakota	SD
Tennessee	TN
Texas	TX
Utah	UT
Vermont	VT
Virginia	VA
Washington	WA
West Virginia	WV
Wisconsin	WI
Wyoming	WY

Mailing a Letter

Addressing Your Letter

You've written your business letter and you're pleased with the result. Now you're probably anxious for it to reach its destination.

Since the envelope is the first thing a recipient sees, it is important to address it properly. The front of the envelope has the name and address of the person to whom the letter is being sent. It also has the return address of the sender. Look at the following example.

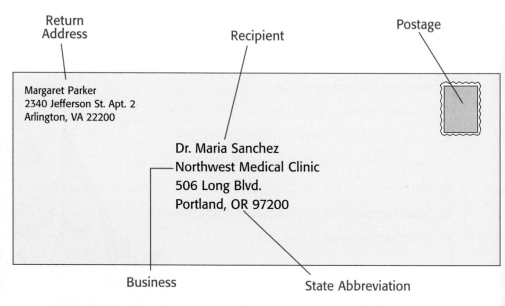

Return Address — Margaret Parker / 2340 Jefferson St. Apt. 2 / Arlington, VA 22200

Recipient — Dr. Maria Sanchez

Business — Northwest Medical Clinic

506 Long Blvd.

State Abbreviation — Portland, OR 97200

Postage

Abbreviations

The Postal Service prefers that you use abbreviations when addressing an envelope. Use a state's two-letter abbreviation rather than spelling out the state name. Also abbreviate words that indicate a street or a multi-unit building, such as an apartment. See the chart of state abbreviations.

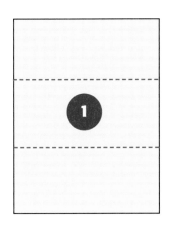

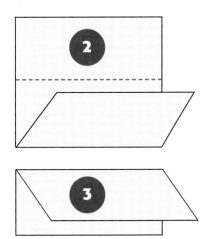

Folding a Letter

When writing a business letter, use standard 8½"×11" paper and a standard business envelope. A business letter should be folded so that when the recipient removes it from the envelope, it will open easily and be ready to read. Sloppy folding and unnecessary creases look unprofessional and distract the recipient.

First, fold the bottom third of the paper so that the bottom edge is a little more than halfway up. Then fold the top third down. If necessary, measure the folds beside an envelope before you crease them. Be sure to keep the left and right edges even. Place the letter into the envelope with the last fold nearest the top.

• Activity A •

Practice folding a business letter, using several sheets of standard-sized paper. Refer to the diagram for the proper method.

Our Wide Wide World

In the mid-1800s many settlers used trails to make the long and difficult journey across the plains and mountains to the Pacific coastline. The most famous trail, the Oregon Trail, was about 2,000 miles long and took travelers through what is now Kansas, Nebraska, Wyoming, Idaho, Washington, and Oregon.

Writer's Corner

Study an envelope from an actual business letter. Determine the sender, the recipient, the business name, the state the letter was sent from, and the state it was sent to. Write your answers in complete sentences.

Enclosures

Imagine that you have discovered that you paid full price for an item that was on sale. If you wrote a letter asking to have the difference refunded, you would need to include a copy of the receipt as an enclosure. An enclosure is something that is put in the same envelope as a letter. Some common enclosures are résumés, certificates, pictures, or pamphlets. It is customary to refer to the enclosure in the body of the letter.

Please see the enclosed photograph to verify the damage to the rear bumper of my car.

You should also list enclosures after the closing. This lets the person reading the letter know what to look for.

Sincerely,

Sally Zhou

Sally Zhou

Enc: résumé, sample photographs

If you are sending something that shouldn't be bent, such as photographs or certificates, you may need to use a cardboard envelope. Put your business letter on top of the enclosures. Heavier items, such as pamphlets, may require additional postage.

• Activity B •

Evaluate the model on page 197 and the envelope on page 214. Answer the following questions.

1. What state is the letter on page 197 being sent to?

2. What is Kathleen Schmidt sending as an enclosure?

3. In what state is the recipient of the envelope on page 214 located?

4. In what state does the sender of the envelope live?

Activity C

Cut two sheets of paper into thirds (the shape of an envelope—about 4 inches by 8 inches per piece). Using both sides of each piece, print out the following addresses. Use your own address as the return address. Remember to use postal abbreviations and correct punctuation.

1. Juliet F. Jefferson, Bronze Tanning Co., 724 Palm Street, Honolulu, Hawaii 96800

2. Dr. Chandra Singh, Saint Charles Hospital, 14 Front Street, Keokuk, Iowa 52632

3. Mrs. Jenny Tan, Camelot Ranch, Rural Route 3, Big Bar, Idaho 83678

4. Mr. Roberto Flores, Kitchen Design Studios, 5525 Penn Avenue, Pittsburgh, Pennsylvania 15201

5. Mr. Howard L. Finkle, The Sentinel Press, 123 Freeman Parkway, Providence, Rhode Island 02906

6. Ms. Carolyn Davis, Kids' Magazines Service, 99 Hampshire Street, Denver, Colorado 80200

Activity D

Identify the types of enclosures that might be included with each business letter.

1. a job application cover letter

2. a letter reporting a defective product

3. an award letter

4. a letter for renewal of a newspaper subscription

Writer's Corner

Choose a business from a phone book. Address an envelope to that business. You can make up the recipient's name.

Speaking and Listening Skills

Congratulatory and Thank-You Speeches

At some point in your life, you will probably have to give a congratulatory speech or a thank-you speech. These speeches can be informal, such as at a party or barbecue, or formal, such as at a graduation or an award ceremony.

Congratulatory Speeches

A congratulatory speech is given to recognize a person's achievement or a major event in his or her life. When giving a congratulatory speech, keep these things in mind.

Audience and Formality

The audience and setting for your speech will influence what you say and how you say it. If you are giving a congratulatory speech at a sports team award dinner, what you say should be formal and respectful. You can be less formal at a party with your friends. Always be aware of what is appropriate to say in your speech.

Introduction

A good way to start a congratulatory speech is with a quick anecdote or story or by thanking the audience for participating. By including the audience, you will keep their attention.

Closing

The closing is your last opportunity to get your point across to the audience, so give your speech a strong finish. Sum up what you have said previously about the subject's achievement. Then invite the audience to join you in extending good wishes or congratulations to the person you are congratulating.

Activity A

Match each speaking situation to its audience. Then indicate whether the speech's tone might be formal or informal.

1. Shen congratulates Emily on her student council president victory at an award ceremony.

2. Mrs. Wright congratulates Ryan on winning the school spelling bee during Language Arts class.

3. Aurelio congratulates his graduating class during his commencement speech.

4. Yeshi congratulates her grandparents at their 50th wedding anniversary party.

A. family members at home

B. students and faculty in the school auditorium

C. students, relatives, and faculty in the school courtyard

D. students in a classroom

Activity B

Write speech introductions for two of the situations in Activity A, imagining yourself or a friend in each situation. Use the audience and tone that you chose for each of those speech introductions.

Activity C

Choose two congratulatory speech topics below. Choose an audience and either a formal or an informal tone. Then write an effective closing for each topic.

- someone's birthday
- a scholarship winner
- a teacher who is retiring
- a winning team

Speaker's Corner

Choose a classmate and think of an award or a tribute you think he or she deserves. List reasons why the person deserves the award.

Thank-You Speeches

There may be occasions when you will have to give a thank-you speech. It might be to thank a group for an award, to thank friends and family for a special gift, or to thank your sports team for nominating you Most Valuable Player. Many of the things that you have learned about congratulatory speeches are important when giving a thank-you speech, such as being aware of your audience and what is appropriate to say. Here are some other things you should keep in mind when giving a thank-you speech.

Giving Special Thanks

When you give a thank-you speech, there might be certain people to whom you wish to give special thanks. For example, if you have won a student council election, you might give special thanks to the people who helped you campaign. Don't, however, feel as though you have to thank everyone you know. Giving special thanks to a lot of people can make a speech too long, which may cause you to lose the attention of your audience. Make a list beforehand of the people and groups you plan to thank. Then stick to it.

Timing and Practice

A brief anecdote or story is often part of a speech. Indicate in your notes where you should pause to give your audience a chance to laugh or to absorb what you have said. When you practice your speech, you can adjust your pauses so that you get your timing just right. Your practice audience can also listen for unintentional double meanings or inappropriate humor in your speech.

Tips for Being a Gracious Listener

Keep these points in mind when listening to a congratulatory or thank-you speech:

- Listen carefully—you may be invited to clap or to extend congratulations.
- Listen actively—you may discover new or interesting information about the subject of the speech.
- Remember, the speaker might be nervous. Show him or her your support by paying attention and applauding at the end of the speech.

Activity D

Read the following movie award thank-you speech and answer the questions that follow.

I have wanted to be an actor ever since I was 11 years old. There have been times when I have almost given up because I was sure that there were other jobs that would do less damage to my ego. I held on to my dream, and now here I am, standing before the best and the brightest in the film community, accepting this award.

There are some people I would like to thank, because without them I wouldn't be standing here tonight. Thank you to writer Charlie Jones, director Amuri Chana, and my amazing costars, Alexander Greene and Laura Del Amico. You all made me look better than I am.

My biggest thanks is to the people assembled here tonight for bestowing this honor upon a young boy who had a big dream. You represent the best that our profession has to offer, and I am honored to be ranked among you.

1. Who is the intended audience for this speech?

2. How does the speaker engage the audience in the introduction?

3. Is this speech formal or informal? How do you know?

4. Explain why the speaker gave special thanks to the people that he mentions.

5. Where might the speaker pause for impact in this speech?

6. Do you think the closing is effective? Explain your answer.

First Engine Operated Over Central Pacific R. R. Out

Speaker's Corner

Use the notes that your partner wrote for the Speaker's Corner on page 219 to develop a thank-you speech. Remember to indicate places in your notes where you should pause. Then take turns with a partner, practicing your speeches. When you feel confident about your timing and delivery, present the speech to the class.

A Thank-You Letter

Prewriting and Drafting

Before writing the first draft of a letter, the writer knows the purpose of the letter, the person to whom it will be written, and what information it will include. Another detail that a writer might be thinking about is the response that he or she hopes to get from the recipient.

Prewriting

Carla's favorite bookstore is Anastasia's Attic. Every time she visits the store, the sales clerk, Ms. Dixon, makes a real effort to help Carla find what she's looking for. One day Carla wondered if Mr. Brody, the store owner, knew how wonderful Ms. Dixon is to all of his customers. With this in mind, Carla decided that she would write a letter.

Your Turn

Think of someone who has done you a favor. Perhaps a family member or a friend helped you work out a problem, or maybe a teacher or coach helped you improve your performance in some way. Maybe there is a person whom you don't know very well, but who went to some trouble to help you in a particular situation. Choose one person whom you would like to thank in a letter.

Gathering Thoughts

Carla sat at the kitchen table and thought about the different times Ms. Dixon had helped her and her friends find just what they were looking for in Anastasia's Attic. She jotted down all the little things she could remember that show how Ms. Dixon takes care of her customers. Here are Carla's notes.

- Ms. Dixon is an excellent employee. She was there when Mom and I first went to Anastasia's Attic.

- She showed Mom where gardening books were; took me to the juvenile book section.

- Helps me pick books for birthday gifts; knows what boys and girls like.

- Mom told Ms. D I didn't like to read. Ms. D made a list of books I might like. I loved every one. Also gave Mom ideas for her reading.

- Once Mom wanted books that she couldn't find anywhere. Ms. D found them and ordered them!

- She showed me how to find out if a particular book is still being printed.
- She puts posters for local events in the windows.
- Once an older woman fell outside. Ms. D brought her in and took care of her and called her daughter.
- My brother Jimmy accidentally tore a page, but Ms. D didn't make him pay for the book.
- Offers customers coffee and juice; does all the clean-up herself.
- Ms. D is the reason I buy all of my books at Anastasia's. I know other customers who feel the same.
- Thanks for hiring such a caring person.

- When Anastasia's first opened, Ms. Dixon showed us around.
- Before I met Ms. Dixon, I didn't like to read. Mom told her that I wasn't a big reader.
- Ms. D made a list of books that I might like. I loved them all.
- Ms. Dixon helped me become a book lover.
- She helps me pick out books to give as gifts. She knows the books that boys and girls like to read.
- Once Mom wanted books that she couldn't find anywhere. Ms. D found them for her!
- One time an older woman fell outside the store. Ms. Dixon helped her inside, gave her tea and called her daughter to pick her up.
- You're lucky to have her working for you. Customers are lucky she's there too.
- Thank you for hiring Ms. Dixon

Your Turn

List the reasons for which you want to thank the person. Jot down the reasons that you are grateful. Did the person do one great act of kindness for you, or does the person regularly do small favors that you wish to acknowledge?

Organizing Ideas

Carla knows that a good letter needs to be short and to the point. She also knows that the reason she is writing should be stated immediately. Therefore, Carla sorted through her notes and selected what she thought were her most important points.

Your Turn

Organize your notes. Work on developing a clear purpose, elaborating on the most important details, and ending with a lasting impression.

Your letter should not be too long. Focus on having a purpose paragraph, a concluding paragraph, and one or two middle paragraphs.

Drafting

Carla went over her notes. As she began writing her first draft, she noticed that using all her details would make her letter very long. She decided to leave out some of the items from her list. Carla double-spaced the body of her draft so she would have room to edit and make changes later.

5244 Sierra Ave.
Seaside, CA 92335

May 3, 20 —

Mr. John Brody
Anastasia's Attic
327 East Front St.
Seaside, California 92335

Dear Mr. Brody,

I'd like you to know why I think that Ms. Dixon at your store is a very special person. Ms. Dixon is always happy to assist me. She helps my friends too. I was in the store Monday. She helped me select a perfect birthday gift book for my friend Jeff I don't know what boys like to read. Ms. Dixon does.

For many years I hated reading. Then my mom and I went to your store's grand opening. Ms. Dixon helped us. She suggested some exciting books for me to read. I read every one. I loved them all. Now I'm a sixth-grade student. I read constantly. I often visit Anastasia's Attic by myself.

Once my mom wanted a three-volume set of gardening tips. She searched high and low for it for two weeks. Ms. Dixon found a set on the Internet and ordered it for her. She must have spent hours looking for it.

Ms. Dixon is a very careful person. One day an elderly lady slipped just outside the door. She fell. Ms. Dixon came to the rescue. She invited the lady inside. She took care of her. She called her daughter to come and pick her up.

Mrs. Dixon has a lot to do with my love for books and reading. You're sure lucky to have her working for you!

Yours truely,

Carla Cameron

Your Turn

Reread your notes and write your first draft. Keep in mind that you probably will want to make some changes, so double-space your draft to leave room for editing.

Remember to think about the person to whom you are writing. Consider your choice of words and the tone you'd like to convey. Think about clarity in your vocabulary and sentence structure. Keep your letter brief. You can continue to eliminate extra information as you see fit during the writing process. Finally, check that all addresses and names are correct.

Content Editing

After writing the first draft of her letter, Carla read it over for content. She understands that content editing letters is just as important as content editing other types of writing. Even though letters are usually not meant for large audiences, ideas should be presented logically and clearly.

Carla used the following checklist as she edited her letter.

Content Editor's Checklist

✔ Is the purpose for writing the letter clearly stated at the beginning?

✔ Do you explain who you are to the recipient?

✔ Do the middle paragraphs offer examples in support of the purpose?

✔ Does the closing paragraph restate the purpose of the letter and ask for action if appropriate?

✔ Is sentence structure varied so that the letter is interesting to read?

✔ Does the language of the letter reflect the tone that is intended?

✔ Does the letter end with a lasting impression?

As in all types of writing, it is helpful to have someone else read over your letter in case you missed something. Carla knew that her friend Rachel was also a big fan of Anastasia's Attic, so she asked Rachel to edit her letter. Since Rachel liked Ms. Dixon, she agreed to help.

Rachel read Carla's letter all the way through once. She then read through it twice more using the Content Editor's Checklist. Rachel made notes as she read so that Carla would be able to read her comments. When she finished, the two got together for a conference.

Rachel agreed with Carla that Ms. Dixon deserved to be recognized. She thought it was a good idea to write to the bookstore's owner. Rachel was certain Mr. Brody would share the letter with Ms. Dixon.

Rachel went on to compliment Carla on her professional-looking business letter. The letter starts off with Carla telling Mr. Brody that Ms. Dixon is a special person. Carla follows with three paragraphs giving examples that support her opinion. In her conclusion Carla restates her appreciation of Ms. Dixon.

Rachel also thought Carla presented a good picture of herself as a positive person and an avid reader. Here's a list of Rachel's suggestions for possible changes.

- You should start off by telling Mr. Brody that you are a customer so that he will know that your opinion is important.

- Mention Ms. Dixon's first name if you can find it. Maybe your mom knows what her first name is.

- It's nice that Ms. Dixon helped you find a birthday gift for Jeff, but maybe you should mention that later.

- "Mom" is too informal a term for a business letter. You should say "mother."

- Your second paragraph has a lot of short sentences. You should combine some of them to make your writing flow more smoothly.

- Your conclusion might be stronger if you compliment Mr. Brody by saying something positive about him or his bookstore. You might thank him for having such a great store for kids like us to go to.

Carla appreciated Rachel's opinions and revised her letter with Rachel's comments in mind.

Your Turn

Reread your first draft, using the checklist as a guide. Then work with a partner and read each other's letter. Use the Content Editor's Checklist as you read your partner's letter. Take notes as you read and then share your comments while your thoughts are still fresh in your mind. Remember, everyone appreciates positive criticism, so be sure to include what you liked about your partner's work before making suggestions for improvement.

Consider your partner's suggestions as you revise your letter.

Revising

Here is Carla's revision to her thank-you letter.

5244 Sierra Ave.
Seaside, CA 92335

May 3, 20 –

Mr. John Brody
Anastasia's Attic
327 East Front St.
Seaside, California 92335

Dear Mr. Brody,

I am a regular customer of Anastasia's Attic, and I want to tell you ~~I'd like you to know why I think that Ms. Dixon at your store is a~~ what a wonderful employee you have in Ms. Janet Dixon. ~~very special person.~~ Ms. Dixon is always happy to assist me. She helps my friends too. I was in the store Monday. She helped me select a perfect birthday gift book for my friend Jeff I don't know what boys like to read. Ms. Dixon does.

For many years I ~~hated reading.~~ was not an avid reader. Then my ~~mom~~ mother and I went to your store's grand opening. Ms. Dixon ~~helped us. She~~ suggested some exciting books for me to read. I read every one, and loved them all. Now I'm a sixth-grade student. and a constant reader. ~~I read constantly.~~ I often visit Anastasia's Attic by myself.

Once my ~~mom~~ mother wanted a three-volume set of gardening tips. She searched high and low for it for two weeks. Ms. Dixon found a set on the Internet and ordered it for her. She must have spent hours looking for it.

Ms. Dixon is a very careful person. One day an elderly lady slipped and fell just outside the door. ~~She fell.~~ Ms. Dixon went ~~came~~ to the rescue. She invited the lady inside and ~~She~~ took care of her. Then she ~~She~~ called the lady's ~~her~~ daughter to come and pick her up.

I'm sure that as a bookstore owner you must be a lover of books. I am. ~~Mrs. Dixon has a lot to do with my love for books and reading. You're~~ too, and Mrs. Dixon has a lot to do with that. You are very sure lucky to have her working for you, and so are all of us bookworms! Thank you for the great store!

Yours truely,

Carla Cameron

Take a look at the changes that Carla made in her letter. She followed most of Rachel's suggestions. Carla thinks the suggestions have helped her develop a more businesslike tone.

- Carla rewrote the first sentence and mentioned that she is a customer of Anastasia's Attic.

- Carla's mom told her that Ms. Dixon's first name was Janet, so she added it in the first sentence.

- Carla wanted to start her letter with the most recent example of how helpful Ms. Dixon is, so she left in the part about Jeff's birthday present.

- Carla changed every *mom* in the letter to *mother*.

- Carla also combined some sentences.

- Carla thought complimenting Mr. Brody was a good idea. She pointed out that they both love books. She also added her thanks at the end.

Your Turn

Using your new ideas and the comments you received from your content editor, make the appropriate revisions to your letter. Remember that you don't need to accept all of your content editor's suggestions. Carla ignored the comment about Jeff's birthday present. You can ignore any suggestion that you feel does not improve your letter. When you have finished, review the Content Editor's Checklist one last time.

A Thank-You Letter

Copyediting and Proofreading

Copyediting

Carla was feeling pleased with her letter after she made her changes. She felt especially good about the last paragraph and the impression it would leave. Now she read her letter for sentence construction and word choice.

She noticed that the first paragraph was choppy and didn't flow well. Carla decided to revise some of the sentences. She changed two short sentences to make one sentence with a compound direct object. She also got rid of some repetitive information in the second paragraph.

Carla realized that *careful* was not the word she wanted to describe Ms. Dixon. The meaning that Carla intended here was that Ms. Dixon cared about others. Carla changed the word to *caring.*

Carla used the following Copyeditor's Checklist to finish editing her letter to Mr. Brody.

Copyeditor's Checklist

✔ Has the letter been checked for rambling and run-on sentences?

✔ Is there variety in sentence length?

✔ Have short choppy sentences been combined into longer sentences with compound parts whenever possible?

✔ Do sentences flow together smoothly and logically?

✔ Are all of the words correct with proper suffixes added as necessary?

Your Turn

Look over your revised draft. Expand sentences by combining short, choppy sentences to make compound and complex sentences. Use compound subjects, predicates, and objects where you can. Use the Copyeditor's Checklist to make sure you have not missed anything. Then read your letter aloud or ask someone else to read it while you listen.

Remember to **SELL** yourself:
    State your purpose.
    Elaborate with details.
    Leave a
    Lasting impression!

Proofreading

Finally, Carla felt that all of her points were presented in a logical manner with correct sentence structure and a smooth flow of ideas. It was time to read for correct spelling, grammar, punctuation, and capitalization. She used the following checklist.

Proofreader's Checklist

✔ Are all the proper parts of the letter included?

✔ Is there appropriate punctuation after the salutation?

✔ Are there spaces between paragraphs?

✔ Are sentences punctuated properly?

✔ Are all words spelled correctly?

✔ Has the writing been checked to make certain that no new mistakes were introduced?

Carla reviewed her letter one more time, using the Proofreader's Checklist as a guide. She then asked her mother if she might give her letter a quick check. Mrs. Cameron was happy to proofread her daughter's letter. She also used the Proofreader's Checklist to help keep track of what needed to be checked.

Carla's mother noticed a few things that weren't corrected in earlier readings.

She found a run-on sentence in the first paragraph. Can you find it?

She reminded Carla that the post office prefers the two-letter state abbreviations and that she will be using the inside address information for the envelope. What change will Carla have to make?

Mrs. Cameron also noticed the punctuation mark Carla used after the salutation and reminded her of the businesslike tone of the letter. What punctuation mark should Carla have used?

Carla's mother pointed out that Carla forgot to change the spelling of a base word after adding a suffix. Carla used a word with an -*ly* suffix in her closing, but what did she forget to do?

Your Turn

Read your paper carefully, using the Proofreader's Checklist. Look for one kind of error at a time. That way it is easier to spot errors. With the extra readings, other types of errors may jump out at you.

When you have finished, trade letters with your partner. Be sure to have the checklist and a dictionary handy.

A Thank-You Letter

Publishing

After a little more revising, Carla was finally ready to send her letter. She printed it out, changing the double-spaced lines to single-spaced. She signed her name below the closing. Then Carla folded the letter carefully and sealed it in an addressed and stamped envelope. When she dropped the envelope into a mailbox, she felt pleased that she was able to tell Mr. Brody how much she appreciates his store and his employee, Ms. Dixon. This is Carla's final letter.

5244 Sierra Ave.
Seaside, CA 92335

May 3, 20–

Mr. John Brody
Anastasia's Attic
327 East Front St.
Seaside, CA 92335

Dear Mr. Brody:

I am a regular customer of Anastasia's Attic, and I want you to know what a wonderful employee you have in Ms. Janet Dixon. Ms. Dixon is always happy to assist my friends and me. When I was in the store last Monday, she spent a half hour helping me select the perfect birthday book for my friend Jeff. I don't know what boys like to read. Ms. Dixon does.

I am a sixth grader at Oceanside Middle School. I was not always an avid reader. Ms. Dixon turned me into one. When your store opened, my mother and I stopped in. My mother told Ms. Dixon that I didn't like to read. Ms. Dixon suggested some exciting books that I might enjoy. I read every one, and I loved them all. Now I'm older, and I often visit Anastasia's Attic by myself.

Once my mother wanted a three-volume set of gardening tips. She searched high and low for it for two weeks. Ms. Dixon found a set on the Internet and ordered it for her. She must have spent hours looking for it.

Ms. Dixon is a very caring person. One day an elderly lady slipped and fell just outside the door. Ms. Dixon went to her rescue and brought the lady inside. She took care of her and called the lady's daughter to come and pick her up.

I'm sure that as a bookstore owner you must be a lover of books. I am, too, and I know Ms. Dixon has a lot to do with that. You are very lucky to have her working for you and so are all of us bookworms! Thank you for the great store!

Yours truly,

Carla Cameron

Carla Cameron

Your Turn

Mailing a letter is much like publishing other types of writing. Once a letter is sent, changes can no longer be made. Before sealing the envelope, proofread your letter one last time. You can refer back to the checklist on page 231 to make sure you don't overlook anything. Here are some additional things to watch for:

- Have you signed your letter?
- Does the address on the envelope match the inside address in your letter? Are they correct?

- Is your return address in the upper left-hand corner of the envelope?
- Is the appropriate postage stamp in the upper right-hand corner of the envelope?

Even though you will send your thank-you letters in the mail, it might be fun for you and your classmates to share them. Think about creating a class display of all the reasons that people might send a thank-you letter.

CHAPTER
7

The trickster is one of humankind's favorite characters. In cultures from North America to Australia, from Africa to Asia, people have told stories of tricksters for centuries. Tricksters were often animals, such as spiders, rabbits, and coyotes, who behaved like humans. The trickster is usually a character who seems weak and has to rely on his or her wit and resources to outsmart someone stronger. Trickster stories are usually clever, comical, and a great deal of fun.

Who are some of your favorite trickster characters of today?

Creative Writing

Rabbit and the Wolves

ong ago in a lush green forest, Rabbit was dozing in the sun. He was having a pleasant dream in which he was showing off his dancing and singing skills, for he was known to excel in both. Suddenly, he felt a presence all around him. As he slowly opened one eye just a slit, his worst fears were confirmed. There, completely surrounding him, were his greatest enemies—the wolves.

Before he could think of what to do, a glowering wolf put his long nose right up to Rabbit and said, "Rabbit, Rabbit, in the grass. Wake up! Wake up! It's you we want for rabbit stew!" With that, Rabbit jumped up quickly and began to nervously tap his foot.

Suddenly he smiled and said very pleasantly, "Why, I wasn't sleeping at all. I was practicing my new dance in my mind. I'd love to share it with you right now if you'd like."

"I'm hungry," growled the biggest wolf. "Let's see how he dances in a pot of boiling water!"

"Wait," cried another wolf. "We know of Rabbit's fame as the greatest dancer of all the animals. Let's let him teach us before we eat him." The others nodded in approval, and they widened their circle around Rabbit.

Rabbit tapped his feet and hummed softly. Then he said sweetly, "Brother Wolves, you must help me. The song goes, *'Ha'nia lil, lil! Hi'nia lil, lil!'* Whenever I sing, *'Lil, lil,'* we will all stomp our feet like this." Rabbit demonstrated and the wolves followed. Then he repeated the song and the stomps several times; each time the wolves did their part.

Finally, Rabbit said, "You are doing so well, I will show you the hardest part of the dance. From now on when I sing, *'Lil, lil,'* you will close your eyes and turn around as you stomp." Rabbit sang louder and louder, repeating, *"Ha'nia lil, lil, lil, lil,"* until he himself was far away from the wolves on the edge of the tall grass. Rabbit finally made a big jump into the tall grass and sped toward a hollow tree stump. He quickly climbed up on the inside where it was very dark and stayed very still. It was a breezy day and Rabbit's footsteps did not even show in the waving grass. The disgruntled wolves had no idea where Rabbit had gone. They slunk away, arguing among themselves.

The biggest wolf said angrily, "The long-eared trickster has fooled us for the last time! Next time we will not let him dance out of our trap!" Rabbit waited and waited until he was sure the wolves were gone, and then he swiftly hopped back home.

What Makes a Good Trickster Tale?

Trickster tales have been around for as long as people have told stories around flickering village fires. This form of narrative fiction usually tells how a weak but clever creature outwits a seemingly more powerful rival. In the Native American trickster tale on page 235, "weaker" Rabbit uses his wits to escape the "powerful" wolves.

Traditionally, the trickster represented a group of people who were oppressed by others. The oppressed people would tell the story as a way of saying, "Even though our enemies are more powerful than we are, we will survive because we are smarter than they are."

Like most narratives, a trickster tale has a beginning, a middle, and an end which provide a plot, an organized pattern of events usually told in chronological order. Here are some things to remember when writing a trickster tale.

Beginning

Many trickster tales begin by introducing the trickster, a cunning and sometimes humorous main character that is often an animal. The beginning might also introduce the "tricked," a victim who is a rival that initially has power over the trickster. The setting, which is often rural, is also introduced in the beginning of a trickster tale.

Middle

The middle of a trickster tale develops a plot in which the trickster tries to outwit its rival to achieve a goal, such as obtaining food or avoiding being eaten. The trickster must often confront obstacles in trying to reach the goal. These obstacles are part of the story's rising action, a series of spiraling events. The rising action leads to an exciting defining moment known as the climax. The plot moves along through literary techniques such as dialog and metaphors.

End

At the end of a trickster tale, there is a resolution. Often the trickster's goal is achieved, but the trickster's plans occasionally backfire, forcing the trickster to learn a lesson. The resolution often leads to a conclusion that answers remaining questions and brings the story to a close.

Activity A

Answer the following questions about "The Rabbit and the Wolves" on page 235.

1. What is the story's setting? In what part of the story is it introduced?

2. Who is the trickster?

3. Who are the victims?

4. What is the trickster's goal?

5. What is the story's climax?

6. What is the story's resolution?

Writer's Corner

There are many examples of trickster tales on television, such as the rabbit that tries to outwit a hunter or the roadrunner that tries to outwit a coyote. Describe in paragraph form the beginning, middle, and end of an episode that you have seen.

Word Choice and Voice

Trickster tales are very informal. The writer uses dialect, the way people speak in their culture. The writer might also include animal sounds, sound effects, or repetition if the story will be shared orally. It can be helpful for writers to keep the following tips in mind when choosing words and creating voice for a trickster tale:

- Be authentic. Use words and phrases that reflect the setting, time period, and culture.
- One purpose of a trickster tale is to entertain. Use original language and appropriate humor.
- Another purpose of a trickster tale is to teach a lesson. Use a confident voice when appropriate.

Our Wide Wide World

Anansi, one of the world's most famous tricksters, is a spider who sometimes looks like a man. Anansi stories come from an area in Africa now called Ghana. There are many stories about Anansi, and sometimes his tricks lead to good things. But at other times he appears greedy and selfish, and the reader doesn't always want him to win.

Activity B

Read this excerpt from a trickster tale about Anansi, the spider trickster of the Ashanti people in West Africa. Make a list of words or phrases that reflect the setting, that are original or show humor, or that have a confident voice.

Anansi and Turtle

Lonely Turtle stopped by the web of Anansi. "Won't you join me for dinner?" asked the spider sheepishly, for Anansi really did not want to share his food, but felt obliged to be hospitable.

When Turtle began to nestle into his shell, Anansi said, "You can't sit at the dinner table with those filthy feet." Turtle trudged down to the pond to wash up. While Turtle was gone, Anansi ate half of the dinner.

When Turtle returned, Anansi told him, "Your feet got dirty again walking back from the pond." Turtle went back down the hill to wash his feet again. When he returned, he took special care to keep his feet clean, but by the time he got back, Anansi had eaten everything. The dinner plate was empty. Turtle was furious, but he politely thanked his host and left. . . .

Write an ending for this story that includes a resolution and answers any remaining questions. Follow the tips on page 238 for determining word choice and creating voice.

Rabbit and the Well

It was a long time of no rain. The streams were all dried up and so were the lakes. All the animals got together and agreed to dig a well—all except lazy Rabbit, who didn't like to get his paws dirty. To all who could hear, Rabbit claimed, "I get enough water by licking early morning dew off of the grass," which he didn't.

The other animals worked hard, and soon the well was finished. They all enjoyed the cool well water, but not Rabbit, who wasn't allowed to drink from the well.

Still, Rabbit never seemed to be thirsty. The other animals suspected that Rabbit was stealing water from the well at night. They decided to catch him in the act.

Fox and Wolf made a tar wolf and put it near the well to guard it. Sure enough, Rabbit came by that night to take some water, but the tar wolf was in the way. At first Rabbit was cautious. He made rabbit noises and got ready to run. Tar wolf didn't say anything. Rabbit shouted and got ready to take off. Tar wolf didn't move. Rabbit got his courage up and ran at tar wolf. It wasn't a good idea. He got stuck to the tar!

The next morning all the animals came by and discussed what to do with Rabbit to teach him a lesson.

"Let's drown him in the well," suggested Gopher.

"Let's roast him and eat him for lunch," Fox urged.

"Yes, yes, those are both good punishments," Rabbit replied. "Just don't throw me into that thorny old briar patch."

Into the briar patch went Rabbit!

Writer's Corner

Choose an animal pair, a goal, and a trick. Brainstorm and write a list of at least three main events that might lead to the trick.

Characters and Setting

Character

Character is one of the most important elements of a trickster tale. A writer needs well-developed main characters—the trickster and victim or victims—in order to determine a setting, a trick, and a plot. Keep these ideas in mind when choosing the main characters for a trickster tale.

- Characters in trickster tales are usually animals.
- The animal characters have human characteristics such as the ability to talk.
- The trickster animal is often perceived as the weaker animal in real life.
- The trickster and the victim are often natural enemies or competitors in real life. The rabbit and the wolves in the model on page 235 are a good example. Other examples could be a cat and a mouse, a dog and a cat, or a spider and a bird.

Once a writer chooses the trickster and the victim or victims, it is time to develop them, either in the writer's mind or as written notes.

Character Checklist

When developing the characters you have chosen for a trickster tale, it can be helpful to do the following:

- Determine each character's appearance. How old is the character? Is the character male or female? Is the character tall or short, strong or weak, beautiful or ugly?
- Determine each character's personality. What are the character's good and bad qualities? Is the character funny, greedy, sneaky, or kind? Keep in mind that the trickster is often not very heroic. He or she might be lazy, as in the story of "Rabbit and the Well," or selfish, as in the story of "Anansi and Turtle."

- Give each character a motivation, a reason for being in the story. Your main characters should always do things for a reason, whether big or small. Is your trickster trying to get some dinner? Does the victim plan to eat the trickster? Consider your characters' motivations, as well as their personalities, as you decide how they will react to conflict in your story.

- Once you determine the trickster's and victim's motivations, choose the trick that either gets the trickster what he or she wants or leads the trickster to learn a lesson.

Remember, all of the character ideas you develop may not be explicitly stated in the trickster tale, but it is important to develop your characters fully so you know the direction you want the story to take.

• Activity A •

Choose an animal from the list to be a trickster for a trickster tale. Use the Character Checklist to develop the character. Make notes about each topic on the list.

Trickster Choices

mouse	clownfish	ladybug	ferret
koala	panda	zebra	monkey

• Activity B •

Choose a victim for the character you developed in Activity A. Use the information on characters to develop the victim. Make notes.

Writer's Corner

Consider two opposing animals that you see in the region where you live. If you live in a city, you might see pigeons and squirrels. In less urban areas, you might see mice and owls. Develop these two animals as main characters for a trickster tale.

Setting

Setting is not only the physical surroundings in which a story takes place. A story's setting also includes the time period in which the action occurs.

Traditionally, a trickster storyteller would use his or her own region and surroundings as the setting, knowing that the people in the community would be the audience. The storyteller would be sure to include sights and sounds that the audience could relate to.

When writing an animal trickster tale, a writer should place the animal characters in their natural habitat. The writer can develop the setting in his or her mind or as written notes.

Setting Checklist

When developing the setting for a trickster tale, it can be helpful to do the following:

- Determine the habitat common to the main characters.
- Choose the time period. Do you want the story to take place long ago or in modern times?
- Determine plants, animals, and weather conditions that are native to that setting. Do research if necessary.
- Know how your main characters interact with the setting, such as their natural forms of shelter or means of finding food. Do research if necessary.
- Consider choosing a weather or climate condition that might relate to the trickster's motivation and trick, such as a drought for a trickster who wants food or a rainstorm for a character who wants to go across a rushing river.

As with character, all the setting ideas you develop may not be explicitly stated in your trickster tale. It is important, though, to develop the setting so it seems natural for your characters to be there.

Putting the Story Together

With fully developed characters and setting, and the trickster's goal and trick, a trickster tale starts to take shape. A writer might then develop more of the story before drafting, such as listing potential main events, a climax, and a resolution. A good writer knows that a plan can change and that a story always evolves from draft to draft.

Activity C

Make notes to write a setting description for "Anansi and Turtle" on page 238. Use the Setting Checklist as you work.

Activity D

Name two opposing animals that could realistically be found in each setting. Write a sentence that describes a natural confrontation between the animals in that setting.

1. a sandy beach on a hot summer day
2. a forest preserve full of picnickers
3. a meadow filled with beautiful wildflowers
4. a mountainside with melting snow
5. a Southwestern desert at dusk
6. an ancient maple tree on the edge of a barnyard
7. an alley in a large industrial city
8. a riverbank on an early autumn afternoon
9. an ice floe in the Arctic Circle
10. a native village in the South American rain forest

Activity E

Choose one setting from Activity D and develop it, using the Setting Checklist. Record your ideas as notes.

Writer's Corner

Make notes to develop setting and plot for the animals you developed in the Writer's Corner on page 239. Use the information from this lesson as you work.

Dialog

Dialog, or conversation between characters, has several purposes in fiction. It helps to develop the characters, it advances the plot, and it helps to draw readers into the story.

Developing Characters

By using dialog in your writing, you can give readers insights into your characters. Read the following line from the opening trickster tale about Rabbit fooling the wolves:

> "I'm hungry," growled the biggest wolf. "Let's see how he dances in a pot of boiling water!"

The storyteller has the biggest wolf make a joke about killing Rabbit. It takes an especially evil creature to joke about killing its victim. Even though a reader might not directly think about the wolves' cruelty, the reader understands that they would not show Rabbit any mercy if he couldn't trick them.

Advancing the Plot

Dialog can also be used to introduce conflict or to move along the story line by adding new information. The following line from "Anansi and Turtle" explains how Anansi gets Turtle to leave the dinner table:

> When Turtle began to nestle into his shell, Anansi said, "You can't sit at the dinner table with those filthy feet."

While Turtle is out washing up, Anansi eats half of the food. However, the greedy spider wants it all.

> When Turtle returned, Anansi told him, "Your feet got dirty again walking back from the pond."

Both times the writer has Turtle react to what Anansi says, and the story moves on from there.

Engaging the Reader

In each of the examples described above, the reader is put into the scene by "hearing" characters talking instead of being told what was said. Readers are made to feel as though they are actually witnessing the action. It is easier for them to picture what is going on in the story.

● Activity A ●

Both sentences in each pair express similar ideas. Write a brief description of a character who might say each sentence. Give each character a name and profession.

1. "We were window shopping."
   "We were chillin' at the mall."

2. "Give me a large coffee and danish."
   "Give me a latté grandé and biscotti."

3. "I ain't takin' no guff from the likes o' him."
   "I won't stand for his insolence."

● Activity B ●

For each line of dialog below, write a response that would advance the story. Make up a character to respond to each.

1. "All the evidence points to James Celito being the murderer," Deputy Osano argued.

2. "You're wasting your time if you think you'll find gold in them hills," the grizzled prospector warned.

3. "My car isn't for sale," Mr. Janisch said.

Writer's Corner

Choose two animals that you like, but that don't always get along with each other. Give these animals human traits, including the ability to talk. Create a situation for them to interact, and write at least six lines of dialog between them.

Dialog Tags

Dialog tags are the words accompanying a quotation that tell the reader which character is speaking.

> *Ben asked,* "Who wants to go to the movies?"
> "I do, but I have no money," *Yvonne responded.*
> "I'll treat," *Ben replied,* "if you drive."

The words *Ben asked, Yvonne responded,* and *Ben replied* let you know who is saying what. However, dialog tags can do more than tell readers who is speaking. Dialog tags can give readers hints about the character's personality or how the character is feeling.

> "Leave me alone," Ida said.
> "Leave me alone," Ida whimpered.
> "Leave me alone!" Ida screamed.
> "Leave me alone," Ida threatened.

The dialog tag *Ida said* is neutral. Readers would need to use the story's context to understand how Ida felt. The other three dialog tags give a more precise idea of Ida's state of mind. To give variety to dialog, it helps to use different dialog tags.

However, it is best not to overdo the variety. Readers will get bored if your characters are constantly moaning, coaxing, stammering, whining, and jesting. Although some variety is important, *stated, replied,* and *responded* generally work well in dialog.

• Activity C •

Make the situations below come alive by creating dialog. Add interesting dialog tags when appropriate. Have each person speak only once.

Example: A lifeguard speaking to a swimmer
"Please don't run around the pool," cautioned the lifeguard.
"Sorry," said Mark. "I was playing a game and I forgot."

1. Two people caught in an elevator during a power failure

2. A person calling the janitor of an apartment building

3. Wendy and Eduardo talking about taking part in a fundraising drive

4. Mr. and Mrs. Lee after a baseball crashes through their window

Activity D

For each verb, make up a character and situation that would fit the dialog tag.

Example: "The baby has finally gone to sleep," Dad whispered.

whispered   demanded   shouted   snapped
declared   protested   cried   groaned

Activity E

Write a conversation between two characters in a fairy tale you know. Choose just one part of the tale to tell, and have each character speak two or three times.

Activity F

The dialog tags below don't match what is being said. Change each tag by using a verb of your own so the dialog tag matches the message.

1. "Please don't talk during the movie," the usher shouted.
2. "Give me all your cash," the bank robber begged.
3. The little boy snickered, "My ice cream fell off the cone."
4. "It certainly is a beautiful day," Granddad demanded.
5. "My big brother is on the varsity team," the boy complained.
6. "Get off my back," the teen coaxed.
7. "Homework over spring break," the whole class giggled.
8. "Way to go, Cougars!" the fans protested.

Writer's Corner

In the Writer's Corner on page 245, you wrote dialog between two animals. Use verbs from Activity D or any others you know to revise the dialog tags so they describe the characters' feelings as they speak. Make any other changes you think would make the dialog more interesting. Save your revision.

Homographs

Homographs are words that are spelled the same but have different meanings. The words might be pronounced the same or differently to reflect the intended meaning. You can identify the correct meaning by the way a word is used in context.

Mr. Akim will *present* the trophy at the awards ceremony.
(to make an award of; *prē-zent'*)

He expects all team members to be *present.*
(being on hand; *prez' ənt*)

Here the pronunciation of the word changes because there is a difference in the first sound and a definite change, or shift, in the accent. The shift in the accent signals a difference in meaning.

When uncertain, use a dictionary to check the meaning of words that might be homographs.

Common Homographs			
Homograph	**Meaning**	**Homograph**	**Meaning**
arms	body parts	gum	chewing candy
arms	weapons	gum	fleshy part of the mouth
ball	a sphere		
ball	a dance	pupil	a part of the eye
band	an orchestra	pupil	a student
band	a strap	swallow	to gulp
duck	a bird	swallow	a bird
duck	to avoid		

Activity A

Complete each sentence with a pair of homographs from the chart on page 248.

1. I had to _____ to avoid the flying _____.

2. To fire some _____ well, you have to have strong

_____.

3. It is not appropriate to throw a _____ at a _____.

4. The tiny _____ couldn't _____ the fat worm.

5. The chewing _____ is stuck to my _____.

6. Each member of the marching _____ wore a red

_____ on his or her arm.

7. The _____ studied the eye diagram, trying to

find the _____.

Activity B

Find each pair of homographs in a dictionary. Write each word in context in a separate sentence. After the sentence write each word's meaning.

1. a. bow (bō)   **b.** bow (bou)

2. a. lead (lēd)   **b.** lead (led)

3. a. live (līv)   **b.** live (liv)

4. a. does (dōz)   **b.** does (duz)

5. a. press (pres)   **b.** press (pres)

Writer's Corner

Read a newspaper or magazine article. Underline at least three words that have homographs. Use each pair of homographs in separate original sentences so that each sentence reflects the meaning of one of the words.

Here are some other common homographs and their meanings.

Common Homographs			
Homograph	Meaning	Homograph	Meaning
bear	an animal	lean	to tilt
bear	to carry	lean	thin
bluff	to trick	left	departed
bluff	a cliff	left	a direction
count	to number	prune	a dried fruit
count	a nobleman	prune	to cut off
firm	hard	socks	knitted footwear
firm	a company	socks	hits

● **Activity C** ●

Write one sentence using each pair of homographs above as in Activity A.

● **Activity D** ●

Write homographs for each pair of word meanings. In words that have more than one syllable, underline the syllable that is stressed. Put an asterisk (*) next to words that are pronounced the same.

1. **a.** 60 seconds
   b. very small

2. **a.** edge of a river
   b. institution where money is held

3. **a.** place of entry
   b. to delight

4. **a.** a meal set out for self-service
   b. to strike repeatedly

5. **a.** to decline
   b. garbage

6. **a.** soft, fluffy feathers on a duck
   b. opposite of *up*

7. **a.** hot, dry place
   b. to abandon

8. **a.** very well
   b. money penalty for an offense

● Activity E ●

Each of these words has one or more homographs. Look up each homograph in a dictionary and write its meaning. Then write sentences to show the meaning of each homograph in context.

1. wind	**7.** lie
2. well	**8.** loaf
3. ring	**9.** mole
4. sewer	**10.** lap
5. pound	**11.** brush
6. close	**12.** can

● Activity F ●

Look back at the homophone lesson in Chapter 5. Write whether the words in each pair below are homophones or homographs. Then use each word in a separate sentence. Use a dictionary if you need help.

1. sow–sow	**7.** content–content
2. thrown–throne	**8.** Polish–polish
3. wound–wound	**9.** sighs–size
4. primer–primer	**10.** two–too
5. waist–waste	**11.** fast–fast
6. toad–towed	**12.** box–box

Writer's Corner

Write a brief narrative that uses at least four pairs of homographs from Activity F. Use context to show the meaning of each homograph.

Rhyming Stanzas

Poetry is a genre of writing in which the way that ideas are expressed is as important as the ideas themselves. Sometimes the way the ideas are expressed is *more* important. Poets work hard to present their work in attractive packages. Instead of ribbons and bows and gift wrap to make their work attractive to readers and listeners, poets use vivid imagery and figurative language such as simile, metaphor, and personification. They also use rhyme and meter.

Rhyme

Rhyme happens when the ending syllables of words sound alike, for example, *imply* and *defy* or *propel*, *tell*, and *resell*. Of course, it's all right if more than one syllable in each word sound alike, for example, *borrow*, *tomorrow*, and *sorrow* or *invention* and *intention*.

Meter

Meter is the rhythm patterns that are created by the stressed and unstressed syllables of words in lines of poetry. Anytime you talk outloud, you stress some syllables and leave others unstressed. You don't worry about rhythm patterns when you talk; but poets work hard to find words that provide rhythmic patterns to their lines of poetry. Note how the syllables are marked in these lines from a Robert Frost poem, "Stopping by Woods on a Snowy Evening." The checks are above the stressed syllables.

     ˘   ✓   ˘ ✓ ˘ ✓ ˘ ✓
Whose woods these are I think I know.

     ˘   ✓ ˘ ✓ ˘ ✓ ˘   ✓
His house is in the village though;

Each line has eight syllables, and every other syllable is stressed. This is a very simple rhythm pattern. Some poems have much more complicated meters.

Activity A

Copy the following poem. Circle the rhyming word pairs. Then count the syllables in each line and mark them as stressed or unstressed. Use a dictionary if you need help.

THE HIPPOPOTAMUS

Behold the hippopotamus!
We laugh at how he looks to us,
And yet in moments dank and grim,
I wonder how we look to him.
Peace, peace, thou hippopotamus!
We really look all right to us,
As you no doubt delight the eye
Of other hippopotami.

—Ogden Nash

Activity B

Pick out the rhyming words in each row. Write two sentences that use each pair as the last words. Don't worry about meter or making the sentences about the same thing.

1. bough	enough	glow	stuff
2. ladle	saddle	cradle	middle
3. whistle	crystal	drizzle	missile
4. ply	pill	mile	isle

Writer's Corner

Look back at previous examples of your writing. Look for three sentences that you feel really good about. Count out their syllables and mark their rhythm patterns. For each one try to write a second sentence with the same number of syllables and the same meter.

Stanzas

Stanzas in poems are like paragraphs in other types of writing. They are each about a single idea. However, instead of sentences, the stanzas are made up of lines. The line might be a complete sentence, or it might be only an image. A stanza must have at least two lines. The poem "Stopping by Woods on a Snowy Evening" is written in four-line stanzas.

Rhyme Schemes

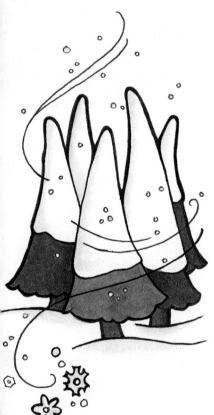

Rhyme scheme is the pattern of rhymes at the ends of lines. The rhyming words at the end of the lines in the first stanza of Frost's poem are *know, though,* and *snow.* To plot the rhyme scheme, we assign the first rhyming words with the letter *a.* The second set of rhyming words is assigned *b,* the third set is *c,* and so on. The first two stanzas of "Stopping by Woods on a Snowy Evening" would be marked this way.

Whose woods these are I think I know.	a
His house is in the village though;	a
He will not see me stopping here	b
To watch his woods fill up with snow.	a
My little horse must think it queer	b
To stop without a farmhouse near	b
Between the woods and frozen lake	c
The darkest evening of the year.	b

The rhyme scheme for the first two stanzas is *aaba bbcb.* The pattern for the next stanza is *ccdc.* The nonrhyming word in each stanza becomes the first rhyme for the next stanza.

Rhyme schemes are not put into poems to make work for students. Poets use rhyme to add beauty and complexity to their work. Rhyme schemes also add another degree of difficulty in writing poems and are a way for poets to show their talent.

• Activity C •

Look at the rhyming word pairs. For each pair, write two sentences or lines with one of the words at the end of each.

1. moon, tune   **4.** dream, seem   **7.** sea, tree

2. heart, apart   **5.** love, glove   **8.** door, before

3. die, cry   **6.** slave, grave   **9.** hairy, scary

Activity D

Look at the rhyme schemes. Write rhyming words that would match each one. The first one has been done for you.

1. abba, bccb   <u>hard, toil, soil, yard   broil, sun, fun, oil</u>

2. abab, cdcd   _____

3. aabb, ccdd   _____

4. aaaa, bbbb   _____

5. aba, bcb   _____

6. aa, bb, cc   _____

Activity E

Read the following lines. By adding some ending rhymes, they could become a poem. Use rhyming words to complete the poem. You may use more than one word to complete a line. The poem doesn't have to make sense, but keep the rhyme scheme the same for both stanzas.

If ever I should see a sight as lovely as a _____,
I think that I would decorate it with a _____.
Then I'd sit and admire its beautiful _____,
While you would envy my happy _____.

But I would share my treasure so _____.
We both could watch as it grows _____.
You in your bonnet, and I in my _____,
Until the day's end or the end of the _____.

Writer's Corner

Write a four-line (or longer) poem about any topic that you choose. You may write it in one four-line stanza, two two-line stanzas, or two three-line stanzas. In your poem, use one of the rhyme schemes that have been discussed in this lesson.

Telling a Trickster Tale

Folktales of all kinds are popular with oral storytellers. Maybe that's because folktales started out as an oral tradition. They were told in many places and in many versions for years and years before they were written down. There was no right way to tell a story. It became each person's own story to tell. The animals may have been changed and the setting may have been altered, but the themes were repeated again and again. These are some things you will want to keep in mind for an oral presentation.

Audience

Think about the ages of the people to whom you are speaking. You will tell the story differently and use different props for an audience of young children and an audience of your peers or adults. Choose your story according to your audience. Adults may lose interest in a story that is intended for children. Children may not understand stories that adults would enjoy. If you are talking to a mixed group, aim for the youngest members of the audience.

Props

If you can think of simple props to use, these can be effective in keeping the interest of the audience. A furry puppet of an animal character might help make the animal come to life. Showing an object that plays a large part in the story adds interest. For example, if you are reading the story about Coyote stealing a blanket, you might wrap a blanket around yourself and move quickly as Coyote did.

Voice and Body Language

Use your voice to help you "be" the characters, especially when you are reading or speaking the dialog. Vary your pitch, loudness, and tone accordingly. Use a different voice for each character. Move your body to imitate your character's actions.

Practice

Read your tale many times before presenting it. You don't have to memorize it word for word, but you should know exactly what the sequence of events is. You should understand each character's motivation as well as his or her personality. Practice in front of a mirror until you are sure you know your story well. Then ask a friend or relative to be your audience. Speak clearly and don't be afraid to exaggerate your voice and movements.

• Activity A •

Read the tale below aloud two times. The first time read without feeling. The second time vary your loudness, pitch, and stress to change the character's emotion. Have your classmates discuss the difference.

"Please, please! Do whatever you want with me, but don't send me into that briar patch," pleaded Brer Rabbit.

Brer Wolf, he up and says, "I'm glad you told me what you don't want me to do, 'cause that's just what I will do!" And he took Brer Rabbit and flung him right into the middle of the thorny briar patch, expecting Brer Rabbit to be yelping from all those thorny thorns.

But Brer Rabbit, he just began to giggling, and he cried out, "Born and bred, I was born and bred in a briar patch and I'm more at home here than a turtle in his shell."

Speaker's Corner

Work with a partner. Make up a short conversation between two animal characters. Role-play the parts of the animals and practice reading your conversation with expression. Present it for your classmates in reader's theater style. You don't have to memorize your part, but be familiar enough with it that you can look at your audience often.

Listening Tips

When you are listening to someone tell a story, these are some of the things you will want to keep in mind:

- Settle in your seat and push all outside thoughts from your mind.
- Picture the setting in your mind.
- Try to identify with the characters as they are described and through their dialog.
- If there is a discussion later, be an active participant.
- Use your imagination to really get into the story, and enjoy yourself.

Activity B

You have probably heard or read the folktale "Stone Soup." Here is a brief summary of the story. Read the story with two partners and discuss ways that you can make it into an interesting presentation.

Once upon a time a lonely traveler came to the end of the day very tired and very hungry. He had just arrived in a small village and decided to see if some kind villager would give him food and a bed for the night.

He tried the first house he came to, and the woman who answered his knock replied that she had no food to spare. The same thing happened as he tried house after house, until finally a woman offered him water.

Smiling as he suddenly thought of a very clever way that he might trick the woman into parting with a morsel of food, he offered to make his magic stone soup with the water. Out of his pocket, he took a smooth stone that he had found along the road. As the water boiled in a big pot with the "magic" stone at the bottom, neighbors came by and inquired about this unusual soup. He told them how delicious it would be, but that it would be even better with some onions. A man quickly offered to go and get some from his cellar. Someone else offered carrots; another offered potatoes. One even brought a big piece of meat. Suddenly everyone had something to donate.

At last the soup was done. There was enough to feed the whole village and still have some for the next day. The traveler slept that night on the softest bed in the warmest cottage.

Activity C

Imagine that the traveler is stirring the pot with the stone in it and he says nonchalantly, "I think you will like my magic stone soup, but it would be better if only we had an onion or two to give it more bite." The woman's next door neighbor replies, "I have some onions that we can add." With your partners, add dialog for the traveler and the other neighbors to contribute the potatoes, carrots, and meat.

Activity D

Now look back earlier in the story and, with your partners, create dialog for the villagers to tell the traveler that they have no food to spare. Have the traveler ask at least three villagers.

Activity E

Choose any of the trickster tales that you have read in this chapter or any other folktale that you particularly enjoy. Work out an oral presentation of the story with at least three separate voices, including the narrator. If possible, include some sound effects. After you have practiced your presentation so that you feel comfortable with it, deliver it to your classmates. Don't be afraid to "ham up" your story. Have fun with it.

Speaker's Corner

In Lesson 3 you wrote dialog for two animals. You added dialog tags to indicate each character's feelings as he or she spoke. Using the dialog tags to guide your presentation, read the animals' conversation to a classmate. Then listen to your partner's animal dialog. See if you each agree with the other's interpretation.

Chapter 7 Writer's Workshop

A Trickster Tale

Prewriting and Drafting

In this chapter you had a chance to read some trickster tales, find out what their special characteristics are, and try your hand at writing some story lines and dialog. Now it's time to apply your writing skills and create your own original trickster tale.

Prewriting

The first stage of the writing process in any genre is to choose a topic. A storyteller's goal is to entertain, so the topic should be something that will amuse an audience. Sometimes the storyteller also wants to teach a lesson. Trickster stories can do both.

Choosing a Topic

Kelly had been reading trickster tales to children at the library. One day, she thought that she could make up a trickster tale herself. She remembered how she had fooled her brother Mike into not eating her favorite candy in a box of chocolates. Kelly decided to write a trickster tale about how she did it.

Your Turn

Is there a favorite family story that you have often heard when everyone is sitting around a holiday meal? Did your father play a joke on one of your aunts or vice versa? Did your mother and an uncle cause some mischief as youngsters? Did your grandparents try to teach their children a lesson only to have it backfire on them?

Use any of these types of stories to give you ideas for your trickster tale, or think of a time when you played a trick on a friend or a friend played a trick on you. Don't choose an unkind prank. Instead select one that made both of you laugh.

As a last resort, if you can't think of any ideas, choose a trickster tale that you know and change the animals and the setting to ones that reflect your own region and situation.

Free Writing

Kelly sat down at the kitchen table and recalled the events of her story in her head. She wrote down the episode as well as she could remember it.

- Mom said that my brother Mike and I could take two pieces of chocolate each.
- took the lid off candy box. diagram on bottom told what type of candy each piece was

- I saw the diagram. Mike didn't.
- We both like chocolate cream. Diagram showed round pieces with squiggle across top had chocolate cream.
- round ones without squiggle = jelly-filled
- took one of each; made a big deal of picking round one with squiggles
- Bit off the top of the jelly-filled piece; told Mike it had squiggle across the top. (I lied.)
- Made face and spit out candy, asked Mike if he wanted to finish the piece
- Mike refused. He doesn't like jelly-filled either.
- Ever since, he leaves squiggly candy in the box . . . for me.

Your Turn

Think of the incident that you want to turn into a trickster tale. Free write all of the events that occurred in the incident. You can write in paragraphs, or you can make a list of the important events.

Converting to a Trickster Tale

Kelly was happy with her story idea so far. Now she wanted to move it from the real world into the world of the trickster. First she thought about animals that could represent her and her brother Mike.

The previous summer, a raccoon broke into her family's attic. Her uncle caught it in a trap and took it away from the city. Kelly thought it resembled Mike and decided that, in her trickster story, Mike would be a raccoon.

Kelly decided that her role would be played by a squirrel. There were two squirrels that visited her backyard on a daily routine. She thought it would be neat to run along the tree branches.

Then she thought about the setting and the plot of her story. Kelly's episode with her brother happened in the family living room. The trick was about a box of chocolates. Squirrels and raccoons live in the woods and rarely get boxes of chocolates. Kelly decided that instead of a box of candy, the treat would be a bush with tasty berries.

Kelly thought about how she fooled her brother. She made him think that he wouldn't like the candy. That was the way for Squirrel to trick Raccoon. Squirrel would make Raccoon think that the berries were no good.

Your Turn

Think about the characters in your story. In real life what kinds of personalities do they have? Can you picture any animals that share their character traits? What kind of environment do the animals live in?

Drafting

Kelly sat down to write. She knew that many things that happened when she tricked her brother would not make sense in a trickster story, so she simplified the way that Squirrel tricked Raccoon. Kelly thought that the trick worked pretty well anyhow. Here is Kelly's first draft.

Squirrel's Bad Berries

One day, Squirrel was using her tree branch highway to avoid running into Fox who had the annoying habit of trying to eat her. Squirrel looked down and saw a new bush growing in the forest. Hanging from its branches were lots of dark brown berries. Squirrel had never seen this type of bush before and so she scampered down the tree trunk to the ground. She tasted one of the berries and was delighted to find that it was delicious. Squirrel greedily set in to eating the sweet fruit as quickly as she could.

She had cleaned off two whole branches when she saw Raccoon coming up the path. Squirrel knew that Raccoon was just as greedy as she was and Squirrel wanted all of the berries for herself, so she thought of a plan. She started talking really loud about finding this new type of bush and wondering how its berries tasted. Then she took one of the berries and popped it into her mouth.

Instead of swalowing it, though, Squirrel spit it out, complaining about how awful it tasted. She spit and spit and then she grabbed her tummy and started to moan about how her belly ached. By now Raccoon had reached the bush, he was laughing at Squirrel's misfortune.

Squirrel said that the berries weren't all that bad and that Raccoon should try one. But Raccoon replied that he couldn't be fooled and that Squirrel should keep the berries for herself.

Your Turn

Use your free writing notes to write the first draft of your story. Make the trick as clear and simple as you can. Be sure, however, that you don't leave out important details. Double-space your work so you will have room to edit and to make changes. Remember that you will probably do more than one rewrite.

Content Editing

Skillful writers know that their writing needs to be edited and revised to make sure that the final product is the best it can be. The first step in editing a creative story is to edit for story content: characters, setting, and plot. This is a checklist you can use when checking the content of your trickster tale.

Content Editor's Checklist

✔ Does your description of the setting give the reader a good mental picture of where the story is taking place?

✔ Do the characters and the setting belong together?

✔ Do your characters each have a distinct appearance and personality?

✔ Do you use dialog to make your characters come alive and to make the story interesting reading?

✔ Does the dialog suit the characters?

✔ Does the trickster have a plan to trick his or her victim?

✔ Does the conclusion satisfy the reader that the right character has been tricked?

Writers edit their own work continually as they write. But sometimes they are too familiar with it to notice something that needs to be changed. That's why it's a good idea to ask someone who isn't familiar with your story to edit it with you.

Kelly's brother Mike often helps her with her homework. He gets high grades in writing. She felt a little guilty asking for his help with her trickster story because he is the raccoon that gets tricked. However despite the tricks they play on each other, they usually get along very well. Mike said that he would look over her story.

He read "Squirrel's Bad Berries" several times—once to get the feeling of the story and two more times using the Content Editor's Checklist to make certain that Kelly followed the guidelines.

Mike made notes of questions that he wanted to ask and suggestions to give Kelly when they went over her story. When he finished, they sat at the kitchen table and had a conference.

First, Mike told Kelly how much he enjoyed her story. He thought that the squirrel played a good trick. "It wouldn't fool most people," Mike commented, "but younger kids will think it's clever."

Then he told Kelly ways that her trickster tale could be improved.

- The setting could use a little more description. Most kids have an idea of what a forest looks like, but a better description will help them visualize the story better. The same is true for the characters.

- One way to describe your characters is to give them some dialog. It would help your story to flow more smoothly too.

- If Raccoon sees Squirrel holding her belly and moaning, wouldn't he be suspicious when she says that the berries aren't all that bad? It seems like Squirrel is pushing her luck.

- The ending is okay, but you should think of a way to make Raccoon even more of a victim. Maybe have him tell the other animals about Squirrel's bad berries.

Kelly thought Mike had some really good ideas. Dialog would help make her story flow more smoothly and would make it more interesting when she read it aloud to the children.

It also wouldn't hurt to describe the setting in more detail. As Mike pointed out, it would help the children see the story better in their minds.

Mike made a great suggestion about the ending. Kelly felt a little guiltier, because his ending made Raccoon look more foolish, and Raccoon is really Mike, even if he doesn't recognize himself.

Kelly decided to leave in the part about Squirrel holding her belly and moaning. She thought it made a funny picture for the children to imagine, and, besides, they probably wouldn't worry about Raccoon being suspicious.

Your Turn

Reread your first draft, looking at the checklist as you do so. Do the characters really come alive? Did you include enough dialog? Do you explain, or do the characters explain, the trickster element?

Work with a partner to edit each other's trickster tales. Take notes as you work and make suggestions for improvement. Be positive in your comments. Make sure you both use the Content Editor's Checklist.

Remember to compliment your partner on the things you liked in his or her writing. You want to appreciate each other's hard work. Consider your partner's suggestions, but the final decisions are yours. You will probably find some more things yourself that you will want to improve each time you read your story.

Revising

This is how Kelly revised her trickster tale.

Squirrel's Bad Berries

One day, Squirrel was using her tree branch highway to avoid running into Fox who had the annoying habit of trying to eat her. The branches gave her a safe route and kept the woods shady and cool. Squirrel looked down and saw a new bush growing in the forest. Hanging from its branches were lots of dark brown berries. "I've ~~Squirrel had~~ never seen this type of bush before," she said, and so she scampered down the tree trunk to the ground. She tasted one of ~~the berries and was delighted to find that it was delicious.~~ "Why, these are delicious," she declared curling her bushy tail with delight and she Squirrel greedily set in to eating the sweet fruit as quickly as she could.

She had cleaned off two whole branches when she saw Raccoon coming up the path. Squirrel knew that Raccoon was just as greedy as she was and Squirrel wanted all of the berries for herself, so she thought of a plan. to fool Raccoon. "Why, look at this bush, she said loudly. She started talking really loud about "and look at those fat berries. I wonder if they taste as good ~~finding this new type of bush and wondering how its berries~~ as they look." ~~tasted.~~ Then she took one of the berries and popped it into her mouth.

Instead of swalowing it, though, Squirrel spit it out, "Oooh, that's awful bitter. Ptui...ptui...ptui," she spit ~~complaining about how awful it tasted. She spit and spit~~ and then she grabbed her tummy and started to moan about how her belly "Oww, oww, oww! My tummy. It hurts." ached. By now Raccoon had reached the bush, he was laughing at Squirrel's misfortune.

~~Squirrel said that the berries weren't all that bad and that Raccoon should try one. But Raccoon replied that he couldn't be fooled and that Squirrel should keep the berries for herself.~~

"What's the problem, Sister Squirrel?" he asked, giggling gleefully. Did you come across some bad berries?"

"No, no, Brother Raccoon. They aren't all that bad." Squirrel said truthfully. "Why don't you try some?"

"Thank you very much, but those berries would not be good for my diet." Raccoon replied, patting his very round tummy. "I believe I'll let you keep them all for yourself." Then he waddled off to tell the other forest animals about Squirrel's foolishness.

When he was out of sight, Squirrel turned back to the bush and finished off the berries, eating slowly and savoring every . . . single . . . one.

Look at the changes that Kelly made to improve her trickster tale.

- She added a brief description of how the trees kept the forest shady and cool to help her audience picture the setting better.

- She also described Squirrel's bushy tail and Raccoon's round tummy to help her audience picture the two characters.

- She added a lot of dialog between Squirrel and Raccoon. The dialog adds to the flow of her story and helps the audience see that Squirrel and Raccoon are rivals even if they aren't enemies

- Kelly understood Mike's point about Squirrel pretending to have a bellyache and telling Raccoon that the berries are good. However, she liked the image and left it in.

- She also liked Mike's suggestion that Raccoon could tell the other animals about Squirrel's "mistake." It makes the trick work even better. As an extra tease, Kelly made Raccoon's last words the same ones Mike used when he turned down the chocolate, "I believe I'll let you keep them all for yourself."

Your Turn

Keep your content editing partner's suggestions in mind as you revise your draft. Use any that you feel will improve the story. Of course, always use your own ideas for improving your work. When you have finished your revisions, go over the Content Editor's Checklist once more to see if you can answer yes to each question.

A Trickster Tale

Copyediting and Proofreading

Copyediting

In the copyediting phase of the writing process, the draft is checked to be sure that the sentences flow smoothly, that the word choice is appropriate, and that the sentence structure is correct. Kelly felt that her revision was much better than her first draft, thanks much to Mike's suggestions. But she knew that there was still room for improvement before her trickster story would be a finished product.

Copyeditor's Checklist

✔ Are there rambling sentences?

✔ Are there run-on sentences?

✔ Is the sentence order logical?

✔ Is there variety in sentence length?

✔ Is there variety in word choice?

✔ Has dialog been added to improve sentence flow?

She noticed that one of her revisions would make a very long sentence. She decided to break it into two shorter ones. How would you divide this sentence?

Squirrel knew that Raccoon was just as greedy as she was and Squirrel wanted all the berries for herself, so she thought of a plan to fool Raccoon.

Kelly also spotted a run-on sentence. See if you can find it. Then she continued using the Copyeditor's Checklist to finish checking her trickster tale.

Your Turn

Use the Copyeditor's Checklist as you edit your revised trickster tale. Pay special attention to the dialog that you wrote. Make it flow like a good conversation. Will it give readers a picture of what the characters are like? Does it help to move your story along? Read your story aloud to someone else. Then have it read to you. Does the dialog sound natural?

Proofreading

Before writing the final copy of a story, a good writer proofreads to check for mistakes in spelling, punctuation, capitalization, and grammar.

A checklist like this one can help:

Proofreader's Checklist

✔ Is the first line of each paragraph indented?

✔ Are capitalization and punctuation correct?

✔ Is the grammar correct?

✔ Is the dialog properly punctuated and indented?

✔ Are all words spelled correctly?

✔ Has the paper been checked to make certain no new mistakes were added?

Writers often find it helpful to have someone else proofread their work because someone who is not the writer can look at it with fresh eyes. Kelly asked Ms. Maniwah, the librarian where Kelly reads to children, to read her trickster tale. Ms. Maniwah used to be an English teacher and was happy to do it.

Ms. Maniwah said that she was impressed with Kelly's trickster tale. It showed a lot of imagination. She read the story several times and saw only a few things that needed to be fixed. There were two misspelled words, one adverb that needed a suffix, and two spots where Kelly needed to add quotation marks. Can you spot these mistakes in Kelly's revision?

Your Turn

Read your paper carefully using the Proofreader's Checklist. Look for only one kind of error at a time. Each time you read, you have another chance to find other errors that you missed. Look especially carefully at the quotation marks enclosing direct quotations. Be sure each one has beginning and ending quotation marks.

When you have finished proofreading with the list, trade papers with a partner. Go through each other's stories in the same way. Be sure to have a dictionary handy.

Publishing

After editing and revising several times, Kelly was pleased with her trickster tale. She decided that it was good enough to tell to the children at the library. Ms. Maniwah said that she would display Kelly's trickster tale on the library bulletin board, so Kelly used her computer to run a spell check before she printed it out. Kelly took her trickster tale to the library and read it for the children. She added sound effects and gave Squirrel and Raccoon their own distinctive voices. The children loved it.

Squirrel's Bad Berries

One day, Squirrel was using her tree branch highway to avoid running into Fox, who had the annoying habit of trying to eat her. The branches gave her a safe route besides keeping the woods shady and cool. Squirrel looked down and spotted a new bush growing in the forest. Hanging from its branches were lots of dark brown berries.

"I've never seen this type of bush before," Squirrel thought, and so she scampered down the tree trunk to the ground. She tasted one of the berries. "Why, these are delicious," she declared, curling her bushy tail with delight. Squirrel greedily began eating the juicy berries.

She had cleaned off two whole branches when she saw Raccoon coming up the path. Squirrel knew that Raccoon was just as greedy as she was. She wanted all of the berries for herself, so she thought of a plan to fool him.

"Why, look at this bush," she said loudly, "and look at those fat berries. I wonder if they taste as good as they look." She took one of the berries and popped it into her mouth.

Instead of swallowing it though, Squirrel spit it out. "Oooh, that's awfully bitter. Ptui . . . ptui . . . ptui," she spit. Then she grabbed her tummy and sat on the ground, moaning about how her belly ached. "Oww, oww, oww! My poor belly hurts so bad!"

By now Raccoon had reached the bush. He was laughing at Squirrel's misfortune. "What's the problem, Sister Squirrel?" he asked, giggling gleefully. "Did you come across some bad berries?"

"No, no, Brother Raccoon. They aren't all that bad," Squirrel answered truthfully. "Why don't you try some?"

"Thank you very much, but I don't think those berries would be good for my diet," Raccoon replied, patting his very round tummy. "I believe I'll let you keep them all for yourself." Then he waddled off to tell the other forest animals about Squirrel's foolishness.

When he was out of sight, Squirrel turned back to the bush and finished off the berries, eating slowly and savoring

every . . .

single . . .

one.

Your Turn

Are you happy with your trickster tale? You've put in a lot of work, and it is probably pretty good by now. Before you print it out, read it through one or two more times and run it through your computer's spell check if you can. This will be the last time that you can improve your story before you turn it in.

Oral storytellers "publish" their stories by presenting them to audiences. Perhaps you would like to volunteer to read your trickster tale to the rest of the class. If you do, practice presenting your story so that you don't have to read too much from the paper.

If you are really proud of your trickster tale, ask if you can present it to the younger children at your school. Perhaps you and some classmates can present your stories as short sketches with different students playing the different characters in each one.

CHAPTER

8

In 1912 Pablo Picasso made a sculpture of a guitar, using scraps of rusty tin. Although it was a simple sculpture, it changed art history forever. Until that time, individual sculptures had been created from solid materials such as bronze, ceramic, or wood. Picasso's guitar sculpture inspired artists to combine a variety of materials to create their sculptures.

What is one of your favorite sculptures?

272

Research Reports

FAAANEWS

FUTURE ARCHITECTS OF AMERICA ASSOCIATION • JULY 26, 2005

Chicago's Own Picasso

THE CITY OF CHICAGO WOULD like to invite the public to attend a festival celebrating Chicago's own Picasso sculpture, beginning at noon on August 15. Who made this unusual sculpture and why? The sculpture was designed by the artist Pablo Picasso for the public to enjoy.

Pablo Picasso was born in Spain in 1881. He did his best-known work while living in France. His early paintings "showed circus performers and the families of the poor," usually painted with one main color (Freudin 387). He is best known for inventing a style called cubism with other artists such as Georges Braque and Juan Gris. By the 1940s Picasso was experimenting with many different artistic forms, such as pottery, sculpture, and new approaches to painting.

William Hartmann, a Chicago architect, originally brought the idea for the sculpture to Picasso, but many thought the world-famous artist would reject the project. According to the Chicago Public Library Web site, when Hartmann met Picasso in France, "it became apparent that the idea of such a major work for Chicago did appeal to him" ("Picasso Statue Unveiled in Civic Center Plaza"). Picasso finished a 42-inch steel model in 1965. The final 50-foot sculpture was built by the United States Steel Corporation and put together in Chicago. Picasso refused payment for the piece and called it a gift for the people of the city.

Please join us on August 15 for an afternoon of food and music to celebrate this great artist and his gift to the people of Chicago. For more information, please contact Thomas Coleman, Future Architects of America Association, at (312) 555-9824. ▲

Works Cited:

Edmund Freudin, *Freudin's History of Art.* New York: Donna Telio Books, 1995.

"Picasso Statue Unveiled in Civic Center Plaza," <www.chipublib.org>.

Research Reports

What Makes a Good Research Report?

A research report is a form of expository writing that presents factual information about a topic in an organized way. It shares ideas that a writer has gathered and interpreted from a variety of sources. Long before drafting, a writer asks questions about a topic and searches various sources for answers.

Writing a good research report takes strong writing skills combined with good detective work. This kind of detective work can be fun, especially when the writer chooses a topic that he or she finds interesting. Just as a detective spends time finding and analyzing clues, the writer spends time hunting down and evaluating good sources of information. Using the planning and writing skills you learned in earlier chapters, you will research and share your discoveries in an organized and well-written research report. These are some things you will want to keep in mind as you write your report.

Narrowing a Topic

Deciding on a topic is the first step. Choose something you can research and write about in a reasonable amount of time. You might first identify a broad topic and then brainstorm a list of narrower ideas about that topic. Be specific. It would be hard to research and write a report on all of American history; the Gettysburg Address would be a more manageable subject.

When you have narrowed your topic, follow your curiosity and think of what questions you would like answered about it. These questions will guide your research.

Research

A good research report is based on thorough research, and thorough research requires reliable sources. Sources are the places you go for information, such as nonfiction books, encyclopedias, and Web sites. Always think about the validity of your sources. Was the information presented by an expert?

You can't remember everything, so you will want to take good, organized notes as you research. Using your topic to guide you, write down everything that is relevant. Your notes will help you organize an effective research report.

• Activity A •

Brainstorming is a good way to narrow topics for a research report. Brainstorm and create a list of narrow topic ideas for these broad topics.

1. explorers
2. the Middle Ages
3. China
4. computers
5. reptiles
6. democracy

• Activity B •

Choose one of the narrowed topics you created for Activity A. Brainstorm a list of questions for the topic that you could research for a report.

Writer's Corner

Use an encyclopedia or a textbook to choose a broad subject. Use your source to come up with three narrow topics on your broad subject. Then pick one topic and come up with three questions you could research.

Maria Tallchief is often regarded as the greatest American ballerina. Born in Oklahoma in 1925, she is a Native American of the Osage people. She began dancing at the age of four and later helped to found the New York City Ballet where she was prima ballerina in her early 20s. She amazed audiences for years with her performances in *Swan Lake* and many other ballets.

Organization

As you research, you will probably find more information than you can use. Developing a thesis statement will help you choose and organize the facts and figures you find. A thesis statement is a sentence that briefly explains or describes the main idea of your report. It should express the important issue that you will explore. The rest of your report will give information that supports your thesis statement.

> Broad topic: healthy snacks
> Narrow topic: almonds
> Thesis statement: Almonds are a healthy snack.

Introduction

As with other kinds of writing, a good introduction catches your reader's interest. You can open with interesting facts you discovered in your research or ask the reader the same questions that interested you in your topic. A good introduction includes a thesis statement.

Body

The body of your research report presents the information that you uncovered. The body can be one or many pages long. Usually each paragraph of the body is about one subtopic, a detail that supports your thesis statement. If your thesis statement is that almonds are a healthy snack, for example, each paragraph might explain a different nutritional aspect of that food. If your thesis statement is that a certain person is a good role model, the information might be ordered chronologically. The person's childhood could be one subtopic, and the person's career could be another subtopic. If your thesis statement is that dolphins are intelligent, each paragraph might answer one question about dolphins' mental capabilities.

Conclusion

A good conclusion briefly summarizes all the information you presented in your report. It leaves your reader with a sense that you covered the topic completely. Don't introduce any new information in the conclusion.

Activity C

Read each pair of research report topics. Tell which one is the better of the two topics. Explain the reason for your choice.

1. **a.** Weather
   b. Hurricanes

2. **a.** Why dinosaurs became extinct
   b. The history of dinosaurs

3. **a.** Jacques Cousteau
   b. Ocean exploration

4. **a.** Irish history
   b. The Irish Potato Famine

5. **a.** The Plymouth Colony
   b. Colonial America

Activity D

Read the following pairs of sentences and choose the one that best works as a thesis statement for a research report. Explain your choices.

1. **a.** Many of us wonder whether or not sharks really do eat people.
   b. While sharks will eat just about anything, certain species of sharks eat some foods more than others.

2. **a.** Air pollution causes many environmental problems.
   b. Air pollution also causes acid rain.

3. **a.** If we didn't have the Internet, most of us wouldn't know how to find locations or phone numbers anymore.
   b. The Internet has gone through many changes since it was first invented in the 1960s.

4. **a.** I would have to say that the Flying Crowbar is my favorite wrestler.
   b. Wrestling is one of the oldest sports.

Writer's Corner

Look back at the topic you chose for Activity A on page 275. Write a draft of a short introductory paragraph for a research report on that topic. Include a thesis statement that tells the reader what you plan to cover in your research report.

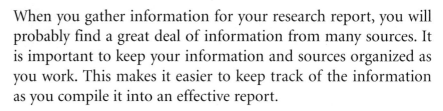

Gathering and Organizing Information

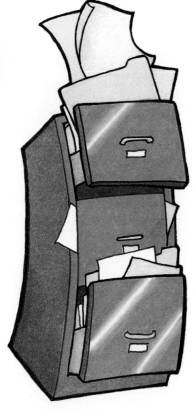

When you gather information for your research report, you will probably find a great deal of information from many sources. It is important to keep your information and sources organized as you work. This makes it easier to keep track of the information as you compile it into an effective report.

Taking Notes

As you research, you will want to write down everything you find that relates to your topic. You will probably collect more information than you can use. Choose information to record by asking yourself if the information answers a question you have about your topic. Even if you collect only relevant information, you probably won't use all of it.

One easy way to keep your information organized is by writing it down on note cards. Write only one idea or piece of information on each card. You may write a phrase, a sentence, or many sentences, but be sure you write only one idea. Write the information in your own words. If you find a quotation that you would like to put in your report, write it with quotation marks. Otherwise, you may forget and accidentally use someone else's words as your own. It is also helpful to write the research question that the information answers at the top of the card.

It is very important to write down your source at the bottom of the card. Be sure to include the title and page number or Web address. This will help you remember where you found the information. It is also helpful to write one extra card for each source that lists all the information about that source. Include the author, title, publisher, and date of publication on these cards. This will help you write a Works Cited page at the end of your report.

The four note cards below were written by the author of the newsletter article "Chicago's Own Picasso" on page 273.

Who made the sculpture?

Pablo Picasso designed a 42-inch model in 1965.

"Picasso Statue Unveiled in Civic Center Plaza."
www.chipublib.org

Why did Picasso make the sculpture?

Asked by Chicago architect William Hartmann. People thought Picasso wouldn't do it. But "it became apparent that the idea of such a major work for Chicago did appeal to him."

"Picasso Statue Unveiled in Civic Center Plaza,"
www.chipublib.org

Who made the sculpture?

Picasso also invented cubism with artists Georges Braque and Juan Gris.

Freudin's History of Art. p. 387

Source

Edmund Freudin. Freudin's History of Art. New York: Donna Telio Books. 1995.

● Activity A ●

Use the note cards above to answer the following questions.

1. What were the two questions the author used to guide his research?

2. How many sources did the author use?

3. From the note cards shown, which source did the author decide to quote directly?

4. Where did the author find the article "Picasso Statue Unveiled in Civic Center Plaza"?

5. What kind of information did the author put on the last card?

Writer's Corner

Go back to the source you used to find a topic and questions for the Writer's Corner on page 275. Use the same source to write four ideas about your topic onto index cards or onto a sheet of paper folded into quarters. Don't forget to include your source at the bottom of each card.

Organizing Your Notes

When you finish researching your topic, you will probably have a lot of note cards loaded with information. It is important to organize these notes in a useful way. Using note cards makes it easy to arrange and rearrange your research.

If you wrote your questions at the top of each card, you can group the cards together by question. You can also decide on the subtopics or paragraphs of your research report and group the note cards together by subtopic or paragraph.

To group cards, you can stack them together and bind them with paper clips or rubber bands. You can also use something colorful to mark different subtopics, such as highlighters or colored dots.

Using Your Organized Notes

Organizing your note cards gives you another chance to check that the information you collected is relevant to your topic. You may find that you have cards that don't fit into any group. This information might have seemed important when you started researching but doesn't seem right for your final report. Keep those notes in a separate pile. As you draft, you may still find some use for them.

Once you gather and organize your notes, it is easier to see the big picture. Sometimes looking at the information you collected will suggest a different thesis statement than the one you started with. Remember that you can change your thesis statement any time before you start drafting.

Using the notes you have organized, you can create an outline for your research report. Outlines are a useful way to organize all the information you have and plan your research report. Lay out your groups of note cards on a large surface and copy the notes on one sheet of paper as an outline. Use what you learned in Chapter 4 to help you write your outline.

Activity B

The information below was collected on note cards for a research report on earthquakes. Decide which subtopic each note card of information belongs to.

Subtopic A: What causes earthquakes?
Subtopic B: Where do earthquakes occur?
Subtopic C: What are the effects of an earthquake?

1. mostly occur along fault lines
2. makes buildings collapse
3. fires and tidal waves can break out
4. great pressure builds at fault lines, then releases
5. usually areas where new mountains have formed
6. shifting of tectonic plates builds pressure in the earth
7. most earthquakes happen under the sea
8. tremendous shaking of the ground
9. in America most common on the Pacific Coast
10. rock bending and folding, until the tension is broken

Activity C

The information below was collected on note cards for a research report about auto racing. Decide which note cards to set aside. Explain why you made each choice.

1. first important race at Grosse Pointe, Michigan
2. Henry Ford created the first assembly line auto plant.
3. Indianapolis 500 first run in 1911
4. motorcycle racing is also very popular, especially in Europe
5. Barney Oldfield one of the first great race drivers

Our Wide Wide World

During the heyday of vaudeville in the 1920s, one blues singer stood out above all the rest. Her name was Bessie Smith. Smith, who poured her heart and soul into every word she sang, was admired as a talented and independent African American woman. Her brief but influential music career earned her the title, "Empress of the Blues."

Writer's Corner

Using the note card information from Activity B, create an outline for a research report on earthquakes.

Citing Sources

When you write a research report, it is important that you let your reader know where you got your information. By providing your sources for the reader, you show that you did good research and that your report is reliable. It also gives the reader suggestions for where to look for more information on your topic. By citing your sources, you give credit to the people who have already done research of their own. Name your sources within parentheses in your report. At the end of the report, add a Works Cited page with more complete details.

Works Cited

The Works Cited page will appear at the end of your report on a separate page. Write or type *Works Cited* at the top of the page. Then list each of your sources alphabetically by the authors' last names or by title if you do not have an author's name. If the information for one source does not fit on one line, indent the following lines. Use the formats below to present the information on your sources. If you use a source, such as a magazine, that is not listed below, ask your teacher or librarian for instructions on how to format your Works Cited entry.

Halcyon-Maddux Books
561 West Oak Street, Carlyle, MO 54687

Copyright © 1995 by Mary Robinson
All rights reserved
Printed in the United States of America
First edition, 1995

Book

For most books you will need the name of the author, title of the book, publisher, location of the publisher, and year the book was published. You can usually find this information on the title page or the copyright page. (See example at left.) The copyright page is the page after the title page. Your entry on the Works Cited page for a book would look like the one below.

Robinson, Mary. <u>A History of Fingerbone Lake</u>. Carlyle, MO: Halcyon-Maddux Books, 1995.

Web Site

Many Web sites do not identify authors. If a Web site article does give the author's name, be sure to include it along with the name of the article, the date that you looked at the Web site, and the Web address. Enclose the Web address in angle brackets (< >).

> Martinez, Tina. "The First FBI Agents." 24 Feb. 2004 <www.fbi.gov/history/agents.htm>.

Encyclopedia

Like Web sites, most encyclopedias do not list the names of the people who wrote each article. For well-known encyclopedias, you will need only the name of the article, the name of the encyclopedia, and the edition or year of the encyclopedia.

> "Grasshopper." <u>World Book Encyclopedia</u>. 2003 ed.

• Activity A •

Write the information for each of these sources the way you would for your Works Cited page. Be sure to underline and use correct punctuation. Indent the second line for each entry.

1. A page called "Wind Cave National Park" that you found on October 2, 2004. You found the article at www.nps.gov/wica, and there is no author listed.

2. The entry for "Greece" in the *World Book Encyclopedia* from 2004. There is no author listed.

3. Chris Mendoza's book *Amazing Grazing.* The copyright page states that the book was published by Boyd Mills Press, which is located in Honesdale, PA. The book was published in 1997.

4. The entry for "Jupiter" written by Sun Li in the *Encyclopedia of Planets and Stars* from 2002.

Writer's Corner

Use books, textbooks, and encyclopedias to write a Works Cited page. Use three sources. Remember to follow the proper format and put the sources in alphabetical order.

Parenthetical Notation

The Works Cited page at the end of your research report should show all the sources used. Any time you pick up a fact, an idea, or a quotation and put it in your report, cite its source in parentheses at the end of the sentence. If you noted the source and page numbers on each index card, this will be easy to do. The important thing to remember is that you must include a parenthetical notation every time you use something from one of your note cards.

Because you will list full source information at the end of your report, you need to use only a short reference in parentheses to guide the reader. For a book give the author's last name and the page number on which the information appeared. If you are not able to get the author's name, use the name of the article or book it comes from. For Web sites you do not need to use a page number unless there is one on the Web site. Just the author's last name or the name of the article will be enough. For encyclopedias just put the name of the article. These short references allow the reader to look at your Works Cited page to find the full source.

Place your notation in parentheses at the end of the sentence containing the information. Put the period for the sentence after the parentheses.

> Mickey Mouse first appeared in a 1928 cartoon called *Steamboat Willie* (Gordan 78).

> Author Gale Holiday claims in her book that Vikings were the first Europeans to reach North America (Holiday 458).

> Country and western music developed in the 1920s out of "the mountain music of Appalachia, the work songs of the coal mines, and the blues of the South" ("Country and Western Music").

Plagiarism

Plagiarism is taking someone's words or ideas and using them in your work as if they were your own. By using parenthetical notations and a Works Cited page, you give credit to people who thought, researched, and wrote on topics so others could learn. To take their ideas and present them as your own is wrong, and can get you in trouble. In school, plagiarism will almost always result in a failing grade or worse. When you use someone else's work in your research report, you must give credit to the author.

• Activity B •

The entries are from a Works Cited page. For each entry write the parenthetical notation that would go in the text of a research report.

1. "Italy." <u>World Book Encyclopedia</u>. 2004

2. Scouten, Rex. "Preface." 8 Jan. 2004
    <www.whitehouse.gov/history/art/preface.html>.

3. Ricardo, Natalie. <u>The Big Book of Sunflowers</u>. Des Plaines, IL: Pearl Garden Publishing, 2001. (from page 63)

• Activity C •

Rewrite the sentences, adding the parenthetical notations you wrote down from Activity B. Match each notation to the correct sentence.

1. The scientific name for the common sunflower is *Helianthus annus*.

2. Gilbert Stuart's portrait of George Washington at the White House "inspires us and evokes calm assurance of national community."

3. The country also includes two large islands—Sicily and Sardinia.

Writer's Corner

Use the note cards you created for the Writer's Corner on page 279 to write a paragraph on a topic. Include parenthetical notations from information on the cards.

Word Study

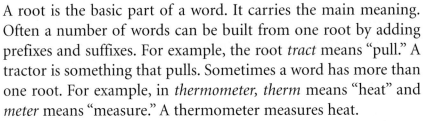

Roots

A root is the basic part of a word. It carries the main meaning. Often a number of words can be built from one root by adding prefixes and suffixes. For example, the root *tract* means "pull." A tractor is something that pulls. Sometimes a word has more than one root. For example, in *thermometer, therm* means "heat" and *meter* means "measure." A thermometer measures heat.

Many roots in English come from either Latin or Greek. For example, *scope* is a root. It comes from a Greek word that means "watch." The prefix *micro-* can be added to it to form the word *microscope*, a device for watching or viewing small things. *Scope* is also a root in the word *telescope*, a device for viewing things that are far away.

In your reading, you will often come across new words. Many times you can figure out what an unfamiliar word means by examining the context and analyzing the word's parts. Then these words will become a part of your vocabulary, and you can use them in your own writing.

You may have encountered the word *bibliography* for the first time in this book. You know now that a bibliography is a list of books. If you had never seen the word before, you might guess its meaning if you knew the meaning of the word parts. The Greek root *biblio* means "book," and the Greek root *graph* means "write." When you *write* a list of *books*, you make a *bibliography*.

You are familiar with the word *biography*. The Greek root *bio* means "life." You know that *graph* means "write." When you *write* about someone's *life*, you write a biography. People often confuse the meanings of *bibliography* and *biography*. You can use the words correctly if you remember the meaning of each word part.

Here are some common Latin and Greek roots and their meanings.

Root	Meaning	Example
ast	star	astronomy
audi	hear	audience
chron	time	synchronize
dict	speak	dictionary
geo	earth	geology
mis, mit	send	mission, transmit
phon, phono	sound	microphone
sol	alone	solitary
tort	twist	contortion
vac	empty	vacant
vid, vis	see	vision

• Activity A •

Copy the chart below, and fill in the missing parts.

	Prefix/Suffix	Root	New Word	Meaning
1.	*trans-* (across)	mis, mit	_____	to send across
2.	*tele-* (far)	_____	telephone	device to send sound far away
3.	*-ion* (act of)	vid, vis	_____	_____
4.	*-tude* (state of)	sol	_____	state of being alone
5.	*-ate* (to make)	_____	vacate	to make empty
6.	*-ible* (able to be)	_____	_____	able to be heard
7.	*pre-* (before)	_____	_____	say in advance

Writer's Corner

Make a list of as many words as you can that have a root that gives a clue to the meaning of the word. Use the roots listed above and try to think of some others that you know.

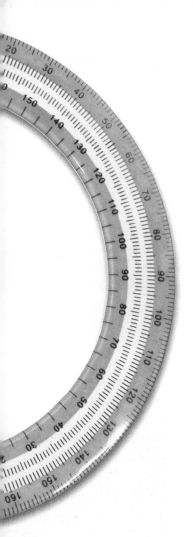

Activity B

Look at the words in Column A. Try to determine the meaning of each word from the root. Match each word in Column A with the correct meaning in Column B. When you have finished, use a dictionary to check your answers.

Column A	Column B
1. soliloquy	a. measurement of surfaces
2. semiannually	b. unable to be seen
3. missive	c. able to be heard
4. geometry	d. a message or letter
5. vacancy	e. occurring every half year
6. homophones	f. an empty space
7. invisible	g. dramatic speech by one person
8. audible	h. words that sound alike but have different meanings and spellings

Activity C

Analyze each root and the pair of words it helps to form. Use the combined meanings of each word pair to determine the meaning of the root. Match the root and words in Column A with the correct root definition in Column B. When everyone has finished, compare your definitions with those of your classmates. Check the dictionary for words no one knows.

Column A	Column B
1. (cycl) bicycle, cyclone	a. flee
2. (pend) suspend, pendulum	b. scrape
3. (opt) optical, optician	c. cut
4. (cise) scissor, incision	d. eye
5. (nov) novice, innovate	e. new
6. (fer) transfer, ferry	f. circle
7. (spec) spectator, retrospect	g. hang
8. (ver) verify, veracity	h. see
9. (fug) fugitive, refugee	i. truth
10. (ras) erase, rasp	j. carry

Activity D

The following words are formed from the same roots given in Activity C. Their connection is not as obvious as the words in Activity C. Work with a partner and determine how the root adds to the meaning of each word. You may use a dictionary to find the meanings of the suffixes and prefixes.

encyclopedia	conifer	append
suspect	centrifugal	verdict
nova	abrasive	concise

Activity E

Read each pair of words and the sentences that follow. Fill in the blanks with the correct words. Discuss the meanings of the roots.

1. indicated, evacuated

   We _____ the building when the fire alarm rang.

   An *X* on the mall's map _____ where we were.

2. incredible, inaudible

   It is _____ that we didn't see each other at the park.

   Parts of the movie were _____ because of the laughter.

3. geologist, biologist

   The _____ studies the earth's surface.

   The _____ studies living things.

Writer's Corner

Brainstorm as a class and try to think of some additional roots that you haven't discussed. List these words on the board. Then make lists of as many words as you can that share the same root. Discuss the words and their meanings. Now choose a group of words that share the same root. Try to use all the words in a paragraph. It can be a humorous paragraph, but it should make sense.

Using the Library and the Internet

Once you have decided on a research topic, you can start gathering information. Two sources that can provide almost all the information that you will need for any topic you wish to write about are the library and the Internet.

Finding Information in the Library

Libraries divide books into two categories: fiction and nonfiction. When you are seeking information for a research report, look in the nonfiction section of your library.

Reference Books

Most libraries keep reference books, such as almanacs, atlases, and encyclopedias, in the same area. These reference books are a good place to start looking for general information about your topic. Encyclopedias give basic information on a wide range of subjects. Almanacs list yearly statistics for everything from sports to the literacy rate of the nations of the world. Atlases contain maps and geographical information.

The Catalog

Every library lists its resources, including books, videos, and CDs, in its catalog. Today most libraries have their catalogs on computer. If your library still uses a card catalog, ask your librarian how to use it to find the books you need.

Computer catalogs allow users to find books in three ways: by title, by author, or by subject. Many catalogs also allow users to find books by keywords. A keyword is a word directly related to the subject. When seeking information for a research report, you want to find books that are about the subject of your report.

All computerized library catalogs use similar procedures. Type the subject of your report into the proper box and click the "Search" button to get a list of books that the library has about your subject.

When you get to the screen that lists books about your subject, you will see information about each one including the book's title and author, the year it was published, and its call number.

• Activity A •

What reference book would you use to find the following information?

1. the total area of Texas in square miles

2. the total population of Alaska last year

3. the main industries in California

4. the states that border Ohio

5. the year that Florida became a state

• Activity B •

Use the sample computer catalog listing to answer the questions.

```
TITLE         The secret of Mary Celeste, and other sea fare.
CALL #        910.453B727S
AUTHOR        Bradford, Gershom
PUBLISHER     Barre, Mass., Barre Pub. Co., 1966
SUBJECT(S)    Mary Celeste
              Sea stories; ghost ships
```

1. In what year was the book published?

2. Who is the author of the book?

3. What is the call number of the book?

Writer's Corner

Look at the topics that you brainstormed for the Writer's Corner on page 275. Use your library's catalog to find one nonfiction book about each topic. Write down the title, the author's name, and the book's call number.

Finding Information on the Internet

The Internet has advantages and disadvantages over the printed resources in your library. New information can immediately be posted on the Internet, while library books might be many years old. Even weekly magazines can't match the Internet's ability to present information as soon as it becomes known.

On the other hand, anybody who is familiar with the Internet can create a Web site. You must decide if the information on a particular site is accurate and unbiased.

Conducting Web Searches

A search engine is a computer program that can be used to locate Web sites for any subject on the Internet. There are a number of search engines. Experiment to see which is easiest for you to use. Just like library computer catalogs, different search engines have different procedures. Fortunately, just like library computer catalogs, the procedures are similar.

In the search field, type in important keywords connected to your subject and then click the "Search" button. If you enter keywords that are too general, you will probably find that there are more Web sites than you can use. You should type more specific keywords into the search field. If the search engine can find no matches, you were probably too specific and you should type more general keywords into the search field.

Evaluating Web Sites

There are billions of Web sites on the Internet. Many sites contain information that is inaccurate or biased. When you use data from a Web site, you must evaluate it for accuracy or bias.

Often you can use the extension of a site's Web address to get a hint of its reliability. The most common extension is ".com," which stands for "commercial." Anyone can own a .com Web site, so you must be careful about verifying information that you find there. A second extension to be wary of is ".org," which stands for "organization." Organizations often have agendas they promote.

You can usually be certain of information that you find on sites with the extension code ".gov," which are government sites. Universities and educational institutions use the ".edu" extension. Information on their sites is usually accurate. Finally, the ".mil" extension is for military Web sites, which are also usually reliable.

Activity C

What keywords would you type in a search field for information about the following topics? Give one example for each topic. You may use words from the topic plus any others you can think of.

1. the monarch butterflies' migration to Mexico
2. how Chinese workers helped build the intercontinental railroad
3. rock music in Europe and Asia
4. different political parties in American history

Activity D

Look at the following topics for research papers and the two Web sites that have information for each one. Decide which site would have the most reliable information. Explain your answer.

1. The Negro Baseball Leagues
   a. Negro Leagues HIST 203 www4.wittenberg.edu
   b. History of Major League Baseball www.sportsfan.com

2. The Interstate Highway System
   a. Federal Highway Administration www.fhwa.dot.gov
   b. American Road Tours www.motelz_r_us.com

3. How Healthy Is a Vegetarian Diet?
   a. Live Longer the Vegan Way www.veganlife.org
   b. Family Nutrition www.healthinsite.gov

4. Is America's Space Program Worth the Cost?
   a. In Defense of Space Exploration www-tech.mit.edu
   b. Next Stop, the Stars www.scifizine.com

Our Wide Wide World

Frida Kahlo was a Mexican artist whose unique self-portraits reflected her difficult life. She survived polio as a young girl and was in a terrible bus accident years later. While recovering from her injuries, she began painting. Over the next three decades, Frida Kahlo painted many self-portraits in a style unlike anyone before her.

Writer's Corner

Use a search engine to find three Web sites for each topic that you looked up in your library's catalog for the previous Writer's Corner. Tell which search engine you used and the keywords you entered to find the Web sites. Write the addresses of the Web sites.

Biographical Reports

A biographical report presents information about the life of a noteworthy person. It explains the important events, periods, and accomplishments that shaped the person.

Choosing a Topic

Do you have a hero, someone whom you admire? If you're a sports fan, you may follow Lance Armstrong's bicycle racing competitions or Tiger Woods's golf tournaments. Perhaps your heroes are not athletic. J. K. Rowling has inspired many young people to read. Maybe you have a hero who is no longer living. Martin Luther King Jr. did much to bring people together at a time when trust between the races was not common.

Any person whom you admire can make a good topic for an oral biographical report. Think of a personal hero whom you would like to know more about.

Researching Your Topic

It is usually quite easy to find information about famous people. If you type a celebrity's or historical figure's name into a search engine, you will probably come up with thousands of Web sites about that person. The encyclopedia will have an entry for almost any historical figure who interests you. Magazines have articles about many famous people. Use the skills that you learned in Lesson 5 to gather information about the person you chose as your subject.

Before you begin, ask yourself questions that you would like answered about the person. Then gather information with these questions in mind. Write your notes onto cards with one idea per card, keeping track of all the sources that you use. Even though an oral report doesn't have a Works Cited page, you want to be able to support your research if anyone asks.

Organizing Your Report

When you have gathered enough information, you can organize your report. Start with your introduction. Explain what interests you about this person. This can be your thesis statement.

The body of your report should tell the major events in the subject's life. It is usually best to organize a biographical report in sequential time order. Begin with your subject's place and date of birth and any childhood influences. Then move on to the events and accomplishments that made the person special. These will be facts supporting your thesis statement.

Your conclusion should summarize the important points of the subject's life. Recap only the most relevant events. Finally, restate your thesis and provide a satisfying concluding statement.

• Activity A •

Look at the following notes taken for a biographical report on Stan Lee. Determine which ones aren't necessary.

1. born Stan Lieber, December 28, 1922, New York City
2. answered ad for Marvel comics right out of high school
3. filled many jobs at Marvel: writer, editor, art director
4. worked under Jack Kirby, Steve Ditko
5. became lead editor at age 17
6. created Spider-Man, The Incredible Hulk, the X-Men
7. Spider-Man's alter ego is Peter Parker
8. made publisher of Marvel Comics in 1972
9. Superman and Batman are D.C. Comics characters
10. now focuses on superhero movies and animation

Speaker's Corner

Use the notes from Activity A to prepare a short speech about Stan Lee. If you wish, you may do research to find more information about his life. Work with a partner and take turns presenting your speeches to one another.

Using Multimedia

You can enhance your biographical presentation through the use of multimedia aids. Use the suggestions below to help you decide what types of media would be most suitable for your speech.

Audio

Audio recordings can be quite helpful in certain biographical presentations. If the subject of your presentation is a musician, you probably own recordings of his or her work. A short song or instrumental can help your audience evaluate the artist's style.

Poets and authors of books often have their works recorded on tape. Sometimes they read their work themselves. Playing a short recorded passage or poem can give your listeners a sense of a writer's "voice."

Video

If your subject is an actor, you could rent a tape or DVD of a movie he or she appears in. Find a scene in which he or she gives a strong performance and play it during your presentation so that your audience can see why you like that artist's work. If your subject is a sports figure, you might be able to find videos of him or her competing in a major event.

Art Samples

Artists have their works reproduced in oversized books and on poster-sized prints. If you admire an artist, you may have reproductions of his or her work on your walls at home or you may have art books with a sampling of the artist's work. Choose several representative pieces and use them to explain why you admire the artist.

Other Media

If the subject of your biographical report is a political or scientific personage, portraits or photographs can help your audience picture the person as you speak. Historical figures can also be made more interesting by using diagrams, such as time lines, to show how they influenced or were influenced by the times in which they lived. Real-life samples can be used for speeches about inventors. For a presentation about George de Mestral, for example, you could display a sample of Velcro.

• Activity B •

Think of a type of medium you could use in a speech for each of the following people. You could choose an audio or a video recording or a picture or a diagram. Tell what particular example you would use in your speech. If you don't know who some of these people are, look them up in the library or on the Internet.

Answers will vary.

1. Charles Lindbergh
2. Wolfgang Amadeus Mozart
3. Margaret Bourke-White
4. Olympia Snowe
5. Akira Kurosawa
6. Billie Jean King
7. Jimmy Carter

• Activity C •

Suggest notable persons whom you could give a speech about. For each person, choose one of the following multimedia aids that would enhance your talk.

video clip

audio clip

photograph or illustration

diagram

real-life sample

Speaker's Corner

Choose a subject for a biographical report. Research at least five facts about the person's life and organize your notes using the information on pages 294–295. Then practice your presentation and be prepared to deliver your oral biographical report to the class.

Research Reports

Prewriting and Drafting

Today you will begin the process of writing a research report.

Prewriting

The first step in writing a research paper is to choose a topic. Once a topic is chosen, the writer can begin to gather and organize information.

Choosing a Topic

Trushar's father is a colonel in the U.S. Army. Colonel Desali is keenly interested in military strategy. Trushar shares his father's interest, and when his history class was assigned a four-page research report, he decided to write about war tactics. His father could give him advice on what to include in his report.

The first advice his dad gave was to narrow his topic. "There are too many variations in strategies," he warned. "Choose one battle and explain how it was fought."

Trushar chose the battle of Marathon, which occurred in 490 BC. It was fought between Greeks and an invading Persian army.

Your Turn

A research report is a chance to learn more about a subject that you like. Pick any topic that interests you. It can be related to history, music, sports, or any other field of knowledge. Be sure that the topic is not too broad to cover in the time that you have.

Researching

Trushar had two questions that he wanted his report to answer: "What were the consequences of the Greek victory?" and "How could the vastly outnumbered Greeks defeat the invading Persians?" These questions led to his thesis statement. "The Greek victory over the Persians at Marathon helped lead to democracy today."

The library had a lot of information on the Battle of Marathon. An encyclopedia provided good general information. Trushar found more details on the Internet and in nonfiction books. He copied many relevant facts onto note cards, keeping track of what source provided which facts.

Your Turn

What questions do you want your report to answer? Look for information about these questions. Start thinking about your thesis statement.

As you research, copy information carefully and write down what you need for a Works Cited page.

Organizing Information

Trushar was surprised at how quickly his stack of note cards built up. He noticed that the cards were mostly divided between battle strategies and political matters, so he divided them into two piles. He reordered the cards in each pile several times before he was happy with the way that the information flowed.

Political

"The victory at the battle of Marathon meant that Greece would not be part of the Persian Empire. Instead it would become the 'Cradle of Western Civilization.'"

direct quote from
The Uncertain March to Democracy, Beals p. 132

Military

Persian forces = 25–30,000 men including archers and cavalry
Greek forces = about 10,000 infantry and 1,000 allies

The Persian Wars, Tillsbe p. 41

Then Trushar used the cards to construct his outline.

The Battle That Saved Democracy
I.   Political Overview
  A. Persian army sent to punish Athenians
    1. Supported Ionian revolt against Persia
    2. Killed Persian messengers seeking tribute
  B. Athens no match for Persia
    1. Small city-state
    2. Few allies
II. Order of Battle
  A. 25,000–30,000 Persians
    1. Cavalry
    2. Archers
    3. Slingers
    4. Light infantry
  B. 11,000 total Greek troops
    1. 10,000 Athenian foot soldiers
    2. 1,000 Greek allies

Your Turn

Organize your notes in a logical manner. If you used note cards, sort them so that cards with related ideas are together. If you copied your notes onto sheets of paper, use colored highlighters, stickers, or any other method you prefer to organize your facts. Then use the information from your notes to make an outline.

Drafting

Using his notes and his outline, Trushar wrote out his first draft. He double-spaced his lines to make room for the revisions he expected to make.

The following paragraphs are from the beginning, the middle, and the end of his first draft.

The Battle That Saved Democracy

Democracy began a long time ago in Athens, a city-state in ancient Greece. If Darius, the king of Persia, had conquered the Greeks almost 2,500 years ago, we might be living in a different world. Athens made Darius angry when it helped one of its neighbors, Ionia, revolt against his empire. Also, Darius had sent messengers to Athens to demand tribute. Instead of paying, the Greeks threw them off of the Acropolis. Darius wanted to punish them (Persian-Hellenic Wars). He sent a great force to conquer them. If his army defeated the Athenians, Greece would be part of the Persian empire. Democracy would not have started there. Maybe it would not have started at all. The Athenians won, however, even though they were badly outnumbered. They had 10,000 foot soldiers against Darius's 30,000. The Persian troops included 1,000 calvary and many archers (Tillsbe 41).

The Athenians marched to meet the invaders at Marathon. They were joined by 1,000 allies but they were still were outnumbered nearly 3 to 1. Because his 11,000 warriors weren't enough to match the front line of the Persians, the Greek General took a chance. He removed men from the middle and put them on the left and right sides. That is usually considered a poor tactic. When the two armies finally clashed, the Persians forced the Greek middle to retreat. When the Persians began to chase them, they unwittingly pushed themselves into a pocket with Greek soldiers on either side. Both sides rushed down onto the suddenly surounded Persians. The Athenians killed many of their confused foes. Perhaps if the Greek middle had held, the Persians would've won the battle. (Herzoff) In the end, the Persians lost nearly 6,500 soldiers killed compared to fewer than 200 on the Greek side.

According to historien Jean Beals, "The victory at the battle of Marathon meant that Greece would not be a part of the Persian Empire. Instead it would become the 'Cradle of Western Civilization'" (Beals 132). Who knows how different our world would be today if the Persian forces had beaten the Athenians? Maybe you and I would be speaking a different language. Maybe we'd be the subjects of a ruler from across an ocean. Maybe America wouldn't even have been discovered. We can thank the Greek victory over the Persians for the Democracy we enjoy today.

Your Turn

Use your notes and outline to write the first draft of your research report. Keep in mind the questions that you asked about your topic as you began your research. Whenever you include a piece of information that comes from a specific source, make sure that you cite that source immediately after the information. Use the style taught in Lessons 2 and 3 of this chapter.

Notes on Citing Sources

As you gathered information for your research report, you probably saw that many sources contain the same information. It is common knowledge, for example, that the Battle of Marathon took place in Greece. When a fact is commonly known, you do not have to cite any of the sources where you read it. Make certain, however, that the fact is stated in several different places that don't credit the same single source. That way you can be reasonably sure that the information is in the "public domain."

Content Editing

After Trushar completed his first draft, he read through it several times. He had found some fascinating information in his research, and he liked the way everything seemed to fit together. His paragraphs didn't stray from supporting his thesis. His sentences were varied and flowed together smoothly. Finally, he read his report against the Content Editor's Checklist.

Content Editor's Checklist

✔ Does the introduction identify the topic and main ideas? Does it include a thesis statement?

✔ Does each main idea support the thesis?

✔ Were different sources used while doing research?

✔ Has credit been given to all the necessary sources?

✔ Does the conclusion sum up the research or leave readers with an interesting thought or observation?

✔ Does the report use formal language and a confident tone?

✔ Is information about each source included in the Works Cited page?

Trushar realized that he hadn't really stated his thesis in his opening paragraph. He would rework the language to make his thesis clearer.

Trushar also decided that his last paragraph would have to be reworked. Using *maybe* so many times made it sound as if he wasn't sure about what he was saying. He wanted a more confident tone in his conclusion.

Those were some improvements that Trushar saw that he could make. He knew that there were probably other things that he didn't notice that would improve his report. Because his father was an expert on historical battles, Trushar asked him to read over his work.

Colonel Desali read through Trushar's report several times using the checklist. He told his son that he was impressed with his work. He could see that Trushar had done good research. Trushar put together a lot of facts from different sources to make a solid presentation. The Colonel noticed, however, some ways that the report could be improved.

should leave it out. If it is someone else's opinion, you need to cite your source.

- In the same paragraph, you credit Herzoff for your information, but you don't say what page of her book the information was on. Your Works Cited page doesn't give it either.

- The quote by Beals is interesting, but the wording seems awkward. Perhaps you can drop the quotation marks and just paraphrase her.

- You might have overstated your thesis at the end. Tone it down a little to make it more believable.

Your Turn

Read through your first draft several times to see how your sentences flow. Then read through it again using the Content Editor's Checklist. Mark any revisions that you think will improve your paper.

Next trade your draft with a classmate. Read your partner's paper for sense and sentence flow. Read it one more time, using the checklist.

When you meet with your partner to discuss your drafts, point out what you like about his or her work and then offer suggestions for improvements. Listen to your partner's suggestions for your paper with an open mind. Use any suggestions that you think will improve your work. Don't use suggestions that you disagree with.

- You use the word *them* so often in the first paragraph, I lost track of who is who.

- The first paragraph shouldn't list the numbers of different troops that both sides had. Statistics should come later in your report, not in the introduction.

- In the first paragraph on page two you state that thinning the center ranks in battle formation is a poor tactic. If this is your opinion, you

Revising

Here are the changes that Trushar marked on his draft.

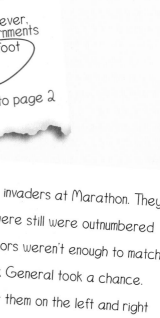

The Battle That Saved Democracy

Democracy began a long time ago in Athens, a city-state in ancient Greece. If Darius, the king of Persia, had conquered the Greeks almost 2,500 years ago, we might be living in a different world. Athens made Darius angry when it helped one of its neighbors, Ionia, revolt against his empire. Also, Darius had sent messengers to Athens to demand tribute. Instead of paying, the Greeks threw ~~them~~ *the messengers* off of the Acropolis. Darius wanted to punish ~~them~~ *the Athenians* (Persian-Hellenic Wars). He sent a great force to conquer them. If his army defeated the Athenians, Greece would be part of the Persian empire. Democracy would not have started there.

Maybe it would not have started at all. The Athenians won, however, even though they were badly outnumbered. Their victory at Marathon helped lead to the *democratic governments we see in the world today.* (Beals 131) They had 10,000 foot soldiers against Darius's 30,000. The Persian troops included 1,000 calvary and many archers (Tillsbe 41).

— move to page 2

The Athenians marched to meet the invaders at Marathon. They *were joined by 1,000 allies but they* were still were outnumbered (insert copy from page 1) nearly 3 to 1. Because his 11,000 warriors weren't enough to match the front line of the Persians, the Greek General took a chance. He removed men from the middle and put them on the left and right sides. ~~That is usually considered a poor tactic.~~ When the two armies finally clashed, the Persians forced the Greek middle to retreat. When the Persians began to chase ~~them~~ the Athenians they unwittingly

pushed themselves into a pocket with Greek soldiers on either side.

Both sides rushed down onto the suddenly surounded Persians. The

Athenians killed many of their confused foes. Perhaps if the Greek

middle had held, the Persians would've won the battle. (Herzoff 141)

In the end, the Persians lost nearly 6,500 soldiers killed compared

to fewer than 200 on the Greek side.

According to historien Jean Beals, "The victory at the battle
of Marathon meant that Greece would not be a part of the
Persian Empire. Instead it would become the 'Cradle of Western
Civilization'" (Beals 132). Who knows how different our world would
be today if the Persian forces had beaten the Athenians? ~~Maybe
you and I would be speaking a different language. Maybe we'd be
the subjects of a ruler from across an ocean. Maybe America
wouldn't even have been discovered. We can thank the Greek
victory over the Persians for the Democracy we enjoy today.~~

It's impossible to determine if the march to democracy would have
been completely stopped or only delayed. One thing is certain: the
Athenian victory allowed the idea of democracy to take root.

Trushar made the following changes to his draft:

- He replaced *them* twice in the first paragraph and made it clear which people he meant.

- He moved the troop statistics to the body of his report.

- He dropped the statement that thinning the center of a battle line is a poor tactic.

- He looked through his notes and found the page from which he had taken Herzoff's comment about how Persia might have won if the Greek center had held.

- He reworked his conclusion to make his language more confident and formal. He also toned down the thesis statement in the conclusion.

Trushar decided not to paraphrase the quote from Jean Beals as his father suggested. He thought the wording was understandable. Besides, part of the assignment was to use a direct quotation.

Your Turn
Use your partner's suggestions and your own ideas as a guide to revise your draft. Keep in mind that you might rewrite your paper several more times. Reread your revisions. What other improvements can you think of?

Chapter 8 Editor's Workshop

Research Reports

Copyediting and Proofreading

Copyediting

Trushar was happy with his report so far. It helped that he had chosen a topic that he really liked. He was pleased with the content. Now he wanted to make certain that his language flowed smoothly with varied sentences and vivid, precise words. He used the following checklist as he copyedited his paper.

Copyeditor's Checklist

✔ Has the writing been checked for rambling sentences and run-on sentences?

✔ Is there variety in sentence length?

✔ Has the writing been checked for overused words?

✔ Has the writing been checked for unnecessary repetition?

✔ Is the language formal?

✔ Have all quotations been checked for accuracy?

✔ Has all other information been stated in the writer's own words?

Trushar's paper had no rambling or run-on sentences. After a full year of *Voyages in English,* he had learned to watch for those mistakes as he wrote. He did see two places where he used informal language, however. Can you spot them?

Your Turn

Look over your revised draft. Read it aloud several times to see how your language flows. Use the Copyeditor's Checklist to guide you as you edit. Look for one type of mistake at a time.

Proofreading

Finally, Trushar felt that he was nearly ready to write out the final version. He was pleased with both the content and the language of his paper. Now he just needed to make certain that his spelling and grammar were correct. His best friend at school was Kelly. Her dad was also in the army. Trushar and Kelly often traded papers to edit or proofread. They traded their research reports. Both of them used the following Proofreader's Checklist.

Proofreader's Checklist

✔ Are the paragraphs indented?

✔ Have all words been checked for spelling?

✔ Is the grammar correct?

✔ Are the sentences capitalized and punctuated correctly?

✔ Has the paper been checked for new errors introduced in the revising process?

Using the checklist, Kelly spotted several errors. Trushar had capitalized words that should not have been capitalized. In fact, he wrongly capitalized one word several times. He also misspelled three words. Kelly noticed that Trushar had made punctuation mistakes in two of his reference notations. Some of the mistakes were in Trushar's original draft, and some were introduced while making revisions. Can you find the errors?

Kelly pointed out the things that she caught, and Trushar showed her the two mistakes he found in her paper. They both went to work writing the final copies of their research reports.

Your Turn

Read through your draft one more time before giving it to a proofreading partner. Then use the Proofreader's Checklist as you go over your partner's paper. Use a colored pencil to mark mistakes in spelling or grammar. After you and your partner have discussed mistakes that you have each noticed, write out the final version of your research report.

Publishing

After several revising sessions, Trushar felt that his research report was ready for publishing. Here are excerpts from the beginning, middle, and end of his report.

The Battle That Saved Democracy

Democracy began a long time ago in Athens, a city-state in ancient Greece. If Darius, the king of Persia, had conquered the Greeks almost 2,500 years ago, we might be living in a different world (Beals 131). Athens made Darius angry when it helped one of its neighbors, Ionia, revolt against his empire. Also, Darius had sent messengers to Athens to demand tribute. Instead of paying, the Greeks threw the messengers off of the Acropolis. Darius wanted to punish the Athenians (Persian-Hellenic Wars). He sent a great force to conquer them. If his army defeated the Athenians, Greece would be part of the Persian empire. Democracy would not have started there. Maybe it would not have started at all. The Athenians won, however, even though they were badly outnumbered. Their victory at Marathon helped lead to the democratic governments we see in the world today.

The Greeks marched to meet the invaders at Marathon. They were joined by 1,000 allies but they were still outnumbered nearly 3 to 1. They had only 11,000 foot soldiers against Darius's 30,000. The Persian troops also included 1,000 cavalry and many archers (Tillsbe 41).

Because his 11,000 warriors weren't enough to match the front line of the Persians, the Greek general took a chance. He took men from the middle and put them on the left and right sides. When the two armies finally clashed, the Persians forced the Greek middle to retreat. When the Persians began to chase the Athenians, they unwittingly pushed themselves into a pocket with Greek soldiers on either side. Both sides rushed down onto the suddenly surrounded Persians. The Athenians killed many of their confused foes. Perhaps if the Greek middle had held, the Persians would have won the battle (Herzoff 141). In the end, the Persians lost nearly 6,500 soldiers killed compared to fewer than 200 on the Greek side.

According to historian Jean Beals, "The victory at the battle of Marathon meant that Greece would not be a part of the Persian Empire. Instead it would become the 'Cradle of Western Civilization.'" (Beals 132). Who knows how different our world would be today if the Persian forces had beaten the Athenians? Maybe the march to democracy would have been completely stopped. Maybe it would only have been delayed. One thing is certain: the Athenian victory allowed the idea of democracy to take root.

Beals, Jean. The Uncertain March to Democracy. St. Louis, MO: Historical Press Inc., 2004.
Herzoff, Sara. Ancient Battlefields. Des Plaines, IL: Mt. Olympus Press, 2001.
"Persian-Hellenic Wars." 14 November 2001 <www.greekhistory/athensu.edu/persia.html>.
Tillsbe, Alexei. Great Victories. Aiken, SC: Rebel Printing Group, 1999.

Your Turn

When you feel that you have polished your research report until it is as good as it can be, it is time to publish. Make your final copy. Print it out on a computer or copy it in your neatest handwriting. Add a cover sheet with your report's title and your name. Before you turn it in, read it through one more time for mistakes that you might have missed. You want your work to be as good as you can make it.

Discuss ways to display your papers with your teacher and classmates. Your class could make a "mini-encyclopedia" by combining everyone's research report under a single cover. Arrange the reports in alphabetical order and create a table of contents.

Another option is to post the reports on your school's Web site.

Grammar

Nouns

Noun Challenge

1.1 Singular and Plural Nouns

A **noun** is a name word. A **singular noun** names one person, place, or thing. A **plural noun** names more than one person, place, or thing.

Add *-s* to most nouns to form the plurals.

Singular	Plural	Singular	Plural
ship	ships	airport	airports

Add *-es* to form the plurals of nouns ending in *s, x, z, ch,* and *sh.*

Singular	Plural	Singular	Plural
gas	gases	watch	watches
fox	foxes	sash	sashes

Some plural nouns are not formed by adding *-s* or *-es.* Check a dictionary if you are not sure of a plural form.

Singular	Plural	Singular	Plural
man	men	sheep	sheep
child	children	moose	moose
tooth	teeth	Chinese	Chinese

Exercise 1

Identify each noun. Tell whether it is singular or plural.

1. Men and women search for treasure under the ocean.
2. Recently searchers discovered jewels on a sunken ship.
3. Experts estimate that the treasure is priceless.
4. The objects are now at the museum.
5. The collection of gems includes many diamonds.
6. Flashes of light reflect off their surfaces.
7. My favorite pieces in the exhibit are the emeralds.
8. The topazes are a beautiful, deep yellow color.
9. The amazing display fascinates children and adults.

Exercise 2

Write the plural form for each noun. Use a dictionary if necessary.

1. lunch   **3.** ox   **5.** mix

2. foot   **4.** coin   **6.** porch

Exercise 3

Complete each sentence with the plural form of the noun in parentheses.

1. The treasure _____ (hunter) discovered the jewels on a sunken ship.

2. We saw the maps and _____ (compass) they used.

3. Kings and queens, princes, and _____ (princess) once owned these objects.

4. _____ (Pirate) stole this treasure in the 1600s.

5. The ship's _____ (record) show it was part of a large fleet.

Exercise 4

Use either the singular or plural form of the word in parentheses to complete each sentence.

1. Our _____ (visit) to the museum was very interesting.

2. Two _____ (woman) led our tour that day.

3. Some _____ (gem) are still at the bottom of the ocean.

4. We saw some _____ (brooch) made of diamonds.

5. A _____ (museum) often contains amazing treasures.

Practice Power

Write a paragraph about a museum you have visited or would like to visit. Circle all of the singular nouns. Underline all of the plural nouns.

1.2 More Singular and Plural Nouns

If a noun ends in *y* preceded by a vowel, form the plural by adding *-s.*

Singular	Plural	Singular	Plural
pulley	pulleys	attorney	attorneys

If a noun ends in *y* preceded by a consonant, form the plural by changing the *y* to *i* and adding *-es.* If a noun ends in *o* preceded by a vowel, form the plural by adding *-s.*

Singular	Plural	Singular	Plural
discovery	discoveries	radio	radios
colony	colonies	portfolio	portfolios

If a noun ends in *o* preceded by a consonant, form the plural by adding *-es.* There are exceptions to this rule. Always check a dictionary.

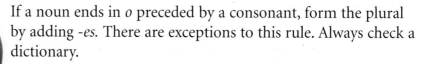

Singular	Plural	Singular	Plural
tomato	tomatoes	mosquito	mosquitoes

Exceptions:

taco	tacos	alto	altos

For most nouns that end in *f* or *fe,* form the plurals by adding *-s.* For some nouns ending in *f* or *fe,* form the plurals by changing the *f* or *fe* to *-ves.* Use a dictionary to be sure.

Singular	Plural	Singular	Plural
roof	roofs	calf	calves
safe	safes	leaf	leaves

Form the plurals of most compound nouns by adding *-s.* Form the plurals of some compound nouns by adding *-s* to the principal word. Use a dictionary to be sure.

Singular	Plural	Singular	Plural
drive-in	drive-ins	brother-in-law	brothers-in-law
eyeball	eyeballs	editor in chief	editors in chief

Exercise 1

Write the plural of each of the following items. If you are not sure of a plural form, check a dictionary.

1. photo
2. grape
3. cherry
4. bush
5. sky
6. soprano
7. journey
8. door
9. loss

Exercise 2

Complete the sentences with the plural form of each word in parentheses.

1. Several _____ (party) of divers are scheduled to leave.

2. The teams consist of _____ (trio) of divers.

3. The _____ (chief) of the expedition have obtained the _____ (supply) needed.

4. There are _____ (compass), underwater _____ (radio), and _____ (knife) for all crew members.

5. The divers will be researching ocean _____ (valley) and coral _____ (reef).

6. Who can predict what _____ (discovery) will be made about the _____ (life) of animals and plants under the sea?

7. The _____ (story) of individual divers will be recorded, and their adventures will be available on _____ (video).

Practice Power

Write the plural form for each noun. Then use the words in sentences of your own.

1. butterfly
2. colony
3. zoo
4. valley
5. thief
6. hero

1.3 Count and Noncount Nouns

Count nouns name things that can be counted. Count nouns have singular and plural forms. To show a specific quantity, a plural count noun can be modified by a number: *three cookbooks, five recipes, eight cups, two and a half teaspoons.*

Singular	Plural	Singular	Plural
cookbook	cookbooks	recipe	recipes
teaspoon	teaspoons	cup	cups

Noncount nouns name things that cannot be counted. Noncount nouns do not have plural forms. To show how much, a noncount noun must be preceded by an expression of quantity.

Noncount Noun	How Much?
bread	a loaf of bread
water	three glasses of water
gas	two gallons of gas

Some nouns can be count or noncount.

I ate a piece of *cake.* (noncount)
She baked two *cakes.* (count)

He has brown *hair.* (noncount)
There's a *hair* on his jacket. (count)

Exercise 1

Identify the noncount nouns. There may be more than one noncount noun in a sentence.

1. The host made soup with rice and beans.

2. He served it in bowls, along with bread and butter.

3. He also prepared beef with vegetables and gravy.

4. The guests had coffee with milk and sugar.

5. The host served ice cream and fruit last.

Exercise 2

Identify all the nouns in each sentence. Tell which are count and which are noncount.

1. The weather was very hot in the afternoon.

2. Mom asked us to help make a batch of lemonade.

3. I measured eight cups of water into a pitcher.

4. My brother squeezed the lemons and added two cups of juice to the water.

5. Mom stirred in several tablespoons of sugar.

6. We poured our refreshing lemonade into glasses.

7. We added ice to our drinks.

8. It was a wonderful way to beat the heat!

Exercise 3

Finish the sentences. Add a word or phrase to tell how much for each noncount noun.

1. For the pasta sauce my sister first fried _____ ground beef in _____ oil.

2. She then added _____ tomato sauce and _____ salt.

3. I asked if she needed to add _____ basil.

4. When the sauce was almost ready, she cooked _____ spaghetti for about 10 minutes in a separate pot.

5. My sister put _____ bread and _____ salad on the table along with the pasta.

6. I added _____ cheese on top of my pasta.

7. We each ate _____ the delicious pasta.

Practice Power

Write down your favorite recipe. When you have finished, circle the noncount nouns.

1.4 *Concrete and Abstract Nouns*

A **concrete** noun names a thing that can be seen or touched. Most nouns are concrete nouns.

bridge	flower	bus
pilot	octopus	movie
Japan	Mount Everest	Dr. Seuss

An **abstract noun** names something that cannot be seen or touched. It expresses an idea, emotion, quality, or condition.

freedom   joy   strength   safety

Most abstract nouns are noncount nouns. However, a few abstract nouns, such as *idea,* are count nouns.

Exercise 1

Identify the nouns in each sentence. Tell whether each noun is concrete or abstract.

1. Martin Luther King, Jr., earned the admiration of many Americans.

2. He was a leader of the movement to ensure basic rights for African Americans.

3. King experienced criticism because of his beliefs.

4. He and his followers marched against segregation in Birmingham.

5. Watchers were shocked at the hatred directed against the marchers.

6. King was arrested, but his determination remained strong.

7. In Washington King spoke about his hopes for better lives for his children.

8. King focused attention on the difficulties of poor people.

9. His honesty and intelligence make him an example to follow.

10. People who believe in justice continue to look up to King.

Exercise 2

Use each of these abstract nouns in a sentence.

1. love
2. democracy
3. independence
4. charity
5. strength
6. truth
7. cleanliness
8. enthusiasm
9. humility
10. cheerfulness
11. confidence
12. vitality

Exercise 3

Many abstract nouns can be formed from other words by adding the suffixes *-hood, -ion, -ity, -ment, -ness, -ship, -ty,* or *-y.* Make an abstract noun from each word by adding the proper suffix. Then use each word in a sentence.

1. friend
2. subtract
3. moral
4. kind
5. honest
6. leader
7. bright
8. celebrate
9. major

Exercise 4

Decide whether each noun is abstract or concrete. Then use each one in a sentence.

1. food
2. nutrition
3. privacy
4. committee
5. carelessness
6. skeleton
7. leader
8. hope
9. ambition
10. honesty
11. wisdom
12. crew
13. computer
14. dollar
15. gratitude

Practice Power

What do you think the traits and characteristics of a good friend are? Write a paragraph explaining your ideas. Use both concrete and abstract nouns.

1.5 Noun as Subjects and Subject Complements

A noun can be the **subject** of a verb. The subject tells what a sentence is about. In this sentence *Hope Diamond* is the subject.

The *Hope Diamond* was originally from India.

A noun can be **subject complement.** A noun used as a subject complement refers to the same person, place, or thing as the subject. It renames the subject.

A subject complement follows a linking verb such as the verb *be* and its various forms: *am, is, are, was, were,* and so on. In this sentence *gem* is the subject complement.

The Hope Diamond is a beautiful *gem*.
(Hope Diamond = gem)

Exercise 1

Identify the subject of each sentence.

1. A merchant purchased a large diamond in the 1600s.

2. King Louis XIV of France bought this magnificent stone in 1668.

3. Jewelers cut the rare diamond and set it in gold.

4. The Hope Diamond disappeared in 1792, during the French Revolution.

5. Henry Philip Hope had the beautiful stone in the 1800s.

6. An affluent woman bought this diamond in 1911.

7. Mrs. Evalyn Walsh McLean owned the stone until 1947.

8. The precious stone changed hands in 1949.

9. This blue-colored gem is now at the Smithsonian Institution in Washington, D.C.

10. Many tourists view the diamond each year.

Exercise 2

Identify the subject complement in each sentence.

1. The Hope Diamond is a steely-blue stone.

2. Jean Baptiste Tavernier was its first owner.

3. The gem was once the possession of King George IV of England.

4. Many people were owners of the diamond throughout its history.

5. The Smithsonian Institution is a famous museum.

6. This museum is the new home of the Hope Diamond.

Exercise 3

Identify the subject and the subject complement in each sentence.

1. The Crown Jewels of England are the most famous gems in the world.

2. The jewels are symbols of the British monarchy's power.

3. All of the objects that make up the Crown Jewels are the property of the monarch and the nation.

4. Their long-time home has been the Tower of London.

5. The ancient St. Edward's Crown is the headpiece for royal coronations.

6. Edward was an English king during the Middle Ages.

7. The Star of Africa, set in the monarch's scepter, is the largest cut diamond in the world.

Practice Power

Write sentences using the following nouns as subject complements.

| jewels | thief | pirates | treasure |

1.6 Nouns as Objects

A noun can be used as a **direct object** of a verb. The direct object answers the question *whom* or *what* after an action verb. In this sentence the direct object is *ships*. It answers the question *What did the pirates sail?*

> Many pirates sailed *ships* during the 1500s and 1600s.

In this sentence the direct object is *cargoes*. It answers the question *What did pirates steal?*

> Pirates stole *cargoes* from ships.

A noun can be used as the **indirect object** of a verb. The indirect object tells *to whom* or *to what*, or *for whom* or *for what* the action is done. In this sentence the indirect object is *members*. It answers the question *To whom did the captains give a share of stolen cargoes?*

> Captains gave crew *members* a share of stolen cargoes.

A noun can be the **object of a preposition.** To find the object of a preposition such as *to, at, from, on, by,* or *into,* ask *whom* or *what* after the preposition. In this sentence the object of the preposition *on* is *Atlantic Ocean*. It answers the question *On what did pirate ships sail?*

> Pirate ships sailed on the *Atlantic Ocean.*

Exercise 1

Identify the direct object in each sentence.

1. As a young girl, Granuaile loved the sea.

2. She joined her father on a sea voyage to Spain.

3. This Irish noblewoman eventually commanded an army of pirates in the 1500s.

4. She and her crew raided ships off the coast of Ireland.

5. Ship captains paid money to Granuaile for safe passage along the coast.

Exercise 2

Identify the indirect object in each sentence.

1. Writers of the time left future generations amazing stories about pirates.

2. Current films often offer viewers a romantic picture of pirate life.

3. Reluctantly captains of merchant ships gave pirates their valuable cargoes.

4. Rulers offered these sea robbers ransom for captured individuals.

5. Nations sent their colonies ships for protection against pirates.

Exercise 3

Identify the object of the preposition in each sentence.

1. Edward Teach was born in Bristol, England.

2. However, Teach was seldom called by this name.

3. The name Blackbeard was given to this merciless pirate.

4. He had a long, black beard tied with black ribbons.

5. Blackbeard raided colonies along the North American coast.

6. A fleet of ships eventually captured Blackbeard.

Practice Power

Write sentences using each of the following prepositions and objects of prepositions.

1. in the ocean
2. on the sea
3. of his ship
4. across the ocean
5. to kings and queens
6. in Europe
7. from ships
8. about many feared pirates
9. in museums
10. by movies and books

1.7 Possessive Nouns

A **possessive noun** expresses possession or ownership. In this sentence the tomb belonged to a ruler. The word *ruler's* is a possessive noun.

> The big pyramid was actually a *ruler's* tomb.

To form the singular possessive, add -*'s* to the singular form of the noun.

> My *friend's* report was on ancient Egypt.

To form the possessive of plural nouns ending in *s*, add an apostrophe only.

> The *kings'* tombs held their mummies.
> *Archaeologists'* work has uncovered the secrets of
>   ancient Egypt.

To form the possessive of plural nouns that do not end in *s*, add -*'s*.

> *Women's* influence on ancient Egyptian government was
>   sometimes very great.

The possessive of proper nouns ending in *s* is usually formed by adding -*'s*.

> *Alexandria Parsons's* book on ancient Egypt has fun
>   activities for kids.

The possessive of compound nouns is formed by adding -*'s* to the end of the word.

> My *brother-in-law's* vacation to Egypt was
>   full of adventures.
> My *brothers-in-law's* vacations
>   were two months apart.

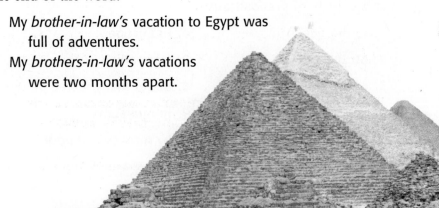

Exercise 1

Identify the possessive noun in each sentence. Name the thing owned or possessed.

1. King Tut's tomb was discovered in 1922.

2. Howard Carter's discovery was one of the most important archaeological finds ever made.

3. Surprisingly, the ruler's tomb and mummy were intact.

4. Tomb robbers' attempts to take major objects had failed.

5. The amazing discovery captured people's imagination.

Exercise 2

Write the singular possessive and the plural possessive form of each noun.

1. baby
2. sparrow
3. wife
4. astronaut
5. classmate
6. woman
7. witness
8. goose
9. captain

Exercise 3

Rewrite each group of words using a possessive noun.

1. mummies of pharoahs
2. tools of the workers
3. mask of Tutankhamen
4. beliefs of the Egyptians
5. sides of the pyramid
6. wrappings of the mummy
7. location of the tomb
8. headdress of the queen
9. work of the artists
10. beauty of the objects

Practice Power

Write about a famous explorer or an important person in history. Include at least three possessive nouns in your writing.

1.8 *Nouns Showing Separate and Joint Possession*

Separate possession occurs when two or more people own things independently of one another. **Joint possession** occurs when two or more people own something together.

To show separate possession, use *-'s* after each noun. In this sentence Ann and Peter each own a boat.

> *Ann's and Peter's* boats are in the marina.

To show joint possession, use *-'s* after the last noun only. In this sentence Tom and Gloria own a boat together.

> *Tom and Gloria's* boat is painted bright blue.

Exercise 1

Read each sentence. Tell whether it shows separate or joint possession.

1. Ana and Carlos's party was a lot of fun.

2. Marisha and Laura's lemonade was delicious.

    3. We all liked Carl's and Peter's cookies.

      4. Todd and Amy's dance was really graceful.

        5. Kim's and Anita's jokes were funny.

          6. We clapped for Frank and Mandy's singing.

            7. Later we played Brian's and Tom's new CDs.

Exercise 2

Rewrite each sentence, changing the spelling and punctuation to indicate separate or joint possession.

1. Ivan and Jaime ideas about music are very different.

2. Jason and Nicole song was performed very well.

3. Fred Martino and Wayne Faber sisters like the Beatles.

4. Ed and Sam sister prefers country western music.

5. Margaret and Claudia band played for the dance.

Exercise 3

Read each pair of sentences. Write a new sentence that shows separate or joint possession.

Examples: The president and secretary worked together.
They made an interesting presentation.
The president and secretary's presentation was interesting.

1. Raphael and Titian each painted pictures.
   Their pictures are considered masterpieces.

2. Rodgers and Hammerstein wrote *Oklahoma!* together.
   Oklahoma! is a famous musical.

3. Lewis and Clark made a journey of discovery together.
   The trip went as far as the Pacific Ocean.

4. Elijah Wood and Ian McKellen each had roles in *The Lord of the Rings.* The roles were difficult to play.

5. Lennon and McCartney wrote songs together.
   The songs were extremely popular.

6. Mozart and Beethoven each composed symphonies.
   The symphonies are music-lovers' favorites.

7. James Watson and Francis Crick did scientific experiments together. Their experiments led to the discovery of DNA.

8. Strunk and White wrote a book together.
   Their book tells people how to write well.

9. Green Bay and Kansas City each have a football team.
   The teams played in Super Bowl I.

10. Harry Potter and Hermione Granger went to the same school.
    Their school was called Hogwarts.

Practice Power

Write five sentences about your home and your family. Use possessives to show separate or joint ownership in each sentence.

1.9 *Appositives*

An **appositive** is a word that follows a noun and explains its meaning. An appositive names the same person, place, or thing as the noun it explains. An **appositive phrase** is an appositive and its modifiers.

In this sentence the noun *site* explains *Sistine Chapel.* It is an appositive.

> The *Sistine Chapel*, a famous *site* in the Vatican, was once called the Palatine Chapel.

The appositive phrase *a famous site in the Vatican* is set off from the rest of a sentence by commas because the phrase is **nonrestrictive.** A nonrestrictive appositive or appositive phrase is not essential to the meaning of the sentence; it merely adds information. The appositive phrase above is not necessary in order to know which church was called the Palatine Chapel.

In this sentence the noun *Peter* explains *apostle.*

> The *apostle Peter* is believed to be buried in the Vatican.

The appositive *Peter* is not set off by commas because it is **restrictive.** The name is necessary in order to know which apostle is buried in the Vatican.

Read each sentence. Tell if the appositive is restrictive or nonrestrictive. Explain your answer in terms of meaning.

1. Saint Peter's Basilica, a huge church in Rome, is a popular tourist destination.
2. The dome is the work of the Italian artist Michelangelo.

You are correct if you said that the appositive in the first sentence is nonrestrictive. The appositive gives more information about Saint Peter's Basilica, but it is not necessary in order to understand the sentence. You are correct if you said that the appositive in the second sentence is restrictive. Without it, you would not know which Italian artist worked on the dome.

Exercise 1

The appositive in each sentence is underlined. Name the noun it explains.

1. The Sistine Chapel was built during the time of Sixtus IV, a <u>pope</u> during the 1400s.

2. Pope Julius II, the <u>nephew</u> of Pope Sixtus IV, had Michelangelo paint the ceiling of the chapel.

3. *The Last Judgment,* the <u>painting</u> over the altar in the chapel, was also painted by Michelangelo.

Exercise 2

Identify the appositive and the noun it explains.

1. Michelangelo used a scaffold, a flat wooden platform on brackets, to paint the ceiling.

2. The Hebrew prophets, figures from the Old Testament, are painted around the edge of the ceiling.

3. Sibyls, ancient Greek prophets, are also in the paintings.

Exercise 3

Rewrite each sentence, adding commas where necessary.

1. Michelangelo a well-known sculptor and architect was not primarily interested in painting.

2. His marble sculpture *Pietà* is located in Saint Peter's Basilica.

3. Michelangelo's statue of David the Old Testament hero is the symbol of Florence, Italy.

4. Michelangelo's finest achievement as an architect was the dome of Saint Peter's the main church in the Vatican.

Practice Power

Write a paragraph about an interesting place you visited. Use appositives to explain the nouns.

A **noun** is a naming word. A **verb** expresses action or state of being. Many words can be used as nouns or verbs.

In this sentence *photograph* is a noun because it names a thing.

> I took a *photograph* of the Cathedral of Notre Dame.

In this sentence *photograph* is a verb because it expresses an action.

> Many tourists *photograph* the cathedral of Notre Dame.

Tell whether the word in italics is a noun or a verb.

1. The *light* of the sun shone beautifully on the altar.
2. They *light* the candles each evening.

You are correct if you said that the word *light* is a noun in the first sentence. *Light* names a thing in sentence 1. The word *light* is a verb in the second sentence. *Light* shows an action in sentence 2.

Exercise 1

Tell whether each italicized word is a noun or a verb.

1. Many tourists *visit* the beautiful beaches of Rio de Janeiro.

2. Some people say the best time for a *visit* is February, summertime in Rio.

3. During carnival time the city is filled with music and *dance*.

4. People *dance* in the streets.

5. Many people *swim* in the ocean off Rio's beaches.

6. A *swim* can be fun, although some beaches can be crowded.

7. Some adventurous people *surf* off the beaches.

8. The *surf* off Rio is suitable for this sport.

9. Tourist brochures *highlight* the major attractions of Rio.

10. A major *highlight* is Sugarloaf Mountain.

Exercise 2

Write whether each italicized word is a noun or a verb. If the word in italics is a verb, write a new sentence using it as a noun. If the word in italics is a noun, write a new sentence using it as a verb.

1. We left our blankets in the *shade* of a beach umbrella.
2. *Cover* the food before we go swimming.
3. A long *swim* will cool us off.
4. Let's *race* to the raft.
5. Don't *cut* yourself on the rocks.
6. Sit in the shade to avoid the *heat* of the sun.
7. The *taste* of the lemonade was refreshing!
8. After lunch we'll *hike* up the dunes.
9. We'll *view* the entire beach from there.
10. We'll all be sleepy on the *ride* home.

Exercise 3

Write sentences using each word as a noun and as a verb.

1. form
2. ring
3. reach
4. view
5. surprise
6. cause
7. pull
8. dance
9. pilot

Practice Power

Imagine you are at the bottom of the sea. Do you see the stones and shells? How do the schools of fish look as they swim past you? How does the seaweed look? Write a short paragraph about your imaginary picture. Include words that are used as both nouns and verbs.

1.11 *Words Used as Nouns and Adjectives*

A **noun** names a person, place, or thing. An **adjective** describes a noun. Many words can be used as nouns or adjectives.

In this sentence the word *constellation* is a noun because it names a thing.

> Ancient people mapped each *constellation*.

In this sentence the word *constellation* is an adjective because it describes the noun *map*.

> The *constellation* map made in China was different from the map of the stars made in the West.

Tell if each italicized word in these sentences is a noun or an adjective.

> 1. Astronomers' *research* helps us learn about the stars.
> 2. *Research* scientists help us understand the universe.

You are correct if you said that the word *research* is a noun in the first sentence. It names a thing. The word *research* is an adjective in the second sentence. It describes the noun *scientists*.

Exercise 1

Tell whether each italicized word is a noun or an adjective.

1. In ancient times Aristotle made a *model* of the solar system.

2. His *model* solar system had Earth in the center.

3. The *night* sky was an object of study for Ptolemy.

4. He studied the sky at *night* and charted the stars during the first century AD.

5. Copernicus's theory of the sun as the center of the universe went against the popular *belief* system of the times.

6. In the 1500s people's *belief* was that the Earth was the center of the universe.

Exercise 2

Tell whether each italicized word is a noun or an adjective. If the word in italics is a noun, write a sentence using it as an adjective. If the word in italics is an adjective, use it as a noun.

1. A *satellite* can give astronomers a lot of information about the planetary system.

2. It is an important source of information in *space* astronomy.

3. In the 1960s and 1970s *radio* telescopes were used to observe the skies.

4. Communication *networks* are dependent upon satellites.

5. The astronomers looked at the *top* of the picture and found a cluster of stars they had never seen before.

6. We looked at an enlarged *picture* of the surface of Mars in brilliant color.

7. A *human* has walked on the moon.

8. Will there be an *alien* colony on Mars in this century?

Exercise 3

Write sentences using these words as nouns and as adjectives.

1. sound
2. winter
3. night
4. plant
5. phone
6. stop
7. top
8. picture
9. country
10. paper
11. summer
12. water

Practice Power

Write a short paragraph about a time you were outside at nighttime. What did you see? What did you hear? How did you feel? Include at least two nouns used as adjectives in your writing.

Noun Challenge

Read the selection and then answer the questions.

1. Would you rather watch a television program or listen to the radio? 2. To some people, news on the radio is dull. 3. They prefer to get a television reporter's on-the-spot remarks. 4. To many people, watching music videos on TV is the better way to listen to the latest music. 5. Some people prefer to listen to music on the radio in order to concentrate on the sound. 6. Both television and radio have advantages and disadvantages. 7. Television presents pictures to its audience. 8. Radio, the earlier invention, gives listeners only sound. 9. A radio is a more portable item, however. 10. You can be doing chores or traveling and still listen to the radio.

1. Which noun in sentence 1 is the object of a preposition?

2. Name two nouns in sentence 2 that are used as objects. Are they direct objects or objects of prepositions?

3. Name a possessive noun in sentence 3.

4. Name two plural nouns in sentence 4.

5. Name the subject of sentence 5.

6. Name four nouns in sentence 6. Which are subjects, and which are objects?

7. What is the direct object in sentence 7?

8. Which noun in sentence 7 is the object of a preposition?

9. Name the appositive in sentence 8.

10. What are the two objects in sentence 8? What type of object is each?

11. Name the subject complement in sentence 9.

12. Is *radio* used as a count or a noncount noun in sentence 9?

Pronouns

2.1 *Personal Pronouns*

A **pronoun** is a word used in place of a noun. Pronouns help avoid repetition. In the second sentence below, the pronoun *he* refers to *Richard.* The pronoun *it* refers to *station.* The word a pronoun refers to is called its **antecedent.** *Richard* is the antecedent of *he. Station* is the antecedent of *it.*

> *Richard* is going to make a weather *station.*
> *He* is going to put *it* in his garden.

Personal pronouns change form depending on **person**—who is speaking, being spoken to, or being spoken about.

They also change form depending on **number**—whether they refer to a singular or a plural antecedent.

Third person singular pronouns also change form to reflect **gender**—whether the antecedent is feminine *(she, her, hers),* masculine *(he, his, him),* or neuter *(it, its).*

PERSONAL PRONOUNS	Singular	Plural
First person (speaker)	I, me	we, us
Second person (spoken to)	you	you
Third person (spoken of)	he, she, it	they
	him, her, it	them

GENDER OF THIRD PERSON PRONOUNS	Male	Female	Neuter
Subject	he	she	it
Object	him	her	it

Exercise 1

Identify the pronoun or pronouns in each sentence. Tell whether each is first person, second person, or third person, and whether each is singular or plural.

1. We asked many questions about tornadoes.

2. For example, can they make houses explode?

3. Jason knew the answer, and he told us that tornadoes don't create a vacuum and so can't make houses explode.

4. A tornado's winds are so strong that they can make a house look as if it is exploding.

5. I thought that tornadoes were the most interesting weather phenomenon that we studied in class.

Exercise 2

Write a pronoun for the underlined word or words. Tell whether the pronoun is masculine, feminine, or neuter.

1. <u>Julia</u> told our class that waterspouts are tornadoes that pass over water.

2. <u>A tornado</u> can actually pull water out of lakes.

3. <u>The wind</u> spins more slowly than in tornadoes that travel over land.

4. <u>Harry</u> saw a waterspout over a lake in Minnesota.

5. Karen was with <u>Harry</u> and took an amazing picture!

6. Karen sent <u>the picture</u> to the newspaper.

7. <u>Mr. Riley</u> put the picture on the front page.

8. He sent <u>Karen</u> a check.

Practice Power

Write a paragraph about an outdoor activity you did with a family member or friend. When you tell what happened, use pronouns to make your writing less wordy. Then reread your paragraph and circle the pronouns you used. Indicate the person and number of each and the gender where appropriate.

2.2 Agreement of Pronouns and Antecedents

The noun to which a pronoun refers is its **antecedent.** The pronoun must agree in person and number with the noun it replaces. In the sentences below, the pronoun *they* refers to the noun antecedent *tornadoes*. Since the antecedent *tornadoes* is third person and plural, the pronoun must also be third person and plural. Therefore, *they* is the correct pronoun.

> Can *tornadoes* occur in January?
> Yes, *they* can, but most occur in April, May, and June.

A third person singular pronoun must also agree with its antecedent in gender. In the sentences below, the pronoun *it* refers to *Tornado Alley*. Because the antecedent *Tornado Alley* is a place, you need to use a pronoun that is third person singular and neuter. Therefore, *it* is the correct choice.

> *Tornado Alley* includes 10 states in the United States.
> *It* is where most of the country's tornadoes occur.

Exercise 1

Identify the antecedent of each underlined pronoun.

1. Eric told us about a tornado that <u>he</u> read about.

2. This tornado began suddenly, and <u>it</u> traveled some 600 miles.

3. People didn't know about it, so <u>they</u> didn't run for shelter.

4. The tornado lasted for three hours. <u>It</u> killed 689 people.

5. Many people in the Midwest have storm cellars. They stay in <u>them</u> for protection until a tornado is over.

Exercise 2

Identify the pronoun that goes with the underlined antecedent.

1. Last summer my brother, Dan, and I visited my <u>aunt</u>. She lives in Kansas.

2. When <u>Dan and I</u> were there, we wondered if a tornado would strike during our visit.

3. My cousin <u>Ted</u> told Dan and me that it was possible. He said they can occur at any time.

4. Ted told me to get out of the <u>car</u> if I saw a tornado, because it might be blown over by the wind.

5. My aunt told me to go to the <u>basement</u>. It is the safest place.

Exercise 3

Complete each item with a pronoun that matches the underlined antecedent. Remember to use the correct person, number, and gender.

1. My <u>brother and I</u> read about tornadoes when _____ got home.

2. We studied the <u>topic</u> because _____ is fascinating.

3. Also, we were amazed by the stories my <u>aunt</u> told about tornadoes. _____ has lived through several of them.

4. A <u>tornado</u> is the most violent of all storms. _____ usually forms under a thundercloud.

5. In the Northern Hemisphere, <u>tornadoes</u> generally twist clockwise, but in the Southern Hemisphere, _____ usually turn counterclockwise.

Practice Power

Write a pronoun that can replace each noun below. Then use each noun and pronoun pair in two related sentences.

brother	pasta	newspapers
pilots	keyboard	student
reports	bulletin board	grass

2.3 Intensive and Reflexive Pronouns

Intensive pronouns and reflexive pronouns end in *-self* or *-selves*. These pronouns must always have antecedents. They agree with their antecedents in person, number, and gender.

INTENSIVE AND REFLEXIVE PRONOUNS	Singular	Plural
First person	myself	ourselves
Second person	yourself	yourselves
Third person	himself, herself, itself	themselves

An **intensive pronoun** is used to emphasize a preceding noun or pronoun. In this sentence *myself* emphasizes its antecedent, the pronoun *I*.

I myself have read many stories about survival.

A **reflexive pronoun** is usually the object of a verb or a preposition. It generally refers to the subject of the sentence. In this sentence *himself* is used as an indirect object. Its antecedent is *Len*, the subject of the sentence.

Len bought *himself* a survival story at the bookstore.

Exercise 1

Identify the intensive pronoun in each sentence. Then identify the antecedent of each intensive pronoun.

1. The students themselves decided on the theme of survival for their current language arts project.

2. Elena chose to read *Julie of the Wolves* after she herself found a review of it.

3. After working hard to make a list of good survival books, David himself offered to share the list.

4. We heard the survivalist herself talk about her book.

Exercise 2

Identify the reflexive pronoun in each sentence. Also identify its antecedent.

1. In many books the characters have to survive by themselves—they are all alone in a difficult situation.

2. In *Hatchet* by Gary Paulsen, the main character finds himself stranded in the Canadian wilderness.

3. The young boy teaches himself skills to survive in the wilderness, such as building a fire.

4. In many of his books, Paulsen's characters find themselves in close contact with animals and nature.

5. When I read *Hatchet,* I put myself in the place of the main character and really experienced the adventure.

Exercise 3

Complete each sentence with a reflexive pronoun. The antecedent for the pronoun is underlined.

1. Jean Craighead George earned _____ many young readers with her book *Julie of the Wolves.*

2. In the book, a young Inuit girl had to teach _____ to survive alone in the cold wilderness.

3. She noticed that the wolves communicated among _____.

4. She figured out for _____ a way to communicate with them.

5. Several of us read *Julie of the Wolves,* and we felt _____ really caught up in the story.

Practice Power

Write a paragraph about a book you read in which you identified with the main character. Write about similarities and differences you share with the character. Use intensive and reflexive pronouns.

2.4 Subject Pronouns

A **subject pronoun** is used as the subject of a sentence or as a subject complement. The subject pronouns are *I, we, you, he, she, it,* and *they.* A **subject complement** follows a linking verb (such as the verb *be*) and renames the subject. In this sentence *I* is part of the compound subject complement, *Jake and I.*

> The students who got lost were *Jake and I.*

A frequent error is not using the subject form when the pronoun is part of a compound subject or subject complement. How would you correct these sentences?

> Harvey and me are looking forward to the class trip.
> The students making all the noise were Janey and her.

You are correct if you changed *me* to *I* in the first sentence. The pronoun is part of a compound subject. For the second sentence, you should change *her* to *she.* The pronoun is part of a compound subject complement.

Exercise 1

Identify the pronoun or pronouns in each sentence. Tell whether each is used as a subject or a subject complement.

1. My class and I went on a trip to the science museum.
2. We all looked forward to seeing the exhibits.
3. The person conducting the tour of the exhibits was he.
4. Have you ever prepared for a trip?
5. The students who forgot their lunches were Irene and he.
6. Vicky was eager to see the museum, and the first in line were she and Al.

Exercise 2

Choose the correct pronoun to complete each sentence.

1. (Us We) first went to the see the weather station.
2. The guide there, Mrs. Lee, showed us the computerized station, and (she her) explained its operation.

3. Sunny and (me I) were surprised to learn that many schools had such sophisticated weather stations.

4. Luis had seen a similar station, and the person chosen to make a weather prediction for our group was (he him).

5. Luis worked with Mrs. Lee, and using data from clouds and winds, (them they) predicted it was going to rain.

Exercise 3

Complete each sentence with the correct pronoun. The pronoun should agree with the underlined antecedent.

1. My <u>classmates and I</u> expected to like the museum, but _____ didn't expect to like the physics exhibit so much.

2. The <u>exhibit</u> illustrated many of the basic laws of physics, and _____ did this through hands-on activities.

3. According to the guide, the laws were discovered by <u>Isaac Newton</u>. _____ was a British scientist of the 1600s.

4. <u>Linda</u> persuaded me to try lifting the 30-pound bowling ball, and both _____ and I were able to do it.

5. The task showed the importance of the <u>pulley</u>: _____ can make lifting much easier—and the more weight, the better.

6. <u>Susan</u> played the panpipe organ, and _____ figured out that shorter pipes have higher pitches.

7. The pitch has to do with sound <u>vibrations</u>: _____ move faster in the shorter pipes.

8. The <u>teachers</u> predicted the trip would be fun, and among those having the most fun were _____.

Practice Power

Write a paragraph about any activity you did with someone else, such as a project at school. Remember to use subject pronouns correctly.

2.5 Object Pronouns

An **object pronoun** can be used as the direct object or the indirect object of a verb or as the object of a preposition. The object pronouns are *me, us, you, him, her, it,* and *them.* In this sentence *them* is the direct object of the verb *read.*

Myths are ancient stories, and people still read *them* today.

In this sentence *her* is the indirect object of the verb *showed.*

Jake showed *her* the beautifully illustrated book of myths.

In this sentence *us* is the object of the preposition *to.*

My mother explained the meaning of the story to *us.*

The sentences below show a common usage error regarding object pronouns. Which sentence is correct?

These books belong to my brother and I.
These books belong to my brother and me.

The object pronoun *me* is correct because the pronoun is the object of the preposition *to.* It is part of a compound object.

Exercise 1

Identify the object pronouns. Tell how each is used.

1. Ancient cultures have given us fascinating myths.
2. Many stories tell of gods and the relationships between them.
3. The Greeks created gods, and the Romans renamed them.
4. One story tells of Ceres, and people have retold it for centuries.
5. According to the story of Ceres and her daughter, we have changing seasons because of them.

Exercise 2

Choose the correct pronoun to complete each sentence.

1. Ceres had a daughter, and fate blessed (she her) and her daughter, Persephone.

2. Then one day the god Pluto saw the beautiful Persephone, and he boldly took her with (he him) to the underworld.

3. Pluto's chariot carried Persephone and (him he) deep into the dark underworld.

4. After Persephone's disappearance Ceres wandered the world in search of (her she).

5. Plants did not grow because Ceres neglected (them they).

6. In the underworld Persephone was unhappy; Pluto offered (her she) many things, but she only wanted to go home.

7. Ceres went to Zeus, the chief god, for help, and a long conversation between (he him) and (she her) took place.

8. In response to Ceres' plea, Zeus gave Pluto and (she her) a compromise judgment.

9. Persephone stayed with Pluto, but Zeus granted (her she) the right to spend six months of each year with her mother.

Exercise 3

Complete each sentence with the correct pronoun. The pronoun should agree with the underlined antecedent.

1. This story explains why there are <u>seasons</u>; Persephone causes _____ by her presence or absence.

2. <u>We</u> owe this classic story to the Greeks and Romans. They gave _____ this explanation for the change in seasons.

3. When <u>I</u> was younger, my parents read this story to my sister, my brother, and _____.

4. My little <u>brother</u> loved the story, but the part with the chariot always frightened _____ and my little sister.

Practice Power

Write a short letter to a friend. Tell him or her about one of your favorite books and why he or she should read it. When you are finished circle all of the object pronouns you used.

2.6 *Possessive Pronouns and Adjectives*

A **possessive pronoun** shows possession or ownership. It takes the place of a possessive noun. Unlike possessive nouns, possessive pronouns do not contain apostrophes.

> This skateboard is *Lucy's*. (possessive noun)
> This skateboard is *hers*. (possessive pronoun)

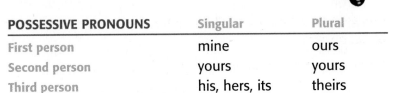

POSSESSIVE PRONOUNS	Singular	Plural
First person	mine	ours
Second person	yours	yours
Third person	his, hers, its	theirs

Words similar to possessive pronouns are **possessive adjectives.** The possessive adjectives are *my, our, your, his, her, its,* and *their.* Don't confuse possessive pronouns with possessive adjectives. Possessive pronouns stand alone. Possessive adjectives always precede nouns.

Possessive Pronouns	Possessive Adjectives
Mine was lost.	*My* scooter was lost.
His is missing.	*His* scooter is missing.

Exercise 1

Identify each possessive pronoun and adjective and tell its person.

1. After the summer storm our task was cleaning the yard.

2. Some of the neighbors' things had blown into our yard.

3. That gardening shovel is theirs.

4. Those orange pots are ours.

5. Mom wears her gloves when she gardens.

6. Those gray gloves under the bench are hers.

7. Is the T-shirt on that bush yours?

Exercise 2

Complete each sentence with a possessive pronoun. The underlined word or words are the antecedent.

1. My <u>sister and I</u> cleaned the basement. That chore was _____.

2. <u>Dad</u> used those old skis. They're _____.

3. <u>Lucy</u> wore this green jacket. It was _____, but throw it out.

4. <u>Jake</u> played with those toy cars. They were _____.

5. <u>I</u> read these books a long time ago. They're _____, and I want to keep them.

6. Do <u>you</u> want these old shoes? They're _____.

7. That old cabinet came from <u>grandmother and grandfather</u>. It was _____. We can't part with it.

8. <u>We</u> used to play these board games. They're _____.

Exercise 3

Rewrite the sentences to correct the use of possessive pronouns and possessive adjectives. Not all sentences have errors.

1. We worked all day to sort ours things in the basement.

2. We wanted to discard the big worn boots, but Dad said that they were his.

3. Mom and Dad said that the big vase had been theirs' for a long time. It was their wedding present from Aunt Sophie.

4. When we saw the old bikes, my sister and I shouted, "Those were ours'. Please keep them."

5. She stored her's in the garage.

Practice Power

Write six sentences of your own about things in your home. Use one of these words in each sentence: *mine, ours, yours, theirs, his,* and *hers.*

2.7 Pronouns in Contractions

Pronouns can be joined with some verbs to form **contractions.** An apostrophe replaces the missing letter or letters in a contraction. In this sentence *They're* is a contraction for *They are.*

Earthquakes occur around the world.
They're often terrifying events.

Pronoun Contractions

I'm = I am	I've = I have
I'll = I will *or* I shall	you're = you are
you've = you have	you'll = you will *or* you shall
he's = he is *or* he has	he'll = he will *or* he shall
she's = she is *or* she has	she'll = she will *or* she shall
it's = it is *or* it has	it'll = it will *or* it shall
we're = we are	we've = we have
we'll = we will *or* we shall	they're = they are
they've = they have	they'll = they will *or* they shall

Possessive adjectives are often confused with contractions. Remember that possessive adjectives express possession. They do not contain apostrophes.

They're studying earthquakes. (contraction—*they are*)
Their topic of study is earthquakes. (possessive adjective)

Exercise 1

Identify the contraction in each item. Tell the pronoun and the verb that form each contraction.

1. Thousands of earthquakes occur every day. They're numerous, but most do not cause damage.

2. Some animals seem to sense the coming of an earthquake. They'll run around in confusion before one actually occurs.

3. You're supposed to stand in a doorway or crouch under a table during an earthquake.

4. Tremors called aftershocks occur immediately after the earthquake is over. They've also been known to occur several weeks or months afterwards.

5. I've read that the movement of an earthquake across the ground looks like waves on an ocean.

6. We've all seen pictures of collapsed buildings and bridges that show the frightening force of earthquakes.

7. Charles Richter devised a way to measure the strength of an earthquake. He's famous for this tool—the seismograph.

8. The Modified Mercalli Intensity Scale measures the amount of shaking. It's been used since 1902 to show how an earthquake affects buildings, bridges, and people.

Exercise 2

Rewrite the sentences to correct the use of contractions and possessive adjectives. Not all sentences have errors.

1. Tidal waves are caused by earthquakes, not tides, and so their name is misleading.

2. Their scientific name is actually *tsunami.*

3. The tsunami gets it's name from the Japanese words for *harbor* and *wave.*

4. Tsunamis can be huge. They're as high as a hundred feet.

5. They're damage can be incredible.

6. I did not know that you're report was also on tsunamis.

Practice Power

Write five sentences, each using a set of two words that can go together to form one of the contractions studied in this section. Exchange your sentences with a partner and rewrite the sentences, using contractions where you can.

2.8 *Demonstrative Pronouns*

Demonstrative pronouns are used to point out things, places, and people. Use *this* and *these* to point out things that are near. Use *that* and *those* to point out things that are farther away.

> *This* is my new sleeping bag.
> *That* is your old sleeping bag.
> *These* are the things for my emergency survival kit.
> *Those* are the instructions for the survival kit in your home.

Read these sentences. Which clothes are more likely to be nearer the speaker?

> *These* are my clean clothes. *Those* are my dirty clothes.

You are correct if you said the clean clothes. *These* usually is used to indicate things that are nearer the speaker.

Exercise 1

Write the demonstrative pronoun that can replace each noun. Use the directions in parentheses to tell whether *this, that, these,* or *those* should be used.

1. papers (near)
2. cars (far)
3. tree (near)
4. flowers (near)
5. book (far)
6. bags (near)
7. present (far)

8. calendar (far)
9. students (far)
10. apples (near)
11. gift (near)
12. key (far)
13. glasses (far)
14. CDs (near)

Exercise 2

Identify the demonstrative pronoun. Tell whether it is singular or plural and whether it refers to something near or far.

1. These are the items we need for our survival kits.
2. Whose radio is this? Does it work?

3. Those are old batteries. Don't use them.

4. The box of bandages on the table is empty. Take these.

5. Is that the broken flashlight?

6. Which box has candles? This has canned food in it.

7. These are the best matches to have in a survival kit.

8. Is this the sleeping bag with a hole in it?

9. Can you open cans with that?

10. Whose boxes of dried fruit are these?

Exercise 3

Complete each item with a demonstrative pronoun. Check to see if you need a singular or plural pronoun. Use the instructions in parentheses to tell whether *this, that, these,* or *those* should be used.

1. Whose backpack is _____? (far)

2. _____ are the flashlights I bought. They are long-lasting. (near)

3. _____ is the right kind of canned food for a home survival kit. You need food you don't have to cook. (far)

4. Whose water packets are _____? (near)

5. The batteries on the table are old. Use _____. (near)

6. _____ are my boxes of juice. (far)

7. Whose blanket is _____? (near)

8. _____ is my poncho. (far)

Practice Power

Write a dialogue between a parent and a son or daughter. The pair is packing things for a picnic. They don't always agree on what to take. Use demonstrative pronouns to indicate items.

2.9 *Interrogative Pronouns*

An **interrogative pronoun** is used to ask a question. The interrogative pronouns are *who, whom, whose, what,* and *which.*

The interrogative pronoun *who* is used when the pronoun refers to a person. It is the subject of a question.

> *Who* is the main character in *The Wizard of Oz?*

The interrogative pronoun *whom* is used when the pronoun refers to a person. It is always used as a direct object, an indirect object, or an object of a preposition. The interrogative pronoun *whose* is used in speaking of persons. It is used to ask about ownership.

> To *whom* did Dorothy go for help?
> *Whose* is this copy of the novel?

The interrogative pronoun *what* is used in speaking of things and in asking for information. *Which* is used in asking about persons or things.

> *What* are you reading?
> *Which* of the characters was the most interesting?

One common error is to use *who* instead of *whom.* Which of the following sentences is not correct?

> Who went to the Emerald City?
> Who did Dorothy see at the Emerald City?

The second sentence is not correct. The interrogative pronoun *whom* should be used because interrogative word is the direct object of the sentence. In the first sentence *who* is used correctly as the subject.

Exercise 1

Complete each sentence with an interrogative pronoun. Tell whether it refers to a person or a thing.

1. _____ wrote the book *The Wizard of Oz?*
2. _____ of the states did Dorothy live in?

3. _____ hit Dorothy's farmhouse?

4. _____ was the dog, Toto?

5. _____ did Dorothy meet on her journey?

Exercise 2

Complete each sentence with one of the following interrogative pronouns—*who, which,* or *what.*

1. _____ was Dorothy's wish?

2. _____ wanted a heart in the book?

3. _____ of the characters wanted courage?

4. _____ did the scarecrow want?

5. _____ was the name of the magical city in the book?

Exercise 3

Complete each of the following sentences with one of the following interrogative pronouns—*who, whom,* or *whose.*

1. _____ has read the novel *The Wizard of Oz?*

2. By _____ was the novel written?

3. _____ is your favorite character in the novel?

4. To _____ would you recommend the novel?

5. _____ are the illustrations in your copy of the book?

Practice Power

Write at least six questions of your own with interrogative pronouns. Ask about something you have studied in class—a book, a science topic, a famous person. When you are finished, share your questions with a classmate and try to answer each other's questions.

2.10 *Indefinite Pronouns*

An indefinite pronoun refers to any or all of a group of persons, places, or things. Most indefinite pronouns are singular but some are plural. A few indefinite pronouns may be singular or plural.

Singular		Plural	Singular or Plural
another	neither	both	all
anybody	nobody	few	any
anyone	no one	many	more
anything	nothing	others	most
each	one	several	none
either	other		some
everybody	somebody		
everyone	someone		
everything	something		
much			

Everyone needs to do a project for the weather unit. (singular)
All are going to work in small groups. (plural)

Anything related to weather is an acceptable topic. (singular)
Many are making weather stations. (plural)

All of the students are working on a project. (plural)
All of our project is completed. (singular)

Exercise 1

Identify the indefinite pronoun in each sentence. Tell whether it is singular or plural.

1. We found that we could make all of the weather instruments ourselves.

2. Each of us was responsible for getting materials.

3. Many of the materials were simple things that we already had, like cups and straws.

4. There was nothing but thermometers that we had to buy.

5. All of us were eager to make the instruments and to start taking weather measurements.

Exercise 2

Rewrite each sentence, adding an indefinite pronoun. You can use information that is true for you. Use the correct verb: the first verb choice is singular in form and goes with singular indefinite pronouns; the second one is plural in form and goes with plural indefinite pronouns.

1. _____ of my family members listens/listen to forecasts.

2. _____ of my friends is/are interested in the weather.

3. _____ complains/complain about the weather.

4. _____ I know talks/talk about the weather.

5. _____ of my friends likes/like snow.

6. _____ of my friends prefers/prefer summer to winter.

7. _____ of my friends prefers/prefer winter to summer.

8. _____ of my classmates takes/take vacations in the summer.

9. _____ of my classmates takes/take vacations in the winter.

10. _____ of my friends has/have ever experienced an earthquake.

11. _____ I know has/have experienced a tornado.

12. _____ of my family members has/have seen a hurricane.

Practice Power

Write a paragraph about an experience your class has had together. You might want to write about a class trip, a class project, or a class play. Refer to groups of people, places, or things by using indefinite pronouns. When you are finished, go back and circle all the indefinite pronouns you used.

2.11 *Indefinite Pronouns and Double Negatives*

Indefinite pronouns such as *no one, nobody, none,* and *nothing* are negative words. In a sentence they should never be used with other negative words, such as *no, not,* and *never.* Combining two negatives in a sentence is an error called a double negative.

Incorrect	Correct
No one don't come to the meeting.	*No one* comes to the meeting.
Nobody brought no refreshments.	*Nobody* brought any refreshments.
Never tell *nobody* your secret.	*Never* tell anybody your secret.

Exercise 1

Choose the correct indefinite pronoun to complete the sentence.

1. There wasn't (nothing anything) to do on the day of the blizzard when we were off school.

2. (Nobody Anybody) was able to go out because the streets were covered with snow.

3. There wasn't (anything nothing) to do that interested me.

4. There was (anything nothing) good on television.

5. (No one Anyone) could find our latest DVD.

6. I couldn't find (anything nothing) I wanted to read.

Exercise 2

Complete each sentence with *no one, nothing, anyone,* or *anything.* Make sure to avoid double negatives.

1. Suddenly the electricity went out, and, of course, _____ electrical in the house worked.

2. "I can't see _____ in the dark," my sister shouted.

3. "Doesn't _____ know where the candles are?" asked Mom.

4. "There's _____ in the kitchen drawer," answered my brother, who eventually found the candles elsewhere.

5. "Now there's really _____ to do," I said.

6. "Since there isn't _____ electrical we can use, let's play a board game," said Mom.

7. However, _____ could find the games.

8. "Isn't _____ where it should be in this house?" complained Dad before we found the games.

9. I decided there's _____ more fun than playing board games by candlelight on a snowy day.

10. _____ wanted to stop when the electricity came back on.

Exercise 3

Rewrite the sentences to correct the use of negatives and indefinite pronouns. Not all the sentences have errors.

1. There isn't nothing we can do about the weather.

2. There was nothing in the forecast about snow.

3. We didn't have nothing warm to wear in the bitter cold.

4. We didn't hear anything on the radio about storms.

5. We can't do nothing until the rain stops.

Practice Power

Write a description of a strange and different world for a science fiction story. Mention things that this world doesn't have that you would expect to find on earth. When you finish, look for indefinite pronouns and check whether you have avoided double negatives.

Pronoun Challenge

Read the selection, and then answer the questions.

1. Helen Keller was less than two years old when she was afflicted by a serious disease. 2. It left her unable to see or hear. 3. For the next five years she wasn't able to speak. 4. She was a frightened and bewildered child who couldn't understand the strange silence around her. 5. Hers was a lonely world. 6. Who could help her and communicate with her? 7. Helen's life began to change when Anne Sullivan became her teacher. 8. Anne worked to teach Helen correct social behavior and manners as well as language, and they spent their days together. 9. Soon Helen learned to understand the names of objects spelled out on her hand. 10. A whole new world opened up for her. 11. Helen's life shows that immense difficulties can be overcome. 12. Few have had to face such enormous obstacles. 13. Helen herself enjoyed a brilliant career helping those with physical disabilities.

1. Name the pronouns in sentences 1 and 2. Give the person, number, and gender of each.

2. What is the antecedent of the pronoun *she* in sentence 1?

3. What is the antecedent of the pronoun *It* in sentence 2?

4. What pronoun is the subject of sentence 3?

5. How is the pronoun *She* in sentence 4 used? How is the pronoun *her* in sentence 4 used?

6. Give the person and number of the pronoun *they* in sentence 8. Name its antecedents.

7. Identify the pronoun in sentence 10. How is it used?

8. Name the indefinite pronoun in the paragraph. What sentence is it in?

9. Name the intensive pronoun in the paragraph. What sentence is it in?

10. Name the interrogative pronoun in the paragraph. What sentence is it in?

11. Name the possessive pronoun in the paragraph. What sentence is it in?

Adjectives

3.1 Descriptive Adjectives

Adjectives describe nouns. Some descriptive adjectives tell about age, size, shape, color, or origin. Other descriptive adjectives describe additional qualities. In this sentence the adjective *beautiful* describes the noun *flowers*.

> Orchids are *beautiful* flowers.

In the following sentences, what does each italicized adjective tell about the noun it describes?

> Many orchids have *pink* petals.
> Some orchids have *pointy* petals.
> Some *tiny* orchids are no bigger than my fingernail.
> *Young* plants do not produce orchids.
> *North American* orchids grow in swamps, forests, and meadows.

Pink describes color; *pointy*, shape; *tiny*, size; *young*, age; and *North American*, origin.

Exercise 1

Identify the adjectives in each sentence. Identify the noun each one describes.

1. Orchids come from a large family: there are thousands of varieties.

2. Orchids grow in tropical forests.

3. Some grow in moderate climates.

4. Arctic orchids actually grow on the tundra.

5. Generally, orchids grow in moist places.

6. Did you know that there are no black orchids?

7. Orchids are not poisonous plants.

8. A lot of orchids have fragrant scents.

9. Orchids are a popular item among florists.

10. The delicate blossoms are favorite decorations for homes.

Exercise 2

Complete each sentence with the correct adjective. Use the clue in parentheses for help. Use each adjective only once.

Asian   mature   tall   triangular   yellow

1. Orchids can look quite different: one type has a large _____ petal to attract insects. (shape)

2. Some orchids have _____ petals. (color)

3. Some _____ orchid plants grow up to 100 feet high. (size)

4. Buy a _____ plant if you want your orchid to bloom quickly. (age)

5. Some _____ recipes use petals from orchids as an ingredient. (origin)

Exercise 3

1. **Use the following descriptive adjectives in sentences of your own.**

   careful   fast   generous   colorful
   brilliant   thoughtful   enormous   modern

2. **Use an appropriate descriptive adjective with each of these nouns.**

   sunset   flower   friend   trip
   book   popcorn   puppy   path

Practice Power

Think of three items you use that were made in another country. Think of at least two descriptive adjectives for each item. Write three sentences in which you use the adjectives to describe the items.

3.2 *Definite and Indefinite Articles*

Articles are a type of adjective. There are two types of articles: definite and indefinite. The word *the* is the only **definite article.** It refers to a specific item or specific items in a group. *The* may be used with either singular or plural nouns.

> I saw *the* whale area at the Metropolitan Aquarium.
>   (specific place—the whale area)
> *The* whales there were rather small.
>   (specific whales—those at the aquarium)

The **indefinite articles** are *a* and *an.* They are used to refer to a single member of a general group. They are used only with singular nouns. The article *an* is used before a vowel sound. The article *a* is used before a consonant sound.

> When I see *a* jellyfish, I am usually startled.
> I saw *an* octopus at the aquarium.

If two or more related nouns appear in one sentence, use an article for each one.

> I saw *a* small jellyfish and *a* large jellyfish.
> *The* bigger jellyfish swam faster than *the* smaller jellyfish.

Exercise 1

Write the correct indefinite article before each noun.

1. ___ umbrella	**5.** ___ zoo	**9.** ___ iceberg
2. ___ guide	**6.** ___ gift	**10.** ___ hour
3. ___ ocean	**7.** ___ human	**11.** ___ egg
4. ___ application	**8.** ___ employee	**12.** ___ swimmer

Exercise 2

Identify the articles in each sentence and tell whether each is a definite article or an indefinite article.

1. Large public aquariums are wonderful places where you can learn about sea animals and the oceans.

2. Many aquariums try to re-create the actual environment in which the sea animals live.

3. An aquarium, for example, may have a tiny coral reef.

4. Some have an oceanarium, which displays large marine mammals such as dolphins and even whales.

5. Of course, the word *aquarium* also refers to little aquariums—like the aquarium you might have in your home.

Exercise 3

Complete each sentence with definite and indefinite articles. Use the directions in parentheses: *D* means to use a definite article; *I* means to use an indefinite article.

1. My family went on _____ (I) trip to _____ (I) aquarium.

2. Our first stop was _____ (I) tank with stingrays and small sharks.

3. _____ (D) stingrays with their flat, wide bodies floated through _____ (D) tank like kites floating in the sky.

4. _____ (I) favorite at _____ (D) aquarium is _____ (I) Pacific octopus, which has thousands of tiny suction cups in its eight arms.

5. We actually saw _____ (D) octopus capture _____ (I) crab.

6. We learned that the octopus is _____ (I) invertebrate—that's _____ (I) animal without _____ (I) skeleton or _____ (I) backbone.

7. Jellyfish are _____ (I) attraction at _____ (D) aquarium, delighting visitors with their odd shapes and varied colors.

Practice Power

Write about your favorite animal. Tell what it eats. Talk about its size, shape, color, and origin. When you are finished, go back and circle each definite and indefinite article.

3.3 *Numerical Adjectives*

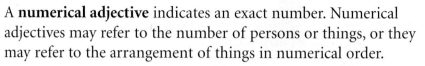

A **numerical adjective** indicates an exact number. Numerical adjectives may refer to the number of persons or things, or they may refer to the arrangement of things in numerical order.

I have *one* sandwich and *two* cookies in my lunch bag.
The *first* day of the week is Sunday.

Exercise 1

Find the numerical adjectives in these sentences. Tell which noun each adjective modifies.

1. I've heard the story of the three little pigs a thousand times.

2. The first pig built a house of straw.

3. Ten bales of straw were needed to build the house.

4. The second pig built a house of sticks.

5. That pig used 16 bundles of sticks.

6. The third pig built a house of bricks.

7. That house was made of three wheelbarrow loads of bricks.

8. It had four sturdy walls and a stout roof.

9. A wolf blew the first house down with three puffs.

10. He blew the second house down with five puffs.

11. No amount of puffing could blow down the third pig's house.

12. After ten attempts, the wolf ran away.

Exercise 2

Choose the correct numerical adjective for each sentence.

1. The (one first) moon landing occurred on July 20, 1969.

2. (Six Sixth) hours after the landing, Neil Armstrong stepped onto the moon's surface.

3. He said, "That's (one first) small step for a man, (one first) giant leap for mankind."

4. The lunar module consisted of (two second) parts.

5. The (first one), or descent, stage had (four fourth) legs and a ladder for climbing down to the moon's surface.

6. The (second two), or ascent stage, carried the crew back to the command service module.

7. The command service module also had (second two) parts, the command module and the service module.

8. The (third- three-) man crew rode in the command module.

9. The crew spent more than (twenty-one twenty-first) hours on the surface of the moon.

10. They picked up (forty-six forty-sixth) pounds of lunar rocks.

11. The (two second) lunar landing took place on November 19, 1969.

12. Its lunar module landed about (182 182nd) meters from a robot spacecraft that had touched down more than (second two) years earlier.

13. The (third three) lunar mission, launched on April 11, 1970, nearly ended in tragedy.

14. About (three hundred thousand three hundred thousandth) kilometers from Earth, an oxygen tank exploded, and the command module was disabled.

15. The (three third) astronauts spent (fourth four) cold, frightening days returning to Earth without ever having landed on the moon.

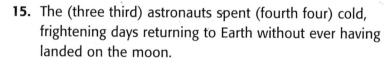

Practice Power

Write two or three sentences about a trip you took to a grocery store. Use four indefinite articles in your sentences. Then rewrite the sentences using numerical adjectives.

3.4 Adjectives as Subject Complements

An adjective usually comes before a noun. An adjective that follows a linking verb and describes or explains the subject is called a **subject complement** or a **predicate adjective.**

> *Hawaiian* waters can harbor the Portuguese man-of-war.
>   (adjective before a noun)
> Some people are *allergic* to its poison.
>   (subject complement)

In this sentence the adjective *dangerous* is a subject complement. It follows the linking verb *are* and describes the subject *animals.*

> Some sea animals are *dangerous.*

The most common linking verbs are *appear, be, become, feel, grow, look, remain, seem, smell, sound, stay,* and *taste.* Can you identify the subject complement and the subject it describes in this sentence?

> Hawaiian waters seem safe.

The subject complement is *safe.* It describes the subject *waters.* The linking verb is *seem.*

Exercise 1

Identify the subject complement in each sentence. Then identify the noun it describes.

1. The state of Hawaii is comparatively small.

2. Its islands are beautiful.

3. Hawaiian vegetation is lush.

4. The temperature there is mild all year round.

5. Its weather is usually sunny.

6. The tourist industry is large.

7. Its inhabitants seem friendly to visitors.

8. The visitors seem happy when they leave.

Exercise 2

Identify the descriptive adjective in each sentence. Tell whether it comes before the noun or is a subject complement.

1. Dan and Jay swam daily in Hawaiian waters.
2. There had been a heavy storm the night before.
3. Now the waves looked placid.
4. Dan saw a violet object near him in the water.
5. The boys remained calm.
6. They had seen a large man-of-war.
7. The boys knew about the powerful sting of a man-of-war.
8. The sting can be painful.
9. The sting of a man-of-war can cause severe reactions.
10. Few stings are fatal, however.

Exercise 3

Add adjectives to complete the sentences. Tell whether each adjective comes before the noun or is a subject complement.

1. The waters of Hawaii are _____.
2. Swimmers enjoy the _____ beaches.
3. Hawaii is _____ even in the winter!
4. The _____ climate brings many tourists.
5. Everyone seems to enjoy the _____ seafood.

Practice Power

Write two sentences for each of the following adjectives. In one sentence, use the adjective before a noun. In the other, use the adjective as a subject complement.

1. delicious
2. warm
3. dangerous
4. beautiful

3.5 Comparative and Superlative Adjectives

Most adjectives have three degrees of comparison: positive, comparative, and superlative. The **positive degree** describes a quality or characteristic. The **comparative degree** is used to compare two items or two sets of items. It is formed with *-er, more,* or *less.* The **superlative degree** is used to compare three or more items. It is formed with *-est, most,* or *least.*

> Elephants are *large* animals. (positive)
> Whales are *larger* than elephants. (comparative)
> Whales are the *largest* mammals. (superlative)

For most adjectives of one syllable and some adjectives of two syllables (generally those ending in *y*), add *-er* to the positive form to get the comparative form, and add *-est* to the positive to get the superlative form. If an adjective ends in *-e,* just add *-r* or *-st.* If an adjective ends in *-y* and is preceded by a consonant, change the *-y* to *-i* before adding *-er* or *-est.* If a single-syllable adjective ends in a consonant preceded by a vowel, double the consonant.

Positive	Comparative	Superlative
narrow	narrower	narrowest
tame	tamer	tamest
funny	funnier	funniest
hot	hotter	hottest

For adjectives of three or more syllables and many adjectives of two syllables, form the comparative by using *more* or *less* with the positive, and form the superlative by using *most* or *least.*

Positive	Comparative	Superlative
courteous	more courteous	most courteous
careful	less careful	least careful

Certain adjectives have irregular comparisons.

Positive	Comparative	Superlative
good	better	best
bad	worse	worst

Exercise 1

Give the comparative and superlative form for each adjective. If you are unsure of a form, check a dictionary.

1. famous   **4.** late   **7.** curious   **10.** gentle

2. noisy   **5.** wet   **8.** good   **11.** careless

3. reliable   **6.** courageous   **9.** harmful   **12.** sensitive

Exercise 2

Complete each sentence with the adjective in parentheses in the form indicated.

1. Australia is the _____ continent. (small—superlative)

2. It has some of the _____ animals in the world. (unusual—superlative)

3. Flightless birds—the emu and the cassowary—are some of Australia's _____ creatures. (strange—superlative)

4. The cassowary is actually _____ than the emu. (large—comparative)

5. In fact, both birds are _____ than most humans. (big—comparative)

6. The platypus and echidna are among Australia's _____ animals—the only mammals that lay eggs. (odd—superlative)

7. Australia's taipan and tiger snake are _____ than most other snakes in the world. (deadly—comparative)

8. The black swan is one of the _____ animals, and it is found only in Australia. (rare—superlative)

9. The blue-tongued lizard has a _____ tail that will regrow if broken. (short—positive)

Practice Power

Compare your favorite animal to two other animals. Use comparative and superlative adjectives in your writing.

3.6 More Comparative and Superlative Adjectives

The **positive degree** of an adjective shows a quality of a noun or pronoun. It is the basic form of the adjective. The **comparative degree** is used to compare two items or two sets of items. This form is often followed by *than*. The **superlative degree** is used to compare three or more items.

An emu is *tall*.
A cassowary is *taller* than an emu.
An ostrich is the *tallest* bird of all.

Be careful not to mix forms. How would you correct this sentence?

The ostrich is one of the most strangest animals.

You are correct if you changed the sentence to *The ostrich is one of the strangest animals.* The use of *most* with *-est* is incorrect.

Exercise 1

Choose the correct adjective form to complete each sentence.

1. The ostrich is the (larger largest) flightless bird in the world; it grows to eight feet tall.

2. The extinct moas of New Zealand were the only birds (taller tallest) than the ostrich; they grew to 10 feet.

3. The only birds (heavier heaviest) than the ostrich were the extinct elephant birds of Madagascar.

4. Ostriches are the (faster fastest) two-legged animal; they can run up to 45 miles an hour.

5. The ostrich has keen eyesight—with eyes actually (bigger biggest) than its brain.

6. The ostrich produces the (more gigantic most gigantic) egg of all animals: it is comparable to 24 chicken eggs.

7. May thinks ostriches are ugly—(uglier ugliest) even than bats.

8. I think, in fact, that they are one of the (cuter cutest) animals.

Exercise 2

Use either the comparative or the superlative form of the adjective in parentheses to complete each sentence.

1. Today the _____ (valuable) part of the ostrich is the skin, which is used for making fine leather products.

2. Ostrich skin makes the _____ (strong) of all leathers.

3. However, ostrich meat is becoming _____ (popular) every day—it is on the menu of an increasing number of restaurants.

4. It is a red meat, but it is _____ (low) in fat than beef.

5. It may be a _____ (healthful) meal than beef or chicken.

6. Some people say that it is _____ (delicious) than they expected.

Exercise 3

Rewrite the sentences to correct any errors in the use of comparative or superlative adjectives. Not all the sentences have errors.

1. I had one of the most weirdest experiences of my life yesterday: I went to an ostrich farm.

2. The animals were even huger than I expected.

3. The excitingest part was feeding the large birds.

4. The farm shop sold ostrich feathers, and these light, airy feathers were more beautifuler than I had imagined.

5. I ate an ostrich burger, and it was the tastier burger I've ever had.

Practice Power

Write sentences using each of the following adjectives.

1. sweetest
2. more exciting
3. most useful
4. most surprising
5. more interesting
6. shorter

3.7 Little, Less, Least *and* Few, Fewer, Fewest

Count nouns name things that can be counted: *birds, trees, naturalists.* They have plural forms ending in *-s.* **Noncount nouns** name things that cannot be counted: *water, food, patience.* They do not have plural forms ending in *-s.*

Use *little, less, least* and *few, fewer, fewest* to make comparisons. Use *little, less,* and *least* before singular or noncount nouns. Use *few, fewer,* and *fewest* before plural count nouns.

> *Few* animals can survive in a city.
> There are *fewer* kinds of animals today than in the past.
> The *fewest* efforts are put into their protection.

> Some people pay *little* attention to natural environments.
> There is *less* space for animals as people take over more.
> The *least* amount of concern is paid to common animals.

Exercise 1

Write phrases with each noun using *least* or *fewest.*

1. attention
2. legs
3. creatures
4. trouble
5. information
6. vegetarians
7. meat
8. farms
9. oxygen
10. plants
11. tourists
12. juice
13. cookies
14. rain
15. phone calls
16. teachers

Exercise 2

Choose *less* or *fewer* to complete each sentence.

1. There are (fewer less) species of animals today than there were 20 years ago.

2. There are (fewer less) koalas in Australia now.

3. Koalas live in eucalyptus trees, and housing developments have left (fewer less) eucalyptus trees.

4. Koalas prefer to eat eucalyptus leaves, so now there is (fewer less) food for them to eat.

5. Koalas drink (fewer, less) water than other animals do.

6. They take (fewer less) drinks a day because they get most of their water in the eucalyptus leaves that they eat.

7. Koalas spend (less fewer) time awake than they spend sleeping.

8. Koalas spend (fewer less) hours awake during the day than they do at night.

9. A koala group's home has numerous home range trees, but (less fewer) food trees.

Exercise 3

Choose *fewer* or *less* to complete the sentences.

1. People in our city work to ensure that there will be _____ animals on the endangered list.

2. We are using _____ land so that animals can keep their natural habitats.

3. New development now takes _____ space.

4. People use _____ pesticides.

5. They also use _____ fertilizers.

6. The reductions in the use of these substances means _____ pollution.

7. These changes should result in _____ loss in the number of animals and the number of animal species.

Practice Power

Choose an endangered animal species. Write at least five sentences about the life of these animals. Be sure to compare how life is different for them today than it was in the past. Use *less* and *fewer* in your sentences. You can use the library, encyclopedias, or the Internet as resources.

3.8 *Demonstrative Adjectives*

A **demonstrative adjective** points out the thing it refers to. The demonstrative adjectives are *this, that, these,* and *those.* They always precede the nouns they modify.

This and *that* point out one person, place, or thing. *These* and *those* point out more than one person, place, or thing.

This and *these* point out things or people that are near. *That* and *those* point out things or people that are far.

Note that demonstratives agree in number with the noun they directly precede. *This* and *that* are used with noncount nouns.

> *this* box of food   *these* boxes of food
>
> *that* cereal

Demonstrative adjectives are similar to and are often confused with demonstrative pronouns. Remember that a demonstrative adjective goes with a noun, but a demonstrative pronoun is used alone.

> *Those* books are mine. (adjective)
> *These* are yours. (pronoun)

Exercise 1

Put the correct demonstrative adjective before each of the following nouns, which name things near at hand.

1. _____ pets
2. _____ birdseed
3. _____ parrots
4. _____ kinds of pets
5. _____ color parakeet
6. _____ collar

Put the correct demonstrative adjective before each of the nouns, which name objects far away.

7. _____ brands of pet food
8. _____ leashes
9. _____ kind of dog
10. _____ instructions
11. _____ behavior
12. _____ snakes

Exercise 2

Identify the demonstrative adjective in each sentence. Tell whether it is singular, plural, or noncount and tell the noun it goes with.

1. It is going to be fun to take care of these hamsters.

2. This corner is not a good place for the cage: it's too sunny.

3. This sawdust is for the bottom of the cage.

Exercise 3

Choose the correct word to complete each sentence.

1. (This These) bag of food was prepared for hamsters.

2. (Them Those) sunflower seeds are a treat for them.

3. You can feed them (that those) pieces of fruit—but don't feed them fruit too often.

4. Put (this those) water bottle in their cage.

5. (These Them) hamsters are mostly small, but some are large.

Exercise 4

Complete each sentence with the correct demonstrative adjective. Use the directions in parentheses.

1. All of _____ (near) equipment is for my new gerbils.

2. _____ (near) wheel is for the gerbils to run on.

3. _____ (far) tubes are for the gerbils to run through.

4. _____ (far) sand is for the gerbils to roll in to clean their coats.

5. The gerbils use _____ (near) little pieces of wood to gnaw on.

Practice Power

Write several sentences describing things in your classroom. Include demonstrative adjectives in your sentences.

3.9 Interrogative Adjectives

An **interrogative adjective** is used in asking a question. The interrogative adjectives are *which, what,* and *whose.* They precede nouns.

Which asks about one or more of a specific set of persons or things. In this sentence *which* asks about a single butterfly of three colors.

> *Which* butterfly is green, gold, and black?

What is used for asking about people or things but is not limited to a specific group or set.

> *What* animals should we have in our classroom?

Whose asks about possession.

> *Whose* snake escaped and was loose in school?

Can you identify the interrogative adjective in this question and the noun it goes with?

> Which snake is easiest to take care of?

You are correct if you said that *which* is the interrogative adjective and that *snake* is the noun it goes with.

Exercise 1

Identify the interrogative adjective in each sentence. Then identify the noun it goes with.

1. Whose chore is it to take care of the lizards?

2. What food do these particular lizards prefer?

3. What country did these lizards come from?

4. Whose lizards are these?

5. Which lizards make good pets?

6. Which members of the lizard family are poisonous?

7. What defenses do lizards have besides camouflage?

8. What predators hunt lizards?

Exercise 2

Complete each sentence with the correct interrogative adjective. More than one choice may be correct.

1. _____ rain forest animals are your favorites?
2. _____ favorite animal is the monkey?
3. _____ layer of the rain forest do monkeys live in?
4. _____ flowers bloom on the emergent layer?
5. _____ habitat is on the forest floor?
6. _____ animals crawl on the forest floor?
7. _____ lizards live in the understory?
8. _____ birds fly through the canopy?
9. _____ plants grow around the trees?
10. _____ home is in the understory?
11. _____ colors are macaws?
12. _____ area of the world does the capybara live in?
13. _____ protection does the frilled lizard have?
14. _____ kind of animal is most numerous in the rain forest?
15. _____ rain forest species are in danger of extinction?
16. _____ actions lead to the destruction of rain forests?
17. _____ countries have large rain forests?
18. _____ products do the rain forests provide humans?
19. _____ malaria medicine comes from a tree?
20. _____ work is aimed at protecting the rain forests?

Practice Power

Find a classmate who likes the same animal that you like. Then write questions using interrogative adjectives so you can quiz each other. Use encyclopedias, books, and the Internet to research. Who got more correct answers?

3.10 Indefinite Adjectives

Indefinite adjectives refer to all or any of a group of persons, places, or things. They precede nouns. These are some of the most common indefinite adjectives: *all, any, both, each, either, every, few, many, most, neither, no, other, several,* and *some.*

> *Several* species belong to the group named crocodilians.

Indefinite adjectives are similar to and are often confused with indefinite pronouns. Remember that an indefinite adjective goes with a noun. In this sentence *some* is an indefinite adjective because it goes with the noun *people.*

> *Some* people would like to visit Australia.

In this sentence *some* is an indefinite pronoun. It is the subject of the sentence and takes the place of a noun.

> *Some* would rather go to Hawaii.

Exercise 1

Identify the indefinite adjective in each sentence.

1. Many people confuse alligators with crocodiles.

2. Both animals have similar characteristics.

3. All crocodiles, however, have narrow snouts.

4. In contrast, the snout of almost any alligator is wider than that of a crocodile.

5. Both crocodilians live in the southeastern states.

6. They can be found in many swamps there.

7. The gavial is one of the largest of all crocodilians.

8. Of all crocodilians, it spends the most time in water.

9. Many gavials are native to India.

10. No crocodilian is more in danger of extinction than the gavial.

Exercise 2

Identify the indefinite adjective in each sentence and the noun it goes with.

1. Like other reptiles, crocodiles are cold blooded.

2. Few males grow larger than 15 feet in length.

3. Most females reach approximately 10 feet.

4. The saltwater crocodile is the largest of all reptiles.

5. Saltwater crocodiles as long as 20 feet supposedly have been caught by a few crocodile hunters.

6. These animals are found in some parts of Australia.

7. They are also found in many Asian countries.

8. All saltwater crocodiles can survive in fresh water.

9. A saltwater crocodile can be readily identified by most crocodile watchers.

10. Every saltwater crocodile has rows of bony scales on its back and neck.

11. Many tourists go to Australia to see these massive reptiles.

12. Few people who have seen these reptiles will ever forget this incredible sight.

13. No viewer can fail to be impressed by these huge creatures.

14. Most nests of the saltwater crocodile are made from mud and plants.

15. Many females lay between 30 and 60 eggs.

Practice Power

Write about the animals in your area. Use indefinite adjectives in your description. When you finish, underline all of the indefinite adjectives in your writing.

3.11 Adjective Phrases

An **adjective phrase** is prepositional phrase that describes a noun or a pronoun.

The butterflies *in the rain forest* can have brilliant colors.
The beauty *of the butterfly* is striking.

In the first sentence above, the prepositional phrase *in the rain forest* describes the noun *butterflies.* In the second sentence the prepositional phrase *of the butterfly* describes the noun *beauty.*

Can you identify the two adjective phrases and the nouns they describe in this sentence?

Some books about butterflies give instructions for butterfly gardens.

You are correct if you said that the adjective phrase *about butterflies* describes the noun *books* and that the adjective phrase *for butterfly gardens* describes the noun *instructions.*

Exercise 1

Identify the adjective phrase in each sentence.

1. The group of insects includes butterflies.

2. They sip the nectar from flowers.

3. The colors of butterflies are their outstanding feature.

4. Their colors can be a means of defense.

5. The colors of some species provide camouflage.

6. In contrast, some butterflies with brilliantly colored wings make themselves conspicuous.

7. Some butterflies' colors stand out, but birds avoid them because the taste of these butterflies is unpleasant.

8. The four stages in a butterfly's life are egg, caterpillar, pupa, and adult.

9. The adults of most species live only a month.

10. The diet of the caterpillar includes leaves and other plant parts.

Exercise 2

Identify the adjective phrase or phrases in each sentence. Then identify the noun each goes with.

1. Some people plan and set up gardens for butterflies.
2. Such a garden needs colorful plants as sources of nectar.
3. An example of a good nectar plant is the azalea.
4. A recommendation from many experts is the zinnia.
5. One requirement for any butterfly garden is sunlight.
6. An adequate supply of host plants gives butterflies a place for their eggs.
7. Host plants are ideal homes for caterpillars.
8. Caterpillars eat leaves from these plants.
9. They then become butterflies in your garden.
10. To fly, butterflies need the warmth of the sun.
11. A butterfly garden also requires some shelter against the elements where butterflies can stay in poor weather.

Exercise 3

Rewrite each group of words as an adjective phrase.

1. forest animals
2. garden hose
3. honey production
4. South American butterflies
5. rose garden
6. defense mechanism
7. expert advice
8. tourist site

Practice Power

Use some of the adjective phrases you wrote in Exercise 3 in sentences. When you are finished, go back and circle each adjective phrase you used.

Adjective Challenge

Read the selection and then answer the questions.

1. The harbor is alive with ships from around the world. 2. Several freighters rock with the tide, graceful liners glide up to the piers, and tugs wander in and out of the harbor. 3. The tugs, which are smaller than the other vessels, look tiny when compared to the black hulls of the freighters. 4. Two pleasure boats cruise up the river. 5. Strains of cheerful music from their orchestras float toward both shores. 6. This port is a vivid glimpse of today's American coastal life.

1. Name an adjective used as a subject complement in sentence 1.

2. What word does this subject complement describe?

3. Name the indefinite adjective in sentence 2.

4. Name the comparative adjective in sentence 3.

5. Name the three descriptive adjectives in sentence 3.

6. Is the word *pleasure* used as a noun or an adjective in sentence 4?

7. Name the article in sentence 4.

8. Name the descriptive adjective in sentence 5. Write the comparative and superlative forms for this adjective.

9. Name the indefinite adjective in sentence 5.

10. Name the demonstrative adjective in sentence 6. Does the demonstrative adjective modify a singular or plural noun?

11. Find an adjective that shows origin in the paragraph.

12. Does the paragraph contain any superlative adjectives?

Verbs

4.1 *Principal Parts of Verbs, Verb Phrases*

Verbs show action or being.

Columbus *explored* the West Indies. (action)
Columbus *was* from Italy. (being)

The four basic parts of all verbs are the **present, past, past participle,** and **present participle.** The present form is also called the base form. The past and past participle of regular verbs are formed by adding *-d* or *-ed* to the base form. The present participle is formed by adding *-ing.*

Present	Past	Past Participle	Present Participle
sail	sailed	sailed	sailing

A **verb phrase** is two or more verbs that work together as a unit. A verb phrase may have one or more **auxiliary verbs** and a **main verb.**

We *have studied* about Columbus in class.

In the above sentence the verb phrase is *have studied.* The main verb is *studied:* it is the past participle form. The auxiliary verb is *have.* Note that the past participle form is often used with auxiliaries, but the past form stands alone.

Some common auxiliary verbs are the forms of *be (am, is, are, was, were),* the forms of have *(have, has, had),* and the forms of *do (do, did).* Other common auxiliary verbs are *can, could, may, might, should,* and *will.*

The verbs in a verb phrase are usually written together. In negative sentences and in questions, the verbs may be separated.

Columbus *did* not *discover* a route to the Far East.
Do you *know* anything about Columbus's early life?

Can you identify the verb phrase in this sentence?

Have you memorized the poem about Columbus?

You are correct if you said that the verb phrase is *have memorized.*

Exercise 1

Identify the verb form for each underlined verb: present, past, past participle, or present participle.

1. We all <u>know</u> the story of Christopher Columbus.

2. People in the U.S. even <u>celebrate</u> a holiday in his honor.

3. Columbus <u>went</u> to sea at the age of 14.

4. He <u>moved</u> to Spain in 1485.

5. He had <u>been</u> in Portugal for many years before that move.

6. Columbus had <u>worked</u> as a mapmaker.

7. He <u>thought</u> that he could sail around the world.

8. He was <u>hoping</u> for a grant to sail to the Far East.

9. King Ferdinand and Queen Isabella of Spain <u>agreed</u>.

Exercise 2

Identify the verb phrase in each sentence.

1. People have praised Columbus as an explorer.

2. He has been called a single-minded entrepreneur by others.

3. Some have considered Columbus a failure.

4. He was looking for a short route to the Far East.

5. He definitely had failed in this goal.

6. He did not reach the Far East and its riches.

7. Nor did he recognize the importance of his discovery.

8. He had succeeded in an unexpected feat of exploration.

9. What else have you read about Columbus?

10. What do you think of his career?

Practice Power

**Write about another explorer's accomplishments.
Underline the verbs and verb phrases in your writing.**

4.2 *Regular and Irregular Verbs*

To form the past and past participle of regular verbs, add *-d* or *-ed* to the present, or base, form.

Present/Base	Past	Past Participle
live	lived	lived
work	worked	worked

If a verb ends in *y* preceded by a consonant, form the past and past participle by changing the *y* to *i* and adding *-ed*.

Present/Base	Past	Past Participle
carry	carried	carried
try	tried	tried

If a single-syllable verb ends in a consonant preceded by a vowel, double the consonant before adding *-ed*.

Present/Base	Past	Past Participle
wrap	wrapped	wrapped
hop	hopped	hopped

There is no general rule for forming the past and past participles of irregular verbs. Check a dictionary for these forms.

Present/Base	Past	Past Participle
bring	brought	brought
drive	drove	driven
put	put	put

Exercise 1

Write the past and past participle forms for each verb.

1. sink
2. want
3. give
4. decide
5. know

6. freeze
7. eat
8. study
9. pass
10. run

11. see
12. cut
13. sing
14. break
15. hide

Exercise 2

Complete each sentence with the verb form in parentheses.

1. The Wright brothers _____ up in Ohio. (grow—past)

2. Mechanics _____ their interest. (draw—past)

3. As boys, they _____ homemade mechanical toys. (sell—past)

4. By the age of 16, Orville had _____ his own printing press. (build—past participle)

5. It was not long before the brothers had _____ to publish their own newspaper. (begin—past participle)

6. After Wilbur had _____ a job at a bicycle shop, the brothers developed an interest in bicycles. (take—past participle)

7. Soon, the Wright brothers not only _____ how to build bikes, they were also designing them. (know—past)

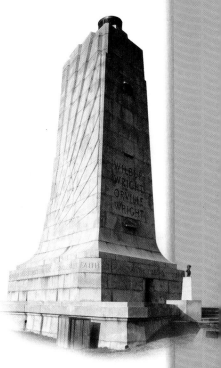

Exercise 3

Complete each sentence with the past tense or the past participle of the verb in parentheses.

1. In 1906 the Wright brothers _____ (receive) a patent for the special design of the wings on their plane.

2. Three years had _____ (go) by before it was granted.

3. Until the patent was granted, the Wright brothers had _____ (keep) a lot about their work secret.

4. This _____ (stop) competitors from copying their ideas.

5. From 1908 the United States War Department _____ (buy) planes from the Wright brothers.

Practice Power

Write two sentences for each verb, one with the past form of the verb and the other with the past participle.

write	send	speak	drink
choose	meet	ride	forget

4.3 *Troublesome Verbs*

The verb *lie (lie, lay, lain, lying)* means "to rest or recline."
The verb *lay (lay, laid, laid, laying)* means "to put something
in a place or situation." It takes a direct object.

> As I *lay* in bed, I daydreamed about becoming a pilot.
> Where did I *lay* my book on Charles Lindbergh?

The verb *sit (sit, sat, sat, sitting)* means "to have or keep a seat."
The verb *set (set, set, set, setting)* means "to place or fix in a
position." It takes a direct object.

> I'd like to *sit* and read my book in peace.
> I think I *set* the book on the television.

The verb *rise (rise, rose, risen, rising)* means "to ascend."
The verb *raise (raise, raised, raised, raising)* means "to lift up,
put up, or elevate," or "to care for to maturity." It takes a
direct object.

> The sun *rose* above the tops of the buildings.
> The airport worker *raised* a flag to direct the pilot.

The verb *let (let, let, let, letting)* means "to permit or allow." The
verb *leave (leave, left, left, leaving)* means "to abandon or depart."

> My dad *lets* me help him with his model airplanes.
> We *left* for the airport at 5:30 a.m.

The verb *teach (teach, taught, taught, teaching)* means "to give
instruction." The verb *learn (learn, learned, learned, learning)*
means "to receive instruction."

> Our instructor *taught* us about the basics of flying a plane.
> We *learned* about pioneers in aviation.

Exercise 1

Choose the correct verb to complete each sentence.

1. (Leave Let) me tell you about Douglas "Wrong Way" Corrigan.

2. He (left let) his name in history for a strange reason.

3. After his first flight at the age of 18 in 1925, he pestered people at the airfield to (learn teach) him to fly.

4. After Charles Lindbergh's flight across the Atlantic in 1927, Douglas (lay laid) plans for his own trip.

5. Douglas worked to (rise raise) money for a plane.

6. His plane was rickety, and aviation officials would not (let leave) him fly across the Atlantic in it.

7. On July 17, 1938, he (sat set) in the cockpit of his plane.

8. He (set sat) some chocolate bars, some fig bars, a quart of water, and a U.S. map down next to him.

9. As his plane (rose raised) into the sky, it was scheduled to go to California but it landed 28 hours later in Ireland.

10. Some have (raised rose) doubts that was a mistake.

Exercise 2

Rewrite the sentences to correct the verbs. Not all have errors.

1. I said to my parents, "Leave me go to the air show."

2. They rose no objections to my going along with my brother.

3. Bill had learned me all about aerial acrobatics.

4. We almost left the house late.

5. My brother forgot where he had lain the tickets.

6. Fortunately they were laying on his desk.

7. When we arrived at the show, we set in the bleachers.

8. Planes rose in the sky, making rolls and climbing.

9. Bill left me get an autograph from one of the pilots.

10. I laid awake all night thinking about the exciting show.

Practice Power

Write one sentence for each of the verbs in this lesson:
lie, lay, sit, set, rise, raise, let, leave, teach, and *learn.*

4.4 Transitive Verbs

A **transitive verb** expresses an action that passes from a doer to a receiver. Every transitive verb has a receiver of its action. The receiver is the direct object. In this sentence, the doer is the subject *Amelia Earhart*. The receiver is the direct object *plane*.

doer	receiver

Amelia Earhart bought her first plane in 1922.

To determine the receiver of the action, ask the question *whom* or *what* after the verb. The word that answers the question is the direct object.

Can you identify the transitive verb in these sentences? Can you name the receiver of the action?

We wrote reports about American aviators.
I chose Amelia Earhart.

In the first sentence the transitive verb is *wrote* and the receiver of the action is *reports.* In the second sentence the transitive verb is *chose* and the receiver of the action is *Amelia Earhart.*

Exercise 1

Identify the transitive verb in each sentence.

1. As a child, Amelia Earhart enjoyed sports.
2. She achieved good grades in school.
3. After high school she studied nursing and medicine.
4. She treated injured soldiers during World War I.
5. She took a short plane ride in the late 1920s.
6. The experience changed her life.
7. Earhart found her life's vocation in flying.
8. A captain offered her a chance for a special flight.
9. She achieved fame for this flight.
10. She crossed the Atlantic Ocean—a first for a woman.

Exercise 2

Identify the transitive verb in each sentence. Then identify the doer and the receiver.

1. Amelia Earhart joined two pilots as a passenger on a transatlantic flight in 1928.

2. On May 20, 1932, she flew a plane across the Atlantic alone.

3. She set a transatlantic record of 14 hours, 56 minutes.

4. President Hoover presented a medal to her for this feat.

5. Earhart also completed a flight from Hawaii to California.

6. Still Earhart sought new challenges.

7. She planned a flight around the world.

8. Earhart chose a route close to the equator.

9. Amélia Earhart had a custom-made plane.

10. The mechanics equipped the plane with large gas tanks.

11. Fred Noonan accompanied Earhart as navigator for this trip.

12. On her first try, Earhart had an accident—her plane crashed.

13. She made a second attempt at a world flight months later.

14. The *Itasca,* a U.S. Coast Guard ship, tracked the flight by radio.

15. Earhart contacted the ship on July 2, 1937.

16. She radioed the ship about a low fuel reading.

17. The *Itasca* received no further communication.

18. Many ships sought Earhart's plane in the following years.

19. No one, however, knows the plane's fate.

20. People still remember Earhart's accomplishments.

Practice Power

Write a sentence for each of these transitive verbs. The verb may be in the present, past, or past participle form.

send	find	forget	protect
make	see	produce	postpone

4.5 Intransitive Verbs

An **intransitive verb** has no receiver of its action—no direct object. An intransitive verb may be followed by an adverb.

> Bessie Coleman *came* from Texas.
> Bessie *worked* diligently.

Some verbs can be **transitive** or **intransitive** according to their use in the sentence.

> Journalists *wrote* about Bessie Coleman. (intransitive)
> Journalists *wrote* stories about her skills (transitive).

Can you identify in which of these sentences the verb *flew* is transitive and in which the verb is intransitive?

> Bessie Coleman flew in air shows.
> Bessie Coleman flew many different planes.

The verb *flew* is intransitive in the first sentence. It is transitive in the second sentence, and the direct object is *planes*.

Exercise 1

Identify the intransitive verb or verb phrase in each sentence.

1. As a child in the early 1900s, Bessie Coleman lived in Texas.

2. As a girl, Bessie helped with the care of her younger brothers and sisters.

3. As a young adult, she moved to Chicago.

4. Like many other African Americans, Coleman's family was hoping for a better life in the North.

5. Coleman worked as a manicurist in the city.

6. After some chance remarks from her brother, Coleman unexpectedly decided on a career in flying.

7. During this time of segregation, blacks did not mix with whites in many places—including some schools.

8. So she went to France for flying lessons in 1919.

Exercise 2

Identify the verb or verb phrase in each sentence. Tell whether the verb is transitive or intransitive.

1. Bessie Coleman came from a large family.
2. She worked hard in school.
3. She went to a local college.
4. She left school because of a lack of money.
5. Coleman dreamed of a better life.
6. She realized her dream of a career in aviation.
7. She obtained her pilot's license in France.
8. She made her debut in an air show in 1925.
9. She sometimes jumped with parachutes.
10. Large audiences attended her shows.
11. She lectured about aviation.
12. Bessie Coleman wouldn't perform before segregated audiences.
13. Everyone used the same gates for her shows.
14. They crowded airfields and race tracks.
15. An estimated ten thousand people showed their respect when she died.
16. They waited in line for hours to file past her coffin.
17. After her death a friend established a flight school in her name.

Practice Power

Write two sentences for each of these verbs, one sentence using the verb as an intransitive verb and the other using the verb as a transitive verb. The verb may be in present, past, or past participle form.

talk	explore	bounce	grow
play	paint	write	fly

4.6 Linking Verbs

A **linking verb** links the subject of a sentence with a subject complement (a noun, a pronoun, or an adjective). The most common linking verb is *be* and its forms *(am, is, are, been, be, was, were)*.

Subject	Linking Verb	Subject Complement
Alan Shepard	became	an astronaut. (noun)
One of the first astronauts	was	he. (pronoun)
The job	was	dangerous. (adjective)

The following verbs can also be used as linking verbs: *appear, become, continue, feel, grow, look, remain, seem, smell, sound,* and *taste*. When these are used as linking verbs, a form of the verb *be* can be substituted for them.

People *felt* excited about the possibility of space travel.
People *were* excited about the possibility of space travel.

Exercise 1

Identify the linking verb in each sentence. Tell whether the underlined subject complement is a noun, a pronoun, or an adjective.

1. Alan Shepard became the first <u>American</u> in space.

2. Shepard had been a test <u>pilot</u>.

3. Then he had become an <u>astronaut</u>.

4. His spaceship was <u>ready</u> for takeoff on May 5, 1961.

5. The time was <u>predawn</u>.

6. Shepard looked <u>strange</u> in his futuristic spacesuit.

7. The cabin of the spaceship was <u>tiny</u>.

8. The name of his craft was <u>*Freedom 7*</u>.

9. The rocket engines seemed extremely <u>loud</u> at takeoff.

10. The time of that first flight was <u>short</u>—only 15 minutes.

Exercise 2

Identify the linking verb and subject complement in each sentence.

1. John Glenn was an engineering student in college.
2. His interest in flying became strong.
3. He was the first person to fly at supersonic speed.
4. It was he who joined the group of seven original astronauts.
5. He became the first American to orbit Earth in 1962.
6. The flight was a great success.

Exercise 3

Identify the verb in each sentence. Tell whether it is a transitive verb, an intransitive verb, or a linking verb.

1. The space age began on October 4, 1957.
2. The Soviets launched the satellite *Sputnik* into space.
3. The United States and the Soviet Union were iron-willed rivals at the time.
4. They became competitors in space exploration.
5. The Russians sent the first human into space in 1961.
6. Yuri Gagarin orbited Earth in the first space flight.

Practice Power

You have just been launched into space in a spacecraft. What do you think you will hear, see, and feel? Write sentences about this experience, using forms of the verb *be* and some of these linking verbs:

look	feel	remain
become	grow	seem
continue	appear	sound

4.7 Simple Tenses

Tense expresses the time of the action or state of being. The **simple present tense** tells about an action that happens again and again and about things that are general truths. The simple present tense uses the present, or base, form of a verb. If, however, the subject is a third person singular noun or pronoun, the verb form takes an *-s* ending.

> Meteor showers *occur* at certain times of the year.
> When a meteor *reaches* the ground, it is called a meteorite.

The **simple past tense** tells about an action that happened in the past. The simple past tense uses the past form.

> Jan and Greg *saw* a meteor shower in November.

The **simple future tense** tells about an action that will happen in the future. The simple future tense uses the auxiliary verb *will* or *be going to* followed by the base form of a verb.

> Another meteor shower *will occur* next month.
> My family and I *are going to watch* for it.

Exercise 1

Identify the verb in each sentence and give its tense.

1. A meteor appears briefly in the sky as a streak of light.

√2. These pieces of stony or metallic material from outer space usually burn on contact with Earth's atmosphere.

3. Materials like those in meteorites formed the planets.

√4. Meteorites will provide scientists with clues on the composition of planets and the formation of the solar system.

5. One big meteor hit the ground about 50,000 years ago.

6. It created the large Meteor Crater in Arizona.

7. The meteor probably disintegrated on impact.

8. Tonight an observer will see five to ten meteors an hour.

9. Many more are visible during a meteor shower.

10. I'm going to observe a meteor shower in November.

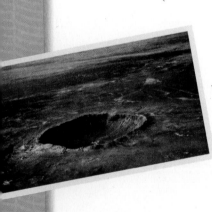

Exercise 2

Complete each sentence with the verb in parentheses in the tense indicated.

1. Comets _____ around the sun. (travel—present)

2. Comets _____ icy balls in the solar system. (be—present)

3. Many people living in 1986 _____ a comet called Halley's Comet. (see—past)

4. People in 1066 also _____ this famous comet. (view—past)

5. The comet _____ into view of Earth approximately every 76 years. (come—present)

6. Halley's Comet _____ in 2061. (return—future)

7. People living now _____ old when it returns! (be—future)

8. In 1986 several spacecraft _____ close to Halley's Comet to study it. (fly—past)

9. Scientists _____ the main part of the comet to be dark black in color, not whitish. (find—past)

10. Dust and rock _____ the comet's icy core. (cover—present)

11. The core _____ about 9 miles across. (measure—present)

12. Edmund Halley _____ the comet in 1682. (study—past)

13. He accurately _____ its return in 1758. (predict—past)

14. A comet's orbit _____ possible predicting the time of the comet's return. (make—present)

15. Another comet _____ in the sky in 1997. (appear—past)

16. Scientists _____ it the Hale-Bopp Comet after its discoverers, two amateur astronomers. (name—past)

Practice Power

Imagine you are marooned on a desert island. Write several paragraphs explaining the situation you are in, how you got there, and what you will do to survive. Use verbs in the present, past, and future tenses.

The **progressive tenses** are formed with a form of the verb *be* (*is, am, are, was, were*) and the present participle.

The **present progressive tense** tells about something that is happening right now. It uses the present tense of the verb *be* (*am, is, are*) and the present participle.

> The students *are asking* the scientist a question.

The **past progressive tense** tells about something that was happening in the past. It uses the past tense of the verb *be* (*was, were*) and the present participle.

> While she *was answering*, we *were taking* notes.

The **future progressive tense** tells about something that will be happening in the future. It uses *will* or *is/are going to* with *be* and the present participle.

> We *will be looking* for meteors tomorrow night.
> We *are going to be lying* on blankets in the back yard.

Exercise 1

Identify the verb in the present progressive tense in each sentence.

1. Meteroids, small particles of matter, are traveling through space.

2. Meteoroids are constantly entering Earth's atmosphere.

3. They are moving at speeds of some 160,000 miles per hour.

Exercise 2

Identify the verb in the past progressive tense.

1. While we were visiting the planetarium, a guide answered our questions.

2. I was wondering about the difference between meteors and comets.

3. He was explaining that people incorrectly call meteors shooting stars or falling stars.

Exercise 3

Identify the verb in the progressive tense in each sentence. Tell whether it is in the present progressive tense, the past progressive tense, or the future progressive tense.

1. Many meteors were flashing across the sky last night.

2. We were watching the sky for only a few minutes when we spotted some.

3. I am hoping to stay up for the next meteor shower!

4. I will be checking the Internet for dates of future showers.

5. We were watching the meteors when the moon rose.

6. We were lying on the ground on a blanket for a good view.

Exercise 4

Complete each sentence with the verb in parentheses in the tense indicated.

1. Scientists _____ meteors and meteorites to learn more about the nature of the planets. (study—present progressive)

2. In the past many people believed that the gods _____ their anger through meteorites. (show—past progressive)

3. When I _____ for information on meteors, I found some facts about meteor showers. (look—past progressive)

4. Earth itself _____ through space about 67,000 miles per hour. (move—present progressive)

5. Meteors _____ through the sky constantly—about 4 billion meteors fall every day. (fall—present progressive)

Practice Power

Write a postcard from outer space. Imagine you are visiting a planet or traveling in a spacecraft. Write what you and others traveling with you are doing now and what you were doing at previous times. Use some present and past progressive forms in your writing.

4.9 Perfect Tenses

The **perfect tenses** are formed with a form of the verb *have (have, has, had)* and the past participle.

The **present perfect tense** tells about an action that happened at some indefinite time in the past or an action that started in the past and continues into the present time. Its form contains *have* or *has*.

Scientists *have called* asteroids minor planets.

The **past perfect tense** tells about a past action that was completed before another past action started. Its form contains *had*.

I *had read* a lot about asteroids before I went to the planetarium.

Exercise 1

Identify the perfect tense verb in each sentence.

1. I had known little about asteroids until I saw a TV program on them.
2. I had already learned the definition of asteroids as small bodies in orbit around the sun.
3. Scientists have described asteroids as "mountains in space."
4. In the past, people had mistaken asteroids for stars.
5. Scientists have identified an "asteroid belt" between the orbits of Mars and Jupiter.

Exercise 2

Identify the verb in the perfect tense in each sentence. Tell whether it is in the present perfect or the past perfect.

1. Asteroids have struck Earth in the past.
2. Scientists have calculated that the chance of a hit is rare.
3. Asteroids and comets have left craters on Earth.

4. By 2000 scientists had discovered about 120 such craters.

5. One of these, in Mexico, has attracted a lot of attention.

6. People have measured the crater as 190 miles across.

7. Scientists estimate that the object from space had hit Earth before the advent of humans some 65 million years ago.

8. Scientists have examined the rock in the crater.

9. They determined that an asteroid had made the crater.

10. It supported a theory that scientists had proposed about asteroids and the disappearance of dinosaurs.

Exercise 3

Complete each sentence with the verb in parentheses in the tense indicated.

1. _____ you _____ the theory of asteroids and the disappearance of dinosaurs? (hear—present perfect)

2. According to the theory, after a giant asteroid _____ Earth, a huge cloud of debris arose. (hit—past perfect)

3. The gigantic cloud _____ in climate changes and chemical changes in the atmosphere. (result—past perfect)

4. Because dinosaurs _____ to adapt to the new environment, they disappeared. (fail—past perfect)

5. Luis and Walter Alvarez _____ this theory of the extinction of dinosaurs years before. (propose—past perfect)

6. Other scientists _____ chemical evidence in rocks to support the Alvarezes' theory. (find—present perfect)

Practice Power

Make up a tall tale about an amazing person. Tell about the amazing things he or she has done. Also tell about the things the person had done by the ages of one, five, and ten. Use verbs in the perfect tenses in your writing.

4.10 Agreement of Subject and Verb

A verb agrees with its subject in person and number. For a third person singular subject, the present tense is the base form with -s or -es added. Note that *is* is the third person singular form of *be*.

> A sixth-grade <u>student</u> usually *studies* about space.
> <u>Students</u> *learn* about meteors, asteroids, and comets.
> Space <u>travel</u> *is* an interesting subject.

Use *doesn't* when the subject is third person singular. Use *don't* in other cases.

> <u>Arnold</u> *doesn't* know what a comet is.
> <u>I</u> *don't* know what a comet is either.

Use *are* and *were* with *you*, whether the subject is singular or plural. Do not use *is* or *was* with the subject *you*.

> *Were* <u>you</u> at the planetarium yesterday?

When *there is* or *there are* introduces a sentence, the subject follows the verb. Use *there is* with singular subjects. Use *there are* with plural subjects.

> *There is* a moon <u>rock</u> at the museum. (singular subject)
> *There are* several moon <u>rocks</u> in one case. (plural subject)

Compound subjects connected by *and* usually require plural verbs.

> <u>Janice and Marie</u> *are* <u>working</u> on a report on asteroids.

Exercise 1

Find the subject in each sentence and tell whether it is singular or plural. Then choose the correct verb.

1. Scientists (studies study) objects in space.

2. The word *meteorite* (describes describe) any space material that strikes Earth.

3. Sometimes a meteor (hits hit) Earth.

4. It (doesn't don't) disintegrate in the atmosphere.

5. That meteor (becomes become) a meteorite.

6. Asteroids and comets also (cause causes) meteorites.

7. (Was Were) you familiar with the definition of a meteorite?

8. On Earth there (is are) many craters from space objects.

9. There (is are) an extremely large crater in Arizona.

10. Visitors (comes come) from all over to see it.

Exercise 2

Complete each sentence with *doesn't* or *don't*.

1. A meteor _____ have an icy core as a comet does.

2. Our local museum _____ have a moon rock.

3. Luis and Tom _____ have binoculars to view the comet.

4. Alicia _____ have binoculars either.

5. You _____ need binoculars to view a meteor shower.

Exercise 3

Complete each sentence with the correct form of the verb in parentheses in the present tense.

1. An astronomer _____ (use) a telescope and other tools.

2. Space probes _____ (get) information from space.

3. Sally K. Ride and Stephen Hawking _____ (work) as astrophysicists.

4. Astronomers usually _____ (study) several sciences.

5. One necessary subject _____ (be) physics.

Practice Power

Write about a job or career that you are interested in or know about. Write about what a person in that field does and the education he or she needs. Check verb agreement in your finished writing.

4.11 Active and Passive Voice

Voice shows whether the subject is the doer or the receiver of the action. When a verb is in the **active voice,** the subject is the doer of the action. In this sentence *astronaut,* the subject, is the doer of the action *placed.* The verb, therefore, is in the active voice.

> An astronaut *placed* a flag on the moon.

In the **passive voice** the subject is the receiver of the action. In the first sentence below the subject *flag* is the receiver of the action *was placed.* The verb, therefore, is in the passive voice. A verb in the passive voice is formed by combining a form of *be* with the past participle.

> A flag *was placed* on the moon by an astronaut.
> The moon rock *is shown* at the museum.
> The samples *were collected* by astronauts.

Which of the following sentences is in the passive voice?

> Millions watched the lunar craft.
> The lunar craft was watched by millions.

You are correct if you said the second sentence is in the passive voice. The subject *craft* is the receiver of the action, and the verb consists of a form of *be (was)* and the past participle of the verb *watch.*

When you write, keep in mind that sentences in the active voice are generally more alive, exciting, and direct than those in the passive voice.

Exercise 1

Identify the verb or verb phrase in each sentence and tell whether it is in the active voice or the passive voice.

1. The goal of a moon landing was set by President Kennedy.

2. He set 1970 as the date for the landing.

3. On July 20, 1969 a person walked on the moon.

4. Kennedy's goal was reached.

5. Three astronauts—Michael Collins, Buzz Aldrin, and Neil Armstrong—traveled in the spaceship *Columbia.*

6. *Columbia* was named after Christopher Columbus.

7. *Columbia* reached the moon in four days.

Exercise 2

Each sentence is written in the passive voice.
Rewrite the sentence so it is in the active voice.

1. The *Eagle* was landed on the moon by Armstrong and Aldrin.

2. Armstrong's first words on the moon are often quoted by people today.

3. Samples of soil were collected by the two astronauts.

4. The astronauts were called by phone by President Richard M. Nixon during their walk.

5. Amazing pictures of Earth and the moon were taken by the astronauts during their space flight.

Exercise 3

Each sentence is written in the active voice. Rewrite the sentence so it is in the passive voice.

1. The astronauts left footprints on the moon.

2. People remember the image of Armstrong on the moon.

3. Other astronauts later visited the moon.

4. Space probes explore the solar system.

5. Scientists and engineers continuously set new goals for space exploration.

Practice Power

Look in textbooks and magazines for examples of sentences in the passive voice. Copy 10 of them.

4.12 Indicative Mood

Mood shows the manner in which the action or state of being is expressed. The **indicative mood** of a verb is used when the speaker is making a statement or asking a question. Most sentences are in the indicative mood.

Sentences in the indicative mood use verbs in the present, past, future, progressive, and perfect tenses. They also reflect active or passive voice.

What *are* the Seven Wonders of the Ancient World? (question—present tense)

I *will research* the Seven Wonders. (statement—future tense)

The Great Pyramid, one Wonder of the Ancient World, *is* still *standing.* (statement—present progressive tense)

I *have read* books about each of the Seven Wonders. (statement—present perfect tense)

Did you *study* about the Seven Ancient Wonders last year? (question—past tense)

The original list of the seven Ancient Wonders *was compiled* in the second century BC. (statement—past tense passive)

Exercise 1

Identify the verb in the indicative mood and give its tense.

1. Where is the Great Pyramid?

2. It rises over the desert near Giza, Egypt.

3. Until the 1800s the Egyptian pyramids were among the tallest structures in the world.

4. There are some 2,300,000 blocks of stone in the Great Pyramid alone.

5. Each stone weighs approximately two and a half tons.

6. At least 112 workers together raised each stone.

7. Perhaps the workers pushed the huge stones up ramps.

8. Engineers are still studying the construction of the massive pyramids.

9. I am hoping to visit the Great Pyramid one day.

Exercise 2

Identify the verb in the indicative mood and its tense in each sentence and identify the correct end punctuation.

1. Were the pyramids originally tombs for the pharaohs

2. A few historians think not

3. Why were they built

4. According to some historians, they originally had been observatories

5. The bodies of early pharaohs were mummified and placed in pyramids

6. The pyramids once probably also contained great riches

7. Did tomb robbers steal the treasures

8. No one really knows for sure

9. In 1997 a team of archaeologists went on a dig at the Great Pyramid

10. Soon they were wandering through the ancient chambers

11. Where had the laborers lived

12. Egyptologists are still studying evidence to prove that a palace must exist

13. Yet no excavation has ever found such a palace

14. Each shred of evidence adds little or no proof

15. It will remain a logical hypothesis for years to come

Practice Power

Divide a sheet of paper into two columns. Write *What I Know about the Seven Wonders of the Ancient World* at the top of the first column and *What I Want to Know about Them* on top of the second. Fill in the columns, using statements and questions in the indicative mood.

4.13 *Emphatic Form of the Indicative Mood*

The **emphatic** form of a verb in the indicative mood gives special force to a simple present or past tense verb. To make an emphatic form in the present tense, use *do* or *does* before the base form of the verb. To make an emphatic form in the past tense, use *did* before the base form of the verb.

> The Seven Wonders of the Ancient World *do fascinate* me.
> I *did read* a lot about one, the Lighthouse of Alexandria.
> The structure *does continue* to stimulate the imagination.

Do not confuse this use with *do, does,* and *did* used as auxiliary verbs in questions or negative sentences.

> What *do* you *know* about Alexander the Great? (*Do* acts as an auxiliary verb in a question.)
> I *didn't know* the answer to the question. (*Did* acts as an auxiliary verb in a negative sentence with *not.*)

Exercise 1

Identify the verb phrase in the emphatic form in each sentence.

1. Alexandria, Egypt, an ancient city, still does exist.

2. I do think that it was named after Alexander the Great.

3. The Lighthouse at Alexandria, a Wonder of the Ancient World, did stand a long time—for about 1,500 years.

4. It did once rise to a height of between 450 and 600 feet.

5. A controlled fire did burn in the lighthouse all day and night to provide both light and smoke.

6. Sailors did see the fire's light from some 100 miles away in the dark of night.

7. During the day they did see its smoke from afar.

8. The lighthouse did help in navigation for centuries.

9. Engineers today do agree that the lighthouse used an ingenious system.

10. A curved mirror did project the fire's light far out to sea.

Exercise 2

Identify the verb phrase in the emphatic form in each sentence. Tell whether it is in the present or past tense.

1. People do find the history of the Lighthouse at Alexandria fascinating.

2. It certainly does rank as one of the most impressive of the Seven Wonders.

3. Alexander the Great did order the building of the city of Alexandria.

4. However, an Egyptian ruler—not Alexander himself—did command the building of the lighthouse in 290 BC.

5. Some historians do attribute the destruction of the lighthouse to an earthquake—not to deterioration.

Exercise 3

Rewrite the sentences to change the italicized verb to the emphatic form.

1. I *find* the Lighthouse of Alexandria a remarkable building.

2. Its structure somewhat *resembled* today's skyscrapers.

3. It *stood* higher than any other man-made structures of the time except for the Egyptian pyramids.

4. Today's engineers *find* its design very clever.

5. Its designer, Sostrates of Knidos, truly *deserves* recognition as one of the greatest engineers of all time.

Practice Power

Write a paragraph that uses sentences in the emphatic form to persuade someone to do something. You might want that person to clean your room for you, go to the movies with you, or rake the leaves for you. When you are finished, identify each sentence that uses the emphatic form.

4.14 *Imperative Mood*

The **imperative mood** is used to express a command or a request. To form the imperative mood, use the base form of the verb. The subject of an imperative sentence is usually understood to be the second person pronoun, *you*.

> *Tell* me about the Seven Wonders of the World.
> *Describe* the Hanging Gardens of Babylon.
> Please *lend* me your book on the Seven Wonders.

Can you identify which sentence is in the imperative mood? Can you identify the verb in that sentence?

> Come to the library with me.
> The Hanging Gardens of Babylon were beautiful.

You are correct if you said that the first sentence is in the imperative mood. It expresses a command. The verb in the imperative mood is *come.*

A command can be given in the first person by using *let's (let us)* before the base form of a verb.

> *Let's use* the Hanging Gardens as our study topic.

Exercise 1

Identify the sentences that are in the imperative mood.

1. Where were the Hanging Gardens of Babylon?

2. Show us the location of ancient Babylon on a map.

3. Explain the reason why the Hanging Gardens were built.

4. How long did archaeologist Robert Koldewey search for the Hanging Gardens?

5. Let's talk about the size of the Hanging Gardens.

6. Tell us about the source of water for the gardens.

7. Special chain pumps brought water up to the gardens.

8. Make a model of the gardens.

9. What materials will you use?

Exercise 2

Identify the sentences that are in the imperative mood. Then name the verbs in the imperative sentences.

1. Help me with my report about the Hanging Gardens.

2. Please give me your book on the Seven Wonders.

3. King Nebuchadnezzar built the Hanging Gardens in the sixth century BC.

4. Why are they called the Hanging Gardens?

5. The gardens' terraces explain the probable reason for the name.

6. Let's list the special features of the Hanging Gardens.

7. The gardens looked like a mountain of green.

8. Ask me anything about the Hanging Gardens.

Exercise 3

Rewrite the following sentences in the imperative mood.

1. You need to decide on a topic for your report.

2. It is a good idea to write down questions about the topic.

3. You should try to answer the questions in your report.

4. You need to do some research for your report.

5. You might look for information at the library.

6. It often helpful to look on the Internet for information.

7. You should type your topic into a search engine.

8. You need to find correct answers to your questions.

9. It is a good idea to check the reliability of sources.

10. You should also include other interesting details.

Practice Power

Design your own special garden. Make a list of instructions for the workers, telling them what to do and where to plant things. Write the instructions in the imperative mood.

4.15 *Subjunctive Mood*

The **subjunctive mood** is used in several ways: (1) to express a wish or desire; (2) to express a command, request, or suggestion following the word *that;* and (3) to express something that is contrary to fact (not true). The subjunctive refers to what is hoped or wished rather than what actually is.

For the verb *be,* the common forms of the subjunctive are *be* or *were. Be* is commonly used with verbs of command, request, or suggestion. Otherwise, the form is typically *were.* The auxiliary verb *would* is used in place of *will.*

> I wish I *were* able to go to the lecture with you.
> (to express a wish)
> He requested that we *be* on time for the lecture.
> (a request following *that*)
> If I *were* you, I *would* leave by 7:30.
> (to express something that is contrary to fact)

Can you identify the subjunctive forms in these sentences? Can you tell how the subjunctive is used?

> If I were Sammy, I would work on my project tonight.
> I wish my project were finished.
> My mother ordered that all my attention be on my homework.

In the first sentence the subjunctive form *were* expresses a contrary-to-fact condition. In the second sentence the subjunctive form *were* expresses a wish. In the third sentence the subjunctive form *be* follows a verb of command.

Exercise 1

Identify the subjunctive verb phrase in each sentence and tell what it expresses, such as a command or a wish.

1. If my report were finished, I would know more about the tomb of Mausolus.

2. Mausolus's widow, Artemisia, insisted that her husband be buried in a magnificent tomb.

3. She demanded that no money be spared in building the memorial.

4. If its structure were not so beautiful, the Mausoleum of Halicarnassus wouldn't have been named one of the Seven Wonders of the Ancient World.

5. I wish that the tomb of Mausolus were still standing.

6. If it were still standing, it would be a marvelous sight.

7. If I were more focused on the mausoleum, I would have finished my report by now.

8. My dad just suggested that I get started.

Exercise 2

Choose the correct form of the verb for the subjunctive and then complete the sentences with your ideas.

1. If I (was were) a traveler through time, I'd _____.

2. If I (was were) older, I'd _____.

3. If I (was were) a movie star, I'd _____.

4. I wish I (was were) _____.

5. My teacher recommends that I (be was) _____.

6. I wish we (were be) _____.

7. If I (was were) a better athlete, I'd _____.

8. My parents insist that I (be were) _____.

9. The speaker suggests that we (be were) _____.

10. If I (was were) in charge of the world, I'd _____.

Practice Power

Imagine you are lost in a rain forest. Write about three things you wish you had with you. Also write about what you would do if you were rescued and got home. Use the subjunctive mood to write your sentences.

Modal auxiliaries are used to express possibility, permission, ability, necessity, obligation, intention, and willingness. They are followed by main verbs that are in the base form.

The common modal auxiliaries are *may, might, can, could, must, should, will,* and *would.*

> Possibility: You *might want* information on the Wonders of the Modern World.
> We *could look* on the Internet for information.
> Permission: Anyone who wants *may use* the computer in the classroom.
> Ability: June *can find* just about anything on the Internet.
> Necessity: We *must finish* the proposal for our project today.
> Obligation: We *should help* June with the research for our project.
> Intention: I *will bring* all my notes to study hall.
> Willingness: *Would* you *help* us with the report?
> I *would* gladly *do* the artwork for you.

Exercise 1

Identify the modal auxiliary and main verb in each sentence. Tell whether the verb phrase expresses possibility, permission, ability, necessity, obligation, intention, or willingness.

1. I can name some of the Wonders of the Modern World.

2. With modern advances in technology, engineers can design amazing structures.

3. Lists of modern wonders might include the Chunnel (English Channel Tunnel).

4. Every list should include the CN Tower in Toronto—the world's tallest freestanding structure.

5. Would you get information on the Petronas Towers?

6. We'll combine our notes for a report.

7. We must complete the work this week.

8. I will do my share of the research online tonight.

9. Could you meet me after school tomorrow?

10. We should proofread and finish it to hand in on Friday.

Exercise 2

Complete each sentence with a modal auxiliary, according to the meaning indicated in parentheses. More than one modal auxiliary may be correct for some sentences.

1. We _____ get more information before we decide on the final format for our report. (intention)

2. We _____ discuss our findings after school. (possibility)

3. _____ you attend the meeting today? (ability)

4. We _____ meet one day this week. (necessity)

5. _____ you look for information on the Petronas Towers? (willingness)

6. The teacher says that our group _____ borrow her book on the Wonders of the World. (permission)

7. We _____ spend at least one hour per person doing the research. (obligation)

8. Some of us _____ want to make visual aids. (possibility)

9. We _____ ask Troy if we can use his video camera. (necessity)

10. We _____ make an outstanding report. (possibility)

Practice Power

Pretend you are a time-travel agent. Write a letter telling your clients what they might do when they visit a Wonder of the Future World and what they should do before leaving for their trips. Use modal auxiliaries in your writing.

Verb Challenge

Read the selection and then answer the questions.

1. Icebergs contain more than half the world's fresh water.
2. Scientists have created a plan for the future that involves towing icebergs from the Antarctic to hot desert countries.
3. The fresh water could irrigate the dry, thirsty land. 4. Imagine it is the year 2050. 5. The plan works this way. 6. Scientists first choose a very large iceberg—at least five miles long and two miles wide. 7. The iceberg then becomes a ship. 8. The crew members of the "ship" live on board the iceberg, which is driven by an engine. 9. After the ship crosses the ocean, it is put into a giant plastic bag. 10. The iceberg slowly melts, and water is piped into the fields to irrigate the land. 11. Scientists have estimated that one iceberg might hold a trillion gallons of water. 12. That is a big ice cube!

1. In sentence 1 what is the verb? Is it singular or plural?

2. Name the verb phrase in sentence 2.

3. In sentence 3 name the receiver of the action of the transitive verb *irrigate.*

4. What is the mood of the verb in sentence 3?

5. In sentence 5 is the verb *works* singular or plural? Why?

6. Name the verb in sentence 6. Give the past and past participle of this verb.

7. Name the linking verb and the subject complement in sentence 7.

8. In sentence 8 what tense is the verb *live?* What is its mood?

9. In sentence 9 is the verb *crosses* transitive or intransitive?

10. In sentence 10 is the verb *melts* transitive or intransitive?

11. Find the verb in the passive voice in sentence 10.

12. In sentence 11 which verb is in the present perfect tense?

13. Name the modal auxiliary in Sentence 11. What does it express?

14. Name the linking verb in sentence 12. Does it link the subject with a noun, a pronoun, or an adjective?

Adverbs

5.1 Adverbs of Time, Place, and Manner

An **adverb** is a word that describes a verb, an adjective, or another adverb.

> The ancient monuments stood *majestically.*
> (describes the verb *stood*)
> Some monuments were *relatively* famous.
> (describes the adjective *famous*)
> The ancients built *quite* skillfully.
> (describes the adverb *skillfully*)

An **adverb of time** answers the question *when* or *how often* and usually modifies a verb. Adverbs of time include *again, already, always, before, early, ever, finally, first, frequently, immediately, later, never, now, often, once, recently, seldom, sometimes, soon, still, today,* and *usually.*

> I *already* knew that the Temple of Artemis was one of the Wonders of the Ancient World.
> (describes the verb *knew*)

An **adverb of place** answers the question *where* and usually modifies a verb. Adverbs of place include *above, away, back, down, far, forward, here, in, inside, outside, there,* and *up.*

> When the ancients looked *inside,* they saw that the temple was made totally of marble.
> (describes the verb *looked*)

An **adverb of manner** answers the question *how* or *in what manner.* It usually describes a verb. Some adverbs of manner are *bravely, carefully, clearly, gracefully, nicely, steadily, quickly,* and *softly.* Many adverbs of manner end in *-ly* and are formed by adding *-ly* to an adjective (*sad—sadly*). Three common exceptions are *fast, well,* and *hard.*

> The Temple of Artemis was not built *quickly.*
> (describes the verb phrase *was built*)
> It was built *well,* however.
> (describes the verb phrase *was built*)

Exercise 1

Identify the adverb in each sentence. Tell whether it is an adverb of time or place.

1. A single column now stands on a site in Asia Minor.
2. The temple of Artemis was built there in the sixth century BC.
3. Outside, magnificent carved columns formed the four walls.
4. A temple had once stood on the site.
5. After the great temple was destroyed in a fire in 356 BC, a new temple was soon built to replace it.

Exercise 2

Write an adverb of manner for each adjective.

1. honest
2. happy
3. foolish
4. neat
5. unexpected
6. smooth
7. patient
8. cheerful
9. tireless

Exercise 3

Identify the adverb of manner and name the verb it describes.

1. John Turtle Wood worked diligently for six years to find the Temple of Artemis.
2. He asked the British Museum for money persistently.
3. Wood excitedly reported the temple's discovery in 1869.
4. He excavated the foundation painstakingly.
5. He and his team carefully shipped some of the remains of the temple to the British Museum.

Practice Power

Choose a photograph to describe. Write five sentences to describe the image. Use adverbs in your sentences that tell *when, where,* and *how.*

5.2 *Adverbs of Degree, Affirmation, and Negation*

An **adverb of degree** answers the question *how much* or *how little*. It describes a verb, an adjective, or another adverb. Adverbs of degree include *almost, barely, extremely, fully, greatly, hardly, less, merely, most, much, nearly, partly, quite, rather, scarcely, too,* and *very*.

> The ancient monuments were *extremely* impressive.
> (describes the adjective *impressive*)

An **adverb of affirmation** or an **adverb of negation** tells whether a statement is true or false.

The adverbs of affirmation include *allegedly, indeed, positively, undoubtedly,* and *yes*.

> You *undoubtedly* know about the Seven Wonders of the Ancient World. (describes the verb *know*)

The adverbs of negation include *no, not,* and *never*.

> I had *never* read about the Colossus of Rhodes. (describes the verb phrase *had read*)

Exercise 1

Identify the adverb of degree in each sentence. Tell the word it describes and its part of speech.

1. The people of Rhodes were very happy with a victory over an enemy and celebrated by building the Colossus of Rhodes.

2. This statue quite imposingly straddled the harbor on the island of Rhodes.

3. It was extremely tall—some 110 feet.

4. Its pedestal also was quite high.

5. A bronze coating totally covered the statue.

6. The statue lasted a rather short time—56 years.

7. An extremely powerful earthquake destroyed it.

8. Very large pieces of it lay in the harbor for centuries.

Exercise 2

Identify the adverb or adverbs of affirmation and negation in each sentence.

1. Yes, Rhodes is an island southwest of Asia Minor.

2. The Colossus of Rhodes is not still standing.

3. The huge statue was undoubtedly magnificent.

4. Yes, the statue was indeed a statement of the power and independence of the people.

5. No, the statue was not of a person but of the god Helios.

6. I have never visited Rhodes.

Exercise 3

Identify the adverb or adverbs in each sentence. Tell whether each is an adverb of time, place, manner, degree, affirmation, or negation.

1. I would indeed like to do some research on the Seven Wonders of the Ancient World.

2. People do not know much about them.

3. The original list of the Seven Wonders of the Ancient World was compiled early—during the second century BC.

4. Many of the Seven Wonders of the Ancient World barely survived to the Middle Ages.

5. Archaeologists resolutely worked to find them, however.

6. Visit the British Museum; you can find remains of several of them there.

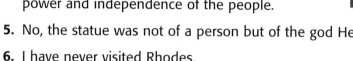

Practice Power

Write sentences that give opinions about current movies, TV programs, songs, or events. Use adverbs of degree to describe adjectives such as *boring, exciting, fascinating, amazing,* and *confusing* in your sentences.

5.3 Comparative and Superlative Adverbs

Some adverbs can be compared. Like adjectives, these adverbs have **comparative** and **superlative** forms.

> The Great Wall of China was built *later* than most of the Wonders of the Ancient World. (comparative)
> The section of the Great Wall built *most recently* is located north of Beijing. (superlative)

The comparative and superlative forms of most adverbs that end in *-ly* are made by adding *more* or *most* (or *less* or *least*) before the positive form of the adverb.

The comparative and superlative forms of many adverbs that don't end in *-ly* are formed by adding *-er* or *-est*.

Positive	Comparative	Superlative
carefully	more carefully	most carefully
fast	faster	fastest

Some adverbs have irregular comparative and superlative forms.

Positive	Comparative	Superlative
well	better	best
badly	worse	worst
far	farther	farthest
little	less	least
much	more	most

Exercise 1

Write the comparative and superlative forms of the following adverbs.

1. slowly
2. soon
3. anxiously
4. hard
5. gracefully

6. clearly
7. well
8. willingly
9. politely
10. late

11. early
12. smoothly
13. quietly
14. intelligently
15. thoughtfully

Exercise 2

Identify the adverb in the comparative or superlative form in each sentence. Identify the verb or verb phrase each adverb describes.

1. The Great Wall of China has lasted longer than most other structures.

2. It extends farther than any single structure—some 4,500 miles.

3. From watchtowers every 100 yards, Chinese soldiers could see the enemy approaching more clearly than ever before.

4. Some historians say that other defenses would have protected the country better than a wall.

5. However, compared with other forms of defense, the wall stood most effectively against China's enemies.

6. Of all of China's early achievements, the wall symbolized most emphatically the power of the early emperors.

7. The magnificence of the Great Wall is seen most easily from aerial photos.

Exercise 3

Complete each sentence with the comparative or superlative form of the adverb in parentheses.

1. Alison worked _____ (hard) of all the students on the project.

2. I finished my project _____ (late) than I expected.

3. I think I could have improved it and written some parts _____ (clearly) if I had had more time.

4. I write _____ (deliberately) of anyone in the class.

5. I need to start on my reports _____ (early) than I tend to do.

Practice Power

Use six adverbs you listed in Exercise 1 in sentences. Tell what degree of comparison each adverb is.

5.4 Adverbs and Adjectives

An adverb modifies a verb, an adjective, or another adverb. An adjective modifies a noun or a pronoun. Remember that the word following and describing an action verb should always be an adverb.

Incorrect: She dressed nice.
Correct: She dressed *nicely.*

A linking verb is often followed by an adjective that refers back to and modifies the subject.

The waves look *rough.*
Mom's stew smelled *delicious.*

To decide whether to use an adverb or an adjective, first determine which word is being modified. If that word is a noun, use an adjective. If that word is a verb, use an adverb.

Noun	Verb
The weeds grew *tall.*	The roses grew *abundantly.*
The man appeared *calm.*	The mayor appeared *early.*

Common Errors

Bad and *badly* are frequently used incorrectly. *Bad* is an adjective. It often follows linking verbs such as *feel, look, taste,* and *smell. Badly* is an adverb.

She feels *bad* because she played *badly.*
This brown shade looks *bad* on the walls.

Good is always an adjective. *Well* is an adverb except when it refers to a person's health.

Incorrect: They work good together.
Correct: They work *well* together.

Incorrect: In spite of his cold, Jim feels good enough to go.
Correct: In spite of his cold, Jim feels *well* enough to go.

Not all modifiers ending in *-ly* are adverbs. Among adjectives that end in *-ly* are *homely, friendly, lovely,* and *kindly.*

Exercise 1

Choose the correct word to complete each sentence. Identify it as an adjective or an adverb.

1. Visitors speak (enthusiastic enthusiastically) about the Great Barrier Reef—one of the Great Natural Wonders of the World.

2. I felt (enthusiastic enthusiastically) about the visit to the reef.

3. The waters around the reef are quite (clear clearly).

4. Snorkeling allows visitors to see the reef (clear clearly).

5. Visitors can also see the sea life (good well) from semi-subs that travel a few feet beneath the water's surface.

6. A guide gave a (thorough thoroughly) explanation of the unusual features of the reef.

7. Coral reefs do not grow (quick quickly)—a few inches a year.

Exercise 2

Rewrite these sentences to correct errors in the use of adverbs or adjectives. Not all sentences have errors.

1. Before my visit to the reef, I could snorkel good.

2. The reef looked quite magical underwater.

3. The world appears quite differently underwater.

4. A marine expert guided us safe under the water.

5. I felt badly when the trip ended.

Practice Power

Use the following pairs of words in separate sentences. Be sure your sentences indicate clearly which are adjectives and which are adverbs.

good, well	quick, quickly
enthusiastic, enthusiastically	different, differently
bad, badly	sharp, sharply

5.5 *Negative Words*

Using two negative words where only one is needed is called a double negative. If a sentence already has a negative word, whether an adverb or an adjective, avoid using another negative word. The most common negative adverbs are *no, not,* and *never.*

> Incorrect: I haven't never seen Mount Everest.
> Correct: I *haven't ever* seen Mount Everest.

> Incorrect: Nobody didn't attend the concert.
> Correct: *Nobody attended* the concert.

The adverbs *barely, hardly,* and *scarcely* have a negative sense and should not be used with other negative terms.

> Incorrect: There wasn't hardly enough food.
> Correct: There *was hardly* enough food.

> Incorrect: We couldn't barely see the screen.
> Correct: We *could barely* see the screen.

> Incorrect: He wasn't scarcely inside the car.
> Correct: He *was scarcely* inside the car.

Can't help but and *haven't but* are double negatives and should be avoided.

> Incorrect: She can't help but wonder who got the part.
> Correct: She can't *help wondering* who got the part.

> Incorrect: I haven't but one dollar left.
> Correct: I *have but one dollar* left.
> Correct: I *have only one dollar* left.

Sometimes a double negative occurs when there is an intervening element between the *not* and the remainder of the clause it is negating.

> Incorrect: Juan didn't think that, because he was the youngest, he shouldn't have to stay back.
> Correct: Juan *didn't think* that, because he was the youngest, *he should have* to *stay back.*

Exercise 1

Choose the correct words to complete these sentences.

1. I hadn't (ever scarcely ever) heard that Mount Everest is considered one of the Great Natural Wonders of the World.

2. There aren't (no any) mountains in the world taller.

3. (No Any) other mountain has so captured our imagination.

4. There aren't (barely any any) people who know the Himalayas better than the native Sherpa.

5. Edmund Hillary, a New Zealander, and Tenzing Norgay, a Sherpa, weren't the first who (ever never) tried to reach its top, but they were the first to succeed.

6. Hillary took a photo of Norgay at the top, but there aren't (no any) photos of Hillary there.

7. I (can't help but can't help) remembering that the pair left (no any) sign other than gifts Norgay left for the gods.

8. Interestingly, both Hillary and Norgay said they didn't have (any hardly any) desire to ever return to the top.

Exercise 2

Rewrite the following sentences to correct any errors in the use of negatives. Not all sentences have errors.

1. I haven't never climbed a mountain.

2. There aren't any mountains near my home.

3. There aren't even no hills.

4. I've never been skiing either.

5. There isn't no sport I would like to try more.

Practice Power

Write 10 sentences about things you haven't done and things you don't ever want to do. Use negative words correctly.

A prepositional phrase is made up of a preposition and its object. When a prepositional phrase is used as an adverb, it is an **adverb phrase** and, like an adverb, modifies a verb, an adjective, or an adverb. An adverb phrase can appear anywhere in a sentence but usually appears next to the word it modifies. Adverb phrases tell *when, where, how,* or *how much.* They also tell *why, to what extent,* and *under what condition.*

In the following sentence *in ancient Greece* is an adverb phrase. It describes the verb *began* and tells where.

> The Olympic Games began *in ancient Greece.*

More than one adverb phrase may be used to modify the same word. In the following sentence both adverb phrases modify the verb *sped.*

> The car sped *through town toward the stadium.*

A **clause** is a group of words with a subject and a predicate. A dependent clause does not express a complete thought. **Adverb clauses** are dependent clauses used as adverbs to describe verbs, adjectives, or adverbs. Adverb clauses answer the same questions as adverb phrases.

In this sentence the dependent clause *after the Olympic flame is ignited* is an adverb clause. It tells when and describes the verb *is carried* in the main clause.

> *After the Olympic flame is ignited,* it is carried by torchbearers to the site of the Olympic Games.

Some common conjunctions that introduce adverb clauses are *although, after, as, because, before, if, in order that, provided that, since, so that, unless, until, when, whenever, where, wherever, whether,* and *while.*

Exercise 1

Identify the adverb phrase or phrases in each sentence. Tell the word that each describes.

1. A temple stood in ancient Olympia.

2. The Olympic Games were played near the temple.

3. Zeus's statue was placed inside the temple.

4. It was named one of the Seven Wonders of the Ancient World by the ancients.

5. The statue was built during the fifth century BC.

6. Zeus's figure sat on a throne.

7. Ivory was used for Zeus's skin, and gold was used for his beard and robe.

Exercise 2

Identify the adverb clause in each sentence.

1. Although Zeus was the king of the gods, his temple was plain.

2. Because the temple was relatively simple, the Greeks decided to build a magnificent statue in honor of the god.

3. When the statue was finished, it stood some 40 feet tall.

4. The statue seemed even more imposing because it reached nearly to the lofty ceiling of the temple.

5. Although copies of the statue were made, none survive.

6. Images on coins, however, remain so that we have some idea of what the statue looked like.

7. The statue survived until a fire destroyed it in AD 462.

Practice Power

Write a short paragraph about a historic place that you would like to visit. Include a little about the history of the place and tell why you want to visit it. Identify any adverb phrases and clauses.

Adverb Challenge

Read the selection and then answer the questions.

1. Lewis and Clark, explorers of the Louisiana Territory, were important pioneers of the western United States. 2. Asked by President Jefferson to explore the possibility of a water route across the continent, these explorers organized a party and bravely undertook the difficult mission. 3. They traveled for two years. 4. Very slowly and patiently they pushed up the Missouri River to its source. 5. Each day they traveled farther into the wild. 6. Their progress was often slow, but with the aid of their guide Sacagawea, a Shoshone woman, they crossed the mighty Rockies. 7. As they descended the Columbia River, they finally sighted the Pacific Ocean. 8. Courageously, the explorers continued until they reached their goal.

1. Name the adverb in sentence 2 and tell what kind it is.

2. Identify the adverb phrase in sentence 3. Tell what word it describes.

3. Find an adverb in sentence 4 that describes another adverb.

4. Find two adverbs of manner in sentence 4.

5. Write the comparative and superlative forms of those two adverbs of manner.

6. Name an adverb of place in sentence 5.

7. Write the positive and the superlative forms of that adverb.

8. In sentence 6 what kind of adverb is *often?*

9. Name the adverb phrase in sentence 6.

10. Name the adverb of time in sentence 7.

11. Identify the adverb clause in sentence 7.

12. What is the adverb clause in sentence 8? What does it describe?

Sentences

The essential elements of a sentence are a subject and a predicate.

The **subject** of a sentence names the person, place, or thing the sentence is about. To determine the subject of a sentence, ask *who* or *what* before the verb.

> *Sequoias* grow more than 200 feet tall.

Question: What grow more than 200 feet tall? The answer is *sequoias*—the subject of the sentence.

> <u>Parks</u> in California are home to many sequoias.

The subject is *parks*. The noun or pronoun about which something is said is called the **simple subject.** The complete subject is *Parks in California.* The **complete subject** consists of the simple subject and all the words that describe it. Two or more simple subjects form a **compound subject.**

The **predicate** tells what the subject is or is doing.

> Sequoias *soar.*

The subject of the sentence is *sequoias.* What do sequoias do? The sequoias *soar.* The predicate of this sentence is *soar.*

> The giant sequoias <u>produce</u> *tiny seeds.*

In this sentence, the word *produce* is the **simple predicate,** or verb. The phrase *produce tiny seeds* is the **complete predicate.** A complete predicate contains the verb, its modifiers, and its complements or objects. A simple predicate may contain more than one word—the main verb and all of its auxiliary verbs; this is called a **verb phrase.** Two or more simple predicates form a **compound predicate.**

Exercise 1

Tell the simple subject and complete subject in each sentence.

1. Sequoias are a type of evergreen tree.
2. The enormous size of these redwoods makes them unusual.

3. Scientists measure the age of trees by counting their rings.

4. A new ring grows around a sequoia's thick trunk every year.

5. The trees are among the largest living organisms on earth.

Exercise 2

Identify the simple predicate and the complete predicate in each sentence.

1. Sequoias grew throughout the Northern Hemisphere before the last Ice Age.

2. The General Sherman sequoia in California was alive at the time of the ancient Greeks and Romans.

3. The circumference of the giant tree named for a general is 102 feet.

4. Most sequoias rise to the height of skyscrapers—as high as 360 feet.

5. Thick bark protects these stately trees from forest fires.

Exercise 3

Identify the complete subject and the complete predicate in each sentence. Then name the simple subject and simple predicate of each.

1. The trees grow only in the Sierra Nevadas now.

2. The government protects most large sequoias.

3. People cannot cut them down.

4. Sequoia National Park in California is home to many sequoias.

5. The largest of sequoias is taller than a 25-story building.

Practice Power

Write down seven facts about a natural phenomenon.
Identify the subject and predicate in each sentence.

6.2 Natural and Inverted Order

A sentence is in **natural order** when the verb follows the subject.

> Niagara Falls lies between Canada and the United States.

The simple predicate is *lies*. Ask *who or what lies?* to find the subject. It is *Niagara Falls*. The verb comes after the subject, so the sentence is in natural order.

A sentence is in **inverted order** when the main verb or an auxiliary verb comes before the subject.

> Between Canada and the United States lies Niagara Falls.

The verb *lies* comes before the subject *Niagara Falls* so the sentence is in inverted order. Ask *who or what lies?* The answer is *Niagara Falls*.

Many questions are in inverted order. Can you explain how the following question is in inverted order?

> Where does Niagara Falls lie?

You are right if you said that the auxiliary verb *does* comes before the subject *Niagara Falls*.

Exercise 1

Tell whether each sentence is in natural or inverted order.

1. Niagara Falls has two main waterfalls.

2. On the Canadian side is Horseshoe Falls.

3. Water roars over the falls into a gorge below.

4. Into the air rise vast amounts of spray.

5. Have you ever been to Niagara Falls?

6. Prospect Point is home to the observation tower.

7. At the edge, between the American and Bridal Veil Falls, sits Luna Island.

8. Each night beautiful lights illuminate the Falls.

Exercise 2

Rewrite each sentence in natural order.

1. Between Lake Erie and Lake Ontario lies Niagara Falls.

2. Over Horseshoe Falls tumbles most of the water.

3. On the U.S. side is the American Falls.

4. Under the falls go sightseers in steamboats.

5. Around the falls stand observation towers for tourists.

6. Over the falls have gone many daredevils.

Exercise 3

Each sentence below is in natural order. Rewrite it in inverted order, writing questions where indicated.

1. About 100,000 cubic feet of water a second flow down Niagara Falls.

2. The name *Niagara* comes from a Native American word for strait. (question)

3. The roar of the falls is deafening. (question)

4. Millions of people visit Niagara Falls each year. (question)

5. Many tourists come for a single glimpse of the falls.

6. Honeymooners, families, and school groups are among the crowds.

7. The pristine water splashes from the sky.

8. Brilliant rainbows appear in the billowing mists.

Practice Power

Write a description of your bedroom or some other place special to you. Describe the things in the room and their locations. Use some inverted sentences for variety in your writing.

6.3 *Types of Sentences*

There are four types of sentences. A **declarative sentence** makes a statement. A declarative sentence ends with a period.

Stonehenge is in England.

An **interrogative sentence** asks a question. An interrogative sentence ends with a question mark.

Shouldn't Stonehenge be considered one of the Wonders of the Ancient World?

An **imperative sentence** gives a command. An imperative sentence ends with a period.

Write a report about Stonehenge.

An **exclamatory sentence** expresses a strong emotion. An exclamatory sentence ends with an exclamation mark.

Stonehenge is magnificent!

Exercise 1

Tell whether each sentence is declarative or interrogative. Rewrite the sentences to show the correct end punctuation.

1. What is Stonehenge
2. Stonehenge consists of a number of large stones placed in a circle
3. The stone structure dates from ancient times
4. Are the stones tall
5. Some stones stand 13.5 feet high
6. Who built Stonehenge
7. When were you there
8. I've never been there myself
9. We're going someday

Tell whether each sentence is imperative or exclamatory. Rewrite the sentences to show the correct end punctuation.

1. What an impressive sight Stonehenge must be
2. Tell me about the placement of the stones at Stonehenge
3. Explain the difficulty of transporting such huge stones
4. Wow, you know a lot about Stonehenge
5. Name some Web sites with good pictures of Stonehenge

Exercise 3

Tell whether each sentence is declarative, interrogative, imperative, or exclamatory. Rewrite the sentences to show the correct end punctuation.

1. Why was Stonehenge built
2. Some archeologists think Stonehenge was an ancient calendar
3. It was probably the site of religious observances
4. Construction of Stonehenge began in approximately 2800 BC
5. That's really incredible
6. Figure out its age with that information
7. The builders placed the huge stones upright in a perfect circle
8. How did they manage that
9. What an amazing feat
10. For me Stonehenge is an amazing work of art
11. What do you think of Stonehenge
12. Check the library for more information about Stonehenge

Practice Power

Write about something in nature that fascinates you. Use at least one of each of the four sentence types: declarative, interrogative, imperative, and exclamatory.

6.4 Simple and Compound Sentences

A **simple sentence** contains a subject and a predicate. Either or both may be compound.

Subject	Predicate
The auroral *lights*	*are* a natural wonder.

(simple sentence with one subject and one predicate)

Spring and *fall*	*are* good times for views of them.

(simple sentence with a compound subject)

Colorful *lights*	*streak* or *hang* in the sky.

(simple sentence with a compound predicate)

A **compound sentence** contains two or more independent clauses. An independent clause has a subject and a predicate and can stand on its own as a sentence. Independent clauses are usually connected by a coordinating conjunction: *and, but, or, nor, yet,* or *so.*

> Auroral lights are associated with the activity of the sun, and they are caused by electrons from it.

This sentence has two independent clauses connected by *and.* Can you find the subject and verb in each clause? You are right if you said that in the first clause *lights* is the subject and *are associated* is the predicate. In the second clause *they* is the subject and *are caused* is the predicate.

Tell whether each of these sentences is simple or compound.

1. Auroral lights sometimes appear as lines in the sky and then change into balls of light.

2. The northern lights are common in Canada and Alaska, but people farther south see them at times.

You are correct if you said the first sentence is a simple sentence. It has one subject—*lights*—and a compound predicate—*appear* and *change.* The second sentence is a compound sentence; it has two independent clauses.

Exercise 1

Identify the subject and predicate in each independent clause in these compound sentences.

1. In the 1600s Galileo saw the lights, and he chose the name *Aurora.*

2. In Galileo's theories the auroral lights reflected the dawn, so he named them after the goddess of dawn.

3. The lights are not reflections of the sun, but they are produced by the movement of electrons from the sun.

4. The northern lights have the name *aurora borealis,* and the southern lights have the name *aurora australis.*

Exercise 2

Tell whether each sentence is simple or compound. Identify the subject and predicate in the simple sentences and in both clauses in the compound sentences.

1. Ancient people saw the lights but did not know their cause.

2. To some Asians auroral lights were dragons in the sky, but to Scandinavians they were reflections off gods' armor.

3. Great storms begin on the sun, and particles shoot out.

4. Particles enter Earth's atmosphere and collide with air molecules.

5. Streamers, arcs, and rays are all forms of the resulting lights.

6. Most auroral lights are green and white, but nitrogen gases can make them red, blue, or purple.

Practice Power

Write sentences using the words as described.

1. *arcs, rays*—as the compound subject of a simple sentence and as subjects in a compound sentence

2. *appear, shine*—as the compound predicate of a simple sentence and as predicates in a compound sentence

6.5 *Punctuation of Compound Sentences*

The clauses of a **compound sentence** are usually connected by a conjunction: *and, but, or, nor, yet,* or *so.* The clauses are usually separated by a comma placed before the conjunction.

> The Grand Canyon is not the deepest canyon in the world, *but* it is one of the most famous.

A semicolon may be used between independent clauses instead of a coordinating conjunction.

> The Grand Canyon is famous for its colorful walls; they make it one of the most beautiful canyons in the world.

If the clauses are short and closely related, the comma or semicolon may be omitted.

> The river flowed and the canyon slowly formed.

Exercise 1

Rewrite the compound sentences to add correct punctuation.

1. The Grand Canyon is now located in the desert yet water erosion was the cause of its formation.

2. Millions of years of water erosion formed the canyon but wind also played a major role in its creation.

3. The ancient Colorado River eroded the rocks of the Grand Canyon and the broad stripes of its walls appeared.

4. The Grand Canyon is still changing it continues to be eroded by rain and windstorms.

5. The canyon's deepest rocks are about two billion years old and the river started to erode them some 60 million years ago.

6. Parts of the canyon aren't easily accessible yet some tourists manage to visit them.

7. The tourists in the early spring come for the view but they often don't stay long because of the cold mountain air.

Exercise 2

Combine each pair of simple sentences to form a compound sentence. Use either a comma and a coordinating conjunction or a semicolon to separate the clauses.

1. The Grand Canyon is about 300 miles long. It is about a mile deep!

2. The width of the Grand Canyon can be less than one mile. It is sometimes 18 miles across.

3. The Grand Canyon has 10 primary layers of rock. There are also many secondary layers.

4. The rock layers are different colors and widths. They give the canyon its unique stripes.

5. The colors of the rock include terra cotta, mustard, white, grayish green, and purple. It is impossible to name them all.

6. The colors look different at different times of day. Some people think the best time to view the canyon is at sunrise or sunset.

7. Native Americans have lived in the Grand Canyon for hundreds of years. Some still live there today.

8. You can get to their village only by river, by foot, or by mule. Many tourists still visit it.

9. The journey to the bottom of the Grand Canyon and back usually takes two days. You have to make it by mule.

10. You can visit the Grand Canyon on foot or by mule. You can take a raft down the river.

11. In 1869 the geologist John Wesley Powell saw the Grand Canyon for the first time. He gave it its name.

12. The Grand Canyon looks durable and unchanging. It is still constantly eroding.

Practice Power

Write about a trip to the Grand Canyon. Use compound sentences to describe the trip, the sights, and your reactions.

6.6 Prepositions and Prepositional Phrases

A **preposition** is a word that shows the relation of a noun or pronoun to some other word in the sentence. The noun or pronoun that follows the preposition is its object.

Common prepositions include the following:

about	before	from	over
above	behind	in	through
across	beside	like	to
after	between	near	under
against	by	of	up
among	down	off	with
around	during	on	within
at	for		

Two or more words are sometimes used together as a preposition. These include *apart from, because of, by means of, in place of, instead of,* and *out of.*

A preposition and the noun or pronoun that follows it form a **prepositional phrase.** The phrase includes any words that describe the object.

Snow still covers Lake Baikal *in early March.*

The prepositional phrase *in early March* includes the object *March* and the adjective *early,* which describes the object. Do not mistake the object of a preposition for the subject of a sentence.

> Incorrect: The main causes of seal population decline is toxins and hunters.
> Correct: The main <u>causes</u> of seal population decline <u>are</u> toxins and hunters.

When a personal pronoun is the object of a preposition, it must always be in the object form. When the object is compound, it remains in the object form.

> Incorrect: I sent the wildlife brochures to Sue and he.
> Correct: I sent the wildlife brochures to Sue and *him.*

Exercise 1

Identify the preposition or prepositions in each sentence. Then name the object of each preposition.

1. Lake Baikal may be the oldest and deepest lake on earth.
2. There are 1,500 species of animals in the lake.
3. It is known for its unusual varieties.
4. They are studied by scientists.
5. The lake is compared to the Galapagos Islands because of its unique creatures.

Exercise 2

Identify the preposition and prepositional phrase in each sentence. There may be more than one phrase in a sentence.

1. The world's only freshwater seal is found in Lake Baikal.
2. These seals are known by the Russian name *nerpas.*
3. The seals probably are relatives of the Arctic seals.
4. Nerpas usually spend the winter under the ice of the lake.
5. They poke small holes in the ice.
6. The nerpas use these small holes for air.
7. They build dens like igloos in the ice.
8. In the summer they spend time on the surface of the lake.
9. The animals feed mainly at night, and during the day they submerge to great depths.
10. With a large blood supply to carry oxygen, nerpas can stay under the water for some 60 minutes at a time.

Practice Power

Write three sentences in which a prepositional phrase comes between the subject and predicate. Then write five prepositional phrases with compound objects.

6.7 Using Prepositions Correctly

At, to *At* shows presence in. *To* shows motion toward.

> Dionne was *at* the Grand Canyon.
> Dionne went *to* the Grand Canyon.

Between, among Use *between* to speak of two persons, places, or things. Use *among* for more than two.

> I can't decide *between* Niagara Falls and the Grand Canyon as the subject of my report.
> I can't decide *among* the Grand Canyon, Niagara Falls, and sequoias as the subject of my report.

Beside, besides *Beside* means "at the side of" or "next to." *Besides* means "in addition to" or "except."

> The Horseshoe Falls are *beside* the American Falls.
> *Besides* the report, do we have any other homework?

In, into Use *in* to show location within something. Use *into* to show motion toward a place or a change of location.

> The diver is *in* the water near the reef.
> The diver went *into* the water near the reef.

Omit unnecessary prepositions.

> Where *is* Maria? *not* Where is Maria at?
> Go *inside* the house. *not* Go inside of the house.

When two or more prepositions have a single object, each prepositional phrase must be correct.

> He gave *to* and took *from* his brother.

Exercise 1

Complete each sentence with the correct preposition, *at* or *to*.

1. Millions go _____ the Grand Canyon.

2. Were you ever _____ Niagara Falls?

3. We climbed _____ the top of an observation tower.

Complete each sentence with the correct preposition, *among* or *between*.

4. _____ all the natural wonders, which is the most amazing?

5. Choose _____ Ayers Rock and the Great Barrier Reef.

6. I can't decide _____ a hiking trip and a rafting trip.

Complete each sentence with the correct preposition, *beside* or *besides*.

7. _____ the Grand Canyon, are there any other natural wonders in the United States?

8. _____ Elaine, Louisa is the only person I know who has been to Mammoth Cave.

9. Visitors to Yellowstone National Park often take pictures of one another _____ one of the many geysers.

Complete each sentence with the correct preposition, *in* or *into*.

10. We got _____ the boat for our trip through the Everglades.

11. Water from the outboard engine splashed _____ the boat.

12. A variety of cactuses grows _____ the southwestern desert.

Exercise 2

Correct the following sentences to eliminate unnecessary prepositions or to insert omitted prepositions.

1. Have you checked inside of your wallet?

2. Here's the friend with whom I went to the movie with.

3. She gave her ticket and walked past the usher.

4. We climbed up the stairs to the top balcony.

5. The award was presented and accepted by the lead actor.

Practice Power

Write a pair of sentences for each set of prepositions in this section. Underline the prepositional phrases.

6.8 Prepositions and Adverbs

Some words can be used as either prepositions or adverbs: *after, around, before, below, down, inside, near, outside, past, through, under,* and *with.*

Fish swam *past* me. (preposition)
Fish swam *past.* (adverb)

What parts of speech are the italicized words in these sentences?

We left for the beach soon *after* dawn.
We left for the beach soon *after.*

You are correct if you said that in the first sentence *after* is a preposition, part of the phrase *after dawn.* In the second sentence *after* is not part of a phrase; it is an adverb.

A preposition is always part of a phrase that ends with a noun or pronoun. So, to determine whether a word is a preposition or an adverb, check whether it is followed by a noun or pronoun. If it is, the word is a preposition; if not, it's an adverb.

Exercise 1

The word italicized in the first sentence in each set is used as an adverb. Use the word as a preposition in the second sentence by adding an object.

1. I swam *near.*

   I swam near _____.

2. It is fun to look *around.*

   It is fun to look around _____.

3. We prepared *before.*

   We prepared before _____.

4. We rested *after.*

   We rested after _____.

5. He said his sister was *through.*

   He said his sister was through _____.

Exercise 2

Tell whether the italicized word in each sentence is a preposition or an adverb.

1. Dive *in* and see some wonders of the world.
2. Slip *under* the water and enter a different world.
3. *With* a snorkel you become part of the world under the sea.
4. With fins on your feet and a mask *over* your face, you're ready.
5. Wear a buoyancy jacket to help float *on* the water.
6. You swim face *down.*
7. The top of the snorkel stays *above* the water.
8. That way you can still breathe *in.*
9. Look *around* and see a world of blue.
10. You might see a school of fish go *inside* a reef.
11. If you have never snorkeled *before,* be sure to stay close.
12. You can go deeper and put the snorkel under the water, but then you can't breathe *through* the snorkel.
13. Look *up* when you surface—don't hit the bottom of a boat.
14. You'll learn that it's hard to walk with fins *outside* the water.
15. You can talk about the underwater experience for a long time *after.*

Practice Power

Imagine that you are a world-famous diver. Write a description of your adventures. Use at least five of the following words as either adverbs or prepositions. Identify them and their use in your writing.

about	between	off
above	down	through
after	from	under
before	in	up

6.9 Adjective Phrases

A prepositional phrase used as an adjective is called an **adjective phrase.**

> Borobudur, a temple *to Buddha,* is a wonderful sight.

To Buddha describes or gives more information about the noun *temple* and is therefore an adjective phrase.

Can you identify the adjective phrases in these sentences and tell the nouns they describe?

> Buddha was the founder of a major world religion.
> Buddha sought freedom from worldly things.

You are correct if you said that *of a major world religion* gives information about the noun *founder* in the first sentence. In the second sentence the adjective phrase *from worldly things* describes the noun *freedom.*

Exercise 1

Identify the adjective phrase or phrases in each sentence.

1. Borobudur is the name of a magnificent temple.

2. The Indonesian temple in central Java is more than 1,400 years old.

3. It is an attraction for many tourists.

4. The temple on the mountainside has three parts, or levels.

5. The three parts are a base with square terraces, a cone with circular terraces, and finally a stupa.

6. The stupa is a bell-like structure with a statue of Buddha.

7. The openings in the stupa give a view of the statue.

8. The stupa at the top of the temple dominates the landscape around the temple.

9. An amazing feature of the temple is its many sculptures.

10. The sculptures at the lower levels retrace Buddha's life.

11. This magnificent marvel of stone especially inspires those who see it in the tropical moonlight.

Exercise 2

Identify the adjective phrase or phrases in each sentence. Name the word that each describes.

1. Ancient pilgrims to the temple climbed the stairs.
2. The climb up the stairs was a symbolic journey.
3. Each of the temple's three levels represents a stage in life.
4. The goal of the journey is access to Wisdom.
5. The eruption of a neighboring volcano covered the temple.
6. Its rediscovery by a 19th-century British official made the temple famous again.
7. The damage to the temple was considerable.
8. A restoration between 1973 and 1984 revealed its glory.
9. The work of restoration was sponsored by UNESCO.

Exercise 3

Complete the sentences with the correct preposition. Identify each adjective phrase and the word it describes.

   about   for   from   of   to

1. Buddha was a man _____ India.
2. His life was a search _____ enlightenment.
3. He sought nirvana, a state _____ happiness and peace.
4. His teachings _____ his followers influenced many lives.
5. Stories _____ his life are important in Buddhism.

Practice Power

Use the following as adjective phrases in sentences.

1. from the top
2. of the trip
3. inside the building
4. with amazing artworks
5. about the natural wonders
6. through the openings

6.10 *Adverb Phrases*

Prepositional phrases that function as adverbs are called **adverb phrases.** Like single-word adverbs, adverb phrases answer the questions *how, when, where, why,* and *to what extent.* They often describe verbs.

> Several volcanoes are found *in Mexico.*

In Mexico is an adverb phrase that describes the verb phrase *are found.* It tells where.

In the following examples, adverbs are replaced by adverb phrases. They all describe the verb *rose.*

> The volcano rose *rapidly.* (adverb)
> The volcano rose *in a rapid manner.* (adverb phrase)
>
> The volcano rose *there.* (adverb)
> The volcano rose *in a field.* (adverb phrase)

Exercise 1

Identify the adverb phrase or phrases in each sentence.

1. For several weeks people heard rumbling sounds.

2. The sounds rolled like thunder.

3. However, the rumbling sounds were coming from the ground!

4. On February 20, 1943, Dionisio Pulido, a Mexican farmer, was working in his fields.

5. Suddenly the trees trembled and the ground shook for no apparent reason.

6. A hole was forming in the ground.

7. He looked into the gaping cavity and saw smoke and ashes.

8. The ground rapidly rose around the hole.

9. Dionisio looked into the hole fearfully but tried to think calmly.

10. He was standing on the edge of disaster.

11. His mind filled with visions of catastrophe.

Exercise 2

Identify the adverb phrase or phrases in each sentence. Tell what each tells about the word it describes—*how, when, where, why,* or *to what extent.*

1. Hot lava rolled over Pulido's field, and ashes blew into the air.

2. Pulido worried about his family.

3. They had been working near him.

4. He got on his horse, and he rode to the nearest town.

5. Fortunately his family already had arrived in the town.

6. During the night the ground rose 30 feet.

7. A volcano had been born in Pulido's field and continued its rapid growth!

8. The name Paricutin was given to the volcano.

9. It continued its eruptions until 1952.

10. Six thousand acres were destroyed by the volcano.

Exercise 3

Use each pair of words in a sentence. Then rewrite each sentence replacing the adverb with an adverbial phrase.

1. appeared instantly
2. ran hastily
3. looked worriedly
4. traveled quickly

5. smiled happily
6. worked patiently
7. listened silently
8. spoke sincerely

Practice Power

Write a story about a camping trip, using these phrases as adverb phrases.

1. into the backpack
2. in the woods
3. by the campfire
4. near the lake
5. into our camp
6. over the mountains

A **complex sentence** contains an independent clause and one or more dependent clauses. An independent clause has a subject and a verb and can stand on its own as a sentence. A dependent clause also has a subject and a verb, but it cannot stand alone as a sentence. It is always used with an independent clause as part of a complex sentence.

independent clause	dependent clause
My friend saw Ayers Rock	when she visited Australia.

Name the subjects and verbs in this complex sentence. You are right if you said that in the independent clause, *friend* is the subject and *saw* is the verb. In the dependent clause *she* is the subject and *visited* is the verb.

One type of dependent clause is an **adverb clause.** An adverb clause acts like an adverb and describes a verb, an adjective, or another adverb. Like adverb phrases, adverb clauses tell *how, when, where, why,* and *to what extent.*

Adverb clauses begin with **subordinate conjunctions.** Some common subordinate conjunctions are *although, after, as, because, before, if, in order that, provided that, since, so that, unless, until, when, whenever, where, wherever, whether,* and *while.*

independent clause	dependent clause
People visit Ayers Rock	because it is so mysterious.

Because it is so mysterious is an adverb clause that describes the verb *visit* in the independent clause. It answers the question *why.* Note that an adverb clause can often come before the independent clause.

Because it is so mysterious, people visit Ayers Rock.

Exercise 1

Indicate whether each clause is independent or dependent.

1. Because the huge rock stands alone in the desert

2. The formation of Ayers Rock took 500 million years

3. An ocean once covered the center of Australia

4. Aborigines are natives of Australia

5. While the rock is a symbol of creation for aboriginal people of Australia

6. Although the aborigines call the rock Uluru

Exercise 2

Identify the adverb clause in each sentence.

1. Ayers Rock changes color when atmospheric conditions change.

2. The colors of Ayers Rock also change as the time of day changes.

3. Although it often appears red, it can also appear blue.

4. Many tourists go at dawn in order that they can view the fabulous changing colors of the rock—red, pink, mauve.

5. Uluru still is 1,142 feet tall though it has eroded.

6. Although the visible rock seems amazingly huge, two thirds of it is under the surface.

7. Because it is sacred to the aborigines, it also seems a holy place to others.

8. If you ever go to Uluru, you will experience the close connection between nature and humans.

Practice Power

Use these adverb clauses in complex sentences of your own by adding independent clauses.

if I go to Australia	before I travel anyplace
whenever I go on a trip	because I'm interested in it
before you buy a bike	because the TV was broken
after I return from a trip	whenever I am really hungry
after I've earned some money	

Sentence Challenge

Read the selection and then answer the questions.

1. In the future, what will cars be like? 2. Cars will probably answer our questions, and they will respond to our commands! 3. You will simply tell your car where you want to go, for example, and it will turn on its engine and start you on the way. 4. Cars will have digital maps that show exactly where you are and where you are going. 5. Cars of the future will be more convenient, and they will be safer too. 6. Automatic sensors will control the steering and the brakes. 7. This automatic system will sense the nearby cars and guide your car through traffic. 8. You will be able to drive faster, yet there will be fewer accidents. 9. Because technology offers so many possibilities, cars of the future will certainly be a breeze to drive. 10. Buckle your seatbelts. 11. Maybe cars of the future will do that for you!

1. Is sentence 1 in natural or inverted order?

2. What is the prepositional phrase in sentence 1?

3. Is sentence 2 a compound or a complex sentence? How do you know?

4. In sentence 5, what is the prepositional phrase? Is it an adjective phrase or an adverb phrase?

5. Is sentence 5 a compound or a complex sentence? How do you know?

6. In sentence 6, name the simple subject and the simple predicate.

7. In sentence 7, identify the adverb phrase.

8. What are the two clauses in sentence 8? Is this a complex or a compound sentence?

9. What is the adverb clause in sentence 9?

10. Find an interrogative sentence.

11. Find an exclamatory sentence.

12. Find an imperative sentence.

Conjunctions, Interjections, Punctuation, and Capitalization

7.1 Conjunctions

A **conjunction** is a word used to connect words, phrases, or clauses in a sentence.

A **coordinating conjunction** is used to connect similar words or groups of words. It typically connects words that have the same use in a sentence. These words may be nouns, pronouns, verbs, adjectives, or adverbs. The coordinating conjunctions are *and, but, or, nor,* and *yet.*

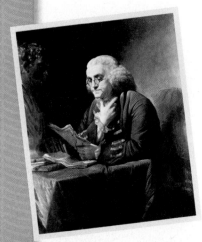

> Do you think Benjamin Franklin was a greater inventor *or* statesman? (nouns)
>
> Franklin also bought *and* ran the *Pennsylvania Gazette.* (verbs)
>
> Ben worked repeatedly *but* consistently to study electricity. (adverbs)
>
> The *Pennsylvania Gazette* was successful *and* entertaining. (adjectives)

Coordinating conjunctions can connect prepositional phrases.

> Ben was known for his intelligence *and* for his hard work.

Coordinating conjunctions can connect independent clauses or dependent clauses. When a conjunction joins independent clauses, use a comma before the conjunction.

> Franklin didn't have much formal schooling, *but* he managed to educate himself. (independent clauses)
>
> Because Franklin was patriotic *and* because he was willing, he served the country in many ways. (dependent clauses)

Exercise 1

Identify the conjunction in each sentence. Then identify the words it connects and tell whether they are nouns, verbs, adjectives, or adverbs.

1. Franklin was a printer and an author.

2. Franklin was civic-minded and diplomatic.

3. He organized and supervised a program to clean the streets of Philadelphia.

4. He started and ran the first public library in this country.

5. He knew that books were both scarce and costly.

6. He worked tirelessly and selflessly for the improvement of the city.

Exercise 2

Identify the coordinating conjunction in each sentence. Tell if it connects prepositional phrases or independent clauses.

1. Franklin had strong interests in science and in electricity.

2. He was famous in the Americas and in Europe for his experiments with electricity.

3. He invented a better stove, but he did not want to get a patent on his invention.

4. Is his fame based on his scientific achievements or on his patriotic service?

5. He worked for the benefit of all, yet he did not seek personal profit.

6. Franklin invented bifocals, and the concept is still in use today.

7. His fascination with politics and with science has made him one of our country's most famous early figures.

8. Franklin was brilliant, but he was also humble.

Practice Power

Write a sentence that contains a coordinating conjunction to connect each pair of words, phrases, or clauses below.

1. muffins, rolls
2. quick, easy
3. from the country, to the city
4. collects, labels
5. slowly, confidently
6. Linda read the map, Andre drove the van.

An **interjection** is a word that expresses a strong or sudden emotion. Interjections may express happiness, disgust, pain, agreement, impatience, surprise, sadness, amazement, and so on. They can also be used in greetings and as attention getters. An interjection is usually set off from the rest of the sentence by an exclamation mark.

My word! I didn't know Alexander Graham Bell invented so many things.

Yes! He invented many things having to do with sound.

You have a new cell phone. *Great!*

Here are some common interjections:

Ah!	Ha!	Oops!
Aha!	Hello!	Ouch!
Alas!	Hey!	Rats!
Beware!	Hooray!	Sh!
Bravo!	Hurrah!	Ugh!
Good!	Hush!	Well!
Goodbye!	Indeed!	What!
Good grief!	My!	Whew!
Goodness!	My word!	Wow!
Gosh!	No!	Yes!
Great!	Oh!	Yikes!

Exercise 1

Identify the interjection in each sentence.

1. Aha! You know a lot about Alexander Graham Bell.

2. Good! You can tell me about the invention of the telephone.

3. Hooray! That Bell worked with people with hearing disabilities isn't surprising.

4. No! I didn't know that Bell experimented with making a better telegraph and that led him to invent the phone!

5. You can tell me more about him later. Fantastic!

Exercise 2

Note the interjections. Tell what feeling or emotion you think each interjection expresses.

1. Well! Alexander Graham Bell worked on many inventions after the telephone.

2. Oh! I didn't know that!

3. Yes! He experimented with using sound waves to detect icebergs under the water.

4. Hey! He even invented a hydrofoil—a vehicle that moves on land and water.

5. Indeed! He received a patent for the hydrofoil when he was 75 years old.

6. Good grief! Bell really was interested in a lot of things!

Exercise 3

Write an interjection at the beginning of each sentence.

1. _____! We're going to visit the science museum.

2. _____! That dinosaur skeleton is huge.

3. _____! With this machine you can see the blood cells move within your eye.

4. _____! There's a video about Mars in the theater.

5. _____! I almost tripped on something in this dark.

6. _____! I can't hear the video.

7. _____! I think I lost my lunch money.

Practice Power

Imagine how funny a TV cooking show might be if the chef kept getting things wrong. Write a paragraph on what might happen. Use interjections to express surprise, pain, agreement, impatience, and so on.

A **period** is used

- at the end of declarative and imperative sentences

  I ordered some special glue for my model.
  Please mail the letter with my order.

- with these common abbreviations

Names

J. F. Kennedy		John Fitzgerald Kennedy	
R. L. Stevenson		Robert Louis Stevenson	

Titles

Pres.	President	Dr.	Doctor
Gov.	Governor	Rev.	Reverend
Gen.	General	Mr.	Mister

Addresses

Ave.	Avenue	Bldg.	Building
Pkwy.	Parkway	Co.	Company
U.S.	United States	Inc.	Incorporated

Time

a.m.	before noon	Jan.	January
p.m.	after noon	Sat.	Saturday
sec.	second	mo.	month

Units of Measure

gal.	gallon	in.	inch
qt.	quart	ft.	foot
pt.	pint	yd.	yard
oz.	ounce	mi.	mile

Periods are *not* used in metric measures.

cm	centimeter	l	liter

Periods are not used after the postal abbreviations for states. Both letters in the abbreviation are capitalized.

CA	California	IL	Illinois	NJ New Jersey

Exercise 1

Add periods where needed in these sentences.

1. Dr Martin isn't a medical doctor He's a dentist

2. His office address is 898 E Edgeware Blvd, Norfolk, CT

3. My appointment card reads Wed, Nov 3, at 3:30 pm

4. His wife, Mrs Sarah Martin, is a friend of my mother's

Exercise 2

Rewrite the following letter. Add periods where needed.

1489 N Ashland Ave
Chicago, IL 60647
April 3, 20—

Edna K Roberts, President
Great Glue Co
1992 Western Hwy
Boston, MA 02127

Dear Ms Roberts:

I recently ordered a large (16 oz) tube of Playtion Glue from your latest catalog When it arrived, however, the package contained a medium (12 oz) jar of your Scrapbooking Paste, which I cannot use at this time

Please send a replacement tube by return mail as well as instructions for how to return the errant jar

Very truly yours,
Robert Josephs

Practice Power

Write a letter to a company to place an order or to return a product. Also address an envelope to the company. Be sure to use periods in abbreviations correctly.

Commas are used to

- separate words or groups of words in a series of three or more

  George Washington studied math, geography, astronomy, and surveying in school.

- set off parts of dates, addresses, and geographic names

  George Washington was born on February 22, 1732.
  Born in Westmoreland County, Virginia, he made that state his home.

- set off an appositive that is nonrestrictive

  George Washington, the first president of the United States, was both a military and a political leader.

- separate the clauses of a compound sentence connected by the coordinating conjunctions *and, but, or, nor,* or *yet*

  George Washington led the U.S. army during the Revolutionary War, and he was later elected president.

  The comma may be omitted if the clauses are short and closely connected.

  The armies met and the battle began.

- set off direct quotations

  "Liberty—when it begins to take root—is a plant of rapid growth," said Washington.

Exercise 1

Give the rule that applies to the use of each comma in the following sentences.

1. James Madison was born on March 16, 1751.

2. He was from Port Conway, Virginia, a very small town.

3. Madison fought against slavery, helped write the U.S. Constitution, and worked for passage of the Bill of Rights.

4. Madison, an experienced statesman, became the fourth President of the United States.

5. He succeeded Jefferson, and he pursued many of the same policies.

6. One of my friends said, "This period in U.S. history was the most exciting."

Exercise 2

Revise the sentences if necessary. Add commas where needed.

1. John Adams a founding father of the United States was born in Braintree Massachusetts.

2. He was born on October 30 1735.

3. He served as a member of the Continental Congress vice-president of the United States and president.

4. Adams arrived in the new capital of Washington D.C. on November 1 1800 and he and his wife took up residence in the White House.

5. As president, he averted a war with France but his presidency saw many rifts among political leaders.

6. The tension between Adams an eloquent promoter of the Declaration of Independence and Thomas Jefferson the writer of the Declaration of Independence followed.

7. Ironically, both men died on July 4 1826 the 50th anniversary of the Declaration of Independence.

8. John Adams once said "The Revolution was in the minds and hearts of the people."

Practice Power

Write two sentences to illustrate each of the rules for commas discussed in this section.

7.5 *Exclamation Points and Question Marks*

Exclamation points are used

- at the end of exclamatory sentences to express a strong emotion or reaction

  The electricity just went out!
  What bad timing this is!

- after interjections and exclamatory words to express happiness, disgust, pain, agreement, impatience, surprise, sadness, amazement, and other emotions

  No! I'm in the middle of drying my hair.
  Quick! Change the fuse in the fuse box.

A **question mark** is used at the end of a question.

  Did Thomas Edison invent the electric light bulb?
  When did Edison live?

Exercise 1

Rewrite the sentences. Add exclamation points where needed.

1. How different life was before there was electricity in homes

2. Wow I can't imagine life without electric lights, let alone electrical appliances.

3. Indeed Electricity runs everything from our hair dryers to our microwaves.

4. Hooray for electricity

Exercise 2

Rewrite the sentences. Add question marks and periods where needed.

1. Did Thomas Edison have an important role in the development of the electric industry

2. His studio at Menlo Park was lit by electricity in 1879

3. Where was the first commercial electric power station

4. What was Edison's role in the design of the first power station in New York

5. It provided the first electricity that went into homes

Exercise 3

Rewrite the sentences. Add periods, exclamation points, and question marks where needed.

1. Wait Thomas Edison didn't invent the light bulb

2. Did Edison improve on an existing idea for a light bulb

3. Yes People had the idea for a light bulb before Edison

4. Wow Someone had the idea for an electric light bulb 50 years before Edison did

5. Amazing I didn't know that Edison had to invent seven other items before he could finish his electric light bulb

6. Did these inventions include on-off switches for lights

7. Yes, indeed Thomas Edison invented on-off switches

8. What was Edison's role in the invention of the light bulb

9. How important his role was

10. It's quite amazing that he was able to find a way to make the light bulb long lasting and practical for home use

Practice Power

Pretend you have won a contest that allows you to spend 15 minutes in a store of your choice selecting as many things as you would like with no charge! Write a short paragraph naming some of the things you would choose. Include exclamatory and interrogative sentences, as well as interjections.

7.6 Semicolons

A **semicolon** is used to

- separate the clauses of a compound sentence when they are not separated by *and, but, or, nor,* or *yet*

  Benedict Arnold is a famous figure from the American Revolution; his name has come down in history as a traitor to the American cause.

- separate items in a series when the items themselves contain commas

  Attending the conference were James Pickett, headmaster of Carter School; Nancy Adams, superintendent of District 85 schools; and Bart Phillips, curriculum director of District 17 schools.

Exercise 1

Rewrite the sentences. Replace the coordinating conjunction and the comma with a semicolon.

1. Benedict Arnold was an American patriot, and for a long time he served the American cause with distinction.

2. Arnold became a general for the Americans, and his men admired his courage and daring.

3. He was a good general, but his promotion to a higher rank did not come quickly.

4. Arnold waited to receive his promotion, and his resentment steadily grew.

5. He was commander of the military post at West Point, New York, and he decided to hand it over to the British.

6. Documents from Arnold were recovered, and they indicated that he had conspired against the Union.

7. John André, a British soldier, was captured, and his capture helped the Americans uncover Benedict Arnold's plan.

8. Arnold fled down the Hudson River on a British ship, and he later defended his actions.

Exercise 2

Rewrite the sentences. Add commas and semicolons where needed.

1. Several times Arnold expected to receive promotions for his army service but he was passed over each time.

2. André was executed as a spy by the Union Arnold fled to safety with the British army.

3. Benedict Arnold was offered a substantial sum of money by the British for his act of treason he was also made a brigadier general in the British army.

4. Arnold fought against the Americans in several battles he eventually went to England.

5. In London some received Arnold as a hero some thought of him as a traitor.

6. Some historians describe Arnold as egotistical and ruthless others describe him as power-hungry.

7. Benedict Arnold became "a man without a country" both the Americans and the British had no use for him.

8. Arnold was generally distrusted he died in debt in 1801.

9. Benedict Arnold was born in Norwich Connecticut owned a business in New Haven Connecticut and traveled to Honduras.

10. Arnold numbers among these famous traitors: Tokyo Rose the United States Henri Petain France and Harold Philby England.

Practice Power

Make each sentence below into a compound sentence by adding an independent clause and a semicolon.

1. **The path on the right leads to the lake.**
2. **The dark clouds gathered quickly.**
3. **Asparagus is my favorite vegetable.**
4. **Fred likes ketchup on his French fries.**
5. **We brought a camera to the parade.**

7.7 Colons

A **colon** is used

- after the salutation of a business letter

  Dear Mrs. McKinnon:

- before a list of items

  Many people think of three things
  when they think of the American flag:
  Betsy Ross, freedom, and liberty.

A colon is never used after a verb.

Exercise 1

Give the rule that applies to the use of a colon in these items.

1. Legend states that three people asked Betsy Ross to make the first American flag: George Washington, Colonel Ross, and Robert Morris.

2. Historians have searched in these places to uncover the truth: government records, George Washington's writings, and personal diaries of the individuals involved.

3. Dear Elizabeth Ross:

4. The colors represent three virtues: courage, purity, and justice.

5. Dear Mr. President:

6. The first American flag had three parts: 13 stars, their blue background, and 13 red and white stripes.

7. Americans usually fly their flags on these days: Flag Day, Veterans Day, and Memorial Day.

8. Dear Sir or Madam:

9. Our present-day flag looks like this: 50 white stars on a blue background, 7 red stripes, and 6 white stripes.

10. American flags of the 1700s and later had a number of variations: five-pointed stars, seven-pointed stars, placement of stars in a circle, placement of stars in rows.

Exercise 2

Rewrite the items. Add colons where needed.

1. Betsy Ross's jobs included the following upholsterer, flag maker, seamstress, and homemaker.

2. Here are some nicknames for the American flag Old Glory, The Star-Spangled Banner, and The Stars and Stripes.

3. Dear Mr. Washington

4. There are special rules of conduct for each of the following actions hoisting the flag, lowering the flag, and passing the flag to another person.

5. The American flag stands for these four ideals our freedom, our land, our people, and our government.

6. Dear Madam Secretary

7. Many people have written about the American flag historians, songwriters, and poets.

8. Some famous songs about the American flag are the following "The Star-Spangled Banner," "Stars and Stripes Forever," and "You're a Grand Old Flag."

9. Here are some rules about flying the American flag don't let the flag touch the ground; don't fly it in bad weather; and don't fly any flag higher than it.

10. Dear Sir

11. Today the American flag flies in the following places on the moon, over the White House, and on Capitol Hill.

12. Dear Senator Robertson

Practice Power

Pretend you are organizing a trip to a zoo or a museum. Write a short letter to participants explaining what they will be able to see and do there and what they should bring. Include several lists in your letter. Use colons where needed.

Quotation marks are used to set off quotations.

The quotation marks are placed before and after every complete quotation and every part of a divided quotation.

> "Great difficulties may be surmounted by patience and perseverance," Abigail Adams wrote. (complete quotation)
> "Great difficulties," she wrote, "may be surmounted by patience and perseverance." (divided quotation)

Commas set off short direct quotations from the rest of the sentence. The comma goes inside the quotation marks. A question mark or exclamation point that is part of the quotation also goes inside the quotation marks.

> "I long to hear that you have declared an independency," wrote Adams to her husband John.
> "If we separate from Great Britain, what code of laws will be established?" she asked in one of her letters.

A question mark or an exclamation point is placed outside the end quotation marks when it is part of the entire sentence.

> Who said, "I'll be back in a minute"?
> I have finished my poem "To Abigail"!

Quotation marks are used to set off titles of songs, short stories, poems, magazine articles, newspaper articles, and episodes of television series.

> "Abigail Adams Writes History" is a magazine article about the letters of Abigail Adams.
> "Women in History" is part of the PBS history series on TV.

Titles of books, magazines, newspapers, movies, plays, operas, TV series, and works of art are usually printed in italic type. When these titles are handwritten, they are underlined.

> I am reading *Abigail Adams: Witness to a Revolution.*
> I found some of Abigail Adams's letters in a magazine called <u>The Historical Woman</u>.

Exercise 1

Explain the use of quotation marks, italics, and commas in these sentences.

1. "How shall we be governed so as to retain our liberties?" Abigail Adams asked.

2. She continued, "Who shall frame these laws?"

3. "The Writings of Abigail" was published in *History Weekly.*

4. "The building of a great empire," wrote Adams, "may now be realized even by the unbelievers."

5. Didn't you say, "I read the biography of Abigail Adams"?

Exercise 2

Rewrite the following sentences. Add quotation marks and underlining where needed.

1. I saw Abigail Adams and Her Times, a TV movie, last night.

2. Abigail asked, Can any government be free which is not administered by general stated laws?

3. The article Women in Colonial Times was by Stephen Lewis.

4. I read the book The Life of Abigail Adams.

5. The Joys and Difficulties of Abigail was published in the magazine Historical Letters.

6. I believe I have tired of politics, Abigail wrote to her husband.

7. May order, continued Abigail, arise from confusion.

Practice Power

Research a favorite historical person. Write a paragraph about this person. Include quotations from your reading as well as the title of the article, book, or magazine.

An **apostrophe** is used

- to show possession

  Ryan's report is on John Paul Jones. *Jones's* story is heroic.
  Does the Joneses' family tree include John Paul?

- to indicate the omission of a letter, letters, or numbers

  John Paul Jones *wasn't* an army commander; he was a naval
  commander.
  My cousin was in the U.S. Naval Academy class of *'04.*

  Study these contractions and note the letter or letters that
  have been omitted from each.

they're—they are	he'd—he would or he had
let's—let us	don't—do not
we've—we have	aren't—are not
she'll—she will	doesn't—does not

- with *-s* to show the plural of a small letter

  There are two *m's* in *commander,* not one.

  An apostrophe is *not* used in forming the plural of a capital
  letter, a number, or an abbreviation that does not have periods.

  Gs   Ms   URLs   10s   180s   fours

Exercise 1

Add apostrophes where needed in these sentences.

1. John Paul Joness real name was John Paul.

2. Hed added Jones to his name when he came to America.

3. Im sure he was born in Scotland.

4. How many os are in the word *commissioned?*

5. When the naval commanders ship was sinking in 1779, he said,
   "I have not yet begun to fight."

Exercise 2

Add apostrophes in these sentences where needed.

1. Its well accepted that John Paul Jones was one of the founders of the U.S. Navy during the late 1700s.

2. The French royal familys cemetery is where John Paul Jones was originally buried.

3. Not long after, however, Frances revolutionary government sold the cemetery, and there wasnt any place for the graves.

4. The naval leaders body was placed in an unmarked grave, and people didnt know what had happened to it.

5. Many wanted their heros remains returned to the United States, and Ambassador Horace Porters search began.

6. Hed begun his search in 1899, but Joness body was not found until 1905.

7. At President Theodore Roosevelts request, battleships escorted Joness remains down the Chesapeake Bay.

Exercise 3

Rewrite these sentences to correct errors in the use of apostrophes. Not all the sentences have errors.

1. We mustnt forget that John Paul Jones was the first person to raise the American flag on a captured warship.

2. He's remembered for taking over an enemy vessel when his own vessel was destroyed in close combat.

3. Richard does'nt remember the date of the battle.

4. Lets get more information on Jones's career.

Practice Power

Write a paragraph telling what your family members do for fun. Use at least two words that show possession with an -'s and at least two contractions.

7.10 Hyphens

A **hyphen** is used

- to divide a word at the end of a line when one or more syllables are carried to the next line

    Francis Marion, the Swamp Fox, changed the momen-
    tum of the Revolutionary War.

    A dictionary shows how a word is divided into syllables correctly. Check a dictionary when you have to divide a word at the end of a line.

- in compound numbers from twenty-one to ninety-nine, when they are written out

    When Marion was forty-four, he was commissioned captain of the Second South Carolina Regiment.

- to separate parts of some compound terms

    His all-encompassing devotion to the American cause was recognized when he was made a brigadier general.

    Some compound terms are hyphenated only when they act as adjectives before the nouns they modify. Other compound terms, such as *mother-in-law, bright-eyed,* and *self-respect* are always hyphenated. Check a dictionary if you are unsure.

Exercise 1

Find each of these words in a dictionary. Use hyphens to show where the words could be divided at the end of a line.

1. lavender
2. affection
3. hedgehog
4. trustworthy
5. locomotive
6. preparation
7. parrot
8. ingredient
9. unemployed
10. catastrophe
11. dandelion
12. enlargement

Exercise 2

Add hyphens to the compound nouns that normally use them.

1. common sense
2. mother in law
3. drive in
4. first aid
5. self respect

6. fire engine
7. forget me not
8. six year old
9. brother in law

Exercise 3

Rewrite these sentences. Add hyphens where needed.

1. The Southern born Francis Marion grew up on a farm.

2. Marion began his military career when he was twenty nine.

3. He helped defend Charleston, South Carolina, against a British led attack.

4. For most of the Revolution, Marion's efforts were largely self directed: he and his brigade focused on communication and supply line disruption.

5. Some members of his ill supplied brigade had to use swords made from old saws.

6. Because Francis Marion was so difficult to catch, a British commander gave him the nickname Swamp Fox.

7. Marion died when he was sixty three years old.

8. He has been called an all American soldier.

Practice Power

Write a paragraph about a favorite performer. Use a hyphen when you give the person's age. Use at least one compound word that requires a hyphen. Check a dictionary for any word you need to break at the end of a line.

7.11 Capital Letters

Use a **capital letter** for

- the first word in a sentence and the pronoun *I*

  In 1777 Sybil Ludington was 16 years old.
  I was 16 years old when I read about her.

- the first word of a direct quotation

  Mr. Lewis said, "This young woman was a hero."

- a proper noun or a proper adjective

  Many say Sybil Ludington is an American hero. A statue of her
  on horseback is in Carmel, New York.

- a title before a name

  Her father was an aide to General George Washington.

- *North, South, East,* and *West* when they refer to sections of
  the country

  She was born in the North.

- each principal word in a title (but not *a, an, the, and,* or *but,*
  or prepositions unless they are the first or last word)

  Have you read *Sybil Ludington's Midnight Ride?*

- the first word of every line of most poems and songs

  Listen, my children, and you shall hear
  Of the midnight ride of Paul Revere.

  Lift ev'ry voice and sing,
  Till earth and Heaven ring.

Exercise 1

**Give the rule that applies to the use of each capital letter in
these sentences.**

1. Sybil Ludington was born in Fredericksburg, New York.

2. In April 1777 the English had planned a surprise attack on Danbury, Connecticut.

3. Sybil's father, Colonel Ludington, learned of the attack and sent her on a ride to alert the men in his regiment.

4. Some people compare her to Paul Revere, I soon learned.

5. My cousin in Danbury said, "She was more important than Revere, and she rode longer too!"

Exercise 2

Rewrite these sentences. Use capital letters where they are needed.

1. since it was planting season, many of colonel ludington's men were at their farms.

2. sybil's ride was long and dangerous; she had to avoid the british soldiers and the british supporters in the area.

3. unfortunately, colonel ludington was not able to save danbury.

4. he was able to attack the british soldiers under general william tryon as they were leaving the battle.

5. sybil rode from eight o'clock in the evening until dawn.

6. one book about her that i read was written by judy hominick and jeanne spreier.

7. the title of the book is *ride for freedom.*

8. another book about her that i found was *sybil ludington's midnight ride* by marsha amstel.

Practice Power

Write a paragraph about an American hero. Do research in an encyclopedia, in reference books, or on the Internet. Proofread your paragraph to make sure you used capital letters correctly. Then underline each capital letter and give the rule that explains its use.

Section 7 Challenge

MANISTIQUE, MI
HOME OF
PAUL BUNYAN

Below is part of a story about the meeting of two legendary characters—Pecos Bill and Paul Bunyan. Pecos Bill wanted some land for the grazing of his cattle; Paul Bunyan wanted it for his trees.

Read about the battle that occurred. Then rewrite the selection on a separate sheet of paper, adding the correct marks of punctuation and capitalizing words correctly. (Some punctuation is already given.)

with the hundred men watching, the fight started. paul bunyan picked up his axe and hit at pecos bill so hard that he cut a huge gash in the earth. people call it the grand canyon of the colorado river

then pecos bill swung his red hot iron missed paul bunyan and scorched red the sands of the desert that was the beginning of the painted desert out in arizona

again paul bunyan tried to hit pecos bill and again he hit the ground instead the scores of strange shaped rocks that are piled up in the garden of the gods in colorado were split by paul bunyans axe in that fearsome fight

pecos bills iron, instead of cooling off, grew hotter and hotter, until with one swing of his iron he charred the forests of new mexico and arizona these trees, burnt into stone by the heat from pecos bills running iron, are now the famed petrified forest

neither man could get the better of the other for the first and only time, pecos bill had met his match. . . . It was the first and only time that paul bunyans crew had seen a man who could stand up to him

finally they paused to get their breath and paul bunyan suggested lets sit down a minute

all right agreed pecos bill and they sat down on nearby rocks.

—From *Pecos Bill and Lightning* by Leigh Peck

Diagramming

8.1 Subjects and Predicates

A **diagram** is a picture of a sentence. It shows how the words in a sentence are related and fit together. A diagram highlights the most important words and clearly indicates the words that go with them. Knowing how to diagram can help you write sentences correctly because it illustrates immediately how the parts of a sentence fit together. For example, you can more easily figure out if a subject and a verb agree.

The essential parts of a sentence are the subject and the predicate. The subject names the person, place, or thing the sentence is about. The verb is the main word in the predicate, and it tells about an action or a state of being.

- Start the diagram by drawing a horizontal line.
- Find the verb in the sentence. Write it on the right half of the horizontal line.
- Find the subject. Write it in front of the verb.
- Separate the subject and the verb by a vertical line that cuts through the horizontal line.

Sentence: Lions roar.

In this sentence the subject is *lions* and the verb is *roar*.

Words that describe the subject or the verb are written on slanting lines under them. Adjectives describe nouns, and adverbs describe verbs, adjectives, or other adverbs.

Sentence: The frightened lion was roaring loudly.

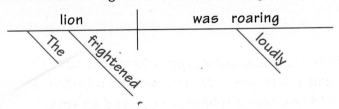

The article *the* and the adjective *frightened* go under the noun they describe, *lion*. The adverb *loudly* goes under the verb it describes, *was roaring*.

Exercise 1

Diagram the sentences.

1. The lilacs were blooming.
2. The bus is waiting.
3. A storm arrived suddenly.
4. Cats purr softly.
5. Light snow was falling.
6. The audience applauded.
7. The band is rehearsing.
8. The old door slammed noisily.
9. The fastest runner won.
10. The little boy was giggling.
11. Aaron is studying.
12. Our fund drive will continue.
13. Six prizes were awarded.
14. Dad's newspaper was soaked.
15. Both girls are performing.
16. The car's engine is running.
17. Jandy's new puppy is playing clumsily.
18. Those boys are muttering unhappily.
19. A cold wind was blowing steadily.
20. Nikki's snowman melted slowly.

Practice Power

Write three sentences and diagram them: one with a subject and a verb; one with a subject, an adjective, and a verb; and one with a subject, a verb, and an adverb.

8.2 *Direct Objects and Indirect Objects*

A **direct object** answers the question *whom* or *what* and receives the action of the verb.

A direct object is written on the main horizontal line to the right of the verb. A vertical line separates a direct object from the verb. The vertical line touches the horizontal line but does not cut through it.

Sentence: Amy saw a rainbow.

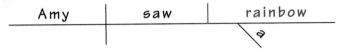

Amy is the subject; *saw* is the verb. The direct object is *rainbow*. It answers the question *Amy saw what?*

The **indirect object** tells *to whom* or *to what* or *for whom* or *for what* an action is done.

An indirect object is placed on a horizontal line under the verb and is connected to the verb by a slanting line.

Sentence: I gave my mother flowers.

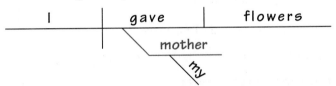

In this sentence *I* is the subject, *gave* is the verb, and *flowers* is the direct object. The indirect object is *mother*. It answers the question *I gave flowers to whom?*

Sentence: Aunt Susan has bought me new red sneakers.

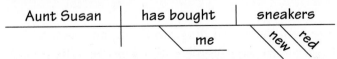

Aunt Susan is the subject; *has bought* is the verb; *me* is the indirect object, and *sneakers* is the direct object.

Exercise 1

Diagram the sentences.

1. The explorers discovered an ancient cave.
2. Lightning struck the tree.
3. We ate spicy soup.
4. Jenny cleaned her room thoroughly.
5. Galileo studied the planets.
6. Jake dropped his chocolate bar.
7. Su Ann read both novels.
8. The choir director is holding auditions.
9. My little sister broke six plates.
10. Mom washed my baseball uniform.

Exercise 2

Diagram the sentences.

1. The shop sells tourists pottery.
2. I showed my friend my new parakeet.
3. Louisa taught me the magic trick.
4. The volunteer read the patient a story.
5. The Constitution guarantees people the vote.
6. Terry gave Mandy all the tickets.
7. Our new teacher assigned the class *Moby Dick*.
8. I brought the whole class popcorn.
9. Mrs. Kim awarded Miguel a gold star.
10. We will give Joni a new skateboard.

Practice Power

Write and diagram four sentences, two with direct objects and two with direct and indirect objects.

8.3 *Subject Complements*

A **subject complement** follows a linking verb and renames or describes the subject. Linking verbs most often are *be* and its various forms. Other common linking verbs are *appear, become, feel, grow, look, remain, seem, smell, sound, stay,* and *taste.*

A subject complement can be a noun, a pronoun, or an adjective. In a diagram a subject complement is written after the verb on the main horizontal line. A line that slants to the left separates a complement from the verb. The slanting line touches the horizontal line but does not cut through it.

Sentence: A junk is a wooden sailboat.

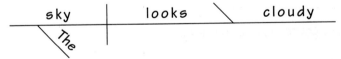

The subject complement, *sailboat,* is a noun and renames the subject, *junk.* The adjective *wooden,* which describes *sailboat,* goes on a slanting line under it.

Can you identify the subject complement in this sentence? What part of speech is it?

Sentence: The sky looks cloudy.

sky	looks \ cloudy

The subject complement is the adjective *cloudy.* It describes the subject, *sky.* Note that the subject complement always goes on the main line, whether it is a noun, a pronoun, or an adjective.

Sentence: The old shed remains sturdy.

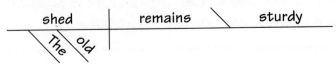

Here again, the subject complement is an adjective—*sturdy.*

Exercise 1

Diagram the sentences.

1. The prize was a bicycle.
2. The evening was cool.
3. A cheeseburger is my favorite meal.
4. A sitar is a musical instrument.
5. The pottery was ancient.
6. The lemonade tasted bitter.
7. The winner was she.
8. Sunflowers grow very tall.
9. The platypus is a mammal.
10. The runner looked tired.
11. My new bike is silver.
12. Our Thanksgiving program was a great success.
13. That mystery is Leif's first choice.
14. Uncle Tony's plane will be late.
15. That newspaper is weeks old.
16. Old Faithful is a famous geyser.
17. George Washington was our first president.
18. "Buenas dias" means "Good day."
19. Those three trees are elms.
20. Ana's library books are overdue.

Practice Power

Write and diagram three sentences with subject complements: one with a noun as a subject complement, one with a pronoun, and one with an adjective.

8.4 Appositives

An **appositive** is a word or group of words that follows a noun or pronoun and explains its meaning. An appositive names the same person, place, or thing as the word to which it refers. In a diagram an appositive is placed in parentheses to the right of the word it identifies. Words that describe the appositive go under it.

In this sentence the appositive is the noun *game*. It renames the noun *jai alai*, which is the subject.

Sentence: Jai alai, a Spanish game, uses long wicker baskets.

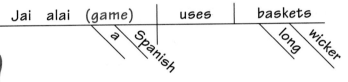

Can you identity the appositive in this sentence? What word does it rename? How does that word function?

Sentence: The painter was Georgia O'Keeffe, an American artist.

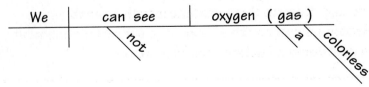

The appositive is the noun *artist*. It renames the noun *Georgia O'Keeffe*, which is the subject complement.

Can you identity the appositive in this sentence? What word does it rename? How does that word function?

Sentence: We cannot see oxygen, a colorless gas.

The appositive is the noun *gas*. It renames the noun *oxygen*, which is the direct object.

Exercise 1

Diagram the sentences.

1. My cousin, a beekeeper, sells honey.
2. Harry Houdini, a magician, made amazing escapes.
3. King Arthur valued Excalibur, his magic sword.
4. We read *The Incredible Journey,* a classic novel.
5. My favorite new dish is pho, a Vietnamese soup.
6. Our new dog is a Labrador retriever, a friendly breed.
7. Leif Ericsson, a bold Viking, visited North America.
8. My sister Dana is a teacher.
9. We watched *ET,* a wonderful film.
10. Our supper was penne, a pasta dish.
11. The mayor honored Juan's father, a police officer.
12. Charles Dickens, an English novelist, wrote *Oliver Twist.*
13. Ms. Tamaro, our neighbor, will be our new state senator.
14. Oriel's favorite instrument, the violin, requires daily practice.
15. Annamarie Karras, a baton twirler, led the parade.
16. We are planning our fall fundraiser, a bake sale.
17. My favorite author, J. K. Rowling, has written another book.
18. Our destination, Disneyland, is a popular theme park.
19. Lindsay won first prize, a gold medal.
20. Dan gave Jamie, his little brother, the old sled.

Practice Power

Write and diagram three sentences with appositives: one describing a subject, one describing a direct object, and one describing a subject complement.

8.5 *Intensive and Reflexive Pronouns*

Intensive pronouns and **reflexive pronouns** end in *-self* or *-selves*. An intensive pronoun emphasizes a preceding noun or pronoun. In a diagram an intensive pronoun is placed in parentheses directly to the right of the word it emphasizes.

In this sentence the intensive pronoun *herself* emphasizes the subject, *Andrea*.

Sentence: Andrea herself planned the party.

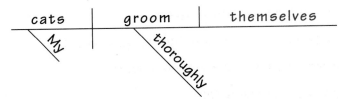

A reflexive pronoun can be the direct or indirect object of a verb or the object of a preposition. It usually refers to the subject of the sentence.

In a diagram a reflexive pronoun is placed according to its function in the sentence. In this sentence the reflexive pronoun is the direct object.

Sentence: My cats groom themselves thoroughly.

What is the role of the *-self* pronoun in this sentence?

Sentence: Evan always makes himself breakfast.

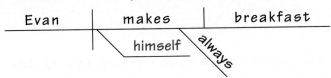

Himself acts as an indirect object in the sentence.

Exercise 1

Diagram the sentences.

1. The students themselves organized the fundraising event.
2. Jackson bought himself new skates.
3. I burned myself carelessly.
4. Sally herself made the cake.
5. Did you hurt yourself?
6. I myself pitched the tent.
7. We ourselves cleaned the school grounds.
8. The cat opened the cabinet door itself.
9. My sister taught herself chess.
10. Napoleon crowned himself.
11. The authors themselves conducted the interviews.
12. I made that pizza myself.
13. I made myself a tuna sandwich.
14. We are planning the whole trip ourselves.
15. The mayor herself delivered the welcoming address.
16. That shaggy old dog is scratching himself.
17. Tamara served the lemonade herself.
18. The cheerleading squad made themselves new outfits.
19. We ourselves climbed the steepest mountain.
20. This old velvet itself feels soft.

Practice Power

Write and diagram two sentences: one with an intensive pronoun and one with a reflexive pronoun.

8.6 Prepositional Phrases

A preposition and its object, the noun or pronoun that follows the preposition, form a **prepositional phrase.** A prepositional phrase can be an adjective phrase, which describes a noun or a pronoun, or it can be an adverb phrase, which describes a verb, an adverb, or an adjective.

In a diagram a prepositional phrase goes under the word it describes.

- The preposition is on a slanting line.
- The object of the preposition is on a horizontal line connected to the line with the preposition.
- Words that describe the object go under it.

What word does the prepositional phrase describe in this sentence? What kind of phrase is it?

Sentence: The walls of the old castle are high.

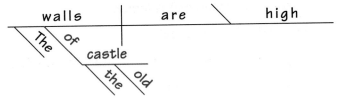

The prepositional phrase, *of the old castle,* describes the noun *walls,* so it is an adjective phrase. *The* and *old* describe the object of the preposition, *castle.* They are positioned under *castle.*

What word does the prepositional phrase describe? What kind of phrase is it?

Sentence: The astronaut walked on the moon.

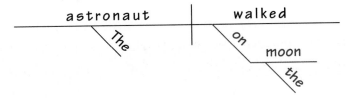

The diagram shows that the prepositional phrase *on the moon* describes the verb *walked,* so it is an adverb phrase.

Sentence: My collection of fossils will be quite valuable someday.

Exercise 1

Diagram the sentences.

1. The capital of Belgium is Brussels.

2. A balloon vendor stood on the corner.

3. The house across the street is very old.

4. We saw a program about apes.

5. I finished my report in the afternoon.

6. Louis Braille was born in 1809.

7. We played car bingo during the trip.

8. The name of the unusual animal is lemur.

9. We lay on the deck of our sailboat.

10. Immigrants to the United States came from many countries.

11. The ball flew over the picket fence.

12. Lincoln Park Zoo is on the lakefront.

13. I need three more books about Greece.

14. The schedule for the day begins at noon.

15. Practice will be held in the old gym.

16. I read an article about glassblowing.

17. Keri was happy about her award in the contest.

18. Arthur congratulated himself on his narrow escape.

Practice Power

Write and diagram four sentences with prepositional phrases: two with adjective and two with adverb phrases.

8.7 Compound Sentence Parts

The subject and the verb in a sentence may be compound. Each sentence part may consist of two or more words connected by a coordinating conjunction: *and, or, but,* or *nor.* Remember that a sentence with a compound subject or verb may still be a simple sentence.

In a diagram compound subjects and verbs are placed on separate lines with the coordinating conjunction on a dashed line between them. The parallel horizontal lines with the compound terms are connected to the main horizontal line.

In this sentence the subject is compound.

Sentence: Laurie and Lynn take their own pictures.

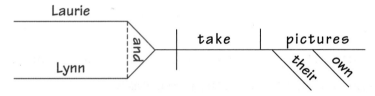

What is compound in this sentence?

Sentence: Lisa reads and writes poetry.

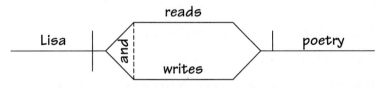

In this sentence the verb is compound, *reads* and *writes.*

What is compound in this sentence?

Sentence: My father and I cleaned the garage and painted it.

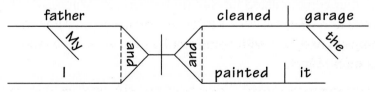

The sentence has a compound subject and a compound verb. Each verb has its own object.

Exercise 1

Diagram the sentences.

1. The holidays came and went.

2. Soccer and baseball are my favorite sports.

3. Prehistoric people lived together and hunted together.

4. Plants and trees need sunlight.

5. I read and reread the notice on the board.

6. Minneapolis and St. Paul are the Twin Cities.

7. Sarah cracked the eggs and beat them.

8. Tomatoes and beans are growing in my garden.

9. The players and the spectators applauded and cheered the winning touchdown.

10. My aunt and my uncle work in the city and design computer programs.

11. Jay and Helen will go to the Art Institute and the Aquarium.

12. Dave and Sally can share the new computer.

13. Saugatuck and Grand Haven are on Lake Michigan.

14. Ice cream and cherry pie are my favorite desserts.

15. Trailside Resort offers swimming and horseback riding.

16. Jeri and Kim washed and polished Mom's car.

17. Red roses and blue forget-me-nots decorated the tables.

18. The harbor is filled with small boats and large ones.

Practice Power

Write and diagram four sentences: two with compound subjects and two with compound verbs, each verb with its own object.

8.8 Compound Sentences

A **compound sentence** contains two or more independent clauses. An independent clause has a subject and a predicate and can stand on its own as a sentence. Independent clauses are usually connected by a coordinating conjunction: *and, but, or, nor, yet,* or *so.*

In a diagram the independent clauses are placed on parallel horizontal lines. Each independent clause has its own horizontal line, with the subject, verb, and any complements or objects. The coordinating conjunction is placed between the clauses on a dashed vertical line at the left edge of the diagram.

Sentence: Max likes adventure stories, but Marian prefers biographies.

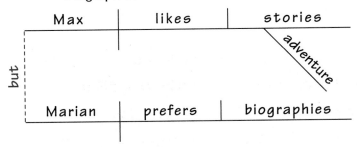

Can you identify the subject and verb in each clause in this compound sentence?

Sentence: Tulips grow in many places, but we associate them with Holland.

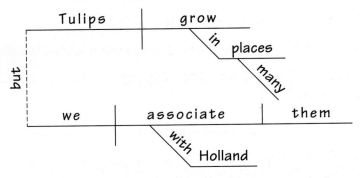

In the first clause the subject is *tulips* and the verb is *grow*. In the second clause the subject is *we* and the verb is *associate.*

Sentence: I like classical music, but Maria prefers the theater.

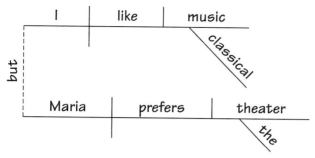

Exercise 1

Diagram the sentences.

1. I take violin lessons, and my sister takes karate lessons.

2. Animals with backbones are vertebrates, and animals without backbones are invertebrates.

3. King Arthur had many knights, but Lancelot was the best fighter.

4. Ottawa is Canada's capital, but Toronto is its largest city.

5. Fog filled the streets, and travel became difficult.

6. Solar energy is used, but it is not very common.

7. We can fish from the boat, or we can fish from the pier.

8. Each snowflake has six sides, but each is different.

9. I bought the fruit, and my brother made the fruit salad.

10. We have two gerbils, and we are getting two hamsters.

11. The movie opens on Friday, and we will go to the first showing.

12. Quidditch is my favorite sport, but I can't fly a broom.

13. One side of the moon is bright, and the other is always dark.

14. We could go to the Illinois State Fair, but the Wisconsin State Fair is closer.

Practice Power

Write and diagram two compound sentences.

8.9 Interjections

An **interjection** is a word that expresses strong or sudden emotion. Interjections may express happiness, disgust, pain, agreement, impatience, surprise, sadness, and so on. They include words such as *Ah, Oh, Well, Sh, Hey, Good, Ouch, Oops, Yikes,* and *Wow.* These words or the sentences in which they appear are usually followed by exclamation points.

In a diagram an interjection is placed on a line that is separate from the rest of the sentence. The line is above, to the left, and parallel to the main horizontal line.

Sentence: Hooray! We won the game!

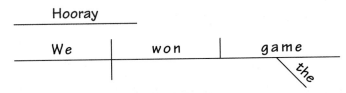

Placement of an interjection is the same whether it is separated from the rest of the sentence by an exclamation point or a comma.

Sentence: Oh, I can see the rainbow!

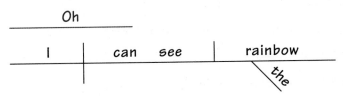

Can you identify all the parts in the following diagram?

Sentence: Oh! Have you heard the news?

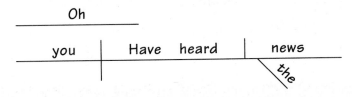

Oh is an interjection and is placed on a separate line. *You* is the subject, *have heard* is the verb, and *news* is the direct object—all placed on the main horizontal line.

Sentence: Sh! Megan will hear you.

```
         Sh
_____

   Megan  |  will hear  |  you
_____|             |_____
          |
          |
```

Exercise 1

Diagram the sentences.

1. Hey! It is raining again.

2. Ouch! I twisted my ankle.

3. Wow! That was a great catch.

4. Oh! I left my homework at home.

5. Bravo! That was a great performance.

6. Sh! The baby is sleeping.

7. Well! You finally arrived.

8. You won tickets to the concert. Great!

9. Ah! The mountains are so beautiful.

10. No! I lost my wallet.

11. Yikes! That was a terrible pun.

12. My, that is a cute puppy!

13. Gee, I have always wanted one of these!

14. Oops! I dropped another one.

15. Wow! Amanda can run fast!

16. Gee, those are great photos!

17. Great! We are in first place.

18. No, I do not want that one!

19. Hey! Lara is next.

Practice Power

Write and diagram two sentences with interjections.

8.10 *Adverb Clauses*

A **dependent clause** has a subject and a verb, but it cannot stand alone. It does not express a complete thought and therefore always accompanies an independent clause.

One type of dependent clause, an **adverb clause,** acts like an adverb and describes a verb, an adjective, or another adverb. Adverb clauses tell *how, when, where, why, to what extent,* or *under what condition.* Adverb clauses begin with conjunctions. Some of the most common are *after, although, as, because, before, if, since, so that, unless, until, when, whenever,* and *while.*

In a diagram an adverb clause goes on its own horizontal line under the independent clause. The conjunction is placed on a slanting dashed line that connects the two clauses. The line goes from the verb in the adverb clause to the word in the independent clause that the adverb clause describes, which is usually the verb.

Sentence: After the snowstorm ended, we played outside.

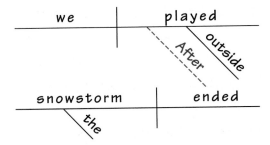

Can you identify the subject and the verb in this adverb clause? What word in the main clause does the clause describe?

Sentence: I cannot go to the movie until I finish my homework.

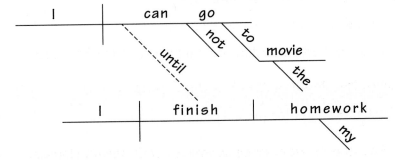

Sentence: Bill babysat while Ana and Lee shopped for groceries.

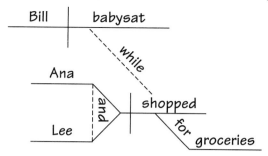

Exercise 1

Diagram the sentences.

1. My keyboarding skills improved after I took the class.

2. If you need the pronunciation of a word, you can look in a dictionary.

3. I am saving money because I want a new skateboard.

4. Although a standing bear appears aggressive, the posture indicates curiosity.

5. Until the rain stops, we cannot have our picnic.

6. After Elaine finished the first Harry Potter book, she quickly read the next one.

7. I had never seen a skyscraper before I visited New York.

8. When the Suez Canal opened in 1869, the Red Sea became an important trade route.

9. Tom will memorize the script while I find the props.

10. Before I made the muffins, I found the ingredients in the kitchen.

11. As soon as Jacqui arrives, we will light the candles.

12. I found the book after Donna left.

13. I need more practice before I play my recital.

14. Dad checked his pockets before he locked the front door.

Write and diagram three sentences with adverb clauses.

8.11 *Diagramming Review*

Can you identify the main elements in this sentence?

Sentence: Lucy sells antiques.

Can you name what else might be written on the main line? Did you remember that both appositives and intensive pronouns go next to the words they explain or describe?

Adjectives, adverbs, and prepositional phrases go under the words they describe. Identify all of the adjectives, adverbs, adjective phrases, and adverb phrases in this sentence.

Sentence: The scientists on the expedition found large fossils of a dinosaur in a rather rocky area.

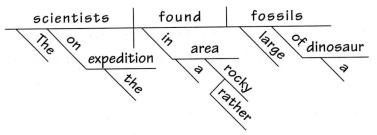

Compound sentences and sentences with adverb clauses have two separate horizontal lines. What kind of sentence is this?

Sentence: Charlemagne was a wise king, and during his reign his territories flourished.

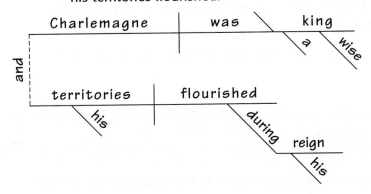

This is a compound sentence, and the coordinating conjunction goes on a dashed vertical line.

Sentence: The auditorium itself has been freshly painted and has been recarpeted.

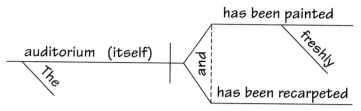

Exercise 1

Diagram the sentences.

1. Ben, a sixth grader, rides his bicycle with his mother.

2. A long path runs along Lake Michigan.

3. The ride on the path is an interesting adventure for Ben.

4. Ben goes to the lake when the water is blue and calm.

5. The lake is choppy on windy days, and water splashes onto the path.

6. Ben gets wet, and his bike makes loud noises.

7. Ben rides slowly and avoids the puddles and muddy patches.

8. Whenever he rides, Ben notices the things around him.

9. Joggers and skaters are also on the path.

10. When Ben is on the bicycle, he enjoys himself.

11. Mr. Moreno, our drama coach, is casting our spring play.

12. I myself will paint the scenery and Jan will be the stage manager.

13. Lori and JoAnn will sell cookies and brownies during intermission.

14. Wow! The audience gave the cast a standing ovation.

Practice Power

Diagram five sentences from a source such as another textbook, a magazine, or a newspaper.

Diagramming Challenge

Study the diagram and answer the questions.

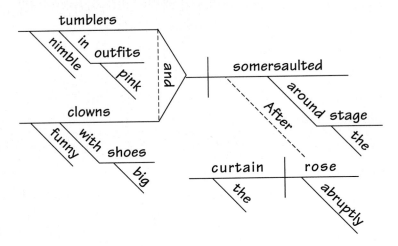

1. What are the two clauses in the sentence? What kinds of clauses are they?

2. Identify the subject and verb in each clause.

3. What is compound in the sentence?

4. What are the prepositional phrases in the sentence? What does each describe?

5. What is the adverb in the sentence?

6. Identify all the adjectives in the sentence.

7. Write out the sentence.

Grammar and Mechanics Handbook

Grammar

ADJECTIVES

An adjective points out or describes a noun.

That building is *tall.*

Adjective Phrases

An adjective phrase is a phrase used as an adjective.
See PHRASES.

Articles

An article points out a noun. See ARTICLES.

Common Adjectives

A common adjective expresses an ordinary quality of a noun or
pronoun: *fast* car, *delicious* hamburger.

Comparison of Adjectives

Most adjectives have three degrees of comparison: positive,
comparative, and superlative.

The positive degree of an adjective shows a quality of a noun or
pronoun.

Elephants are *large* animals.
The actor is *famous.*
Those rings are *valuable.*

The comparative degree is used to compare two items or two
sets of items. This form is often followed by *than.*

Whales are *larger* than elephants.
The dancer is *more famous* than the actor.
The bracelets are *less valuable* than the rings.

The superlative degree is used to compare three or more items or sets of items.

> Whales are the *largest* mammals.
> The singer is the *most famous* performer in the show.
> The necklaces are the *least valuable* of all the jewelry.

The adjectives *few, fewer,* and *fewest* are used to compare count nouns. Note that the nouns are plural in form.

> Kara made a *few* cookies for the bake sale.
> Joel made *fewer* cookies than Kara did.
> Keesha made the *fewest* cookies of anyone in class.

The adjectives *little, less,* and *least* are used to compare noncount nouns. Note that the nouns are singular in form.

> Kara has *little* time to bake cookies.
> Joel has *less* time than Kara.
> Keesha has the *least* time of us all.

Demonstrative Adjectives

A demonstrative adjective points out a definite person, place, or thing. Demonstrative adjectives always precede the nouns they modify and agree with them in number.

Singular	Plural
this plant	*these* plants
that plant	*those* plants

This and *these* point out things or persons that are near. *That* and *those* point out things or persons that are farther away.

> *This* plant is healthy. (singular and near)
> *Those* plants need water. (plural and far)

Descriptive Adjectives

A descriptive adjective gives information about a noun or pronoun. It tells about age, size, shape, color, origin, or another quality.

> This *African* violet has *small, pink, pointy* petals.

Indefinite Adjectives

An indefinite adjective refers to all or any of a group of persons, places, or things. Some of the most common indefinite adjectives are *all, another, any, both, each, either, every, few, many, most, neither, no, other, several,* and *some.* Note that *another, each, every, either,* and *neither* are singular and the others are plural.

> *Every* student has a pencil.
> *Several* students have rulers.

Interrogative Adjectives

An interrogative adjective is used in asking a question. The interrogative adjectives are *which, what,* and *whose.*

Which is used to ask about one or more of a specific set of persons or things. *What* is used to ask about people or things but is not limited to a specific group or set. *Whose* asks about possession.

> *Which* backpack is yours?
> *What* supplies do you carry in your backpack?
> *Whose* backpack is under the chair?

Numerical Adjectives

A numerical adjective indicates an exact number. Numerical adjectives may refer to a number of persons or things, or they may refer to the arrangement of things in numerical order.

> My family has *two* cats.
> The *first* day of the week is Sunday.

Position of Adjectives

Most adjectives go before the words they describe.

> *Many dedicated* gardeners live on *my* block.

Adjectives may also directly follow nouns.

> Their flowers, *tall* and *colorful,* brighten every yard.

An adjective can follow a linking verb as a subject complement.

> The results of their work are *spectacular.*

Possessive Adjectives

A possessive adjective shows possession or ownership. Possessive adjectives have antecedents. They must agree with their antecedents in person, number, and gender.

> John has a skateboard. *His* skateboard is silver.
> Jo and Luis have bikes. *Their* bikes are new.

Possessive adjectives change form depending on person and number. Third person singular possessive adjectives change form depending on gender—whether they are masculine *(his)*, feminine *(her)*, or neuter *(its)*.

	Singular	Plural
First Person	my	our
Second Person	your	your
Third Person	his, her, its	their

Proper Adjectives

A proper adjective is formed from a proper noun: *Roman* ruins, *Mexican* food.

Subject Complements

An adjective may be used as a subject complement. See SUBJECT COMPLEMENTS.

ADVERBS

An adverb modifies a verb, an adjective, or another adverb. Adverbs indicate time, place, manner, degree, affirmation, or negation.

Adverbs of time answer the question *when* or *how often.*

> The chorus *frequently* sings for us.

Adverbs of place answer the question *where.*

> The tenors walked *forward.*

Adverbs of manner answer the question *how.*

> They begin to sing *loudly.*

Adverbs of degree answer the question *how much* or *how little*.

The sopranos had *very* clear voices.

Adverbs of affirmation tell whether a statement is positive or expresses consent or approval. Adverbs of negation express something negative or a refusal.

Yes, we enjoyed the concert.
We *never* miss hearing them sing.

Adverb Clauses
An adverb clause is a dependent clause used as an adverb. See CLAUSES.

Adverb Phrases
An adverb phrase is a phrase used as an adverb. See PHRASES.

Adverbial Nouns
An adverbial noun is a noun that acts as an adverb. An adverbial noun expresses time, distance, measure, weight, value, or direction.

The trip will take only a few *minutes.* (time)
The post office is just five *blocks* away. (distance)
The box is a *foot* long. (measure)
The package weighs six *pounds.* (weight)
It's worth twenty *dollars.* (value)
Look this *way.* (direction)

Comparison of Adverbs
Most adverbs have three degrees of comparison: positive, comparative, and superlative.

Tom *works carefully.*
Eddie works *more carefully* than Tom.
Luz works *most carefully* of anyone in class.

Wiley ate *rapidly.*
Frank ate *less rapidly* than Wiley.
Allison ate *least rapidly* of anyone.

Carla walks *fast.*
Lisa walks *faster* than Carla.
Ping walks *fastest* of us all.

ANTECEDENTS

The noun to which a pronoun or a possessive adjective refers is its antecedent. A pronoun or possessive adjective must agree with its antecedent in person and number. Third person singular personal, possessive, intensive, and reflexive pronouns and possessive adjectives must also agree in gender. See PERSON, NUMBER, GENDER.

APPOSITIVES

An appositive is a word (or words) that follows a noun and helps identify it or adds more information about it. An appositive names the same person, place, or thing as the noun it explains. An appositive phrase is an appositive and its modifiers.

An appositive is restrictive if it is necessary in order to understand the sentence. It is nonrestrictive if it is not necessary. A nonrestrictive appositive is set off by commas.

> The poet Langston Hughes also wrote stories and plays.
> Toni Morrison, the American writer, won the Nobel Prize.

ARTICLES

An article points out a noun. *The* is the definite article. It refers to a specific item or specific items in a group. *The* may is be used with either singular or plural count nouns and with noncount nouns.

> We went to *the* beach yesterday.
> *The* beaches in California are beautiful.
> *The* sand is very white.

A and *an* are the indefinite articles. Each is used to refer to a single member of a general group. *A* and *an* are used only with singular count nouns. The article *an* is used before a vowel sound. The article *a* is used before a consonant sound.

> We sat on *a* blanket under *an* umbrella.

CLAUSES

A clause is a group of words that has a subject and a predicate.

Adverb Clauses

An adverb clause is a dependent clause used as an adverb. An adverb clause can tell *how, when, where, why,* and *to what extent.*

> We locked all the doors *before we left.*
> We went *where we could see the beach.*
> We didn't tell anyone *because it was a secret.*

Dependent Clauses

A dependent clause cannot stand on its own as a sentence.

> *While we were loading the car,* my cell phone rang.

Independent Clauses

An independent clause can stand on its own as a sentence.

> *We drove off* after I answered the phone.

CONJUNCTIONS

A conjunction is a word used to connect words, phrases, or clauses in a sentence.

Coordinating Conjunctions

A coordinating conjunction is used to connect similar words or groups of words. The coordinating conjunctions are *and, but, or, nor,* and *yet.*

> My cousin is a swimmer *and* a sailor. (nouns)
> She is quick *but* methodical. (adjectives)
> She doesn't hike *or* backpack. (verbs)
> She is known for her kindness *and* for her sense of humor. (prepositional phrases)

Coordinating conjunctions can connect independent or dependent clauses.

> She spends a lot of time alone, *yet* she has many friends. (independent clauses)
> She is popular because she is kind *and* because she has a good sense of humor. (dependent clauses)

Subordinate Conjunctions

A subordinate conjunction is used to connect a dependent clause and an independent clause. Some common subordinate conjunctions are *although, after, as, because, before, if, in order that, provided that, since, so that, unless, until, when, whenever, where, wherever, whether,* and *while.*

> She is popular *because* she has a good sense of humor.
> *After* she moved away, I e-mailed her every week.

DIRECT OBJECTS

The direct object of a sentence answers the question *whom* or *what* after the verb. A noun or an object pronoun can be used as a direct object.

> My mom made *lemonade.*
> I helped *her.*

GENDER

Third person singular personal, possessive, intensive, and reflexive pronouns and possessive adjectives change form depending on gender—whether the antecedent is masculine *(he, him, his, himself)*, feminine *(she, her, hers, herself)*, or neuter *(it, its, itself)*.

INDIRECT OBJECTS

An indirect object tells *to whom* or *for whom,* or *to what* or *for what,* an action is done. A noun or an object pronoun can be used as an indirect object.

> I gave my *dad* a birthday present.
> I made *him* a birthday card.

INTERJECTIONS

An interjection is a word that expresses a strong or sudden emotion, such as happiness, disgust, pain, agreement, impatience, surprise, sadness, amazement, and so on.

> *Ouch!* I stubbed my toe.
> *Oh, no!* I lost my keys.

MOOD

Mood shows the manner in which the action or state of being of a verb is expressed.

Indicative Mood

The indicative mood is used to make a statement or ask a question. Most sentences are in the indicative mood.

> Do you like to play baseball?
> I learned to play last year.
> Baseball is my favorite game!

The emphatic form of the indicative mood gives special force to a simple present or past tense verb. To make an emphatic form, use *do, does,* or *did* before the base form of the verb.

> I *do like* to play baseball.
> He *did hit* a home run last night.

Imperative Mood

The imperative mood is used to express a command or a request. The imperative uses the base form of a verb. The subject of an imperative sentence is usually understood to be the second person pronoun, *you*.

> *Catch* the ball!
> Please *hand* me that bat.

A command can be given in the first person by using *let's* before the base form of a verb.

> *Let's play* another game tomorrow.

Subjunctive Mood

The subjunctive mood is used to express a wish or desire; to express a command, request, or suggestion following the word *that;* or to express something that is contrary to fact (not true). The subjunctive refers to what is hoped or wished rather than what actually is.

For the verb *be,* the subjunctive forms are *be* and *were. Be* is commonly used with verbs of command, request, or suggestion. Otherwise, *were* is typically used. The auxiliary *would* is used in place of *will.*

> I wish I *were* a better player. (a wish)
> The coach requested that we *be* here on time.
> (a request after *that*)
> If I *were* you, I *would* arrive at 6:00.
> (something that is contrary to fact)

NOUNS

A noun is a name word. A singular noun names one person, place, or thing: *boy, city, book.* A plural noun names more than one person, place, or thing: *boys, cities, books.*

Abstract Nouns

An abstract noun names something that cannot be seen or touched. It expresses an idea, emotion, quality, or condition: *belief, fear, independence, beauty.*

Appositives

An appositive is a word (or words) that follows a noun and helps identify it or adds more information about it. See APPOSITIVES.

Collective Nouns

A collective noun names a group of persons, animals, or things considered as one: *team, herd, bunch.*

Common Nouns

A common noun names any one member of a class of persons, places, or things: *sailor, town, telephone.*

Concrete Nouns

A concrete noun names something that can be seen or touched: *queen, river, baseball.*

Count Nouns

A count noun names something that can be counted. Count nouns have singular and plural forms: *women, towns, cars.*

To show how many, a plural count noun can be modified by a number: *three women, five towns, eight cars.*

Noncount Nouns

A noncount noun names something that cannot be counted. Noncount nouns do not have plural forms: *cheese, bread, water.*

To show how much, a noncount noun must be preceded by an expression of quantity: *two pounds of cheese, a loaf of bread, three glasses of water.*

Possessive Nouns

A possessive noun expresses possession or ownership.

To form the singular possessive, add -'s to the singular form of the noun.

friend	friend's report
scientist	scientist's excavation

To form the possessive of a plural noun ending in s, add an apostrophe only.

kings	kings' treasure
archaeologists	archaeologists' work

To form the possessive of a plural noun that does not end in s, add -'s.

women	women's influence

The possessive of a proper noun ending in s is usually formed by adding -'s.

James	James's research

The possessive of a compound noun is formed by adding -'s to the end of the word.

brother-in-law's vacation
brothers-in-law's vacations

Separate possession occurs when two or more people own things independently of one another. To show separate possession, use -'s after each noun.

Ann and Peter each own a boat.
Ann's and Peter's boats are in the marina.

Joint possession occurs when two or more people own something together. To show joint possession, use -'s after the last noun only.

Tom and Gloria are the owners of three boats.
Tom and Gloria's boats are all painted bright blue.

Proper Nouns
A proper noun names a particular person, place, or thing: *George Washington, White House, Continental Congress.*

NUMBER

The number of a noun or pronoun indicates whether it refers to one person, place, or thing (singular) or more than one person, place, or thing (plural).

PERSON

Personal, possessive, intensive, and reflexive pronouns and possessive adjectives change form according to person—whether the antecedent is the person speaking (first person), being spoken to (second person), or being spoken about (third person).

PHRASES

A phrase is a group of words that is used as a single part of speech.

Adjective Phrases

An adjective phrase is a phrase used as an adjective.

> The clown *with the red hair* was folding balloons.

Adverb Phrases

An adverb phrase is a phrase used as an adverb.

> She threw the balloons *into the air.*

PREDICATES

The predicate of a sentence names an action or a state of being.

Complete Predicates

The complete predicate of a sentence is the verb or verb phrase along with its modifiers and complements or objects.

> The boy *carried his books slowly down the street.*

Compound Predicates

Two or more predicates joined by a coordinating conjunction form a compound predicate.

He *stopped* and *waited for his friends.*

Simple Predicates

The simple predicate of a sentence is the verb or verb phrase.

His friends *were racing* their bikes on Main Street.

PREPOSITIONS

A preposition is a word that shows the relationship of a noun or a pronoun to another word in a sentence.

Adjective Phrases

A prepositional phrase can be used as an adjective.

The woman *in the red dress* is my mother.

Adverb Phrases

A prepositional phrase can be used as an adverb.

She is walking *across the street.*

Objects of Prepositions

The noun or pronoun that follows a preposition is the object of that preposition.

Did you jump over the *log* or walk around *it?*

Prepositional Phrases

A prepositional phrase is a preposition, its object, and any words that describe the object.

We walked *through the dark, silent woods.*

PRONOUNS

A pronoun is a word used in place of a noun. The noun to which a pronoun refers is its antecedent. A pronoun must agree with its antecedent in person and number. Third person personal, possessive, intensive, and reflexive pronouns must also agree in gender. See PERSON, NUMBER, GENDER.

Demonstrative Pronouns

A demonstrative pronoun points out a particular person, place, or thing.

Singular	Plural
this	these
that	those

This and *these* point out things or persons that are near. *That* and *those* point out things or persons that are farther away.

> *This* is my favorite sweater. (singular and near)
> *Those* are my old ski boots. (plural and far)

Indefinite Pronouns

An indefinite pronoun refers to any or all of a group of persons, places, or things. Some indefinite pronouns are *anybody, many, both, none, few, everyone.*

Most indefinite pronouns are singular. The indefinite pronouns *both, few, many,* and *several* are always plural.

> *Everyone* in the class is invited to the party.
> *Few* of the students are going to miss it.

The indefinite pronouns *all, some,* and *none* may be singular or plural, depending on whether they refer to count or to noncount nouns.

> *All* of the children are here.
> *All* of the class is here.

Indefinite pronouns such as *no one, nobody, none,* and *nothing* are negative words. In a sentence they should never be used with other negative words, such as *no, not,* and *never.*

Intensive Pronouns

Intensive pronouns end in *-self* or *-selves*. An intensive pronoun emphasizes a preceding noun or pronoun. It must agree with its antecedent in person, number, and gender.

> She made the whole dinner *herself.*
> I *myself* have never cooked an entire meal.

Intensive pronouns change form depending on person and number. Third person singular intensive pronouns change form depending on gender—whether the antecedent is masculine *(himself)*, feminine *(herself)*, or neuter *(itself)*.

	Singular	Plural
First Person	myself	ourselves
Second Person	yourself	yourselves
Third Person	himself	themselves
	herself	
	itself	

Interrogative Pronouns

An interrogative pronoun is used to ask a question. The interrogative pronouns are *who, whom, whose, what,* and *which.*

Who refers to persons. It is often the subject of a question. *Whom* also refers to persons. It is the object of a verb or a preposition.

> *Who* is starring in the play?
> *Whom* did you see at rehearsal?
> To *whom* did they sell the tickets?

Whose is used to ask about possession. *Which* is used when asking about a group or class. *What* is used for asking about things or for seeking information.

> *Whose* is the script on the chair?
> *Which* of the actors missed his entrance?
> *What* did he leave on stage?
> *What* did the director tell him?

Object Pronouns

An object pronoun can be used as the direct object or the indirect object of a verb or as the object of a preposition. The object pronouns are *me, you, him, her, it, us,* and *them.*

> Carla met *him* at the party. (direct object)
> Tom gave *her* a present. (indirect object)
> The house was decorated by *them.* (object of a preposition)

Personal Pronouns

Personal pronouns change form depending on person and number. Third person singular pronouns change form to reflect gender—whether the antecedent is feminine *(she, her)*, masculine *(he, him)*, or neuter *(it)*.

	Singular	Plural
First Person	I, me	we, us
Second Person	you	you
Third Person	he, she, it, him, her	they, them

Personal pronouns also change form depending on whether they are used as subjects *(I, you, he, she, it, we, they)* or objects *(me, you, him, her it, us, them)*.

Possessive Pronouns

A possessive pronoun shows possession or ownership. It takes the place of a possessive noun. Possessive pronouns must agree with their antecedents in person, number, and gender.

> Maria and Tom have pets.
> *Hers* is a cat, and *his* is a hamster.

Possessive pronouns change form depending on person and number. Third person singular possessive pronouns change form to reflect gender—whether the antecedent is masculine *(his)*, feminine *(hers)*, or neuter *(its)*.

	Singular	Plural
First Person	mine	ours
Second Person	yours	yours
Third Person	his, hers, its	theirs

Reflexive Pronouns

Reflexive pronouns end in -*self* or -*selves*. A reflexive pronoun can be the direct or indirect object of a verb or the object of a preposition. It generally refers to the subject of the sentence. Reflexive pronouns must agree with their antecedents in person, number, and gender.

> I consider *myself* a good reader. (direct object)
> He bought *himself* a new book. (indirect object)
> They read it by *themselves.* (object of a preposition)

Reflexive pronouns change form depending on person and number. Third person singular reflexive pronouns change form depending on gender—whether the antecedent is masculine (*himself*), feminine (*herself*), or neuter (*itself*).

	Singular	Plural
First Person	myself	ourselves
Second Person	yourself	yourselves
Third Person	himself	themselves
	herself	
	itself	

Subject Pronouns

A subject pronoun can be used as the subject of a sentence or as a subject complement. The subject pronouns are *I, you, he, she, it, we, they.*

> *She* painted that picture. (subject)
> The subject of the portrait is *he.* (subject complement)

SENTENCES

A sentence expresses a complete thought. The essential elements of a sentence are a subject and predicate.

Complex Sentences

A complex sentence contains an independent clause and one or more dependent clauses.

> As soon as Marta comes, we will leave for the movie.

Compound Sentences

A compound sentence contains two or more independent clauses. Independent clauses in a compound sentence are usually connected by a coordinating conjunction. A semicolon may be used instead of a coordinating conjunction.

Marta will be here soon, and then we'll leave.
Tom is going to drive; he has the biggest car.

Declarative Sentences

A declarative sentence makes a statement. It ends with a period.

Elephants are the largest land mammals.

Exclamatory Sentences

An exclamatory sentence expresses a strong emotion. It ends with an exclamation mark.

That elephant is huge!

Imperative Sentences

An imperative sentence gives a command. It ends with a period.

Find out how much that elephant weighs.

Interrogative Sentences

An interrogative sentence asks a question. It ends with a question mark.

Did you ask the keeper what the elephant weighs?

Inverted Order in Sentences

A sentence is in inverted order when the main verb or an auxiliary verb comes before the subject.

Across the exhibit walked the baby elephant.
Have you seen the new elephant at the zoo?
There are now three elephants in our zoo.
Here is my DVD of *Dumbo*.

Natural Order in Sentences

A sentence is in natural order when the verb follows the subject.

The baby elephant walked toward its mother.

Simple Sentences

A simple sentence contains a subject and a predicate and expresses a complete thought. Either or both may be compound.

> The baby and its mother watched the keeper.

SUBJECT COMPLEMENTS

A subject complement follows a linking verb such as the forms of *be*. A noun or pronoun used as a subject complement renames the subject of the sentence; it refers to the same person, place, or thing. An adjective used as a subject complement describes the subject of the sentence.

> My sister is a *doctor.*
> The winner of that award was *she.*
> Her job can be very *rewarding.*

SUBJECTS

The subject of a sentence names the person, place, or thing the sentence is about. To determine the subject of a sentence, ask *who* or *what* before the verb.

Complete Subjects

The complete subject of a sentence is the simple subject and all the words that describe it.

> *The small, shaggy dog* barked loudly.

Compound Subjects

Two or more subjects joined by a coordinating conjunction form a compound subject.

> *The dog* and *its owner* walked through the park.

Simple Subjects

The simple subject of a sentence is the noun or pronoun that names the person, place, or thing the sentence is about.

The small *dog* with the red collar is mine.

TENSE

The tense of a verb expresses the time of the action or state of being.

Perfect Tenses

The present perfect tense tells about an action that happened at some indefinite time in the past or an action that started in the past and continues into the present. It uses *have* or *has* and the past participle.

I *have finished* all my homework.
She *has lived* in that house for a year.

The past perfect tense tells about a past action that was completed before another past action started. It uses *had* and the past participle.

I *had finished* my homework before my dad got home.

Progressive Tenses

The present progressive tense tells about something that is happening right now. It uses the present tense of the verb *be* (*am, is, are*) and the present participle.

The students *are working* on a science project.

The past progressive tense tells about something that was happening in the past. It uses the past tense of the verb *be* (*was, were*) and the present participle.

They *were doing* math an hour ago.

Simple Tenses

The simple present tense tells about an action that happens again and again or about things that are general truths. The simple present tense uses the present, or base, form of a verb. If the subject is a third person singular noun or pronoun, -s is added to the base form.

> I *like* ice cream.
> He *eats* ice cream every day.

The simple past tense tells about an action that happened in the past. The past tense uses the past form.

> We *walked* to the ice cream shop.

The simple future tense tells about an action that will happen in the future. The simple future tense uses the auxiliary verb *will* or *be going to* followed by the base form of a verb.

> I *am going to buy* a quart of ice cream.
> We *will eat* it for dessert tonight.

VERBS

A verb shows action or state of being. See MOOD, TENSE, VOICE.

> Carlo *opened* the present. (action)
> He *was* very excited. (state of being)

Auxiliary Verbs

An auxiliary verb combines with a main verb to form a verb phrase. Auxiliary verbs help show voice, mood, and tense. Some common auxiliaries are the forms of *be (am, is, are, was, were)*, the forms of *have (have, has, had)*, and the forms of *do (do, did)*. Other auxiliary verbs are *can, could, may, might, should,* and *will*.

Intransitive Verbs

An intransitive verb has no receiver of its action—no direct object. An intransitive verb may be followed by an adverb or adverb phrase.

> She *comes* from Cleveland.
> She *writes* well.

Irregular Verbs

The past and the past participle of irregular verbs are not formed by adding *-d* or *-ed*.

Present	Past	Past Participle
sing	sang	sung
write	wrote	written
put	put	put

Linking Verbs

A linking verb links the subject of a sentence with a subject complement (a noun, a pronoun, or an adjective). The most common linking verbs are *be* and its forms *(am, is, are, been, be, was, were)*. Other verbs that can be used as linking verbs include *appear, become, continue, feel, grow, look, remain, seem, smell, sound,* and *taste.*

> My cousin *is* a poet.
> The poet who won the prize *was* she.
> She *looks* very happy.

Modal Auxiliaries

Modal auxiliaries are used to express possibility, permission, ability, necessity, intention, and willingness. They are followed by main verbs in the base form. The common modal auxiliaries are *may, might, can, could, must, should, will,* and *would.*

> You *might find* that information on the Internet. (possibility)
> The librarian *could help* you find it. (possibility)
> Anyone *may use* the computer in the library. (permission)
> June *can help* you set up your Web site. (ability)
> We *must finish* this project by tomorrow. (necessity)
> You *should help* June with her report. (obligation)
> I *will help* you after lunch. (willingness)
> Tom *would help* if you asked him. (willingness)

Principal Parts

The four basic parts of all verbs are the present, or base form; the past; the past participle; and the present participle. The past and past participle of regular verbs are formed by adding *-d* or *-ed* to the base form. The present participle is formed by adding *-ing.*

Present	Past	Past Participle	Present Participle
sail	sailed	sailed	sailing

Regular Verbs

The past and past participle of regular verbs are formed by adding *-d* or *-ed* to the present, or base, form. If a verb ends in *y* preceded by a consonant, the past and past participle are formed by changing the *y* to *i* and adding *-ed.* If a single-syllable verb ends in a consonant preceded by a vowel, the past and past participle are formed by doubling the consonant and adding *-ed.*

Present	Past	Past Participle
walk	walked	walked
smile	smiled	smiled
try	tried	tried
hop	hopped	hopped

Transitive Verbs

A transitive verb expresses an action that passes from a doer to a receiver. Every transitive verb has a receiver of its action. That receiver is the direct object.

George *passed* the test.

Verb Phrases

A verb phrase is two or more verbs that work together as a unit. A verb phrase may have one or more auxiliary verbs and a main verb. The verbs in a verb phrase are usually written together. In negative sentences and in questions, the verbs may be separated.

He *has finished* cleaning the garage.
He *did* not *mow* the lawn.
Will he *rake* the leaves?

VOICE

Voice shows whether the subject of a sentence is the doer or the receiver.

Active Voice

When a verb is in the active voice, the subject is the doer of the action.

Marietta *wrote* this poem.

Passive Voice

When a verb is in the passive voice, the subject is the receiver of the action. A verb in the passive voice is formed by combining a form of *be* with the past participle.

This poem *was written* by Marietta.

Mechanics

CAPITALIZATION AND PUNCTUATION

Apostrophes

Use an apostrophe to show possession.

John's   the Joneses'   the boys'

Use an apostrophe to indicate the omission of a letter, letters, or numbers.

aren't   we've   the class of '05

Use an apostrophe to show the plural of a small letter.

i's   *m*'s   *u*'s

Capital Letters

Use a capital letter to begin the first word in a sentence.

The boy is lost.

Use a capital letter to begin the first word in a quotation.

A woman said, "The boy is lost."

Use a capital letter to begin a proper noun or proper adjective.

America   American

Use a capital letter to begin a title before a name.

General George Custer

Use a capital letter to begin *North, South, East,* and *West* when they refer to sections of the country.

She was born in the South.

Use a capital letter to begin the first and last word and each principal word in a title.

"The Battle Hymn of the Republic"
Harry Potter and the Order of the Phoenix

Use a capital letter to begin the first word of every line of most poems and songs.

> "The time has come," the Walrus said,
> "To talk of many things."

> O beautiful for spacious skies,
> For amber waves of grain.

Colons

Use a color after the salutation of a business letter.

> Dear Mr. Monroe:

Use a colon before a list of items.

> I bought three things for my vacation: a backpack, a tent, and a lantern.

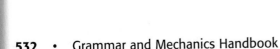

Commas

Use a comma to separate words in a series of three or more.

> We had roast beef, carrots, potatoes, and salad.

Use a comma to set off parts of dates, addresses, and geographic names.

> He was born in Des Moines, Iowa, on February 3, 1990.

Use a comma to set off a nonrestrictive appositive.

> Thomas Jefferson, our third president, was an inventor.

Use a comma to separate the clauses of a compound sentence connected by a coordinating conjunction.

> Thomas Jefferson wrote the Declaration of Independence, and he was elected our third president.

Use a comma to set off a direct quotation.

> Thomas Jefferson wrote, "All men are created equal."
> "I admire Thomas Jefferson," Allison remarked, "because he was so inventive."

Exclamation Points

Use an exclamation point at the end of an exclamatory sentence and after interjections and exclamatory words.

> We won the game!
> Quick! Let's congratulate the coach.

Hyphens

Use a hyphen to divide a word at the end of a line when one or more syllables are carried to the next line.

> When the game was over, everyone congrat-
> ulated the coach.

Use a hyphen in compound numbers from twenty-one to ninety-nine.

Use a hyphen to separate parts of some compound terms.

> brother-in-law   drive-in   six-year-old

Periods

Use a period at the end of a declarative or an imperative sentence.

> The birdhouse is almost finished.
> Please hand me that hammer.

Use a period after many abbreviations.

Dr.	a.m.	Oct.
Fri.	ft.	min.
Gov.	gal.	Co.

Question Marks

Use a question mark at the end of a question.

> What are you going to do next?

Quotation Marks

Use quotation marks to set off quotations. Quotation marks are placed before and after every complete quotation and every part of a divided quotation. Commas set off direct quotations from the rest of the sentence. The comma goes inside the quotation marks. Periods also go inside quotation marks.

> "I'm going to go to the movies," said Marilee.
> "Call me when you're ready to leave," Carol responded, "and I'll meet you there."

A question mark or exclamation point that is part of the quotation replaces the comma that sets off the quotation and goes inside the quotation marks. A question mark or exclamation point that is part of the entire sentence goes outside the quotation marks.

> "What time are you planning to leave?" Janet asked.
> Who said, "Meet me at five o'clock"?

Use quotation marks to set off titles of songs, short stories, poems, magazine articles, newspaper articles, and television shows. Titles of books, magazines, newspapers, movies, plays, television series, operas, and works of art are usually printed in italics. When these titles are handwritten, they are underlined.

> The article "My Favorite Cookie Recipes" appeared in the magazine *Cooking for Today.*
> The lyrics to "America the Beautiful" were reprinted in the <u>Charleston Tribune</u>.

Semicolons

Use a semicolon to separate the clauses of a compound sentence that are not connected by a coordinating conjunction.

> George Washington was our first president; he is called the Father of Our Country.

Use a semicolon to separate the items in a series when the items themselves contain commas.

> I have lived in Baltimore, Maryland; Little Rock, Arkansas; and Fargo, North Dakota.

Index

A

Abbreviations, 214, 217, 462–63, 533

Abstract nouns, 320–21, 516

Active voice, 406–7, 530

Addresses, 198, 214

Adjective phrases, 382–83, 450–51, 492, 506, 518, 519

Adjectives
  adding to sentences, 138–39, 141
  adverbs vs., 426–27
  common, 506
  comparison of, 370–73, 506–7
  definition of, 334–35, 362–63, 506
  demonstrative, 376–77, 507
  descriptive, 362–63, 507
  diagramming, 482–83
  indefinite, 380–81, 508
  interrogative, 378–79, 508
  and nouns, words used as, 334–35
  numerical, 366–67, 508
  position of, 508
  possessive, 348–49, 509
  predicate, 368–69
  prepositional phrases as, 382–83, 450–51, 492, 506, 518, 519
  proper, 478–79, 509, 531
  as subject complements, 368–69, 486–87, 509, 525
  suffixes of, 206–7
  troublesome, 426–27

Adverb clauses
  definition of, 430–31, 454–55, 500, 510, 512
  diagramming, 500–501, 502–3

Adverbial nouns, 510

Adverb phrases, 430–31, 452–53, 492, 510, 518, 519

Adverbs
  adding to sentences, 138–39, 141

  adjectives vs., 426–27
  comparison of, 424–25, 510
  definition of, 420–23, 509
  dependent clauses as (*see* **Adverb clauses**)
  diagramming, 482–83
  nouns as, 510
  prepositional phrases as, 430–31, 452–53, 492, 510, 518, 519
  and prepositions, words used as, 448–49
  suffixes of, 206–7

Almanacs, 290–91

Among/between, 446–47

Antecedents, 338–39, 340–41, 342–43, 511

Apostrophes, 350–51, 474–75, 531

Appositive phrases, 330–31

Appositives
  commas and, 464–65, 511, 532
  definition of, 330–31, 488, 511, 516
  diagramming, 488–89

Articles, definite and indefinite, 364–65, 506, 511

Atlases, 290–91

At/to, 446

Audience
  business letters, 202–5
  congratulatory speeches, 218–19
  current-event reports, 180–81
  descriptions, 85
  how-to articles, 46, 49
  how-to talks, 66
  oral personal narratives, 28
  personal narratives, 8
  persuasive articles, 122–23
  persuasive speeches, 142, 145
  trickster tales, 256

Audio aids, 104–5, 296–97

Auxiliary verbs, 386–87, 527

B

Bad/badly, 426–27

Base form, of verbs, 386–87, 398–99, 527, 529

Be
  as auxiliary verb, 386–87, 527
  as linking verb, 322, 344, 368, 396, 486, 525, 528

Beside/besides, 446–47

Between/among, 446–47

Biographical reports, 294–97

Body
  business letters, 198–99
  expository articles, 160–61
  oral personal narratives, 28
  personal narratives, 8–11
  persuasive articles, 122–23
  persuasive speeches, 142
  research reports, 276

Body language, 143, 256–57

Books, citing, 282–85

Business letters
  audiences, 202–5
  body, 198–99
  closing, 198
  language of, 203–5
  purposes of, 200–201
  salutations, 198, 470–71, 532
  structure, 198–99
  tone, 202, 204–5
  See also **Thank-you letters**

C

Can/may, 96–98

Capitalization, 168, 478–79, 532

Catalogs, in libraries, 290–91

Character, 240–41, 244

Charts
  flow, 62–63
  KWL, 174–75
  sensory, 85, 109

Checklists
  content editor's, 36, 74, 112, 150, 188, 226, 264, 302

D

Acknowledgments

Literature

"Stopping by Woods on a Snowy Evening" from *The Poetry of Robert Frost,* edited by Edward Connery Lathem. Copyright © 1951 by Robert Frost. Copyright 1923, © 1969 by Henry Holt and Company, Inc.

Excerpt from *My Side of the Mountain* by Jean Craighead George. Copyright © 1959, 1988 by the author. Published by Puffin Books, a division of the Penguin Group.

"The Hippopotamus" from *The Selected Poetry of Ogden Nash.* Copyright © 1995 by Black Dog & Leventhal Publishers, Inc.

Excerpt from *Pecos Bill and Lightning* by Leigh Peck. Copyright 1940 and © renewed 1968 by Leigh Peck. Reprinted by permission of Clarion Books/Houghton Mifflin Company. All rights reserved.

Excerpt from *The Red Pony* by John Steinbeck. Copyright © 1935, 1937, 1938, 1961, 1966 by the author. Published by Viking Penguin, Inc.

Illustration

Anni Betts: 10(t), 14(t), 17(t), 17(r), 22, 26(t), 46, 49, 51, 57, 63(r), 65, 87, 89, 93, 99, 125, 128, 135, 140, 161, 167, 172, 176, 183, 203, 208, 213, 218, 242, 249, 254, 259, 278, 285, 286, 292, 295

Antiquarium, Pompeii, Italy/Lauros/Giraudon/Bridgeman Art Library: 82

© 2004 Banco de México Diego Rivera & Frida Kahlo Museums Trust. Av. Cinco de Mayo No. 2, Col. Centro, Del. Cuauhtémoc 06059, México, D.F./SuperStock, Inc.: 293

Private Collection/Bridgeman Art Library: 196

Corbis: 84, 90, 98(l), 124, 169, 200, 210, 221, 234, 240, 304

Paul Downie: 238(r)

Getty Images: 127, 166

Royal Library, Copenhagen, Denmark/Bridgeman Art Library: 258

Photography

British Museum, London, UK/Bridgeman Art Library: 20

Corbis: 6, 44, 68, 83, 102(l), 132, 144, 149(r), 157(r), 173, 175, 180, 202, 215, 244, 276, 289, 291, 297, 306, 308, 411, 412, 421, 430, 450, 453, 456, 458, 460, 462, 464, 465, 467, 468, 470, 473, 474, 477, 479, 480

The Crosiers/Gene Plaisted, OSC: 158

Getty Images: 4-5, 58, 120, 136, 145, 157(l), 170, 211, 253, 273, 281, 294, 310-311, 445

The Lotte Jacobi Collection, University of New Hampshire: 284

Phil Martin Photography: 16, 30, 35, 60(c), 60(b), 78, 80(br), 101(t), 101(b), 108–117 (popcorn pieces), 111(cr), 142, 164, 165, 197(br), 199, 252, 274, 290

© 2004 Estate of Pablo Picasso/Artists Rights Society (ARS), New York/SuperStock, Inc.: 272

Verulamium Museum, St.Albans, Hertfordshire, UK/Bridgeman Art Library: 50

Loyola Press has made every effort to locate the copyright holders for the cited works used in this publication and to make full acknowledgment for their use. In the case of any omissions, the Publisher will be pleased to make suitable acknowledgments in future editions.